AMERICA
STRIKES BACK

AMERICA STRIKES BACK

A RECORD OF CONTRASTS

BY

GUSTAVUS MYERS

Author of
"The History of Tammany Hall," "The History of The Great
American Fortunes," "The History of American Idealism,"
"The History of the Supreme Court of the United States,"
etc., etc.

NEW YORK
IVES WASHBURN, INC.
PUBLISHER

PRINTED IN U. S. A.

PRESS OF
BRAUNWORTH & CO., INC.
BOOK MANUFACTURERS
BROOKLYN, NEW YORK

CONTENTS

THE SWAY OF LEGEND

LEGENDS have a mysterious longevity. In the course of a few generations law, institutions, economic and governmental systems may, and often do, greatly change because the ideas affecting them have changed. But bare assertion, when repeated often enough, becomes established as seeming truth; and the mere scrutiny of it may then be looked upon as presumption.

The range of legend includes peoples as well as individuals and eras. Through that medium a people looms as something it both was and was not. Our notion of "the glory that was Greece," for example, has a basis in the classic beauty of Greek art, which contains few reminders of the misery of a helot population. If judged by the extent of Roman power, "the grandeur that was Rome" is not legendary; but the definition of that grandeur is not allowed to include the degradation and oppression of Rome's plebeian masses.

Legends drawn from antiquity arose at a time when written knowledge was scarce. Yet the avalanche of books and the wide reading of modern times provide us no guarantee against the growth of new legends. Quite the contrary. The more widely error is published and imbibed, the greater its claim to unquestioned acceptance. Thus there has been affixed to America the character of a nation sodden with materialism.

Why has no examination been made into the nature of these assertions? At any time either common sense or knowledge could have prompted the taking of well-grounded exceptions to a campaign of assertion which singled out one country alone as the pernicious exponent of materialism. At any time, too, inquiry could have been made into the consecutive arraignment, both imported and domestic, of America as mercenary; the land of mediocrity, deficient in culture; the country ruled by a reckless, incompetent democracy. Why have these accusations been vested with such authority as to preclude any serious effort to test them by consulting the facts?

Long after it had achieved political independence, America, in a literary sense, remained a colonial dependency. Over a long period American writers looked reverently to Europe for precedent, authority and approval, imitated European modes of style and treatment, and echoed European judgments. I am not, of course, the first to point out this fact: three generations have passed since a noted American author, in a message to his countrymen, dwelt upon the strange, pervading deference of many Americans to foreign opinions of their ways and institutions. In general, this attitude has since persisted among a class of American writers who have seen fit to stigmatize their own country as primitive, crude, commercial. These writers have seemed to possess no knowledge of the antecedents of their attitude, nor any realization that they are but trailing after an old fashion.

Coincident with America's emergence as a nation, foreign critics, in suspicious unison, declared that this country furnished a singular exhibition of money mania. The burden of their complaint was that materialism, as practiced in America, was somehow a native product, spontaneously local in its origin and pursuit. These assertions, however, conformed exactly to the custom, then habitual among European aristocracies, of traducing democracy as low and mercenary in its motives. No inquiry was made, and none suggested, into anterior conditions in Europe, or into the state of affairs in America when, as colonial possessions, it was dominated by European countries. Of many things America may rightfully claim invention; but assuredly materialism is not on the list.

During all the years when Americans allowed themselves to be susceptible to this critical invective, they themselves were supplying the best refutation of it. Theirs was not the European method: concealment of iniquities. As the continuing record of legislative, aldermanic and Congressional investigations attest, Americans were assiduously exposing their own official venality and business corruption. Nor were these disclosures buried in secret reports; there was no prohibition of their use by newspapers; they were given the widest publicity.

But that very merit, which long remained peculiar to this country, was turned to America's disrepute by hostile critics who professed to see in it only a self-admission of debasement. Those critics said no word of the subtle systems of corruption in Europe; nothing of the systematic suppression of public disclosures there prevalent if scandal did arise; nothing of drastic laws forbidding the publication of proceedings which rulers or parliamentary bodies wished to keep secret. Uninformed about such practices elsewhere, and faced by corruption at home, many Americans assented when the denunciation was propagated that American social, political and governmental systems were peculiarly ignominious and full of innate evils. "They do these things better in Europe." So they were told; and so they are still being told.

As to modern times the question is: Have other nations been less materialistic than America? Have not some, indeed, been more so, while glozing over their materialism by creating an illusion about themselves—and by damning America as the nefarious example? What is the pretence and what the actuality?

In respect of this our own historians have not shown a questioning disposition or the curiosity to explore the records of other countries, and hence they have supplied neither enlightening information nor needed comparison. Widely-read American authors, professing to write American history, treat stock-watering, stock-jobbing and other speculative practices as distinctly American phenomena, outgrowths of an unscrupulous American "get-rich-quick" mania. Such transactions were commonplaces of European acquisitive arts when America was still largely a wilderness.

When the trading nations of Europe explored and settled primitive America, the way was open here for the establishment of European codes and creeds—and for the instantaneous implanting of European materialism. In that search for riches the transplanting of beliefs, ideas and customs occupied an incidental or minor place. The engrafting of materialism in the New World was the first, the preponderating and the long-pursued object of various European nations.

This book, however, concerns itself with facts, not with

formulations of purpose or policy. An additional word of explanation is required. As will be seen, I have had to give preponderant attention to British writers and to British conditions. This arises from no desire to emphasize either, but is the consequence of two compelling facts. Because of the identity of language most of America's foreign critics have been British; and compared with the scant and generally unavailable archives of other nations, Britain's are copious and accessible.

GUSTAVUS MYERS

PART ONE

THE HALLMARK OF MATERIALISM

CHAPTER I

FROM LEGEND TO FACT

WHEN America became a nation every phase of its democracy was obnoxious to the nations of Europe. They at once set out to defame democratic government by seeking to discredit the people that had introduced it into world politics. One of a variety of themes selected for this purpose was the representing of America's business men as thoroughly dishonest and more greedy than those of any other nation.

Thrust forward on every possible occasion as proof of America's materialism, these accusations came down through the decades, with many to repeat them in one way or another and no one to controvert them systematically. This point is not brought out here, of course, with any view of exonerating American business, which was infested with fraudulent practices. The representations of American business thus spread abroad were, in effect, a falsehood not so much because of the charges they contained, although these were much exaggerated, as because of their suppressions. The entire onus was placed upon American turpitude; no mention was made, for example, of British precedent or responsibility.

British writers loftily assumed that the character of British business was one of traditional fair dealing, and they were successful in diffusing this pretence. The misrepresentations of America then set afloat soon became part of a great literary tradition, grew curiously inveterate, and have continued to exercise their world-wide adverse influence down to the present day. But when British writers began self-righteously to reprobate American commercial practices, what had long been, and still were, the methods of business in their own country?

This campaign of British and other defamers was greatly helped by the growth of a legend which assisted in giving their declamations a plausible show of verity. The long-enduring

3

handicraft age had then passed, or nearly so, and the age of steam machinery had come in. Repelled by the mechanical processes, the speed and ugliness of factories, a succession of British writers, without ever venturing to look into the facts, idealized the conditions of the handicraft age. Then was the time, they rhapsodized, when superior artisans made superior products, and did not know how to make any other kind. Then was the time, they chorused, when both master and worker were united in amicable relations and in solicitude for fine quality of work.

This notion became generally accepted, and totally hid the truth. Numbers of present-day writers, European and American, have followed the lines thus set by extolling the past as an age gloriously differentiated from the unscrupulous materialism of today. Thus in one of his books,[1] as devoid of facts as it is full of declamation, Guglielmo Ferrero, the Italian historian, views the past as the qualitative, and contemporary times as the quantitative age.

Actually, however, the worst kind of business materialism existed in Europe before America was ever discovered; and it was rife in Europe centuries after America's settlement. From medieval times—the first times about which documentary information is obtainable—business was extensively based upon fraud in both manufacture and sale. Displays of excellent furniture and other goods made in the handicraft age are merely exhibitory and incidental, proving no more than that some sound, artistic and durable articles were produced. But as testimonials of a general condition these specimens are grievously misleading. They do not attest the kind of goods made for mass or even for class use.

Turning from legend to fact, inquiry exhumes conditions so continuously flagrant that in the long succession of efforts to remedy them law after law was passed. There is no reason to believe that vicious conditions in England were not paralleled in other European countries. But in England the form of government was adapted to the perpetuation of records. From the thirteenth century the English Parliament had functioned; its body of laws was kept intact and in later times collected and published, while in other countries decrees and administrative orders affecting such affairs were often lost.

For more than five centuries Parliament was steadily occupied in the attempt to overcome frauds in British business. These frauds included deceit both in the making and selling of goods. We shall take up each industry as a group.

Recorded legislation dealing with goldsmiths and silversmiths in England began in 1300, when a statute forbade goldsmiths from making spurious wares and passing them off as good; sixty-three years later another such law was enacted.[2] Fraud among goldsmiths was clearly not an isolated practice; a law, in 1403, told of "many fraudulent artificers, imagining to deceive the common people, do daily make locks, rings, beads, candlesticks, harness for girdles, hilts, chalices and sword pommels, powder boxes and cups of copper and of latten, and the same overgilt and silver like to gold and silver, and the same sell and put in gage to men not having full knowledge thereof, for whole gold and silver, to the great deceit, loss and hindrance of the common people." This law prescribed penalties for deceit, and another law in the same year ordered the honest marking of sterling silver, and penalized any city or town allowing sale of any silver unless sterling fine.[3]

A law passed in 1363, and which remained a statute until the time of Henry VIII, itemized seven different social classes, beginning with knights, esquires and gentlemen and going down the scale to merchants, clerks, handicraftsmen, yeomen, servants, plowmen and others of "mean estate" or "low degree." [4] In the "Statutes at Large" upon which I depend the fact is clearly brought out that this law prescribed the apparel which the different classes should wear and the diet to which the "lower orders" were restricted; but there was no provision on the matter of possessing jewelry.

We now turn to a disclosure contained in a law passed in 1464. "Whereas," this law stated, "before this time in the occupations of cloth making the laborers have been driven to take a great part of their wages in pins, girdles and other such unprofitable wares under such price that it did not extend to the amount of their lawful wages" and thus and otherwise workers had been discouraged from keeping at their tasks. Payment in money wages was therefore ordered.[5] This law supplies a competent commentary upon a system of double cheating. The makers of jewelry turned out fraudulent goods which, under pretence of being true gold and silver, were foisted upon workers in lieu of wages—with the worker left to find out that all he had in return for his labor was spurious stuff.

But acts respecting the making of goldware and silverware were so evaded that enactment of new laws was constantly found necessary. The nature of these laws shows that they did not deal with frauds upon the common people who, needless to say, were not purchasers of gold and silver plate. The aristocracy and the rich merchants had efficacious ways of obtaining action upon grievances; and while, as we shall see, merchants in every line of business were practicing fraud and profiting from fraud, they were quick to raise an outcry whenever they were defrauded.

A law, in 1487, declared that fraudulent assaying of gold and silver had become "such an abuse" as to necessitate the strict definition of the rate of fineness allowed and to compel its marking.[6] The power of Parliament was pitted against the wit of adroit minds, and devious wit conquered every time. After passing an act the lawmakers rested content; but while the law stood stock still, ingenious ways of getting around it were constantly being contrived. A long interval ensued when goldsmiths were secure from further laws, and then, in 1576, came another outburst of legislation vehemently beginning: "Whereas certain evil-disposed goldsmiths deceitfully do make and sell plate and other gold and silver wares, to the great defrauding of her Majesty and her good subjects . . ." and going on to ordain that any goldsmith who used falsehood or deceit should forfeit the whole value of the thing sold.[7]

Now goldsmiths, it should be noted, had a power far surpassing that of any other branch of English industry. They had become custodians of funds; the banking business of the mercantile class was in their hands. They loaned those funds to the government at exorbitant profit to themselves, which practice finally brought upon them a summary reprisal.

When, in 1672, Charles II secretly began another war against Holland, without consent of Parliament, he obtained the needed cash by confiscating the funds the goldsmiths had loaned to the Exchequer. By this arbitrary proceeding he ruined many of the goldsmiths and their clients. In 1694 came the establishment of the Bank of England which put banking in England on a different footing. However, others of the goldsmiths escaped disaster; the revenues made by them had been so great that they still had large resources, and these were extended by a settlement made in the reign of William III by which the debt to the goldsmiths was compromised by a one-half payment. From their various operations a number of the goldsmiths amassed great fortunes, some of which, in banking businesses or in other ways, have continued to this present time.

In the eighteenth century, Parliament, amid a plethora of legislation aimed at a mass of other trade frauds, was still endeavoring to overcome frauds in the gold and silverware business. Six years after George I ascended the throne it was found needful to reaffirm the foregoing law of Queen Elizabeth's reign; and so in 1739 another strenuous effort was made to prevent "frauds and abuses in gold and silver wares." This law opened by declaring straightway that "great frauds and abuses are still daily committed" in the making of silver plate. Reaffirming all laws on the subject from the reign of Edward I to that of George I, this law made new provisions. It required official assaying of wares; it granted heavy costs to defrauded persons; and it inflicted fine and imprisonment upon offenders.[8]

The sequel came eighteen years later in a Parliamentary admission that, despite the severity of laws already passed, "great quantities of gold and silver plate of a base and inferior standard, with such forged, counterfeit or transposed marks, stamps or impressions, are frequently vended in this kingdom, *and also exported to foreign lands.*" The forging, counterfeiting and transposing of hallmarks had become a consummate art; a highly lucrative business which sold its wares both in Great Britain and other countries. In the effort to efface these frauds Parliament did its sternest; anyone con-

victed was to suffer death as a felon.[9] But later—in 1773—a
happy thought occurred to Parliament. Any sort of live man
in the colonies was better than a dead man at home; so forthwith there was issued another law changing the sentence from
death to transportation.[10]

In feeling, then, British manufacturers were no doubt ardent
nationalists—but in sharing the practice of fraud many rose
superior to native prejudices. As a case in point take this law,
passed in 1698 and entitled: "An act for the exporting of
watches, sword-hilts and other manufactures of silver." Let
the preamble to that law relate conditions in its own words:

"And whereas great quantities of empty boxes, cases and
dial-plates for clocks and watches have been exported without
their movements, and in foreign parts made up with bad movements, and thereon some London watchmakers' names en-
graven, and so are sold abroad for English work; and also the
like ill practices in England by divers persons, as well as by
some professing the art of clock and watch-making, as others
ignorant therein, in putting counterfeit names, as also the
names of the most-known London watchmakers on their bad
clocks and watches, to the great prejudice of the buyers and
the disreputation of the said art at home and abroad." [11]

The denunciation, however, was stronger than the law's enforcing clause which forbade export of all boxes, cases and
dial-plates not containing the movement, and decreed forfeiture of goods for violation. During this period and prior
periods, however, manufacturers of clocks and watches frequently and loudly complained of the purloining and disposal
of their goods by workmen, and caused the passage of many
severe laws. To mention but one of these, enacted in 1754, it
need only be said that the fines imposed were terrific; £20 for
the first offence, £40 for each subsequent offence—crushing
sums considering the paltry wages of that time.[12]

(An essay might appropriately be interpolated here on the
subject of what are called antiques. Traffic in these, even in
classic times, has ever been a business invested with sentimental interest. Things surviving from olden days—how
quaint they seem and how their quality appears tested and
confirmed by the verdict of Time! No suspicion is ever

aroused, provided they are relics and not a modern simulation, that there could have been any fraud in making or marking in the "good old days"; the face value is taken as real value; and our simple faith in their genuineness gives cause for charging fancy prices. But we cannot linger on this subject, alluringly ironical though it be.)

If one particular law be taken as proof, as a recent biography of Henry VIII has represented, that England was crowded with foreign artificers, the resulting inference may be that English manufacturers had largely to depend upon alien skill in producing bad articles. True, a law of the reign of Henry VIII did complain that foreign artificers and handicraftsmen were becoming too numerous and were "practicing deceits and falsehoods in their handicrafts, to the loss and damage of natives." This law further complained that when officials tried to enforce laws the aliens secretly warned one another, defeating the law's purposes. Furthermore, so it said, some of these interlopers made too much money and returned to their own countries to invest it in lands and tenements. (Lest there be a tendency to identify unspecified foreigners as Jews, let the reminder be made here that in 1290, under Edward I, Jews had been driven from England, and that for more than three and a half centuries thereafter they were not allowed in that country.) The preamble went on to tell how many other foreign artificers had been idle and had consequently gone into crime; moreover, the scarcity of food at this time was attributed to the amount consumed by swarms of aliens. This law set out to regulate the movements of foreign artificers.[13]

All of which presents one side of a condition, that of deceitful work by foreigners. But there was another side implicating natives themselves. Here we turn to a long complaint made to Henry VIII and Parliament, in 1533, by various protesting master pewterers who set forth: That previously many laws had been passed for the purity of processing pewter and brass vessels and to insure honest weight. These vessels made in England had been in good demand in other countries. But "now of late evil-disposed persons, being the King's subjects born, which have been apprentices and brought up in the exercise of said craft of pewterers, have now of late, for their singular lucre, repaired into strange regions and countries, and there do exercise the said craft of pewterers, teaching strangers not only the cunning of mixing and forging all manner of pewter vessels, but also do teach all things belonging to the said craft of pewterers." Makers of pewter vessels in other countries, the preamble went on to declare, were thus enabled to send out great quantities of platters, pots, basins, flagons, goblets, dishes and other wares "which are untruly mixed and made of tin," and so English trade was being ruined.

Parliament came to the rescue by forbidding a number of practices. No one was allowed to buy any wares made of tin outside of England; any foreign wares could be seized; no pewterer was permitted to teach his trade in a foreign land nor could he thenceforth take any alien as an apprentice or journeyman.[14] But the dealers in fraudulent pewter wares were so little suppressed that eight years later there was promulgated another law which restated penalties and made "perpetual" the provisions of the previous law [15]—a piece of legislation mocked by a line of resourceful frauds who as perpetually were devising new kinds of illicit strategic methods.

The survey thus far is indicative of but a few groups of industries, and were it to confine itself to these the objection could rightly be made that the frauds noted were not symptomatic of all groups. The need of complete exposure in this case is proportionate to extravagant representations of the handicraft period, and to the altogether untrue contrast with modern materialism they present.

For decades print has been saturated with such unchallenged effusions as: "There was the opportunity then as there is not now for the worker to give a high degree of technique and a valuation of his workmanship." [16] "But industrial methods have certainly made work more remote from instinct and have destroyed the joy in craftsmanship which gave handicraftsmen something of the satisfaction of the artist." [17] These are typical specimens from books; as for the swarm of articles this characteristic panegyric will suffice: "Before the rise of the factory system, back in the days of hand production, the average worker was deeply interested in the quality of his work and in the general management of his job." [18] For the additional reason, therefore, of showing the parentage of subsequent materialism, amplification of medieval and later practices is necessary.

There is another reason too for this enlarging. In the nineteenth, and into the twentieth century, American industrialism was steeped in fraud. Adulteration of foods, medicines and liquors, shoddy clothing, blankets and other articles with lying labels, flimsy shoes, poor furniture veneered to look good and sound—these and a multitude of other wares were poured forth, were sold under misrepresentation and brought swelling profits into the treasuries of manufacturers whether individual, firm or corporation. But these abuses, be it noted, were only a continuation of practices in colonial times in America when handicrafts did the work. Before America ever became independent of Britain there were brisk frauds in exporting bad flour and in falsely marking flour and bread casks; there were frauds in adulterating potash and pearl ash; frauds in selling bar iron of very bad quality, and in the sale of poor leather.[19] These frauds were only a few transplantations of a large number long established in Europe, of which England gives a plenitude of recorded examples.

Detailed reference to the long list of English statutes aimed at adulterations and false weights and measures would be a tedious compilation. In 1266 came a law against selling short-weight bread, "corrupted" wine and impure meat and fish. A session in the pillory ordered by this law for infractions deterred so slightly that a little later a new law prescribed regulations and penalties: Every baker was compelled to put his own mark upon his bread, and if he overcharged a fine and the pillory were to be his punishment; any butcher selling unwholesome flesh was subject to fine, the pillory for the second violation, imprisonment for the third, and for the fourth offence he was compelled to leave the town.[20]

From that time to the nineteenth century law after law was passed against adulteration and fraudulent weighing. In 1430 a law told how, by fraud in weighing of cheese, "the poor people of the realm be greatly deceived." [21] In time the farmers well learned the tricks of fraud; the preamble of a law, in 1662, gave full particulars. Hilderkins, firkins and pots of butter and cheese were given "false heavy weight" by loading them with stones, iron wedges, bricks and other heavy articles. "Much bad and decayed butter is mixed and packed . . . with sound and good butter and immoderate quantities of salt, to the spoil of the same . . . to the great wrong and abuse of the navy, of merchants, traders and all householders." [22] Notwithstanding penalties, these frauds persisted, as related by a law thirty years later.[23]

Another deep grievance was the making of bad malt. Various persons, declared a law in 1548, "tendring more their own private gain, lucre and profit, have now of late by their insatiable, covetous and greedy minds, accustomably and commonly made much malt impure and unseasonable"; they rushed its making in eight or nine days, whereas it needed at least twenty-one, and not being well dried the malt became musty and full of weevils; this impure stuff was mixed with good, and the result was unpalatable.[24] In the reign of Queen Elizabeth the continuance of these frauds called forth another punitive law.[25]

The celebrated "brown October ale" of merry old England was not, as we see, then much renowned. In 1604 a law ordered forfeiture of corrupt hops; any English brewer using such substances was to forfeit the value of the hops.[26] Only four years prior to the enactment of this, another law had been passed prohibiting dealers from putting in Spanish wine any isinglass, brimstone, raisins, herb or other ingredients. There must have been much feeling over this fraud; penalties were made unusually heavy—£100 fine for every adulteration offence, and a £40 fine for retailing such doctored liquor.[27]

In the course of centuries many changes took place in religion, politics and taste; but no revolution of any kind affected the career of trade fraud. How somnolent the legislative mind was inclined to become in this domain was disclosed by a law in 1709. For nearly five hundred years the statute which had been passed in 1266 was depended upon to stop frauds in the weight and price of bread. In 1709 Parliament woke up to the fact that "many of the provisions in that old law are obscure and impracticable"; taking advantage of the same, "covetous and evil-disposed persons have, for their own gain and lucre, deceived and oppressed her Majesty's subjects, and more especially the poorer sort of people." [28] The law was modernized, and heavy fines and other penalties inflicted. But so ineffective were these that all through the reigns of the four Georges and far beyond need constantly arose for further punitive laws aimed at adulteration of meal, flour and bread.

Nothing that could be adulterated escaped the process. Adulteration of oil was old and common. A law of the reign of Queen Elizabeth complained that deceitful mixtures were put in honey, which was sold in casks of deceitful size. The same law related that "a great part of the wax made and melted in this realm hath of late been found to be very corrupt by reason of the deceitful mixture thereof" with resin, tallow and turpentine. At a time when candles were a chief means of illumination this fraud was condemned as especially heinous; so, as a positive way of identifying culprits, every wax melter was required to put his mark upon his product, and the defrauded person was allowed half of the fine mulcted for adulteration.[29]

New ways of defeating law were ever slily found. What was sold as tobacco and snuff is made clear from the title, and clearer from the text, of a law in 1715. "An act to prevent the mischiefs by manufacturing leaves or other things to resemble tobacco and the abuses in making and mixing snuff" told how tobacco was one of the chief products of Virginia and Maryland, and how walnut-tree, hops, sycamore and other leaves and herbs, plants or materials resembling tobacco had been manufactured and sold for that product. A fine was ordered for every pound sold, and a like penalty for exportation, besides the seizure of such goods and jail for persons making them. Under penalty of fine and forfeiture the law forbade coloring of snuff, and mixing it with fustick, yellow ebony, torchwood or any other sort of wood, or dirt, sand or tobacco dust. Four years later another act was necessary.[30]

According to a preamble of a law in 1781, "great frauds . . . to the great injury of the fair trader" and the encouragement of smuggling had been carried on by the frequent importation into Great Britain of damaged coffee and cocoanuts sold as good quality. Also, in England, tea-dealers, who had permits certifying the good quality of their tea, perpetrated great frauds by substituting inferior tea while in the act of removing the goods at night to places of other dealers. The law forbade the selling of damaged coffee or cocoanuts above certain prices for home consumption, and prohibited nocturnal transportation of more than six pounds weight of any tea from one town to another.[31] This is the first law in the records, it may be mentioned, that contains any reference to the fair trader, or any distinct recognition of loss to him from the practices of fraudulent competitors.

CHAPTER II

"AN ESSAY UPON NATIONAL CHARACTER"

WAR profiteering, through the supplying of bad equipment, has an ancient history. It was in malignant operation in England in 1405, a preamble of a law of that year detailing: "Because arrowsmiths do make many faulty heads for arrows and quarels, defective, not well, nor lawful nor defensible, to the great deceit and jeopardy of the whole realm." Ordained, therefore, that henceforth all arrow and quarel heads should be well-boiled or brazed, and hardened at the points with steel. Failure to do this, and to place the maker's mark on each piece, was made punishable by forfeiture of goods and imprisonment. Enforcement was provided for by giving Justices of the Peace in every county and bailiffs in every borough examining duties and punishing power.[1] In the next century another kind of fraud was evidenced; that of making weapons and tools from billow-iron resembling steel and sold as steel. By this fraud, said a law in 1548, "necessary things having value are of little or no value or goodness, to the great hurt of the King's loving subjects." A fine was put upon every piece so sold.[2]

Scandals from the equipment of English naval and merchant vessels with spurious material were many. "For their own private lucre, certain evil-disposed persons are deceivably making" cables, ropes and other tackle, began a law of the year 1529.[3] Penalties did not discourage fraud; in 1593 came forth another law the preamble of which thus explained conditions:

"Forasmuch, as it is found by common experience, that sundry persons using the trade of making cables, halfors and other kinds of cordage within this realm, have of late, for their own private lucre and gain, used to make the same of old, cast and worn-over cables, halfors and cordage, and yet have craftily and deceitfully uttered and sold the same, being tarred as new, good and strong, and as made of new and perfect stuff, cover-

15

ing and hiding the false and corrupt making thereof, by tarring of them before the same be put to sale:

"By reason whereof, not only divers ships, vessels and goods as well of her Majesty's as of sundry of her Highness' subjects, but also the lives of divers of her said subjects, have been lost, perished and cast away." [4]

The remedy ordered was a fine treble the value of the fraudulent cordage, and imprisonment during the Queen's pleasure. Soon—in 1604—another kind of fraud had to be dealt with—"the deceitful making of mildernex and powledavies, whereof sail-cloths for the navy and other shipping are made." The preamble of the law directed at this fraud told that these goods were made in France until the time of Queen Elizabeth, when the weaving of them was successfully introduced in England. The preamble went on to say that many Englishmen who were not trained in this trade had, notwithstanding, "upon desire of gain," made of poor material such cloths, which were neither well woven nor of the proper length and breadth. These practices resulted "to the great damage of his Highness' navy, the chiefest strength of the realm." This law permitted weaving only by apprentices who had served seven years, or by men with a full knowledge of the trade; prescribed materials and quality; and ordered fines for transgression.[5] But the frauds did not cease, or at least were resumed, as was shown by the passage of more laws in the years 1736 and 1751.[6]

And here the question naturally arises: What of England's chief industry in those days—the manufacture and sale of woolens?

In the thirteenth century England exported much wool and made some fine linens. But the main business was controlled by foreigners, and the finances were conducted by Italians. The English did little navigation to other countries, and England's produce—raw wool, lead, tin—was carried away by foreigners in foreign ships, especially to Mediterranean ports. In 1381 came an act prohibiting all English subjects from conveying merchandise except in English ships, and eighteen years later the importation of woolen cloths into England was forbidden.

How the truth about conditions in this and later times has been wholly subverted is shown by such volumes as Richard Chevenix's "An Essay upon National Character," published a century ago in England. In the England of his time, standing out as "the most renowned seat of industry," great interest was shown in the history and glorification of its industry and commerce. Chevenix included a sketch of the origin and growth of the woolen industry, making this positive statement: That the fifteenth century was a disastrous period in England; "still, however, she found means to apply much attention to her woolen manufactures; and a long list of foreign wares, prohibited in 1463, shows that their fabrication at home had made their importation useless. These, too, principally consisted in woolens. . . ." Chevenix's paean was hailed as a classic, and has since been much cited as authoritative.

The truth was precisely the opposite of the situation he represented. We shall pass over statutes of the years 1433 and 1439 against the selling of cloth defective in make and measurement,[7] and let the preamble of a law of the year 1464 recount what actually was happening: "Whereas, many years past, and now at this day, the workmanship of cloths and things requisite to the same, is and has been of such fraud, deceit and falsity, that the said cloths in other lands and countries be had in small reputation, to the great shame of this land; and by reason thereof, a great quantity of cloths of other strange lands be brought into this realm, and here sold at a high and excessive price, evidently showing the offence, default and falsehood of the making of woolen cloths of this land." [8] The law ordered the examining and marking of all goods, and the confiscation of those fraudulent in make or measure. It prescribed fines for fraud, and put penalties upon the Keeper of the Seals if he failed in his duty and marked any inferior goods as perfect.

While Richard III was busy with intrigue, murder and battle, Parliament was contending with other troubles. The preamble of a law, passed in 1483, was a reproach and an arraignment. England, in the past, it said, had been greatly enriched by the making and draping of woolen cloth whereby many people were kept at work and not fallen to idleness as daily they were now. "It is so now that the woolen cloths which in late days have been made, and being made, are unperfect and deceivably made and wrought, keeping neither length nor breadth." Further, the preamble complained, cloth was stretched instead of pre-shrunk; it was made of substitute materials; and poor dyes were used.[9]

In the reign of Henry VIII law after law was enacted against adulteration of worsteds, deceit in making woolen cloths, and the false weighting of fleece with clay, lead, stones, sand, tails and other substances.[10] "Forasmuch as great infamy and slander hath risen of late years in sundry outward parties beyond the sea of the untrue making of woolen cloths within this realm, to the great derogation of the common weal of the same, and the no little hindrance of the sale of the said commodity." Thus read the preamble of a law in 1535,[11] which closed one of the loopholes left in previous laws and provided new penalties. "Where heretofore divers and many goodly statutes have been made for the true making of cloth within this realm, which nevertheless forasmuch as clothiers, some for lack of knowledge and experience, and some of extreme covetousness, do daily more and more study rather to make many than to make good cloths, having more respect to their private commodity and gain than the advancement of truth and continuance of the commodity in estimation, according to the worthiness thereof, have and do daily—" but let us interrupt this preamble of 1552. Therein it is obviously enough set forth that contemporary critics of the since much exalted handicraft times did not in the least think theirs a "qualitative" age. No indictment of our machine-age "quantitative" production could be more severe than that incorporated in this preamble, setting forth how industry was then bent upon turning out numbers rather than good quality of cloths. The aim of unscrupulous mass production, as we here indubitably see, much preceded any age of machinery.

That preamble had more remarks on the ways of cloth-makers who, "instead of truth, practice falsehoods, and instead of substantial making of cloth, do practice slight and slender making, some by mingling of yarns of divers spinning in one cloth, some by mingling fell-wool and lambs-wool, or either of them, with fleece-wool, some by putting too little stuff, some by taking them out of the mill before they be full-thicked, some by over-stretching them upon the tenter, and then stopping with flocks such bracks as shall be made by means thereof; finally, by using so many subtile sleights and untruths, as when the cloths so made be put in the water to try them, they rise out of the same neither in length or breadth as they ought to do, and in some places narrower than some, besides such cockeling, bandoning and divers other great and notable faults, as almost cannot thought to be true."

By what inducements were the clothmakers able to procure official complaisance in selling their spurious goods? The persuasive means were not disclosed, but the fact that cloth manufacturers did obtain it was most clearly stated: "And yet, nevertheless, neither fearing the laws in that case provided nor regarding the estimation of their country [the cloth makers] do not only procure the aulneger [a royal officer who examined cloth in guarantee of its quality or measure] to set the king's seal on such false untrue and faulty cloth, but do themselves weave into the same the likeness and similitude of the King's highness' most noble and imperial crown, and also the first letter of his name, which should be testimonies of truth, and not a defiance of untruth, to the great slander of the king our sovereign lord, and the shame of this land, and to the utter destruction of so great and notable a commodity, as the like is not seen in any foreign nation." [12]

Increasingly heavy fines, forfeiture of goods and the punishment in the pillory ordered by this law did not decrease frauds. Two laws of Elizabeth's time were, however, variations from the general run. One of these, in 1585, gave the first legislative sanction to the making of "a base and coarse kind of goods" for the use of "the poorer sort of people"; parts of previous statutes prohibiting the putting in of hair, flocks or other such materials were repealed. This law said that the intention was to make statutes more applicable to the needs of trade.[13] Clothmakers now had authorization to do what they had always illegally done. In 1597 another law of unusual tenor came in response to a petition of York, Lancaster and some other clothmakers themselves, who complained: That despite the many wholesome laws compelling the making of good cloths, abuses had not only not been restrained but rather had increased. This was due either to defects in the laws or to lack of their enforcement. The quality of cloths made in Northern England "do yearly and daily grow worse and worse . . . to the great deceit of all nations where the said cloths and kersies are sold and to the great shame and slander of the country where the same is made." This law accordingly ordered every Northern cloth manufacturer to affix a seal of lead to every piece of cloth attesting quality and quantity, provided heavy fines and forfeitures for violations, and granted recovery of damages to defrauded persons.[14] The York manufacturers themselves, who helped in procuring this law, became guilty of the worst kind of frauds, as a later law showed.

The fact has ever to be borne in mind that increased penalties brought no results. In 1605 a law of James I declared for a "true and just commerce without fraud or deceit"; [15] and another in 1623 recounted that "many ill-disposed persons for their own private gain and lucre and in deceit of the buyers of cloth" were putting deleterious foreign substances into woolen cloths. The powers granted by this law exceeded those of all previous statutes, in allowing inspectors to enter any man's house suspected of containing fraudulent cloth; and warrants could be issued for the arrest of any person even suspected of making such cloth. Provisions for fining were drastic.[16]

A detailed resumption of the fraudulent making and selling of woolen goods would entail a needless account of a multitude of punitive laws passed in the seventeenth and eighteenth centuries. Suffice it to say that law after law bemoaned the inefficiency of previous legislation. Laws adopted in 1662, 1708, 1711 and 1719, 1723, 1724, 1726, 1734 and 1738 all successively sought to prevent the making of defective goods, including stockings, their improper dyeing and false certification. Each of these laws in turn decreed severer penalties for enforcement.[17] Finally, as a summary of the whole, we come to a law enacted in 1766, applying to York manufacturers and deploring the ineffectuality of all previous laws in removing some of the frauds which were still practiced. Evidently despairing of compliance from the manufacturers, this law concentrated its punitive efforts upon inspectors and other official examiners of cloth. These officials were made subject to heavy fines for each offence in falsely stamping and fraudulently sealing defective cloth, and were liable to removal from office.[18]

Conspicuously through these centuries stands out the grim resolution of British industry in contesting with law and its proficiency in strategems for evading the statutes. Historians have noted the prevalence of other kinds of lawlessness in Britain during these eras, but have had nothing to say of the defiant and incurable lawlessness of rampant materialism. In an essay "On Fraud," Bishop Thomas Wilson, an eminent English prelate of the eighteenth century, noted: "But the sins of injustice which are most common, and least taken notice of, are such as are committed in the way of trade and bargains." If, he added, the degree of crimes was to be measured by the opinion the world had of them, then "we should only make a jest of taking advantage of and cheating one another, as it is too common."

PART TWO

MERCANTILE DOMINATION

CHAPTER III

ACANADA

WHEN Spanish explorers first gazed at the mouth of the St. Lawrence River "lined with mountains and covered with snow" they named the uninviting country *Acanada*—"Here is nothing."[1] But this judgment turned out to have been unfounded; from the contiguous waters and from inland came a great supply of valuable products. The fisheries attracted a multitude of European traders assured of large profits from the great demand for fish especially in Roman Catholic countries, and, with a single whale frequently yielding as many as four hundred barrels of oil, profits from whaling were temptingly large.

From Spain, England, France and Holland came vessels to load themselves with abundant sea-spoils. Following Cartier's example in 1541 of manning his armed ships with convicts from French jails, some French mariners obtained crews by getting official permission to commandeer men and women prisoners from Brittany and Normandy; but many of these individuals, mendicants by profession and imprisoned for that offence, could not stand the rigors of winter voyage, and died.[2] In 1578 there were thirty to fifty English fishing sail, and perhaps two hundred vessels from Spain on the Newfoundland Banks; twenty Biscay vessels were engaged in whale hunting. Seven years later the fishing fleet mounted to three hundred Spanish, French, English and Dutch vessels. A quarter of a century later the French fishing fleet alone comprised six hundred vessels, or thereabouts.

From the fishing industry there ensued a traffic at first auxiliary but subsequently becoming the principal trade, yielding great profits, inciting conflicts, having its influence in fomenting wars, and directly or indirectly causing a great and continuous sacrifice of human life. This was the fur trade, the main and long-continued source of primitive accumulation of

25

wealth in vast parts of the North American continent. During centuries the great bulk of this wealth from Canada and other sections went to European beneficiaries to be successively invested in land, banks, trade, factories, and transportation systems, in Europe and other continents.

Upon going ashore in Canada to dry fish, traders soon learned both of the prevalence of fur-bearing animals and the absurd cheapness with which these furs could be bought from the unsophisticated Indians. A needle, a harness bell or a tin mirror could be traded for a beaver skin.[3] Potations of liquor assisted the arts of persuasion. When, upon their return to Europe, fishing traders displayed their cargoes of furs and told how they were obtained, the more quick-minded merchants of the seaports were greatly excited by the wealth-producing certainties of the fur trade.

At first more or less of an individual venture, fur-trading soon became an enterprise carried on by charter. A French corporation, Champlain's Company, the shares of which were apportioned among merchants of Rouen and St. Malo, was chartered in 1614 upon condition of certain colonizing performances. These the company did not take seriously, sending but a solitary family to Canada. Its monopoly was abolished in 1620, and the next year a charter, requiring colonization by settlers and missionaries, was granted to the Company of De Caen, organized by William De Caen and his nephew, Rouen merchants. Champlain's Company and the Company of De Caen united in a trading agreement, continuing operations until 1633 but having to meet the competition of the Company of New France established in 1627 by Cardinal Richelieu.

Differing from the previous companies, the backers of the Company of New France were not small-town merchants; its leading stockholders were Parisians. The company was granted a full monopoly lasting fifteen years and complete trading control of the entire St. Lawrence Valley, and was required to introduce three hundred colonists annually. This obligation was only nominally performed, yet somehow the Company of New France contrived to hold its monopoly until 1663 when its charter was revoked. Then followed the Company of the West Indies, chartered by Louis XIV in 1664. The ostensible

object for which this company was empowered was the con-
version of Indian tribes to Christianity, but its privileges com-
prehensively covered trading rights on the West Coast of
Africa, the East Coast of South America, and in Canada, Aca-
dia and Newfoundland. Apparently the officials of this company
were more concerned in stock-jobbing than in directing the
routine of trade; while they were thus pocketing booty the
company's affairs languished, and its charter was canceled in
1675. There came into being various other French companies,
the most important of which was the French East India Company, having the sole privilege of exporting beaver from
Canada.

There are no extant reports of the profits made by the various French companies from the fur trade, but ample records
exist showing the methods followed and giving some indication of the traffic's magnitude. To a considerable extent the
companies had to depend upon itinerant traders who penetrated
afar among the Indian tribes and brought back their bales of
furs. But as no one could trade with the Indians without an annual license, and as such permits were made a matter of favoritism and jobbery by French officials who granted or annulled
them at will, the state of the fur trade was entirely lacking in
system. Having only precarious licenses, French traders could
make no permanent establishments of any importance, but
roamed wherever opportunities of fur-gathering were greatest.

The debauching of Indians with intoxicating liquor, chiefly
brandy, entailed such demoralization, conflicts and atrocities
that, on April 17, 1664, the Sovereign Council of Canada, composed of French officials, issued a drastic decree prohibiting
barter of liquor or giving it in trade to Indians.[4] Safe from the
reach of enforcing officers, traders did not diminish their debauching operations. The failure of this decree prompted the
Sovereign Council four years later to give permission to all
Frenchmen in Canada to sell and deliver liquor freely to Indians; the justification advanced was that freedom of sale
would cause less demoralization than a restraint the attempted
enforcement of which was impracticable.[5]

Another effort, this time partial, to curtail the evils was made
in the next year, when a proclamation prohibited traders from

lying in wait in the woods for Indians, or going to meet them there.[6] Frequent energetic protests also were made by prelates and missionaries in Canada against traders' methods of making the Indians drunk so as to get their furs for little or nothing; and the protest graphically set forth the rôle of liquor in devastating settlements and engendering immorality, theft and murder.[7]

Animosity among officials aroused by differences as to their priority and respective sphere of authority, or disputes caused by contentions over rival trading groups, likewise provoked disclosures. In 1670 one Perrot was appointed Governor of Montreal. Although on a small salary, he managed by benefit of illegal trade with the Indians to become speedily wealthy. Jacques Duchesenau, Intendant of Canada's Police, Justice and Finance, formally accused Perrot of having thus illegitimately pocketed 40,000 livres (approximately $10,000), then an enviable sum, in a single year.

In one of his arraignments Duchesenau declared that "the desire of making money everywhere" had led Perrot and others, including relatives, to violate their own official edicts by shipping on canoes an enormous aggregate of beaver furs to English dealers who gave double the price paid by French fur merchants in Quebec. "Violence, upheld by authority, decides everything," Duchesenau reported. "The force the Governor [of Montreal] has at his hand sustains his interests, and he employs it only to intimidate the people, so as to prevent them from complaining. . . ." [8] Functionary DeMeulles complained to the king, in 1684, that in the course of Governor Perrot's partnership with Quebec merchants and their aim to monopolize all the trade of the West, Perrot had incited war with the Iroquois. But the year before, it appears, DeMuelles himself had advised attacking the tribe, "who must be humbled or annihilated in the interests of trade." [9]

A remonstrance made by Bishop Laval to Louis XIV, in 1677, against the widespread debauchery of Indians was followed by the ordering by Colbert, Louis' Minister of Finance, of "Twenty Principal Inhabitants" of Canada to make inquiry. All of these persons, however, were themselves engaged in the fur trade. Their report accordingly minimized the extent of the use of liquor in fur trading, and declared that its interdiction "would ruin trade, without any equivalent and without remedying the evils" because in territories in far west Canada in which the English operated, and in areas south controlled by English and Dutch, those nationalities "will sell it [liquor] freely to the Indians, and will attract to themselves both the Indians and the trade in furs." [10] Indignantly criticizing this report, the author of Bishop Laval's biography asked what were the returns for so many hideous evils arising from the debauchery of Indians? "A few dozen rascals enriched, returning to squander in France a fortune shamefully acquired." [11]

Opposition of conscientious clergymen in Canada to the infamies of such a trade was overcome by the merchants who sent specious and successful pleas to the king at Versailles, and represented that the brandy traffic gave France an advantage over Holland and England. Frequent memorials to King Louis' ministers set forth the horrors caused by the Indians' imbibing of brandy. For example, the Marquis de Demonville wrote, in January, 1690, to the Marquis de Seignelay: "There is no crime that they do not perpetrate in their excesses. A mother throws her child into the fire; noses are bitten off; this is a frequent occurrence. It is another Hell among them during these orgies, which must be seen to be credited. . . ." [12] Several Indian tribes and a number of chiefs had earnestly and pathetically implored French officials not to allow liquor among them. Siding with the merchants, however, the royal government instructed the Bishop of Quebec, in 1691, to prevent the clergy from "disturbing consciences." [13]

With little actual money circulating in great parts of Canada, beaver furs became the accepted medium of exchange, although at times the want of currency was made up by a fiat issue called "card money." Transported to Europe, however, furs brought payment in gold and silver. Almost the entire population of Canada, 18,000 or 20,000 in all, was engrossed in the fur trade. "Beaver," wrote Intendant Randot of Canada in his "Memorial" to Versailles, July 16, 1708, "have always been looked upon here as a mine of gold of which everyone wanted to take his share. The settlers spent their time hunting in the woods, preferring a life of adventure in the woods, which brought them large profits with little toil, to the cultivation of the land which requires assiduous labor." [14]

Although, to a small extent, the utilization of Canada's rich timber resources had begun in 1686 when Quebec merchants built a ship to carry boards to La Rochelle, France, and there was some slight cattle-raising and wheat cultivation, the fur trade long remained dominant. Randot urged the French Government, by finding a market for the products, to induce the people to take up agriculture, lumbering, ship-building, to develop the greater possibilities of the fish and whale oil trade, and to exploit the coal, feldspar and gypsum deposits of Cape Breton.[15] But with powerful interests in Canada, reflected in the Government of France, feverishly involved in the get-rich-quick opportunities of the fur trade, the course advocated by Randot was treated as absurd.

During the entire time when the Dutch and English, Spanish and French ruled American territory—during the period of Canada's domination by the French, and of its passing under British sovereignty—European publications made no criticism of the wealth-seeking spirit rampant in those possessions. Encouraged by European governments, that spirit fostered the eager aim of European merchants and corporations, and was generally applauded in Europe as natural and gratifying. So long as European nations owned and domineered over those lands this course was approved as proper and requisite.

But when American colonists increasingly defied British restrictive acts, declared for democratic rule, and later revolted and achieved independence, there arose a new standard of judgment. In no sense, of course, did Europe relinquish any of the money-making aims which had so long instigated its activities. European critics of Americans on the other hand, converted into odium what European nations had acclaimed in themselves as a high merit. The development by Americans of their natural resources was listed as one irrefutable proof of the avarice passionately imbuing the American temperament. Throughout the centuries when colonists of European nativity, employment or attachment roved promiscuously to gather furs, no European criticism was made of a mode of life ensuring products and profits to European beneficiaries. But in the later eighteenth century and in the early nineteenth, when hosts of Americans uprooted themselves from eastern homes to pioneer settlement in the Middle West, this migration was scathingly condemned by European critics as attesting the instability and money-lust of the American character.

CHAPTER IV

THE LORDS OF TRADE

THE practically-minded English ruling and trading classes took early steps to make the development of trade and jurisdiction over it a regular and systematic branch of government. Unlike other nations, the English were sagaciously alert to the folly of leaving deliberations respecting trade to the ignorance of nondescript assemblies or to ministerial functionaries experienced only in political machination. Although, as a matter of caste pride, England's aristocracy might profess to disdain trade as sordid, this attitude did not deter a number of nobles from joining in the move to create government trade boards under the guidance of which England's already large trade could be swelled.

So there came into existence the Council of Trade, established by Charles II, on November 7, 1660, to determine ways and means of extending English trade and navigation. Less than a month later was initiated a body of far wider and more authoritative scope—the Council of Foreign Plantations. This comprised a notable array of peers—the Earl of Southampton, the Earl of Manchester, the Earl of Marlborough, the Earl of Lincoln, Viscount Say, Lords Hyde, Dacre, Willoughby, Roberts and Berkeley—associated with whom was a group of keen merchants.

Royal instructions to the Council for Foreign Plantations endued it with comprehensive powers of supervising the produce, shipping, trade and related affairs of all colonies, and the regulation of them by one management giving orders from London. The conventional provision requiring "effectual care in propagating the Gospel" was not omitted. England's colonies were already numerous; and in 1664 its wresting of the Province of New York from the Dutch added another section to the tier of American colonies subject to the powers of the

Council for Foreign Plantations. All of these, and still greater powers, were finally lodged in the Board of Trade, which in 1696 was established on a permanent basis.

The Board of Trade was an extraordinary institution. It kept scrutiny upon every phase of England's trade, and exercised sweeping and arbitrary powers in American and other colonies. Officially and otherwise it was always impressively addressed as "The Lords of Trade." British governors in America had minutely to report to it every public happening of whatever nature. The Board of Trade passed upon and either approved or rejected colonial legislation, and decided the fate of land grants in America. It vetoed a New York Charter of Liberties and Privileges; commanded what should be the quotas of soldiers furnished by the respective colonies; passed upon colonial acts for paying debts; and made a multitude of other such decisions.[1]

Succeeding Benjamin Fletcher as Captain-General and Governor of New York and Massachusetts Bay, Lord Bellomont reported to the Board of Trade, on June 22, 1700, that he, Bellomont, had been offered a bribe of £10,000 in money to confirm title to a vast area in New Hampshire claimed by Colonel Samuel Allen. In other reports Bellomont gave the specific facts dealing with huge areas that Fletcher had been bribed to grant. Captain John R. N. Evans had been presented with an estate, running forty miles one way and thirty the other, on the west bank of the Hudson. Nicholas Bayard, said to have been intermediary in arranging the price that sea pirates paid for Fletcher's protection, received a grant of the same size in New York. Colonel Henry Smith obtained from Fletcher an area fifty miles in length on Nassau—now Long Island. To Henry Beekman went a grant of two New York tracts, one sixteen miles long, the other twenty miles along the Hudson and running eight miles inland. Also by Fletcher's grace, Peter Schuyler and associates had conjointly secured a grant of land fifty miles long in the Mohawk Valley. Lord Bellomont reported these to the Board of Trade as some of the enormous estates created by "Colonel Fletcher's intolerable selling away of the lands of this Province"; bribes paid to Fletcher, Bellomont intimated, totalled at least £4,000.[2]

Bellomont succeeded in having the New York legislature nullify the grants to Evans and Bayard, and two small grants. A subsequent legislature repealed the voiding act, but the Board of Trade ordered that the invalidating act should stand. Bellomont's efforts to confiscate the other extravagant grants were thwarted, and the Board of Trade took no action upon his plea to restrain all colonial governors from granting, without express royal permission, more than a thousand acres to any man. In a formal complaint to Secretary of State Vernon, in London, the outspoken Bellomont charged that one of the members of the Board of Trade regularly sold appointments to offices in America "to any sort of trash that will give him money." [3]

An order, on September 26, 1722, of the Board of Trade to procure an act voiding remaining exorbitant grants was never carried out. The desideratum most influencing that body was the aim to get and reserve for the British navy the fine timber growth on those lands. Most of the grants however, remained in possession of the grantees and of their heirs; Lieutenant-Governor Cadwallader Colden, in a communication on September 20, 1764, to the Board of Trade, told how three of the grants each contained more than 1,000,000 acres, and several others 200,000 each. Under the terms of the grants, the proprietors were virtually made hereditary members of the legislature, while the owners of other great grants were so opulent that they commanded their own constant election to the legislature. [4]

Meanwhile, expanding in all directions, English materialism had not overlooked Canada. Ten years after establishing the Council of Trade, Charles II, in 1670, granted to a group of intimates, servitors and merchants a perpetual charter for the exploitation of western Canada. The incorporators of the Hudson Bay Company—formally styled "The Governor and Company of Adventurers Trading into Hudson's Bay"—were Prince Rupert, Count Palatine of the Rhine, Duke of Bavaria, Cumberland, etc.; the Duke of Albermarle, otherwise General Monk, who had been the chief instrument in restoring Charles to the throne; the Earl of Craven, Lord Arlington, and Lord Ashley, together with Sir John Robinson, Sir Charles Vyner

and other knights and various London merchants. Granted
upon the nominal condition of the company's discovering a new
passage to the South Sea,[5] the charter endowed the company
with an exclusive monopoly of trade and commerce of all waters
and lands in whatever latitude, within and adjacent to the en-
trance of Hudson's Straits, provided such territories are "not
now possessed by any of our subjects or the subjects of any
other Christian Prince or State."

At the identical time that Charles munificently conferred
this charter, Canada was claimed as French territory; in fact
the king of France, forty-three years previously, had granted
a like charter to a French company. Not until more than a
century after the grant of the Hudson Bay Company charter did
Canada come by conquest under British sovereignty. In later
times when the legality of the Hudson Bay Company was attacked, this asserted usurpation was made one of the strongest
arguments. Familiar with the historic boundaries of Canada,
William McD. Dawson, head of the Crown and Forests Branch
of the Government at Toronto, insisted before an investigating
committee that the early boundaries of Canada or New France
indisputably included the whole of Hudson's Bay, and a petition from the Toronto Board of Trade made the same declaration.[6]

Exclusive trading and commercial rights were, however,
only part of the sweep of powers granted to the Hudson Bay
Company. It was given possession of lands, mines, minerals,
timber, fisheries and other resources in its huge domain. Empowered with governing functions it could, suiting its will or
purposes, appoint all officials, including judges, and make or
revoke laws, ordinances and regulations. Also, it could freely
inflict penalties and punishments, "provided the same are
reasonable, and not repugnant to the laws of England." This
qualifying provision did not detract from the company's arbitrary powers, exercised as they were in a far-away region,
whence news could only with difficulty reach England. To ensure adequate protection of its properties the company was
granted the right to build forts, employ an armed force, and
take other forcible measures. In return for its colossal powers
all that the charter required was a ceremonious triviality:

whenever the king or any of his successors entered the company's territories, the royal visitor should receive two elks and two black beavers.[7]

So was launched, equipped with mighty and extensive powers, a corporation the enormously profitable career of which, in one way or another, has continued to the present time. The Hudson Bay Company ranked among the foremost of England's overseas corporations as a ceaseless source of wealth. This wealth was an important part of the capital successively invested in English industries and finance, and in Canadian or foreign enterprises. Apart from the English stockholders, a line of the Hudson Bay Company's directing officials in Canada emerged to become in course of time magnates controlling or swaying huge land possessions, and great banking and transportation systems.

From the Hudson Bay Company's inception its capacity to ensure profits caused jubilation among the interested in England. The dimensions of those profits is not assumed; exact or fairly exact facts were set forth in the subsequent statement of J. H. Pelley, sometime Governor of the Hudson Bay Company. A summons from the Lords of the Committee of Privy Council for Foreign Trade ordered him, in 1838, to inspect the company's old ledgers and report findings. In a communication stamped Hudson Bay House and dated February 7, 1838, Pelley informed the committee: "Between the years 1670 and 1690, a period of twenty years, the profits appear to have been very large, as, notwithstanding losses sustained by the capture of the company's establishments in the year 1682 to 1688, amounting to £118,014, they [the Company] were enabled to make a payment to the proprietors in 1684 of 50 per cent, and a further payment in 1689 of 25 per cent."

At the time of their distribution these dividends were praised as a brilliant showing for a company in its merest beginnings, and were heralded as a forerunner of still greater benefits. Enthusiasm took the substantial form of lavish stock-watering. In the year 1676 the amount of the company's stock was £10,500. Fourteen years later, by sheer manufacture of additional shares, the capital stock was expanded to £31,500, and simultaneously stockholders received a payment of 25 per cent on the new stock. Later, by the same inflation, the stock was again trebled, making £94,500; and a slight new subscription of £3,150 in funds was converted into thrice the amount in stock. Such was the extent of the stock-watering that of the total capital of £103,950 on December 23, 1720, only £13,150 represented payment in money.[8]

After examination of the company's returns during more than its first century of operations, as nearly as he was able to ascertain from the "defective state of the books," Pelley submitted data which sufficiently evidenced the company's steady prosperity, irrespective of setbacks. French capture, in the years 1692–1697, of some of its posts and their contents, had entailed losses to the company of £97,500; consequent depletion of funds made necessary the borrowing of money at six per cent. Nevertheless, so rapidly did mounting profits overcome these factors that the company was able, in the year 1720, "again to treble their stock with a call of only 10 per cent on the proprietors." And despite more losses incurred in the year 1782 from French aggression, the company, as indicated by its ledgers, apparently paid dividends of 5 to 12 per cent, amounting to an annual average of 9 per cent and showing, Pelley explained, "during the past century, profits on the originally subscribed capital stock, actually paid up, of between 60 and 70 per cent per annum for the years 1690 to 1800." [9]

How was the Hudson Bay Company able to transform the wastes of a remote region into vast profits? By the force of its trading methods. The company's rigorous exploitation of Indian tribes was its chief persistent end, but auxiliary to this was an oppression of its employes, then classed in the menial and submissive station of "servants." Any independent motion on their part was punished by a beating, if not worse; and if any white man, without authority from the company, was detected trading with the Indians, he was lashed. The Hudson Bay Company's methods of trading with Indians both followed and exceeded those of other companies. For furs the company bartered brandy, tobacco, blankets, beads and other wares; its domain was a wide outlet for imposing upon natives the

spurious goods made in England. Shortweight in sale of goods
to Indians was also a fixed practice. Lashing was the reprisal
wreaked upon Indians if they complained of having been
cheated.

At first liquor was shipped from Europe in large barrels, but
difficulties in overland transportation taught the convenience
of using small kegs. When these reached their destination, the
contents were liberally diluted with water, the larger bulk
manifestly bringing greater returns in furs. Excesses in cruelty
and in debauchery of Indians eventually led to disclosures
brought to England by employes who had been either sufferers
from brutality or witnesses of its perpetration. A Parliamentary
investigation in the year 1749 resulted. In his book published
in 1752, Joseph Robson, fresh from experiences in Hudson
Bay territory, declared that the company never gave orders
for "virtue and sobriety until after several hearings in which
its barbarity to the natives and their [the company's] servants
was proved by sundry affidavits." [10]

As events proved, this display of reformation was superficial
and ephemeral. It was done for public effect following the 1749
investigation. Reserving to itself the exclusive right not only
to sell but to raise produce, the Company forced Indians to
trade with it on its own hard terms or otherwise subsist upon
hunting. But the Indians had become wholly accustomed to
the use of guns, and from the company only could they buy
ammunition. Denial of this brought either starvation or recourse to cannibalism, both of which tragic results were not
uncommon.[11]

In no respect, though, did the Parliamentary investigation of
1749 impair the Hudson Bay Company's power and standing.
Harrowing as were the disclosures, knowledge of them was in-
terred in records the contents of which never reached the general public. Although constitutional liberty was considerably extended during the reigns of the early Georges, it did not ensure
freedom of the press. Parliament's hostility to publication of
its proceedings had long been inflexible and long remained so.
If editors circuitously managed to get information and published it even in the most guarded and innocuous way, they were
subject to arrest and penalizing.

The Board of Trade, on the contrary, energetically sought to supply the fullest information on existent trade and to point out means of facilitating its greater growth. In an elaborate report, in 1721, on the "State of the British Colonies in North America," the Board of Trade had gratified British business by its survey of prevailing profitable results and by its indication of prospective opportunities. The colonies dealt with were the ten then formed from New Hampshire to Carolina, with Nova Scotia added. Newfoundland and Hudson Bay were not classed as colonies. The report computed that Britain exported annually at least £1,000,000 sterling in British and other goods to American colonies, the West Indies and other Atlantic Islands and to Africa. Of this total, the American colonies took fully £500,000 a year. Glowingly the report expatiated upon "the advantages accruing to Great Britain from so large an exportation to the colonies on the continent of America from whence, as hath been shown, there doth arise a balance of £200,000." Further, the report pointed out in congratulatory terms, many of the commodities received by Britain from America were such that otherwise they would have to be bought from foreign nations, and that in the re-exportation from Britain of tobacco, sugars and other goods "there is a very great profit."

The triumphant progress of Britain's trade, notably with the American colonies, was vaunted in the report. The three years 1714–1717 had shown an aggregate of 899 British ships clearing for the American colonies; the number of ships engaged in trade with Jamaica, Bermuda and other Atlantic lands brought the total to 2,014 ships of 226,762 tons. Employed in what was called the "plantation" trade, this fleet was more than a sixth part of all British ships sailing from English ports to all foreign countries, and it was even "very probable," the report noted, "that the trade which is carried on between England and the American plantations employs at least one-fourth part of the shipping annually cleared from this kingdom." Analyzing further, the report took account of the number of ships carrying American colonial goods re-exported from Britain to Germany, Holland and other countries; "consequently, it may be concluded that one-third of the shipping employed in the foreign trade of this kingdom is maintained by the plantation trade." [12]

Nothing less than complete monopoly crushing all of America's native trade satisfied British manufacturers and merchants, who would not brook the slightest infringement of their paramount rights. Parliament, in 1699, had by act prohibited exportation of American woolen goods to any place. Later acts forbade manufacture in the American colonies of a variety of articles, the exclusive trade in which was insisted upon by Britain. Colonists were even restrained from exporting natural resources. The Board of Trade prohibited exportation of timber for ships to foreign countries. When, despite this restriction, New England merchants shipped timber from Massachusetts and New Hampshire to Spain and Portugal, Lord Bellomont was wrathful at the openly-displayed spirit of defiance. "These people laugh at your Lordships' order, and so they would at an order from the King." So, on January 2, 1701, he notified the Board of Trade; and he advocated as an intimidating remedy an act of Parliament to make colonial participation in the trade a penal offence.[13]

Authority, as embodied in the Board of Trade, was thrown into a continuing state of perturbation by the refusal of American colonists to heed its orders. Likewise, British officials in America were trying desperately to find some way of subduing a people unawed by menace of law. This spirit, Colonel Robert Quary, a crown official in America, informed the Board of Trade on June 16, 1703, was due to the democratic influence and institutions of Massachusetts. Abolish colonial local governments, he counseled, and put all colonies under command of one strongly centralized government.[14]

In England kings and queens and partisan administrations with their shifting policies came and went, but there never was any deviation in the Board of Trade's assiduous object to keep every possible particle of trade in British hands. Its 1721 report most carefully itemized every detail of each American colony's trade, and the social and political conditions affecting such trade. That Massachusetts settlers had always worked their own wool into cloths, coarse though these were; that those settlers made homespun linen, half cotton though it was; and that they also made goods from leather, were matters of pro-

found concern to the watchful Board of Trade. Scanning closely
the products, and also judging the institutions, of other American colonies, the Board of Trade vented its exasperation in
threatening proposals. It denounced American colonies for
having had the temerity to disobey its orders; "they have
broken through the laws of trade and navigation, and made
laws of their own contrary to those of Great Britain . . . and
have carried on a trade destructive to that of Great Britain."
Such independent temper, the Board of Trade urged, must
be suppressed by elimination of colonial governments all too
assertive of their privileges, and by the subordination of all
colonies under the absolute governing power of a single Lieutenant-Governor.[15]

The great bulk of British manufactures exported to the
American colonies consisted of woolen goods in the making of
which, as we have seen, fraud was ineradicable. The remainder
of Britain's exports included more wares in the manufacture
of which fraud was often notorious—linens, sailcloth, cordage,
silk, iron products, pewter and other goods. Colonial exports to
Britain were mainly furs and skins, tobacco, turpentine, rice,
sugar, logwood, train oil and whale fins.

As the richest of all traffic, the fur trade and its greater
possibilities constituted a subject over which the Board of
Trade pondered much. It was in this trade that the British encountered intense competition from the French. With its influential ramifications in Britain, the Hudson Bay Company
did not have to fear an accounting there for its malefactions.
Its difficulties lay in Canada itself. French raiding within its
territories was occasional. But claiming, as the company did,
sovereignty over lands far from its chartered bounds, its trading agents came into collision with French traders more adept
in winning the favor of outlying Indian tribes. And by either
penetrating into Britain's northern American colonies or inducing Indians there to go to French posts, the French traders
outwitted many of the British in the capture of Indian trade.

This French success was imputed by British officials in
America and, in turn, by the Board of Trade, to the adroitness
of French missionaries in making their propaganda serve the

double purpose of advancing religion and trade. The frequent
and severe aspersions upon those missionaries were but the reflection of the bitterest bigotry then prevailing in England and
in most of its American colonies, where priests were outlawed
and Roman Catholics banned and disfranchised. Following
England's lead, nearly all the colonies had enacted laws dis-
abling Catholics from holding public office, and forbidding
entry to priests. Without specifying all the various laws, one
of a number enacted in New York shows the extremes to which
the virulence of passionate bigotry could go. By a New York
law of August 9, 1700, all priests were compelled to leave New
York province before November 1; any thereafter remaining
and preaching his faith was to be deemed "an incendiary and
a disturber of the public peace and safety," and was liable
to suffer perpetual imprisonment.[16]

The Board of Trade strongly pressed the advisability of
extending the Indian trade "as far westward as lakes and rivers
behind the mountains," doubtless meaning the Alleghenies.
British traders were advised to emulate the tactics of the
French. These had furthered their interests, the Board of
Trade set forth, by encouraging intermarriage with Indians;
and although the English had formerly sought to propitiate
Indian chiefs by giving presents, this ingratiating practice had
been discontinued by the English while the more politic French
traders had adhered to it as a regular custom. But the Board
of Trade's recommendations for the "cultivation of good understanding with the Indians" were not as essential as that body
thought. Already the British possessed the means to a growing
ascendency in the fur trade. British traders resumed giving
presents to the chiefs, but economic advantages conferred a
much stronger hold than gratuities or amicability.

British power to undersell the French was one uppermost
factor. The British were able to sell cloth cheaper, and by turning to rum they could supply a liquor less costly than the
brandy upon which the French had wholly to depend. The
French Government, in 1708, had complained to its functionaries in Canada that, in addition to higher prices paid by the
English for beaver, the English sold merchandise at a lower

rate than did the French.[17] For this "unfortunate state of things," the French Government demanded a remedy which never came and could not come. The goods most wanted by Indians were made in England. After buying them there, the French had to have them conveyed to France, from whence they were shipped to Canada, only to meet more transportation costs and difficulties in transit via the St. Lawrence River. The largest, most valuable part of French cargoes to Canada for the Indian trade consisted of duffels, blankets and other woolens which were bought at a price much cheaper in England than the price demanded in France. And strouds (blankets made of a coarse warm cloth), prized by the Indians more than any other article of clothing, were made in England alone.

These facts explanatory of the situation were contained in Cadwallader Colden's "Memorial on the Fur Trade" submitted on November 10, 1724, to Governor William Burnett of New York. Colden described the predicament of the French who, desiring rum in place of brandy for the Indian trade, had no commodities in Canada which could be exchanged in the West Indies markets for rum. In fact, as a supplementary and near source, the British set up a rum distillery in New York. French traders were left with no alternative but that of using the costly brandy;[18] and in 1726 French officials in Canada mournfully acknowledged the effective methods of the British traders in "furnishing them [the Indians] goods at a very low rate, and supplying them with rum, which is their [the Indians'] favorite beverage." [19]

Not until nearly forty years later did the Board of Trade, impressed by the horrors of the French and Indian War, prohibit in colonial America the debauching of Indians with liquor. Whereupon, it is curious to note, a remonstrance signed by many of New York's foremost merchants—Henry Bleecker, John DePuyster, Abraham Schuyler and sundry other founders or scions of rich families—was forwarded in 1764 to the Board of Trade. They lamented the considerable decrease of trade already resulting, and, with a high air of considerateness for the Indians, pronounced the order a violation of Indian rights to "liberty of trade." Further on the petition avowed with brutal candor the real object sought: "Whereas, when the vent of liquor is allowed among them it spurs them to an unwearied application in hunting in order to supply the trading places with furs and skins in exchange for liquors." [20]

CHAPTER V

RAGING SPECULATION

THE numerous new trading areas acquired throughout the world by England in the seventeenth century had opened a dizzy era for English manufacturers and traders. In that century Holland was Europe's financial and commercial center, and from stock speculation methods at Amsterdam other European nations learned lessons. In England company after company was formed, and upon powers conferred by Government and the roseate visioning of enormous profits, extravagant quantities of stock were issued. There ensued outbursts of speculation to the obvious excesses of which no official attention was given until after an acute commercial crisis in 1696–1697.

War costs and stock inflation had ushered in a period of disaster, bringing ruin to a number of companies. The only public opinion which then had power to make itself audible was that of the investing class, recruited from various divisions of the propertied class. The Board of Trade gave heed to the investors' laments. With an outspokenness that rarely marked its comments, it submitted, in 1696, a scathing arraignment, under the non-committal title of "Report on the Present State of Our Trade." This report deplored "the pernicious art of stockjobbing" which "hath of late so wholly perverted the end and design of companies and corporations created for the introducing or carrying on of manufactures to the private profit of the first projectors." What use had these made of their powers and grants? Commonly, the report stated, no other than the selling of their stock "to ignorant men, drawn in by the reputation, falsely raised and artfully spread, concerning the thriving state of their stock."

Hence we note that in essentials there was then in dextrous operation the decoying contrivance commonly regarded as a concoction of the financial schemers of recent times. Substitute

45

the present colloquialism "unloading" for selling, and the picture of seventeenth-century frauds upon gullibles becomes still more clarified. And, also, the species of predacious promoters, now usually considered an outgrowth of modern industrialism, were then in successful activity. "Thus," the report went on, referring to promoters, "the first undertakers, getting quit of their company, by selling shares for more than they are really worth, to men allured by the noise of great profit, the management of that trade and stock comes to fall into unskillful hands."

Conventional accounts have reverenced that time, and slightly later, as an era when masters of industry, giving life service to it, knew its processes thoroughly and adhered to it with unshaken fidelity. That Board of Trade report, however, presented verities. It set forth the calamitous as well as the scandalous "effects of this stock-jobbing management" in causing companies starting "from very promising beginnings to dwindle away to nothing." They had fallen into "a worse condition than if they were left perfectly free and unassisted by such laws and patents." The distressing state of the paper and linen manufacturers was one example given. Another was that of the fisheries; even in this line stock-juggling companies were numerous. The affairs of fisheries would not be bettered, the report declared, until there was formed a responsible company so properly conducted "as may secure the management of it from the destructive shuffling of stockjobbing." [1]

Although at this time there was not any regularly constituted Stock Exchange at London, transactions were carried on by brokers congregating in a space in the Royal Exchange. Their shady dealings caused antagonism, and their growing numbers became a nuisance. Ejected, they made their headquarters in a thoroughfare called Exchange Alley and in adjoining coffeehouses.

Acting upon a charge in the Board of Trade report that brokers "confederated themselves to raise the price of stocks," Parliament, in 1697, set out to regulate their activities. The preamble of a law then passed sketched the existing condition of market manipulation of bank, industrial and other shares; various stockbrokers "do unlawfully combine to raise and fall

the value of such securities for their own advantage." Applying
for three years, this law excluded from the brokerage business
anyone not licensed by the London city authorities, and restricted the number of brokers to an even hundred. No broker
could charge more than 10 per cent, and for violation of the
law there were heavy penalties.[2] Renewed for another seven
years, the law, at the end of that time, was permitted to lapse,
with Parliament uninfluenced by agitation for its re-enactment.
In 1708, however, Parliament decided that by a law putting a
40 per cent tax on stockbrokers it had taken adequate means
to compel them to disgorge fat profits.[3] But a few years later
the brokerage tax was reduced to a slight amount,[4] whereupon
stockbrokers waxed in profits and saw no barrier to their
frauds, since they could easily recoup the amount of any fines
they might incur.

In 1710, after a financial panic caused by speculation in the
stocks of dubious insurance companies, the public treasury was
exhausted. The Premier, Robert Harley, Earl of Oxford, managed to get £3,000,000 for it by two public lotteries, but this
sum was wholly insufficient to fill the gap. Premier Harley now
devised a scheme intended to serve the double purpose of providing the Government with money to pay its debts and of
establishing British commerce in desired regions.

Virtually of Government inception, the South Sea Company
—formally called the "Company of Merchants of Great
Britain Trading to the South Seas"—was, however, chartered
in September, 1711, as a private company. The nature of this
enterprise was regarded as affording an ingenious means to
British trade for the penetration of all of Spain's American
ports, and as giving no opportunity to continental European
trading nations to complain of overt British aggression. The
company's bankers were mainly rich merchants, confident that
the prospects of huge profits from trade and from the gold and
silver mines would magnetize the small investor.

The program of this company was practically the first in
which any direct and systematic effort was made to draw in
petty investors; heretofore they had been ignored and scorned.
The appeal to them was colored with fervent patriotism. It

represented the company as coming to the rescue of the empty public treasury, and was deemed all the more persuasive on that account.

Of the real and full career of the memorable South Sea Company there has been no adequate historical account. Fragmentary sketches and outlines are, perhaps, familiar, but they are meager, inaccurate and omit many vital facts. They have mainly depended for their information upon biographies and other books written after the event. But it is only by patient excavation and consultation of official and other public records of the time itself that the correct and complete story is obtainable.

Its charter granted to the South Sea Company exclusive trading rights, with certain exceptions, to the East Coast of South America throughout its entire length, and a monopoly of trading in the Pacific Ocean, including the whole American coast. If any British interloping ships presumed to engage in commerce in its domain, the company was empowered to seize them by force and confiscate them. The company was granted further arbitrary powers in the right to make its own laws wherever it traded, and to judge and punish employes and others by fines and imprisonment. It was declared the sole owner of all islands that it might discover. Its stock (which in a few years was expanded almost to £40,000,000) was exempted from all taxes.

In return for these rights, estimated as having a great present and colossal future value, the company agreed to take over nearly £10,000,000 of the national debt. On this they were to receive 6 per cent interest, or £600,000 a year, and an allowance of £8,000 for expenses of arranging the transaction. Britain's public debt consisted of various kinds of securities and notes. In exchange for money loaned to it the Government issued what were called annuities, giving the lenders fixed incomes for life or assured for a specific period. There were also Treasurers' orders or Exchequer tallies, representing money loaned to the public treasury, for payment of which the Government was responsible. By the terms of the charter the company was given three further hugely valuable rights. All Government debentures taken over by it were to be deemed and passed as public money; they were to be made part of the company's capital stock; and the company could demand annuities for the debentures that it took over. Another of the charter's provisions allowed the company's members to be members of Parliament.[5]

The South Sea Company's plan seemed so plausible and so advantageous to debt holders that, within three months after the granting of the charter, possessors of more than £9,000,000 of Government debts had assented to the company's arrangement. Headed by the Earl of Sunderland, who was at the same time Britain's Premier, the company now reached out for greater spoils. Britain's entire debt was £30,000,000. In 1719 the directors came forward with a plan to take over the full national debt, offering the Government £3,500,000 for the privilege. The offer was hailed as a great proof of their public benefaction, in that they were relieving investors of debt holdings which the Government had no funds to pay, and were giving in exchange South Sea stock which already had a substantial market value and promised much larger accretions. However, underneath the fair appearance of the company's ostensible intent and benevolent pose was the covert aim of ensnaring annuity holders. By issuing for the occasion a comparatively small amount of South Sea Company stock at a high premium, the company, by the terms of the bargain, would receive a large amount of annuities which could then be retired. In addition to the company's great profits from this transaction, the Government would pay it a large sum in interest and charges.

But the South Sea Company now encountered two powerful antagonists in the Bank of England and the East India Company. Beginning a quarter of a century previously without a pound of cash capital, the Bank of England had become eminently rich by grace of Government favors and funds and by exemption from taxation on its capital stock. It naturally objected to a scheme threatening to give the South Sea Company a monopoly, or almost so, of Britain's money supply and banking business. And, although the South Sea Company's charter, with a view to safeguarding the East India Company's interests, expressly prohibited trading in East Indian goods, the East

India Company was alarmed at the rise of a new company which might seriously trench upon its power.

The Bank of England offered the Government £5,000,000 for the same privileges requested by the South Sea Company, which now in turn raised its bid. As the sequel showed, several of the Cabinet ministers were heavily bribed, and the South Sea Company's offer was accepted. But it was necessary to obtain an enabling act from Parliament, in both houses of which were beneficiaries or supporters of the Bank of England and the East India Company. The passage of the desired act, in April, 1720, was, as also shown by the sequel, secured by a general bribery of members. Connivance of the king's German mistresses was gained by presenting them with a share of the corruption fund.

CHAPTER VI

MONEY MANIA IN FRANCE AND ENGLAND

MEANWHILE, there was growing in France a great gambling mania which, through the medium of the South Sea Company, soon spread its infection to England.

France was loaded with a public debt amounting to 2,000,-000,000 livres, on which sum its Government had been unable to pay interest. The Duke of Orleans, then Regent of France, and his advisers were completely nonplussed as to how or where to raise money, when there came to Paris a man with a scheme. This welcome individual was John Law. The son of a goldsmith and banker, Law had been born in Edinburgh in 1671. When twenty-three years old he was condemned to death for killing his opponent in a duel in London, but escaped to the continent where for years he led a roving life, partly in gambling and partly in trying to enlist various governments in the adoption of his theories and financial ideas.

When still callow Law had written a book on money and trade; and to the ideas he there maintained he clung with unswerving fanaticism, advocating them forcefully on every possible occasion. His theory was that the value of money was based wholly upon public confidence. Since in his opinion this was so, he argued that paper or any other token would serve the purpose as well as gold: both paper and gold alike represented nothing more than signs or evidences of wealth. Better than silver as a basis for money, Law declared, was land; and with this stable foundation the currency of a country could properly be expanded to the whole value of its lands. His contention was that such an increase of currency would not cause depreciation of that currency but would bring a lowering of interest, thus stimulating trade and augmenting wealth.

Under the auspices of the Duke of Orleans, Law with associates established the Banque Générale, with a capital of 6,000,-

000 livres, divided into 1,200 shares of 1,000 crowns each. The notes of Law's bank commanded a premium over specie and were accepted in payment of taxes. To this early success of the Banque Générale two factors mainly contributed. First, the Government had repeated an old artifice of manipulation: it had called in and restamped its gold currency, issuing as worth twenty livres coins for which, when paid back to it, it had given only sixteen livres. By paying a higher price for these coins than did the Government, Law's bank naturally received money for its notes. The other factor was the Government practice of altering at its will the value of the marc of silver in proportion to the livre which was the coin commonly used. These frequent changes gave an element of uncertainty to contract settlements. Law judiciously made his bank's notes payable in livres of the same weight and fineness as those of the coin currently passed at the date of the note. Added to these factors was the convenience of carrying paper money, which met with wide popular favor.

With prestige acquired and public confidence gained, Law set out on a more ambitious scheme. Considerably before this time a company had been incorporated for trading purposes to Louisiana and Canada, but it was regarded as having forfeited its rights. In 1717 these rights were transferred to Law for the foundation of a new company which was organized as the Company of the West or Mississippi Company. The plan contemplated was that of paying the national debt, then rated at about 30 per cent of its nominal value, by the united operations of the company and the bank.

Asserting that prospects of vast profits fully justified the course, the Mississippi Company issued 100,000,000 livres of stock, in units of 500 livre shares, payable for a part of the public debt. On this issue of stock the Government paid the company 4 per cent interest, which enabled the company to declare a dividend for the same amount on its capital. With this value injected into the stock the market price of shares rose from 160 to 500 livres. Paying off the original stockholders, the Regent, in 1718, converted the Banque Générale into a royal bank, and in the following year the French East India Company was amalgamated with the Mississippi Company.

To give appearance of reality to the company's trading operations a few ships were bought, and, in the redoubled propaganda put forth, the number was magnified.

The next move was the company's contracting with the Government to farm all of the public revenues. (Farming long remained a European and longer still an Asiatic customary practice, whereby rulers empowered individuals to collect taxes and other dues. The revenue farmers paid the Government a certain percentage of the amount collected, or fixed sums, and retained the surplus of their collections.) As a condition of obtaining this farming contract, the Mississippi Company agreed to lend the Government 1,600,000,000 livres at 3 per cent, and the company assured the public that it was now able to pay the splendid dividend of 200 livres a share. The market price of stock at once rose to 5,000 livres a share. At the same time the bank was industriously operating the printing presses, manufacturing bank notes which, by October, 1719, reached the gigantic total of 2,696,400,000 livres. Simultaneously more shares were created. The new stock was bought by the Regent with the notes of his bank, and then, by borrowing the company's same notes, he paid the public debt. This accomplished, the bank and the Mississippi Company were, in February, 1720, reunited.

Looking on, the public had seen men make immense fortunes from the rise in the price of stock from 170 to 5,000 livres in a single year. Now came a general frenzy for quick riches from speculation and stockjobbing. The company's propaganda— or, at any rate, eulogies of its marvelous success and prospects —were not confined to France. They were spread broadcast in many European capitals. One of a number of pamphlets, intended chiefly for British consumption but printed in both French and English, told how "in Paris money grew so common that people did not know where to put it out at 3 per cent." The pamphlet further represented that the business of Parisian tradesmen had wonderfully improved and workingmen's wages had increased. "Many noblemen," the pamphlet further related, "repaired their broken fortunes; and others grew very rich. . . . Numbers of people, never known in the world, and sprung from nothing, were all of a sudden seen riding in their coaches, only by striking into this trade, by which in a very few months they gained vast sums." An appendix to the pamphlet gave a description of Louisiana, asserting that French settlers did not doubt the existence of gold and silver mines there; that the Indians had shown them some of the ore.[1]

Daniel Defoe in England could see nothing wrong in the South Sea Company's scheme (he himself, it was said, had suggested it to Premier Harley) but he wrote a pamphlet denouncing the Mississippi Company scheme. It unavoidably would "blow up," he declared. "The people of France are made the instruments of putting a cheat upon themselves." He explained the speculative mania as caused by "the volatile temper of the French whose levity only can account for what we are now to take notice of, and the warmth of the French temper must indeed be answerable for the running up of an imaginary stock." It was this temper, in his view, "which prompts them to push things to an extremity," and the mounting stock prices were caused by the "fluttering, rash disposition of the people of France." Of the Mississippi Company scheme he predicted: "Great will be the fall of it."

To Defoe's warning no credit was given, but his descriptions of the Paris speculation rage and its results only the more inflamed cupidity in England itself. When Defoe's pamphlet was penned Mississippi Company stock had gone up to 2,050 livres. "So eager," he wrote of scenes in Paris, "were the people to throng in their money into the stock that they were ready to tread one another to death to get to the books, and it was the greatest favor in the world to be admitted. . . ."[2]

Speculative fever now broke forth in Britain. As Law's Mississippi Company, once it sensed public ripeness for speculation, had quickly responded by putting out more and more stock, so now the directors of the South Sea Company and many other British promoters hastened to take advantage of a British public ready to be deluded. And as Law had shown the way to elevating himself in public estimation into a financial hero and a producer of national prosperity, so the South Sea Company's directors instigated impressive praise of their acumen, probity and patriotism. "They were esteemed," wrote a pamphleteer, "too wise to be deceived themselves and too honest to deceive their friends. Thus qualified for mischief they soon began it." [3]

When South Sea stock rose 100 per cent in a single day, the same pamphleteer wrote of the feeling in Britain, "a man of moderate fortune now seemed poor by all the riches about him so suddenly acquired. . . . The merchant who, through a long diligence and a great variety of hazard had gained a small estate, grew mad to see so many idle fellows enrich themselves in a day or two. The honest country gentleman who, by good management and wise economy, had been an age in paying off a mortgage, or saving a few small portions for his younger children, could not bear the big discourse and insults of this new race. Both laid aside their prudence, and at last became unhappy converts to South Sea. . . . The one despised his trade and sold his effects at any rate [price] to try his fortune, the other mortgaged what he could, or sold it for a little stock. . . ." [4]

Himself a speculator in South Sea stock, riches from which placed him for a time on the pinnacle of wealth, Dr. James Houstoun left in his "Memoirs" one of the best contemporary accounts. Of the uproar in Exchange Alley stock buying he wrote: "From the first quality [of rank] to the meanest tradesman, bustling and jostling together, and dealing for thousands of pounds in a minute; credit was so extensive that it was in the hands of everybody; they only wanted your name for it. . . . All were brothers in prosperity. . . . For during the violence of this raging distemper, the daily transactions in and about 'Change Alley amounted to a greater sum than the whole circulating cash of Great Britain amassed together." [5]

So speedily did the price of South Sea Company stock go up that many eager men of insufficient resources came in the market too late. But, they were assured, the South Sea Company's directors were men of public spirit and desirous of helping everybody. The price of South Sea stock, these late comers were further assured, would unfailingly reach £1,500; "they were advised to enlarge their capital and their success . . . in proportion would be much greater. Thus deluded into enlarging their capital they borrowed on the stock." [6]

Within a year the market price of the South Sea Company stock rose to £1,050 a share; Dr. Houstoun affirmed that it went as high as £1,300. Seeing such opportunities to gull the public, promoters of scores of other bubble schemes introduced and manipulated their stocks.

As the Mississippi Company speculation in France had given furious impetus to South Sea Company and other speculation in Britain, so now the gathering troubles besetting the Mississippi Company presently had a cooling effect in Britain. The rise of Mississippi Company stock to 10,000 livres a share did not and could not last long. During the time when the price ranged between 5,000 and 10,000 livres, many of the original holders or "insiders" sold their stock, flooding the market with shares, lowering prices, and interfering with the Government's sales of its Mississippi stock. The stupendous output of paper money caused its depreciation and drove gold and silver from France. Various expedients devised by the Government and the bank to retain these within that country were futile. By May, 1720, France's paper money circulation, amounting to the colossal sum of 2,235,000,000 livres, could not be sustained. Whereupon a royal edict ordered that its value be reduced one-half by immediate monthly reductions. This measure brought the French people face to face with realities; its instant effect was to make them refuse to accept bank notes, which were no longer seen in circulation. The significance of these moves, involving technical matters of finance, were not generally understood in Britain. For Law's bank and his Mississippi Company still functioned, and there had been no official extinction of the bank notes.

It was not until October, 1720, that the British public had a clear idea of what a catastrophe had come to France. But by early summer of 1720 some London financiers saw the situation clearly enough. And so great was the number of flimsy, illegal or fraudulent stockjobbing companies in Britain and so vast their stock issues, that alarm was manifested in high places.

The Lords Justices, on July 12, 1720, set out to put a stop to "those pernicious practices." The resolutions of those judges were confined to the operations of scores of mushroom companies which were stigmatized as "bubbles." A long list was given. The Lords Justices declared that "the sums intended to be raised by these airy projects amounts to a little less than £300,000,000, a sum so immense that it exceeds the value of all the lands in England." [7] In particular, writs were issued against various illegal concerns, among which were the English Copper Company and the Welsh Lead and Copper Company. The Prince of Wales, later George II, was the head, then called governor, of the English Copper Company. When formally notified that the company had no legal standing he asked the directors to choose another Governor.[8] Before he withdrew, it is chronicled, he pocketed £40,000.[9]

Some perceptive individuals who saw the explosive effects of the situation both in France and at home were selling South Sea Company stock in June and July, 1720. By August 17 the price had fallen to £830. The tricks to which the South Sea Company's directors now resorted were fully detailed in the Parliamentary records. To force up the price they immediately sent agents into Exchange Alley to buy up a considerable quantity of stock, the price of which thereupon rose to £880. Two days later it had fallen to £820.

Notwithstanding successive declines in price the spell of South Sea stock upon the public was unbroken. Crowds still surged in the company's offices which, although they had been enlarged, could not accommodate the swarms eager to exchange annuities for stock. For transaction of business it had been found necessary to put tables and desks in the streets. Careless of what the market price was and believing the price would rebound, crowds continued to do business directly with the company. "And the directors observing that great quantities of stock had been bought [on August 17 and 18] at £1,000 and even at higher prices" decided to close the transfer books, and five days later open other books for the selling of £1,000,-000 of capital stock, at the rate of £1,000 for every £100 share. This sum was to be paid in money, 20 per cent down, the remainder in installments. When subscriptions were opened at South Sea House on August 24 "there was such a vast crowd of subscribers, and amongst them not a few of the prime nobility, that in less than three hours more the intended sum was subscribed; and that very afternoon this fourth subscription was sold in Exchange Alley at 30 or 40 per cent advance." [10]

This was but a flash. Pressure of secret selling from various of the company's directors and officers for their personal account sent the price of the stock down in two days to £800, and a little later to £700. To silence outcries of hosts of annuity holders who had bought stock at much higher prices, the company's directors now executed a bold stroke. Although, as investigation later showed, the South Sea Company had no money to pay therefor, the directors passed a resolution "that 30 per cent in money should be the half year's dividend, due at Christmas next, and that from thence for twelve years further, not less than 50 per cent in money should be the yearly dividend on their stock." [11] At first, this declaration raised the price of stock to £800, yet it soon sagged, and kept on declining.

To appease a growing number of stockholders looking with dismay upon dubious shares for which sounder annuities had been exchanged, the South Sea Company's directors now staged a move for public effect.

A general meeting of the company was called for and held on September 8, 1720, and precautions were taken to crowd it with upholders of the company's policies. The proceedings began with a laudatory speech by James Craggs, secretary of the company, who fervidly maintained that no company "had ever performed such wonderful things" as had the great South Sea Company. It had, he went on, accomplished the miracle of reconciling all parties in one common interest and the equal marvel of extinguishing domestic animosities. With bland assurance Craggs ignored the falling market price of the company's stock and the mounting losses confronting legions of stockholders. He warmly described how "by the rise of its stocks the moneyed men had vastly increased their fortunes; the country gentlemen had seen the value of their lands treble in their hands; and they [the company] had at the same time done good to the church, not a few of the reverend clergy got great sums from this project. In short they [the company] had enriched the whole nation."

To the surprise of the company's officials who believed that they had the meeting completely in hand, a couple of persons ventured "to speak in favor of the annuities, and [proposed] to censure the directors, but they were presently hissed to silence." Saying that he knew of no reason why anybody should not be satisfied, the Duke of Portland made a motion for a vote of thanks, which resolution was enthusiastically adopted.[12]

This overwhelming vote, the directors expected, would certainly have a soothing effect upon the public. But slight as was the opposition at that meeting, the suppressing of it was noised abroad and awakened alarm among such of the public as saw the implications. On the next day the price of the stock fell to £640, making a sheer drop to £550 on the day following. The directors were in a quandary. They had used great sums in manipulating the stock market, and had committed the company to payment of preposterous dividends. Above all, they needed connection with a source of large cash supply. "Under the influence and interposition of some persons of the highest figure and station," the South Sea Company directors made overtures to the East India Company for a union of the two corporations. The proposal was rejected. Then the South Sea Company directors approached the Bank of England for assistance. Only conferences, or rather talks, were held on the morning of September 12, but upon the strength of these, the report was circulated as a fact that an agreement had been reached. South Sea stock thereupon rose to £670; in a few hours, when a denial was issued, the price fell to £580. A week later it was £400. Through September down and down went the market price, until by the end of the month it was £150.[13]

These great declines, together with the discrediting of the South Sea Company's securities, caused a furious run upon the largest goldsmiths and most "eminent" banking houses. Some of these had loaned great sums upon South Sea Company stock and upon that of other corporations. Goldsmiths and bankers precipitately closed their places and hastened to abscond. News of this spreading—and the news traveled fast—added to the general consternation and anger. Immediate action was taken to adjudge bankrupt the missing money custodians. Another threatening crowd made a fierce run upon the Sword-Blade Company, the banking auxiliary of the South Sea Company.

CHAPTER VII

WHEN BUBBLES BURST

WITH the loud bursting of the two giant bubbles in France and England a multitude of lesser bubbles vanished. In October, 1720, Law's bank was formally suppressed by the French Government, and the Mississippi Company became a nullity. The accounts of this combined scheme of jobbery and fraud were in so bewildering a state that the unraveling of the confusion took a long time and arduous application. All told, the bank had issued the prodigious quantity of 2,696,000,000 livres of bank notes. Of these 700,000,000 were found in the bank; the public had the remainder. Cash in the bank, amounting to 90,-000,000 livres, was used to pay off an equal amount in bank notes. For part of the balance of outstanding notes the Government paid holders at the rate of one-half of their nominal value; the other part was a total loss to holders. Of the Mississippi Company's 200,424 shares of stock, it was found, the public held 200,000 shares, and the Regent the insignificant remainder. The loss to the stockholders was estimated at 1,863,000,000 livres.[1]

Numbers of people were plunged from the heights of affluence or from the comfortable plane of easy circumstances to the depths of poverty. France, dispirited, was resounding with the cries of woe of a disillusioned, embittered population. Business was shattered and for a long time stagnant; there was a dearth of any medium of exchange. The deluge of paper money had forced from France to other countries an amount of coin computed at 500,000,000 livres. In all of the channels of trade confidence was lacking, and nobody trusted the Government. As much reviled now as formerly he had been extolled, Law was driven from France, and his estates were confiscated. He returned to England in the year following the South Sea Company's collapse, and there had the grim satisfaction of looking on at the baleful consequences of another monstrous bubble which no one could charge to his theories. Four years later he went to Italy, and died in Venice in 1729.

Of the total losses directly and indirectly caused in Britain by the mass of fraud and stockjobbery no approximation is obtainable. In Britain there was no accompanying increase of currency such as saturated France. On the other hand, stock schemes were far more numerous in Britain, and losses in that regard were correspondingly much greater. Conditions there were calamitous. The dislocation of trade affected all classes; the British people, or at least the sections which had possessed or could borrow money for stock investment or gambling, were "reduced to dejection and ruin." Noble families of ancient lineage and venerated as the country's honor—so lamented one pamphleteer—were "brought to ruin and beggary, and their estates [are] in the possession of sharpers." Numerous worthy gentlemen, tempted by extraordinary promises of profit to sell their estates and buy South Sea Company stock "have been stript of both money and lands." British merchants had been "obliged to quit their habitations and be vagrants in those parts of the world where [whence] they had formerly imported treasure to these kingdoms."

Further, "our middle sorts of persons are shutting up their shops; our artificers and poor are starving." The many who had borrowed for stock purchases were now pressed by creditors, who seized even household articles. "Are not," asked one pamphleteer, "their misfortunes great enough already who are thus reduced, who from plenty now scarce have bread? Must the last poor morsel be wrested?" This pamphleteer commented upon the general hardness of heart in this bitter adversity, every man thinking of his own skin. Another pamphleteer declared: " 'Tis owing to this sin of avarice we may justly impute our present misfortunes." [2]

Impressed by the money craze in which he had been a participant, Dr. Houstoun wrote in ironic vein: "My riches and grandeur did not last above seven or eight months before I was sunk into a deeper abyss than ever." He had lost everything and was £5,000 in debt. To escape his creditors—thousands of others were fleeing likewise—he had to go abroad where he obtained the post of physician and surgeon-general, first to the Royal African Company, then to the South Sea Company. Every time he even set foot in England his creditors hounded him. During his banishment he amused himself by writing a play which he entitled "Money, the Emperor of the World." The Emperor sat on a throne of great magnificence, and about him was a continual flow of money from an inexhaustible source. "The whole world," Houstoun wrote describing this part of his play, "is addressing his Imperial Majesty by turns; kings, courtiers, divines, lawyers, physicians and tradesmen. At a distance is placed a great multitude of the populace. All, from the knights to the cobbler, harangue this great monarch to serve their different views and designs in their own way." In various places in his book he expressed himself on money's power: "In short, sir, money is the devil, the very devil we all talk of and most worship." "We find by experience that money is the only lawgiver of Europe." [3] Dr. Houstoun also cherished the consoling reflection that there were great as well as little fools; he instanced the case of the Duke of Chandos, who lost "an immense sum of money" in Royal African Company stock speculation.[4]

Members of both houses of Parliament were in a bitter mood; charges were made and recriminations flung with irate frequency. A debate in the House of Commons, on December 8, 1720, was interspersed by the repeated use of the word criminal; and Lord Molesworth said that he "looked upon the contrivers and executors of the villainous South Sea schemes as the parricides of the country," and would be satisfied to see them treated in the ancient Roman way—that is, sewn in a sack and thrown in the river.[5] A few days later the House of Commons assented to this declaration: "That the present calamity is mainly owing to the vile arts of stockjobbers." [6] Both houses of Parliament ordered investigations. Public excitement was intense; and there had been a minority in Parliament, under the leadership of Sir Robert Walpole, which all along had opposed the South Sea scheme. The investigations were, accordingly, not of the usual leisurely or nominal kind, but were pushed with great rapidity.

When on January 21, 1721, it was found that Robert

Knight, cashier of the South Sea Company, had fled, the House of Commons at once ordered a strict search of all ports and coasts; later he was arrested at Antwerp. On the same day General Rosse of the House of Commons Committee of Secrecy, which was investigating, informed that body: "That they had already discovered a train of the deepest villainy and fraud that ever contrived to ruin a nation." [7] Three days later the House of Lords passed a resolution declaring that the taking of stock by any member of Parliament without paying for it was "a notorious and dangerous corruption." [8] The standards of the times are well shown by this resolution. Provided a member paid for stock, his voting in Parliament on measures affecting the company in which he held stock was entirely legitimate. This standard long continued that of the British Parliament.

A few days later the Select Committee of the House of Lords passed a resolution stating that the South Sea Company directors, on pretence of keeping up the price, had ordered great quantities of stock to be bought for the company. At the same time several of the directors and other officers of the company, "having in a clandestine manner sold their own stocks to the company, such directors and officers are thereby guilty of a notorious fraud and breach of trust." [9] On February 2, 1721, both houses of Parliament adopted resolutions denouncing as frauds various of the company's transactions and artifices to raise the price of stock. The promoting of the third issue of stock was done "to cheat the public"; the declaring of the 30 and 50 per cent dividends, when the company had no money to pay them, was "a villainous artifice to delude and deceive" and "a notorious fraud." [10]

The Committee of Secrecy's findings showed that £70,000 of South Sea Company stock had been handed to John Aislabie, Chancellor and Under-Treasurer of the Exchequer. This transaction was denounced as "a most notorious, dangerous and infamous corruption in the said Mr. Aislabie" who had "encouraged and promoted the dangerous and destructive execution of the late South Sea scheme with a view to his own exorbitant profit." A resolution was passed to expel him from the House of Commons and commit him to the Tower. [11] The finding further showed that before the act of April, 1720, was passed for the benefit of the South Sea Company, £50,000 of the company's stock had been given to the Earl of Sunderland, a member of the House of Lords; he, be it recalled, was Prime Minister and First Lord of the Treasury.[12] To James Craggs, Sr., Postmaster-General, £40,000 of the stock had been given. Craggs died soon after the company's collapse; his estate showed that he left £87,000 of South Sea stock, £34,000 of East India Company stock, and £1,000 of the Bank of England stock; and the committee denounced him as "a notorious accomplice and confederate of Robert Knight." [13] The Committee of Secrecy handed in seven reports in quick succession; these showed that large specified amounts of stock had been distributed among members both of the House of Lords and the House of Commons; many names of recipients were given.[14]

The estates owned by the directors of the South Sea Company amounted to a total of more than £2,000,000. When Parliament proceeded to confiscate those estates two of the directors implored leniency, upon which Mr. Shippen in the House of Commons said that "a whole injured nation called aloud for vengeance." [15] But less than a month later Parliament did modify its confiscatory rigor by allowing the directors to retain about one-sixth of their estates.[16] To making any allowance to Grigsby, one of the directors, a member of the House of Commons objected: "Since that upstart was so prodigally vain as to bid his coachman feed his horses with gold, no doubt but what he can feed on it himself. I, therefore, move that he [Grigsby] be allowed as much gold as he can eat, and the rest of his estate might go towards the relief of the sufferers." A motion to remit to Grigsby £10,000 was amended and passed to allow him £2,000.

The company's directors had loaned £11,000,000 on their own stock; among the numerous borrowers were 138 members of Parliament. In the case of bona fide buyers of the stock Parliament remitted this debt to the company upon payment of 10 per cent of sums borrowed, and made the same provision for the benefit of persons who had borrowed money from the company upon subscriptions. And of the £7,000,000 due from the company to the Government, £5,000,000 was remitted for the relief of sufferers from the South Sea scheme.[17] A number of the personages chiefly implicated opportunely died while the investigation was in progress, and various others escaped punishment.

Astonishing as it may seem, the South Sea Company managed to extricate itself and remain solvent. Its capital stock, still remaining at nearly £40,000,000, was, however, subjected to various changes in the course of years. Its monopoly of trading rights remained intact. For the surrender of certain of these, interfering with Spanish aims, the Spanish government, in 1750, paid the company £100,000 and an end then came to its commercial career. But its chartered privileges were as strong in law as ever, and prevented a number of rising British concerns from carrying out ambitious trading plans. In 1802 and 1807 the South Sea's exclusive rights, as also those of the East India Company, were modified by the passage of acts permitting any British ship to engage in fisheries in the Pacific Ocean without a license from either company. And in 1805 Parliament enacted a law declaring that the interests of general British commerce demanded the South Sea Company's surrender of its sole and exclusive trading rights. As compensation for the relinquishment of these, the Government paid the company £610,464.[18]

In 1834 the South Sea Company's holdings amounted to £10,144,584, of which £3,662,784 was company stock and the remainder annuities. On all of these the Government had paid the company regular interest, now totaling more than £304,000 annually, which was distributed among the stockholders.[19] Parliament decided in 1852–1853 to terminate the anachronism. It ordered the compulsory commuting of the company's holdings by their exchange for Government money payments or securities.[20] This done, the South Sea Company passed out of existence in 1854.

But to recur: So effectively had the French nation disabused itself by its Mississippi Company experiences that for fifty-six years thereafter no one had the hardihood to propose establishing a bank with power to circulate its notes. For an even longer time the French people, seared with memories, were immune to speculative fevers. This exemption, however, did not apply to Louis XV and his courtiers, who shamelessly speculated in wheat.[21] But a new and self-confident generation to which lessons of the past were obscured came upon the scene. Finding a spirit of acquiesence, or at any rate meeting no opposition, promoters succeeded, in 1776, in founding in Paris a new bank for the double purpose of making loans to the Government and discounting mercantile paper. Seeing a public ready and in fact eager to speculate, the bank's directors promoted the process by old devices made to look new, and in 1784 and 1785 a great public speculation broke forth. The French Revolution effaced the bank.

In England the public long shunned Exchange Alley. Professional speculation still went on with its frauds as vigorous as ever before. Seeking again to accomplish what previous laws had failed to bring about, Parliament, in 1733, passed another law for suppression of stockjobbing frauds.[22]

In a chapter on "Honesty in Trade," Daniel Defoe thought that possibly "the time may come, in spite of companies and companies of sharpers, that honesty may be able to appear upon 'Change again; and whether ever it may in the Alley or not, I dare not say." [23]

As the shock of the South Sea Company's collapse and the impoverishing effects of its stockjobbing operations gradually wore away, conditions improved. Marauding continued the partner of trade in India, and wealth poured into the coffers of Britain's possessing classes. By 1745 British commercial affairs were in such good shape that Horace Walpole could satirically note: "We have taken infinite riches; vast wealth in the Indies, vast from the West; in short, we grow so fat that we shall soon be fit to kill." [24]

CHAPTER VIII

SECRET FRAUD AND THE REVOLUTION

SOON after America had become a nation there were corruption scandals which were given much publicity. Legislatures were bribed to grant bank and other company charters, and to bestow upon corporations and speculators gifts of tens of millions of acres of public lands. A number of America's leading public men and jurists were instrumental in securing or validating those grants.[1] But British critics especially were pleased to take the pose of regarding these corruptions as something uniquely sinister, and of condemning them as the progeny of the American form of government. To the plain fact that such corruptions were only a continuation of the practices under British rule of America those critics were wholly oblivious.

The so-called representative form of government functioning in the British Parliament was aristocratic, with the lords in the upper body, and the lower house containing many of their relatives. Bribery, fraud and intimidation in elections had long been a commonplace. By the end of the eighteenth century a total of sixty-five statutes to prevent such corruption and fraud had been enacted in Britain. These laws were evaded by various devices, one of which was the employing of third persons to do the bribing; there was no law applying to them. Under the "rotten borough" system in operation until 1832, a handful of propertied voters elected the majority of the members of Parliament. This fact, according to a statement made in the House of Commons in 1790 by Henry Flood, a noted Irish politician, had been given as a reason for refusing representation to the American colonies; "when the American complained that he was not represented in the British House of Commons he was told that only a small part of the people of England were represented, and that he was therefore in the same state as an infinite number of the people of England." Flood added that the English were in the habit of regarding Americans as "an inferior species of beings who ought to be content with their station, though they did not at all partake of the elective capacity." [2]

Corruptly elected members of Parliament were accessories to all kinds of corrupt measures. Even those of the public who were able to read had no means of learning what actually went on in the sacred precincts of St. Stephen's. Browbeaten by the punitive laws, printers were compelled to resort to a variety of subterfuges. Such of the debates as they dared print were presented in a frightfully mutilated way, and usually were published six months or more after the debates had taken place. One has only to consult the news sheets and magazines during the reigns of the first three Georges to see the evasive, often amusing, contrivances that printers were obliged to employ. Names of Parliamentary speakers were hidden by the substitution of classical appellations, or concealed by the use of asterisks, or blurred by the elision of letters in names. Speeches thus printed were clothed in a ludicrously pompous phraseology, a monotonous flow of rounded sentences. They were the work of writers who took such bits of speeches as they were able to get and elaborated upon them. Not infrequently adept writers went further and invented entire speeches. [3]

While in Britain the press was thus gagged, the efforts of British officials in America to enforce British libel laws were not successful. Upon a charge of seditiously libeling the royal governor Lord Cornbury, John Peter Zenger, editor of the "New York Weekly Journal," was arrested and tried in 1735. His criticism, in reality, was aimed more at the British Government than at the governor. The jury ignored the charge of the prejudiced and instructed judges, and acquitted him. New York City residents saluted Zenger with cannon, and the municipality presented him with the freedom of the city in a gold box. Thereafter in America there were some further prosecutions but no jury would convict.

In the year following the outbreak of the American Revolution there was a lively debate in Parliament on a motion made by Temple Luttrell to admit reporters (referred to in the Parliamentary proceedings as "strangers") to the gallery of the

House of Commons. Luttrell, on April 30, 1777, urged the abolition of the long-standing order excluding reporters. Most of the laws, he stated, had been passed in the House "with a clandestine privacy, like lettres de cachet from the Court of Paris." Richard Rigby (a sinecurist holding many offices) arose and announced that he had always voted against admitting reporters and would continue doing so. "What good," he asked, "could result from strangers being in the gallery? Only to print speeches in newspapers of all sorts." Sir William Meredith, another member of the House of Commons, urged: "None but members ought to be present during the debates in the House. . . . The world at large, even our immediate constituents, have no just claim to be apprised of the minutiae of the debate." Luttrell's motion was defeated by a vote of 83 to 16.[4]

When the question again came up on January 29, 1778, the fact developed that the Speaker had somewhat relaxed the strict order against admittance of reporters, but this was a capricious decision not in the least impairing his power to bar reporters at any time. One member—Townshend—protested that it was unconstitutional to shut the doors generally against the people whom members represented, while another member—Vyner— thought that, as every member had the right to order strangers to withdraw, there was no need of enforcing it to an extreme.[5]

While the American Revolution was in progress a bill was introduced in the House of Commons, on April 13, 1778, to exclude men who held Government contracts from sitting as members. Sir Philip Jennings Clarke said that he could name many instances. Sir Cecil Wray explained that the bill was not one aimed at decent contractors but was intended to prevent the foul deeds of men leagued with Government officials to rob the public. Colonel Barre demanded open contracts, the awarding to be to the highest bidder. The debate was exceedingly bitter and even vituperative on the part of Government supporters. When the bill was again discussed, on May 5, following, Clarke said that proof had been presented showing how one contractor had obtained more than £35,000 above the ordinary profit on one contract; the contractors [profiteers], he declared, naturally wanted the war with America continued.[6] The bill was defeated by a vote of 115 to 113. Clarke, however, kept pushing the bill, with denunciations of "the influence of contractors on elections and of their immense profits." In the next year the bill was adopted. But, as was soon shown, whether or not profiteers sat in Parliament they were able to carry on their operations effectually.

We are now to acquaint ourselves with a hitherto unwritten chapter of the American Revolution. That the following facts have not been presented in conventional history is one of the most extraordinary of omissions. Of privations and deeds of the American Revolutionary army much has been recounted; suffering from want of adequate supplies and for a time ill-disciplined, that army won its way to victory against supposedly well-provided and disciplined troops backed by the resources and skill of the wealthiest of nations.

But the American Revolutionists had a virtual ally within Britain itself in the profiteers who plundered army and navy funds, and committed great frauds in every direction, particularly in foisting bad equipment upon Lord Cornwallis' army in America. Parliament could intimidate reporters and editors but it could not squelch rumor. As the years passed, exasperation increased at failure to suppress the American Revolution which the British people generally had been led to believe was carried on by designing leaders heading licentious mobs and by generals commanding disordered troops. Dissatisfaction in Britain with the heavy mounting costs of the war became acute. Rumors spread thickly of groups of army and navy officers and influential men making fortunes in a short time from war contracts. Nor were these rumors without visible substantiation— the spectacle of some of the war profiteers vaunting their wealth in gaudy display. The pressure of public opinion from without, and the indignant demands of some of its own members, moved the House of Commons, on November 10, 1780, to order an examination of the public accounts and a full report thereon.

Now came a series of sensational disclosures, the extent of which was not anticipated even by those who had a fair knowledge of the profiteering in process. The Commissioners appointed performed their task with deadly earnestness. Explaining first the machinery of army profiteering, the Commissioners related that the Quarter-Master General's function was to provide wagons, horses and their attendants and appendages for the army. When necessary, the Quarter-Master General could also hire vessels. In their departments the Barrack-Master General and the Chief Engineer exercised the same powers. The report went on:

"It is the duty of these officers to make contracts for the articles, and to see these contracts honestly and substantially performed. . . . But it has been the usage, so far back as our inquiry has gone, for the officers in these departments to be themselves the proprietors of, or to have shares or interests in, a great number of the vessels and the smaller craft, and in almost all the wagons and horses employed in these services. These officers have purchased or procured them upon their own account, and let them out to the Government at a fixed price of hire. The same persons, employed by and acting for the public, contracts, on the part of the public, with himself, for the hire of his own property, controls his own actions, and pays himself with the public money entrusted to his charge. . . .

"This practice has a manifest tendency to corrupt and endanger the service of the army; it weakens the military discipline; it infuses into the soldier the thrift for his own gain, and diverts his attention from honor and his country's service to the pursuit of wealth, and that, too, by intrenching upon the treasure of his country." [7]

The report showed that in supplying horses, wagons and attendants to Lord Cornwallis' army in America, the profiteers made a clear profit in three and a quarter years of £241,960. On December 23, 1780, Lord Cornwallis ordered a change in methods; he testified later that on several occasions he had found the horses and wagons supplied "in bad condition and unable to perform the service required"; and he issued orders that the Quarter-Master General should have no property in either horses or wagons, and should charge the Government no more than the amount actually paid.[8] Whether Cornwallis' instructions were carried out was not clear to the Commissioners. Hence they computed that if the same system of profiteering was continued to June 18, 1782, the profiteers reaped an additional profit of £175,902, making a total clear profit for horses, wagons and attendants of £417,592.[9] The profit thus paid from the public treasury, the Commissioners stated, represented sums beyond what the cost would have been had the horses and wagons belonged to the Government.

The sum mentioned was, however, only part of the loot in the Quarter-Master General's Department and in allied departments. These paid in the hire of vessels (exclusive of charges for pilotage and various contingencies) for the British army in America the sum of £127,483 from December, 1776, to March 31, 1780. The Commissioners further reported that in the list of owners of these vessels the names of subordinate officers in the Departments of the Quarter-Master General, Barrack-Master General and Commissary-General did appear. But in cases in which head officers were owners or had shares, care was taken not to record their names; the names of the vessels' captains were inserted in their stead. How lucrative the business was to the profiteers was shown by the Commissioners. A vessel of 100 tons, hired to the Government at 13 shillings per month per ton, yielded the owner £780 a year. "If possessed," the Commissioners went on, "of 50 large wagons and 200 horses (and the wagons and horses were in general the property of a few officers only), he [the owner] will have, as long as he can continue them in the service of the Government, a clear income of £9,885 secure from all risk." [10]

Successive Quarter-Masters General from 1776 to 1781 were Lieutenant-Colonel William Shirreff, Sir William Erskine, Lord William Cathcart, Brigadier-General Dalrymple and Captain Henry Savage. To them had been issued a sum totaling £1,688,379. To three Barrack-Masters—Major-General James Robertson, Lieutenant-Colonel George Clark and Major William Crosbie—had been issued a total of £662,419.[11] Profiteering was so great that, in his order of December 23, 1780, Lord Cornwallis directed that all necessary craft should thereafter be purchased for Government account, and that all unnecessary vessels hired to the Government should be dispensed with. At the same time Cornwallis ordered the Commissary-General to charge no more for fresh provisions, flour and Indian meal than what those foods cost him.[12] From 1776 to 1781 there was issued to three Commissaries-General a total of £1,521,076.

The allowance of vouchers without sufficient examination "pervades every branch of the expenditures under our consideration," the Commissioners reported. "Of the £10,000,000 and upwards that have been issued for these [army] services within the last six years, accounts of a few officers only, amounting to £1,100,000, have as yet been rendered to the proper office. The accounts of about £8,760,000 still remain to be accounted for." [13] From 1776 to 1780 the total sums issued for British army supplies and provisions in America—including £322,308 to the Chief Engineer's Department—were £4,194,-183. Dealing with the plundering of a large part of this, the Commissioners suggested the possibility that "the public might be enabled to obtain restitution where they have been defrauded, and security against imposition and peculation for the future." [14] Need it be said that the profiteers were able to keep their loot?

But these were not the only startling facts the Commissioners found as to peculations of Government army funds. Calling for all records the Commissioners received and examined old as well as recent accounts. From the past came proofs that peculations were of long standing and of magnitude. Henry, Earl of Lincoln, Paymaster-General, had received from the Exchequer in six months from December, 1719, to June, 1720, the sum of £473,127 of which, the Commissioners reported, no account was ever given, nor could the money be traced in any way; "neither book nor paper relative to this account is to be found" in either the Paymaster's or Auditor's office.[15] As the Commissioners reported in another case uncovering an old peculation, there was no reason for probing further into the distant past; their inquiries were concerned with recent years and the present. Having stumbled upon the Earl of Lincoln's defalcation they did not pursue investigations of the accounts of early or mid-eighteenth century Paymasters-General.

"It has been the practice of the Paymasters-General, when they went out of office," reported the Commissioners, "to take with them the books and papers that relate to their accounts, as their own private property, although these official books are, and should be considered as the property of the public, and, as such, left and deposited in the Pay Office, for the use and information of posterity." [16]

In the years immediately preceding 1768 the successive Paymasters of the Forces were Lord Henry Holland, Charles Townshend, Lord North, George Cooke and Thomas Townshend. The private retention of public money by Paymasters of the Force after they had left office, was, the Commissioners reported, "a usage of office." At the time of his resignation a Paymaster-General took with him a sum of public money which he kept in his possession until his accounts were passed by the Auditors of the Impost.

Of the loss to the public the Commissioners reported: "A computation of interest at four per cent per annum, upon these balances every year, from six months after they had severally resigned the office, proves that the loss of money left in the hands of Lord Holland amounts, at simple interest, to £248,394; of Mr. Charles Townshend to £24,247; of Lord North and Mr. Cooke [jointly] to £18,775; of Mr. Cooke and Charles Townshend [jointly] to £3,419." These sums, with odds of shillings added, totaled £294,836 actual loss to the public in loss of interest.

The Paymasters-General, the Commissioners further reported, constantly had in their hands sums much larger than were needed for army service. Nearly £46,000,000 was issued to Lord Holland; not until seven years after his resignation was his final account handed in to the Auditor. It was eleven years after his resignation that Charles Townshend accounted for the £2,000,000 in his hands; and twelve and eleven years after they had left office before the subsequent Paymasters-General turned in their accounts.[17]

Of the funds that they took with them upon quitting office, four Paymasters-General returned the balances to the Exchequer about twelve years after their resignation, and then only upon peremptory orders of the Commissioners. When leaving office Lord Holland, for example, took £460,000; thirteen years passed and his representatives paid back £200,-000 into the Exchequer; two more years went by and then

upon demand of the Commissioners £256,000 more was returned. During all of this time Lord Holland had the benefit
of the interest.[18]

Proved malfeasances or peculations in the Navy Department
reached far back. The records disclosed a hitherto unknown
and unsuspected fact, namely that Lord Anthony Falkland,
Navy Treasurer in the late seventeenth century, left an unpaid
balance of £27,611 due from him to the Exchequer. "We did
not misspend our time in a pursuit where there was so little
probability of benefit to the public," the Commissioners reported. "A debt that has subsisted for near a century may be
presumed desperate." [19]

Confining its researches to recent times the Commissioners
dealt with the accounts of Navy Treasurers Grenville, Lord
Barrington, Lord Howe, Sir Gilbert Elliot, and of the incum-
bent Welbore Ellis. The report stated that for nearly nineteen
years considerable sums of public money had remained in the
hands of these men or of their representatives. Three of the
Treasurers had received for Navy service upwards of £33,000,-
000 the accounts of which were not yet settled. This failure to
render final accounts equally applied to Grenville's more than
£25,000,000, and to Wellbore Ellis' £16,000,000 of public
funds. "By this delay in making up the accounts," the Commissioners commented, "the public loses the use at least of
considerable sums of their own money, not that the principal
itself has always been safe." [20] When a Navy Treasurer retired
he could refuse from pique or other reasons to make payments.
By that means he could hold up, for eight months or more,
payment of all seamen at the various ports. Grenville acted
thus.

Simultaneously, in all departments, there was a system of
fees and emoluments some of which were based upon needs of
ancient times, but for the continuation of which there was no
longer justification. For instance, poundage fees derived from
the times when transactions were carried on by delivery of
actual coin of various denominations and weight, and often
clipped or of doubtful weight. Weighing or "poundage" of those
coins was then necessary. But for decades before the time here
dealt with payments were made in paper, cash notes, drafts or

bills of account. Yet the old charges for "poundage" were still made. In the year 1778 alone the Paymaster-General received £32,587, and in later years even more for "poundage" fees; the Paymaster-General for some years was Richard Rigby, the same who, as we have seen, objected in Parliament to newspapers reporting its proceedings.[21]

Other kinds of fees were exacted from persons doing business in the Paymaster-General's office. In 1780 these additional fees amounted to more than £23,000 which were apportioned among the heads of the office; the cashier's salary and fees of £8,389 in that year give an indication of the lucrative division.[22] In the Navy pay office there was a list of fees and perquisites paid by persons transacting business there.[23] The Auditor of Receipts in the Exchequer or Treasury was appointed for life; the Duke of Newcastle, occupying the post, received in 1780 a nominal salary and fees making a total of £16,880, of which he paid various sums to clerks and in taxes, making his net official income for the year more than £14,000.[24] In the same year "poundage" fees of £62,225 (and that sum included only what the Commissioners were able to discover) were paid to Exchequer officials on a banknote issue of £16,000,000.[25] In the Exchequer's office the position of Usher was a life appointment; he was allowed a profit of 40 per cent on the purchase of certain supplies—stationery and some other articles—and a large profit on workmen's bills for repairs; his net income in 1780 was £4,200. The Commissioners reported that the office of Usher was superfluous; that during the year, because of the profits connected with it, the public paid £14,440 for supplies really worth only £9,187.[26]

These are but a few of the many facts brought out in the Commissioners' reports. The later Tammany Hall system of grafting, which British critics have made the occasion for frequent taunts at America, had its full-fledged progenitor in this British system. The Commissioners thus described the system of fees or gratuities: "It is a species of emolument in every way liable to abuse. It may be a reward for civility, favor or extra service; it may be also the purchase of undue preference, expedition and, in some cases, of procrastination. Flowing at first from the liberality of opulence, the ostentation of vanity or the design of cunning, it very soon assumes the name of custom. . . . The public voice unites with that of individuals in demanding a suppression of a species of emoluments so easily perverted to purposes injurious to the interests of both." [27]

Throughout the nineteenth century and into the twentieth many European critics, chiefly British, sneered at the incompetence of American democracy, and some even in the United States looked back longingly to the times when a capable aristocracy, "trained to rule," had directed public affairs. During the American Revolution, Britain was run by an aristocracy intrenched in important offices.[28] Of the incumbents of those offices the Commissioners reported, in part: "Educated in and accustomed to the forms in use, they are insensible of their [the forms'] defects, or if they feel them, have no leisure, often no ability to correct them. Alarmed at the idea of innovation, they resist the proposal of a regulation, because it is a change, though from a perplexed and intricate to a more simple and intelligent system." [29]

It was the findings of these Commissioners that gave weight to denunciations such as Henry Flood's, when he declared in the House of Commons—March 4, 1790—that it was partly "the influence of corruption within doors" which had continued the American Revolutionary War, swept away so much of Great Britain's territory, cost Britain £100,000,000 and caused the sacrifice of 40,000 lives.[30]

PART THREE

BAITING OF AMERICA BEGINS

CHAPTER IX

AN ONRUSH OF CRITICS

THE European industry of turning out books critical of America and Americans began in force with the visit to America in 1795 of a British youth, Isaac Weld, Jr. His father held a lucrative Government office in the Irish customs, and Isaac Jr. had been born in Dublin. He was educated in an aristocratic private school; some of his fellow students later inherited titles or estates. When he came to America he was barely twenty-one years old. At such an immature age he manifestly had no understanding of the real import of the great changes which the American system had introduced. His ideas had been formed by his training and environment, and his conclusions were those of a trivial observer, impressed by superficial appearances. Yet the two volumes written by him were hailed and long used in Europe as those of an unimpeachable authority.

Weld spent the years 1795, 1796 and 1797 in America, traveling "pretty generally" through Pennsylvania, Delaware, Maryland, Virginia, New Jersey and New York. In the preface to his volumes he professed that his motive in visiting America had been to ascertain whether or not the accounts of a "happy and flourishing" America were true, and whether America was an eligible place for Irish emigration. Considering the text of his volumes, the further wording of the preface hardly seems the handiwork of a mere youth, and rouses the suspicion that a mature and adroit mind had a directing share in the shaping of it. Weld asserted that he had gone to America "thoroughly prepossessed in favor of the people and the country," and he asked his readers to bear in mind: "If it shall appear to anyone that he has spoken with too much asperity of American men and manners, the author begs that such language may not be ascribed to hasty prejudice and a blind partiality [sic] for everything American."

81

On his visit to America Weld was accompanied by a servant, who ministered to him everywhere with the deference customary in England. Of the effect of this sight upon farmers, workmen and tradesmen, Weld does not seem to have had the slightest realization. He apparently did not sense why they balked at catering to the expectations of a "young gentleman." At any rate, in America Weld saw three monstrous defects: the lack of good manners among "the lower sort of people"; an American disputatiousness and quarrelsome disposition over politics; and the settlers' roving proclivities, which he interpreted as proof of a money-making obsession.

On the score of bad manners he included "the generality of the lower sort of people in the United States and particularly those of Philadelphia." Disclaiming any parallel with the deference paid by the lower classes in Britain, he went on: "In the United States, however, the lower classes of people will return rude and impertinent answers to questions couched in the most civil terms, and will insult a person that bears the appearance of a gentleman on purpose to show how much they consider themselves on an equality with him. Civility cannot be purchased from them on any terms; they seem to think it is incompatible with freedom, and that there is no other way of convincing a stranger that he is really in a land of liberty, but by being surly and ill-mannered in his presence."

At that time and for many years later there was in America a widespread popular sense of national pride in the newly established equality, and a consequent expression of individual manliness and freedom. Sometimes, no doubt, these manifestations were overdone to the point of vaingloriousness. But toward prying and critical strangers the course of the manifestation depended upon the strangers' conduct. Weld filled his volume with sneers at "the lower orders." When in America he could hardly have divested himself of that outlook in his bearing, and, it is not unreasonable to suppose, in his remarks.

In principle, as embodied in declarations and the substance of many laws, equality for whites had been instituted. Although titles of nobility were prohibited, rank of position still prevailed socially, and suffrage was still restricted to the propertied classes. But in various other respects equality of standing was shown in ways that were as enlightening to American gentry as they were disconcerting to European critics. A few years before Weld's visit, an American, signing himself "A Gentleman," wrote with astonishment how in a Philadelphia celebration the procession comprised all classes and professions marching in equality. "These circumstances," he commented, "distinguished this procession from the processions in Europe. . . . Such is the difference between the effects of a republican and a monarchial Government upon the minds of men!" [1] At that time, however, there was still the force of propaganda behind the vilifying of "the lower orders," the depreciation of them as ignorant churls. "The American Museum or Universal Magazine," the patrons of which were America's leading public men, from George Washington down, warned its readers in April, 1792: "The idea of the necessity of a nobility for preserving decorum in and giving éclat to a nation has been assiduously propagated throughout the world."

To many Americans politics was naturally a subject inciting to discussion and vehemence. Weld could not in the least understand this: in Britain, as we have seen, Parliamentary seats depended upon relatively few voters, too often bought and sold. At the time of Weld's visit to America the rift was widening between the aristocratic forces headed by Alexander Hamilton and those of democracy led by Thomas Jefferson. The significance of this great opening struggle, to widen in later years, Weld did not understand, nor did he even glimpse the grounds for the fierce passions that it evoked.

The predominant spirit of America in those days was the pioneering; there was a steady movement of settlers westward and southward. But almost wherever they went pioneers encountered great speculative companies claiming or owning the land. Until the year 1800 public lands could not, under the laws, be bought from the Government in tracts of less than about 5,000 acres. Even after the laws were changed the path of the pioneer was beset with difficulties. Albert Gallatin, Secretary of the Treasury, reported to Joseph Nicholson, Chairman of the House Committee on Public Lands, on January 2, 1804, that poor persons could not purchase less than 360 acres; that in order to become freeholders they had to pay $160, and became bound for $480 more, payable in four years. If they had no other resources, it was impossible for them to draw means of payment from the produce of the land.[2] Wages were so low, and money so scarce, that for the average farmer or laborer to raise a few hundred dollars was an almost insuperable task. If he managed to borrow money he had to pay usurious interest.

On the other hand, by shifty bargains with the simple Indians and by official favor or connivance land companies obtained enormous areas. A brief résumé of the monopolizing of these areas and of the methods of the land companies is essential, to explain how Weld came to the most fallacious conclusions in passing judgments upon the motives and conduct of settlers in general.

In New York State the Phelps and Gorham Company possessed in a single holding 2,600,000 acres, bought from the Seneca Indians for so paltry a price that each individual member of that tribe received only a dollar.[3] For the insignificant payment of $100,000, Robert Morris acquired more than 4,000,000 acres in New York west of the Phelps and Gorham purchase. To the Holland Company, headed by the banking firm of Willinck & Strapporst, of Amsterdam, Holland, Morris sold more than a million acres comprising all or parts of many counties.[4] The Dutch bankers in the Holland Company had made large profits from the American Revolution, and they reinvested the further profits from land speculation in America in American transportation enterprises.[5] The Holland Company also secured large areas in western Pennsylvania.

The Ohio Company laid claim to more than 1,000,000 acres, and sold much of the land, including the site of the City of Cincinnati, before it was even able to prove its ownership claim by obtaining a patent.[6] To promote the sale of the lands which it claimed, and for invidious purposes as the sequel showed, the Ohio Company organized a separate concern, the Scioto Company, which sold considerable of the Ohio land to companies and individuals in France.[7]

Another huge stretch of land on the Illinois and Wabash rivers was claimed by the Illinois Company which contended that, in 1773 and 1775, the company, then composed of Lord Dunmore and various British and American lawyers and mer-

chants, had bought it from the Indian tribes; the purchase price
was an assortment of strouds, blankets, beads, guns and other
articles.[8]

On January 7, 1795, the Georgia Legislature, over the Governor's protest, had passed an act granting to four companies,
composed of American capitalists and politicians in both North
and South, an area comprising 35,000,000 acres extending to
the Mississippi River—a domain then included in the State of
Georgia. Disclosures soon came of the legislature having been
bribed; a number of the legislators themselves confessed it.
Thoroughly indignant, the people of Georgia elected a new
legislature pledged to repeal the act, but this repeal was later
voided by the Supreme Court of the United States which held
that the original grant was a contract incapable of annulment
by subsequent legislation.[9]

These were some of the great monopolistic land holdings.
But they were sometimes conditioned by laws obligating companies to make actual settlements within a prescribed period.
In Pennsylvania, for instance, the limit was two years. To
evade the law and claim immediate title the Holland Company
brought in crowds of dummy settlers, each of whom often
claimed as many as twenty locations, or settlements as they
were then called. But when real settlers, refusing to recognize
these fraudulent settlements, came and tried to establish themselves, there resulted conflict, and even riot and bloodshed.[10]
Ejected by force, the bona fide settlers had to move on to other
territory where they could safely settle. In Ohio the same
necessity confronted many settlers. The Ohio and the Scioto
companies fell to quarrelling as to which held the title to land
sold to French settlers. In consequence, these settlers found
themselves with bad titles, and had to petition Congress for a
grant of land elsewhere on which they could settle.[11]

In various countries there has been some spectacular period
which, taken by itself, seemed to impart a maleficent cast to
the nation involved. Such, for example, was the period of the
wild South Sea Company speculation in England and the
Mississippi Company excitement in France. But on such occasions England and France were not undergoing visitations by
critics. This was, however, the case with America after the

Revolution. Weld saw the extrinsic things, and the hot-pressed speculation in land was obvious. Not only companies in a large way but a host of individuals in a small way were participants. This jobbing in land was a result to be expected from the methods of the time and the conditions of a country where immense areas of land lay vacant. In the Old World, excepting in France after the French Revolution, the land was largely held in great estates which for centuries had been entailed or otherwise held by generations of possessors. There, so far as land was concerned, there was little or no disturbance, and there could be no speculation.

It is important to enlarge upon twenty-one-year-old Weld, for it was he who largely was instrumental in diffusing the notion of a money-mad America. That land companies in America inordinately hoisted the price of land was a most common complaint. He could not help seeing this plainest of facts, and he formed an immediate assumption. "The wealth," he wrote, "that has been accumulated by particular persons in the United States, in this manner, has been prodigious." He did not know, of course, that to carry such great land holdings companies or individuals had been constrained to borrow large sums. While Weld was still in America a number of these promoters became insolvent; Robert Morris, for example, was haled before a court upon the charge of seeking to defraud creditors and imprisoned in Philadelphia for inability to pay the judgment decreed.

To these developments and their significance Weld was blind. But the bankruptcy of some original promoters merely meant the transfer of the unsold lands to their creditors. A Senate Committee, on February 9, 1812, estimated that not less than 30,000,000 acres of uncultivated lands in the States and Territories west of the Allegheny Mountains was held by individuals.[12] Weld did not see that exorbitant prices demanded for land, and fraudulent operations of land companies, were powerful reasons which kept settlers in motion and drove them from one locality to another in the aim to find free or cheap land. The custom of the British upper classes, in admonishing the lower "to be content with their station," had created in Weld an antagonism to the pioneering movement in America. The rushing about of men and families, uprooting themselves and wandering to new spots, was a violation of the European code—a menace to regulated forms of society.

This opposition to freedom of movement by the "lower orders" was one of the most palpable European aristocratic antagonisms. Yet, of the long list of European critics visiting America, Alexis de Tocqueville was the only one qualified by judicious perception to give it application. In his notable and comprehensive study "Democracy in America," first published in 1835, he found it needful to point out that immigrants to America were not a new species of human beings but Europeans themselves. He explained their motives and their evolution in America. "Emigration," he wrote, "was at first necessary to them as a means of subsistence; and it soon becomes a game of chance which they pursue for the emotions it excites, as much as for the gain it procures. In Europe we are wont to look upon a restless disposition, an unbounded desire for riches, and an excessive love of independence as propensities very formidable to society. Yet these are the very elements which insure a long and peaceful duration to the republics of America. Without these unquiet passions the population would collect in certain spots and would soon be subject to wants like those in the Old World which it is difficult to satisfy." Elsewhere in the same volume Tocqueville wrote: "The perpetual change which goes on in the United States, those frequent vicissitudes of fortune, accompanied by such unforeseen fluctuations in private and in public wealth, serve to keep the minds of the citizens in a perpetual state of feverish agitation which admirably invigorates their exertions, and keeps them in a state of excitement above the ordinary level of mankind. The whole life of an American is passed like a game of chance, a revolutionary crisis in a battle."

But to Weld the whole American scene presented itself as an appalling scramble for money. Thus he sweepingly indicted Americans: "The American, however, does not change about from place to place merely to gratify a wandering disposition; in every change he hopes to make money. By the desire of making money, both the Germans and the Americans of every class and description are actuated in all their movements; self-interest is always uppermost in their thoughts; it is the idol which they worship." [13] Further: "The American, however, is of a roving disposition; he takes his wife with him, goes to a distant part of the country, and buries himself in the woods. . . . In the back parts of the country you always meet numbers of men prowling about to try and buy cheap land; having found what they like they immediately remove." Making a comparison with conditions in sedate England and not allowing for the unavoidable crudities and hardships of pioneering conditions in America, Weld descanted on how much more comfortably the English farmer lived than the Pennsylvania or Middle West farmer. "That," was his comment, "the farmers do not live better in America, I hardly know whether to ascribe to their love of making money, or to their real indifference about better fare; it may be owing in some measure to both." [14]

To deepen his disparagement of the American "lower class of people" Weld dwelt at length upon their gambling habits, and their cruelty and violence, instancing what he saw in Virginia. He reprobated the prevalent gambling, indignantly told how cockfighting was a favorite diversion, and depicted "the common people in taverns" as easily coming to blows. "They fight like wild beasts. . . . It is by no means uncommon to meet those who have lost an eye in a combat, and there are men who pride themselves upon the dexterity with which they can scoop one out. This is called gouging." [15] Of this kind as well as other kinds of brutality there were not lacking actual instances, but Weld's book conveyed the impression that such practices were universal characteristics of Americans.

What then, at the same time, was the quality of Britain's civilization? Did it possess such refinements that a critic from its realms was justified in being shocked at occasional brawls in American taverns? The reply to these questions was supplied by denunciations in Parliament itself.

At the solicitations of humanitarians a bill was introduced in Parliament, on May 24, 1802, to prevent the "barbarous custom" of bull baiting and bull running. Sir Richard Hill depicted "the shocking cruelties" involved in these practices. Another member—Mr. Windham—did not spare aristocratic susceptibilities. He sarcastically declared that the influence of horse racing was more pernicious; that the crowds at horse races "consisted of riff-raff from every part of the country;" that from amusements enjoyed by the rich the poor were excluded by their poverty and the law's rigors; he, therefore, would move to prohibit hunting, shooting, fishing and all of the sports of the higher classes. A third speaker—Mr. Courtenay—described how in Britain bears were trained to dance to music in the streets by putting a hot iron under their feet, the pain making the animal associate movement with music. Still another member—Colonel Grosvenor—uttered his view, most unkind to the sons and cousins of peers sitting in the House of Commons, that the "lower orders" were as much entitled to their bull amusements as were the higher classes to the sports they called their pleasure.[16]

Nearly thirty years later cruelty to animals was still an agitated subject in Britain. A report of an investigating Parliamentary committee told of the British sport of dog fighting in dog pits, and of the not uncommon performance of making dogs, often wounded and exhausted, draw burdensome trucks. The committee also gave its attention to the practice of skinning cats and dogs when alive, and it dealt with the evils of cockfighting, which cruel sport, it pointed out, was "patronized by persons of rank." [17] As for gambling in Britain, Parliamentary reports on it were frequent in the early nineteenth century. In London alone, say in 1815, the sums waged in gambling exceeded those in the whole of America; in the single item of lotteries, not to mention other forms of gambling, millions of pounds were staked. Originating in the upper classes, the habit of gambling so thoroughly infected the lower that on London streets, especially on Sunday, even gangs of children had their unrestrained and boisterous gaming parties. As to the astounding prevalence of drunkenness in Britain and its consequences, as shown by Parliamentary investigations, the facts will be given later.

Almost invariably, when a book was published by a youth, European reviewers treated it jestingly or dismissed it with a few caustic lines. But the bitterness among Tories in Britain toward America since the American Revolution and the enmity among European aristocracies in general against the nascent

American democracy were factors prompting the wide approval of Weld's volumes. These gave European deriders of America the material that they eagerly craved. Published in 1799, in London, Weld's volumes ran through many editions in that city. A French translation was brought out in Paris in 1800, and a German translation at The Hague in the next year. In their attacks upon American ways and institutions, British and other publications for years used Weld's production as their basis.

But his was not the only book to serve their purpose. In the years that Weld was in America the Duc de La Rochefoucauld-Liancourt also was on a scanning tour here. Rochefoucauld was a monarchist professing liberal principles; his reputation as a philanthropist came from his interest in prison reform and from his founding on his estate, Liancourt, near Clermont, a school for the education of poor soldiers' children. His whole idea of philanthropy, however, was the patronizing one of aristocratic bounty. He had been devotedly attached to the person of Louis XVI, and had tried in the French Revolution to prepare for Louis' flight from France. Rochefoucauld emigrated from France shortly after the storming of the Tuileries, on August 10, 1792.

His four volumes on America were published in France in 1798, and the next year in England. In the translator's preface to the London edition, H. Neumann told how, although Rochefoucauld favored mild principles of political reform, he was a victim to the French Revolution and an outcast. "Throughout the whole of his American journies," translator Neumann further wrote, "there appears to have reigned in the mind of this illustrious exile a melancholy cast of imagination, with a peevish irritability of feeling, such as is very natural for misfortunes like his to produce. Every scene of beneficent conduct from great landholders toward their dependents brings to his remembrance his own endeavors to enlighten and bless the peasantry upon those estates in France which once were his own."

In dealing with Rochefoucauld's attitude when in America, Neumann added: "He complains of a dirty room, a hard bed, a scanty meal, as if it were a grievous misfortune. He has a peculiar quickness of eye at discerning sloth, knavery and mischief wherever he travels. The wounds which his spirit had suffered were still fresh or suffering; and were therefore liable to be grievously inflamed and irritated by the slightest degree of new laceration." Nevertheless, Neumann accorded Rochefoucauld's book the virtue of being free from all affectation. "He appears to have been content to ride on horseback, without a servant, and to travel without aught of the pomp of greatness, or the luxury of opulence, just as if he had never been more than a plain farmer or manufacturer in France." [18]

As an experienced, conciliatory traveler, Rochefoucauld, unlike Weld, invited no rebuffs and received none. He wrote that in every part of America "the obliging civilities that I have experienced proved how false and groundless are those prejudices which the French and the English so obstinately entertain to the disadvantage of the Americans." And he elaborated: "Were I in this instance to form my ideas from my own personal experience alone, they also might in like manner be branded with the appellation of prejudice; but I have found my opinion corroborated by that of every traveler whom I have had the opportunity of seeing, and who thought proper to judge for himself, uninfluenced by partiality." [19]

But Rochefoucauld could not detach from his writings an habitual aristocratic hauteur. He repeatedly expatiated upon "the inferior class of the American people." The most common vice among that class, he asserted, was drunkenness. This was only relatively true, for among the rich inebriation was both a habit and a social custom. But for the drunkenness of "the inferior class" he concluded that "there are, without doubt, fewer crimes committed in America than among an equal number of people in Europe." [20] He charged that, in some measure, prolixity was the common fault of American orators—which was all too true—and he grew ironic over a Congressional declaration that Americans were "the most enlightened nation in the whole world." It was itself, he remarked, "a proof of that good opinion they have of themselves."

But the note most loudly struck in Rochefoucauld's volumes was the greed he attributed to Americans. "The desire for

riches is their ruling passion, and indeed their only passion."
This assertion he frequently repeated. "Excessive avidity of
becoming rich is the common characteristic of the American
people and especially in the inhabitants of cities." (His pronouncement, it need hardly be pointed out, differed from that
of Weld, who saw money the passion of farmers and settlers
in particular.) With an air of judicial qualification Rochefoucauld went on: "But this disposition does not hurry them on
to avarice. They know how at proper times to be expensive
[sic] even without ostentation, and they do not refuse to assist
the unfortunate, when proper opportunities occur." [21] Rochefoucauld made no effort to compare the actions of the American trading class with those of the European trading classes,
the money absorption of which was notorious. He wrote as a
nobleman echoing nobility's scorn of trade.

At that time he was accused by at least one British magazine [22] of filling his work with vilifications of Britain, so as to
ingratiate himself with the Directory, then governing France,
and get back his estates. (In fact, after becoming First Consul,
Napoleon authorized the Duke to return to Liancourt, which
was restored to him.) Dealing with every condition in America,
political, industrial, geographical, climatic and other, Rochefoucauld's volumes had an enormous influence in France and
in England. In America they were considerably read. However
critics in Britain at first resented his comments upon British
policy and laws, they soon overlooked these aspersions, and
selected from his work those parts which they could appropriately cite to prove the greed of the American character.

Among the British visitors to America was another whose
book likewise was used as a verification of American greed.
Richard Parkinson, author of "The Experienced Farmer,"
knew about cattle and pigs, and about farming conditions and
problems as they were in England, but he was void of knowledge on any other subject. The result of his tour in America,
in 1798, 1799 and 1800, was a work of two volumes published
in 1805, on American society, manners and agriculture. His
dedication of the book "To His Royal Highness, the Duke of
York" began: "Sir, In times like these, when the wicked in-

tentions and wild chimeras of misguided or designing men have so widely disseminated principles of a fallacious equality as to shake all Europe to its foundation, it becomes the duty of every reasonable person, especially the inhabitant of this truly free nation [Britain], to manifest a love of order by proper expressions of regard for high station and illustrious ancestry." [23]

In his book Parkinson made grievous complaints of "the disrespectful manners of white servants toward masters," which behavior he ascribed to "notions of equality," and he wailed about his having had to clean his own boots and shoes, even though there were four servants in the house. "The idea of liberty and equality there," he wrote, "destroys all the rights of the master, and every man does as he likes." [24] He pronounced land in America almost worthless for agricultural purposes: "The produce is so small and the expense so great that I never saw any land worth having in America." And, "To look at America in the most favorable way you can, as a nation, there is nothing but extent of territory to entitle it to the consequence it assumes." [25] Parkinson averred that Americans were such sharp traders that Jews could not do well in America. "All of the men in America," he wrote, "make money their pursuit." [26]

Charles William Janson, a lawyer, had made a fortune in England. He lost some of this by speculating in American securities. To America he came to recoup himself by land speculation, in which he again suffered losses. While in America he lost still further by investments in a shipping concern. His losses soured him. Apart from that, he had deep, unalterable prejudices against the social and political innovations America had introduced. Despite his residence for a time in Rhode Island, in which State he took up the profession of councilor at law, he made no attempt to change in the least degree his caste attitude. On his return to England he wrote a book, which he published in 1807.

In the preface he declared of himself: "Among the lower orders, in spite of his endeavors to adapt his behavior to their satisfaction, he was regarded as proud and haughty." He continued: "Though the Americans declaim in favor of liberty and equality, yet nowhere are those terms more unworthily prostituted. That equality, the establishment of which was a favorite object of the revolutionary republicans of France, is still the idol of the mob in the United States. The meanest plebeian would be quite ungovernable did he barely suspect you of harboring the idea that he was inadmissable to equal rank with the best-informed of his fellow citizens. Hence you are accosted by people of the lowest description with familiarity, and answered with carelessness. This, it is obvious, cannot be a very enviable state of society for a person educated in European notions of the decorum necessary to be observed in civilized life." [27]

The text of Janson's book was in keeping with the tone and view of the preface. To him the new rights of man became "the deplorable effects of uncontrolled liberty," and to suit this view he magnified and misrepresented every incident. "One of the great evils of a republican form of goverment is a loss of that subordination in society which is essentially necessary to render a country agreeable to foreigners. . . . The meaning of liberty and equality in the opinion of the vulgar, consists in impudent freedom and uncontrolled licentiousness, while boys assume the airs of full-grown coxcombs." Janson pictured America as a land peopled with fraudulent land speculators, fraudulent merchants and sharpers, and as a place of duplicity and extortion.

A year after the appearance of Janson's book, Thomas Ashe's three volumes were published. A few characteristic extracts will suffice to give an adequate idea of the malevolence filling these. America was a country "where sordid speculators alone succeed." The American States through which he passed were "unworthy"; in the Southern States "society was in a shameful degeneracy." These conditions were "an additional proof of the pernicious tendency of those detestable principles of political licentiousness" which "make men turbulent citizens, abandoned Christians, inconstant husbands, unnatural fathers and treacherous friends." An American's "sluggish faculties required palpable and active objects to give them exercise." Americans were "a race of impudent, selfish, sordid individuals, without either principle or common humanity." M. Buffon "was perfectly right in his assertion that man and beast degenerated in America." [28]

A few years later John Bradbury, a London naturalist, made a tour of the entire Louisiana and of the Middle Western regions. He was not concerned with criticizing people but with collecting plants. In his book he sought to caution European critics against hasty judgments of Americans and snobbish conduct. West of the Alleghenies, he wrote, the settlers were from almost every country in Europe, and from such a people not yet amalgamated it was absurd to expect the forming of a general character. He then gave this instruction and warning:

"That species of hauteur which one class of society in some countries show in their intercourse with one another is here [in America] utterly unknown. By their constitution, the existence of a privileged order, vested by birth with hereditary privileges, honors or emoluments, is forever interdicted. If, therefore, we should here expect to find that contemptuous feeling in man for man, we shall naturally examine those clothed with judicial, or military authority; but we should search in vain. . . .

"Travelers from Europe in passing through the western or indeed any part of the United States, ought to be previously acquainted with this part of the American character, and more particularly if they have been in the habit of treating with contempt, or irritating with abuse those whom accidental circumstances may have placed in a situation to minister to their wants. Let no one here indulge in abusing the waiter or hostler at an inn; that waiter is probably a citizen, and does not, nor cannot conceive a situation in which he discharges a duty to society, not in itself dishonorable, should subject him to insult; but this feeling, so far as I have experienced, is entirely defensive. I have traveled near 10,000 miles in the United States, and have never met with the least incivility or affront." And Bradbury added: "Other European travelers have experienced this liberal spirit of hospitality, and some have repaid it by calumny. These calumnies have reached them [the Americans]; they are well acquainted with what Weld and a person who calls himself Ashe have said of them." Bradbury inserted a footnote on Ashe's book which, he said, was "full of malignant false-hoods." [29]

Similarly, another British visitor, John Palmer, who later came to America to study the soil and farming, scorned current misrepresentations of America. "Most of the travels I have seen," he wrote, "are full of prejudice and invective against America and Americans, which in some instances, the authors could scarcely feel; and who, perhaps, inserted them for no worse motive than to make their publications palatable to readers. This is particularly the case in 'Janson' and 'Parkinson' and 'Ashe.' " [30]

Any book favorable to America was ignored or sneered at by British reviewers. But the books condemnatory of America were given profuse space and approval. How these books, especially Weld's and Rochefoucauld's, were used as authoritative justification for damnation of Americans was exemplified by a long diatribe in "The Quarterly Review," one of the most influential of British publications.[31] Variously, as suited its purpose, it cited or amplified both Weld and Rochefoucauld, and burst forth thus:

". . . There is, however, both in the physical and intellectual features of the Americans a trace of savage character, not produced by crossing the breed, but by the circumstances of society and of external nature. It is only in the great cities and their vicinity that the accompaniments of civilization are found; in the new settlements everything partakes more of savage than of civilized life. The back settlers, useful as they are when considered as the pioneers of civilization, are a worse race than the Indians upon whose border they trespass; inasmuch as they have been better taught, possess greater powers of doing mischief, and are without principle . . .

"Men in this semi-savage state crave like savages for spiritous liquors. Ale, cider and wine are insipid to their coarse and blunted sense; they are without taste, and must have something which the palate can feel."

At this point some parenthetical remarks are necessary. Among the "lower classes" in England and Wales ale was the popular drink, and so widespread was the addiction that in

1806 there were about 50,000 licensed alehouses in England and Wales. London alone made annually more than 68,000,000 gallons of porter, strong ale and beer, and in that city there was one public house or saloon to every thirty-seven families. In England and Wales it was customary for workers to spend their leisure time in alehouses. Whiskey was the general liquor in Scotland and Ireland. But England made millions of gallons of hard liquors which were shipped to all parts of the world; in London itself there were sixty-one distilleries, and one hundred and thirty-three in the whole of England, not to mention illicit stills.[32]

To resume "The Quarterly Review's" onslaught on Americans: "Intoxication with them is not social hilarity betrayed into excess; it is too rapid a process for that interval of generous feeling which tempts the European on. Their pleasure is first in the fiery stimulus itself, not in its effect—not in drunkenness but in getting drunk. . . . Hence the ferocity with which Americans decide their quarrels; their rough and tumbling; their biting and lacerating each other; and their *gouging,* a diabolical practice which has never disgraced Europe, and for which no other people have a name." (Where Weld had distinctly attributed gouging to the "lower classes" in taverns, it is soon after, as we see, applied to American settlers generally.)

"Living in this semi-savage state, the greater part of the American people are so accustomed to dispense with the comforts of life which they cannot obtain, that they have learned to neglect even the decencies which are within their reach. This is not meant to allude to the custom of bundling . . . but it applies to the detestable state of the inns which are as disgraceful to America as they are disgusting to the unlucky European whose fate it is to travel there. . . . His chamber is filled with beds in which men and women, if women happen to be traveling, lie promiscuously; and when he has fallen asleep in foul sheets, he may think himself fortunate if some dirty American does not awaken him by turning in by his side. In these beastly taverns the stranger must be an unwilling spectator of riot and drunkenness and its bloody effects. . . . The Americans have overrun an immense country, not settled it."

Here, apropos of the charge of American incapacity for settle-

ment, the facts about the Sierre Leone Company call for inter-
jection. Composed of British bankers and wealthy merchants,
this company, under the pretence that it was introducing civilization in Africa, obtained from Parliament grants of money
totaling £109,000. In 1807 the company was denounced in
Parliament as having failed in all of its projects, and the proposal was made that, accordingly, it should refund the sums
for which it had produced no results.[33]

To return to "The Quarterly Review"; as to the gambling
spirit in America it delivered this blast: "It is not confined to
their speculations in land by which so many emigrants have
been duped and ruined; it extends to their commercial dealings
and the Americans have a worse character than those of any
other nation."

Were this an isolated specimen it could be allowed to remain
buried. But it was typical of the scurrility in many British
publications, and it was reasserted in many different ways. The
whole, together with the books on America which were widely
circulated, made a mass of opinion moulding the mentality of
men and women who, as visitors to America in later years, went
with jaundiced preconceptions.

Meanwhile, in America the literary fashion of sneering at
America's institutions and American ways had established itself. The leader of this group was Joseph Dennie, who founded
"The Portfolio" (Magazine) in 1801, at Philadelphia. Dennie
was born in Boston in 1768, but of his life little can be learned;
we have to depend upon an oration delivered some time after
his death at a Union College Commencement by Gulian C.
Verplanck, one of the Regents of the University of the State
of New York, for a description of the influences that swayed him
and others, and of the consequent effect upon many Americans.
In speaking of a danger that then beset the American literary
man, Verplanck said: "Familiar with the glories and beauties
of European literature, his ambition is early fixed to imitate
or to rival its excellence. He forms to himself grand plans of
intellectual exploits, all of them probably incongruous with the
state and taste of his country, and most of them doubtless
beyond his own ability." Such aspiring souls, Verplanck went

on, discerned that the world rated their talent very differently from their own estimate of it, or else that the state of society about them was wholly adverse to its exercise in the direction and on the scale their ambitious fancy had anticipated.

"Disappointed and disgusted, they are now tempted to ascribe their disappointment to the republican institutions of their country. The scholar who gives way to this temptation dwells with a sort of complacent disgust at every imperfection of our social state. He gradually becomes a rebel in heart to our glorious institutions. His affections and secret alliance transfer themselves to some other form of government and state of society, such as he dreams to have formed the illustrious men and admirable things of his favorite studies.

"The early history of American literature affords a distinguished example of this influence upon a most elegant, accomplished and brilliant mind. . . . It is that of one once called the American Addison, and still justly regarded as a father of our native literature, the late Joseph Dennie. . . . He was a genuine enthusiast in his love of literature, and he made it the business of his life to propagate the same taste among his countrymen. In this he accomplished much, but he would have accomplished very far more, had he not yielded to a strange, unwise and unhappy morbid dislike for the institutions and social order of his own country. This discolored his views and distorted his judgment. . . ."

Dennie wrote under the pseudonym of "Oliver Oldschool," and the contributors to "The Portfolio" were mainly anonymous. This is an extract from a typical article: "The bulk of mankind are fools. The proportion of men of sense and integrity to men ignorant and knavish, is perhaps as five to ninety-five. . . . The ninety-five ignoramuses will vote wrong, and thus constitute a powerful majority. The minority ought in all cases to carry the vote." [34] Pronouncements in the Declaration of Independence of the equality of men were ridiculed, and predictions made that American democracy would soon degenerate into a despotism. Year after year such attacks deriding every phase of American life continued. Finally, in 1811, a year before Dennie's death, a strong protest, in the form of a letter signed "The Stranger in New York," was sent in to "The

Portfolio," and somehow or other was actually published in that magazine.

"The effect," said the letter in part, "which the misrepresentations of European travelers have had in degrading the character of the people of the United States, is well known to you. A Weld, a Bülow, a Janson, a Moore, a Parkinson, and many others have successively dipt their pens in the gall of malignity to revenge some slight neglect, trifling incivility or fancied insult. They have exhausted the stores of invention to render the American people ridiculous and contemptible; and their spite has even extended to the abuse of their soil and natural productions.

"We are told by Mr. Parkinson (an illiterate adventurer) that [American] civilization is retrogressive and approaches nearer to a Russian than an English level. . . . Moore, the poet . . . informs us that the [American] people, from the form of their government and the influence of Republican sentiments, are strangers to taste, refinement and the arts of imagination; are vulgar, unsocial, insolent and avaricious. But these censures are perfectly mild and merciful when compared with the animadversions of a Prussian traveler, by the name of Bülow. This arrogant, illiberal and conceited foreigner not only pronounces the manners of the American people rude and ferocious, but their hearts narrow, selfish and corrupt to the core. The first settlers of America he is pleased to denominate the rabble and offscourings of the earth, whose principles and vices have descended to their posterity. The American Revolution he declares to have been prompted by no generous or praiseworthy motives, to have been dignified by no lofty or magnanimous feelings, and to have been conducted to its termination without ability, spirit or patriotism; that science and genius are scarcely to be found in this country; and that the people are a mean, groveling, avaricious and barbarous herd, without sense or hospitality.

"When such a distorted picture of America is delineated by the pencil of falsehood, the erroneous impressions which prevail in regard to the character of its inhabitants, must cease to excite astonishment. . . ." [35]

Under a different editorial management "The Portfolio"

(thereafter published in New York) changed its attitude. In a review of John Melish's "Travels in the United States of America, in the Years 1806–1811," it said, in its issue of February, 1813: "Here is a kind of phenomenon. Two whole volumes on America without any material errors; with no palpable falsehoods; no malignant abuse of individuals; no paltry calumnies on the institutions of the United States, Mr. Melish has indeed sinned beyond forgiveness against the common law of American traveling. He had the good sense to visit a large portion of our country, without quarreling with tavern keepers or servants, but has taken things as he found them—made proper allowances for the natural inconveniences of a young country—and been treated with civility—because he knows how to behave himself on the road."

The effect of Dennie's writings, according to Verplanck, was a recoil upon literature itself. Dennie's course "identified in the minds of the unlettered the cause of elegant literature with that of attachment to foreign principles and contempt for our own." Verplanck went on: "Honest men reasoned, and correctly too, though from false premises, that if literature could be gained only at the expense of patriotic feeling, it is best we should go without it. It lessened, too, the merit and value of his writings as literary compositions; for it tended to strip them of the original American air they would otherwise have had, and to give them the common cast of mere English literature. Hence, instead of ranking with those of Irving, at the head of our literature, both in time and merit, his works are already passing into oblivion. . . . Let the student take warning from his great and single error." [36]

CHAPTER X

IN THEIR OWN LANDS

In none of the books or articles antagonistic to America was even the bare suggestion made that in great parts of Canada settlement conditions either paralleled or resembled those in America. That Canada more or less duplicated such conditions in its newly-settled areas was an obvious fact. But Canada was under full British sovereignty, governed by British overlords; it held fast to European institutions, ideas, laws and ceremonials, including in all parts a superimposed official administration, and in some portions a distinct feudal régime surviving in all its force from French control. Not until 1854, more than sixty years after feudalism had been abolished in France, did the Legislative Assembly of the Province of Quebec pass an act opening the way for the suppression of feudal tenures and duties. Critics from Europe were not interested, however, in dissecting and condemning Canadians; their quarry was Americans. Yet in Canada the newly-settled regions showed all of the rudimentary stages common to freshly-peopled countries.

While sundry British critics were so fiercely assailing American settlement conditions, what, at the same time and later, was the situation in Britain's colonies? Two examples will be instanced. The settlement of Australia was largely compulsory, strictly regulated by the Colonial Department in London. In Australia there were three classes of settlers: free settlers; indentured servants from Britain; and the swarms of offenders convicted, under the hard British laws, of transgressions many of which are now recognized as nothing more than minor misdeeds or misdemeanors. Degraded in England, few of the indentured servants had ever been afforded the opportunity to learn even to read and write, and their slum environment left in them ineffaceable characteristics. In Australia many of these indentured servants had, so reported the supreme British official there, "habits of the lowest description"; drunkenness and "irregularities" were common.[1]

From Britain went a procession of hulks crowded promiscuously with offenders, called convicts and sentenced to transportation. Men and women, boys and girls, the aged and infirm as well as the physically fit, were cold-bloodedly condemned to a protracted voyage and dumping in a far distant land. On the average the direct voyage to Australia lasted 127 days; by way of the Cape of Good Hope the voyage dragged over 146 days. Salt pork and bread, the one often unpalatable, the other often mouldy, were the rations. Many of the unfortunates died on the way. A very large proportion of the convicts were not criminals in any real sense; they were workers from Britain's manufacturing districts and the spawn of the cities, products of poverty, driven more by need than by inclination to violating some law or other. Callous to the horrible living conditions of the poor, the aristocracy ruling England, and the judges enforcing the laws made by aristocracy, were hardened to the fate of the great numbers branded as convicts. These, once herded in the hulks, were given no further thought; such official reports of their treatment both on the voyage and in Australia as were turned in were made in an unfeeling, matter-of-fact way, and were received by official dignitaries with the same unconcern.

Totally unsuited to agricultural labor, many of the convicts were placed on the large estates in Australia. The huts in which they were lodged were indescribably filthy. Law did not require estate masters to furnish soap, and consequently none was supplied. The persons of the convicts were foul, a condition partly caused by the scarcity of water on many of the estates and the distance from which it had to be procured. Any infraction by a convict brought upon him a magistrate's sentence of 50 to 100 lashes, at times as many as 500 lashes. Driven frantic, many convicts took to the wilds, became "bush-rangers" and existed like beasts. Other convicts accumulated in cities and were sunk in drunkenness, poverty and wretchedness. Only a few, literate and enterprising, managed to acquire property, and attained some local office, as to which latter development a British investigator much complained. This is not in the least an overdrawn account. It is strictly consonant with the facts given in a comprehensive report, on May 6, 1822, of John Thomas Bigge, Commissioner of Inquiry into the State of the Colony of New South Wales, to Earl Bathurst, Secretary for War and the Colonies.[2]

While Australia was Britain's dumping ground for transgressors, Canada provided the convenient place for shipment of paupers from English and Irish parishes. Having acquired great areas of land in Canada, British proprietors were interested in zealously promoting emigration to that country, as also were Canadian high officials, many of whom bought for trifling sums tracts each ranging from 20,000 and 50,000 to 100,000 acres in Ontario. In the Province of Quebec officials, from the Governor down, obtained similar large tracts by grant or purchase. Nearly the whole of the 1,400,000 acres of Prince Edward Island was given in a single day to grantees mostly living in Britain: Lord Westmoreland, Sir James Montgomery, Lord Selkirk and others were among the beneficiaries. At various times corporations such as the British American Land Company and the Canada Company obtained for a nominal price millions of acres in sections of Eastern Canada. Nearly all of Canada's governing officials were deep in land speculation.[3]

Both voluntary and involuntary immigrants to Canada were packed into pestilential ships, the noxious conditions in which caused ravages from typhus and other diseases. Testimony given at the time by immigration officials at the port of Quebec showed the state of swarms of newcomers. On leaving England voluntary immigrants had a little money; but the extortions of ship captains robbed many of their last shillings, and they landed at Quebec destitute.[4] After 1815 the arrival of both voluntary and involuntary and pauper immigrants at the port of Quebec became greatly accelerated; in the subsequent fifteen years the number was 168,615.[5]

Impoverished upon landing, numbers drifted aimlessly for weeks and degenerated into vagrancy or mendicancy. Others with families resorted to the large towns where they eked a paltry existence by day labor and begging. As for such immigrants as had contrived to retain some money, they, according to Lord Durham's elaborate report on the state of affairs in Canada, sought refuge in low taverns and squalid boarding houses or established themselves in cellars.[6] Few of the immigrants had any agricultural experience. Reporting on a particular shipload of immigrants, Sir James Kempt strongly protested against the cruelty of the practice of relieving English and Irish parishes by sending such hordes of paupers to a distant colony and pitilessly turning them adrift.[7] If, maddened by want, any immigrant turned to crime, he was cruelly punished under merciless laws borrowed from England. Laws in Ontario were severe enough, but they were more so in the Province of Quebec. For petty larceny, a woman's punishment was twenty-five lashes on the bare back; men, for the same offence, often similarly received fifty lashes. Even during the first decade of the nineteenth century, grand larceny was punished by branding the palm of the hand with a red-hot iron. The pillory was also long a common method of punishing offenders of all ages and races.

Following English law, poor children in Nova Scotia were torn from their parents and bound out as apprentices by the overseers of the poor; beggars and wanderers were summarily arrested and hired out for a term not exceeding seven years; and idle persons or tramps were treated as "rogues and vagabonds," and imprisoned. For even the most trivial "felonies," the letter T was burned on the offender's left thumb; and the committing of the pettiest larceny entailed a prison term of seven years at hard labor. Further, in Nova Scotia, stocks and lashing were applied for misdemeanors. In Montreal fifty-four persons—some mere boys—were hanged between the years 1812 and 1840 for various offences, only seven of which involved murder. The majority of hangings were for horse, cattle or sheep stealing, robbery and burglary. A case is mentioned of a boy—B. Clement—not quite fourteen years old who, in 1813, was hanged for stealing a cow.[8]

One potent reason for the slow settling of Canada was the fact that, attracted by better conditions and higher wages in the United States, such immigrants as could gradually manage to go there availed themselves of the opportunity.[9]

Moreover, the great wild areas of Canada presented a sanguinary state to which there was not then any parallel in America. Not until some years later did John Jacob Astor's American Fur Company begin to rival the bloody operations of the fur companies in Canada. Competitor as it was of the powerful Hudson Bay Company, the North West Company, composed of Canadians, was so successful that many of the men in it amassed "great and rapid fortunes," as Lieutenant-Governor Milnes, ranking British official in Canada, wrote in 1802. He reported how the North West Company's opulence had led, in 1800, to the establishment of another Canadian fur-trade company, called the X. Y. Company, headed by Sir Alexander Mackenzie and associates. Between these companies, each seeking supremacy in more or less the same territory, there set in a furious conflict in which human life was wantonly sacrificed.

In disputes over territory jurisdiction, employe often murdered employe; how many Indians were murdered was never known—and no inquiry made. To outdo the other in the effort to secure the fur trade each of the companies went to the uttermost extremes; prodigious quantities of rum were used to debauch the Indians, and every method was employed to intimidate and overawe them. But the richer and more formidable of the two, the North West Company, with a force two-thirds larger than that of the X. Y. Company, was able to pursue such methods more effectively. Indians were incited to fire upon the X. Y. Company's canoes and to pillage its goods; its employes were often enticed by promises or driven away by threats; and its property was destroyed by treachery and other underhand acts.[10]

In proposing to Lord Hobart the establishing of courts of justice in the fur-trading regions to deal with this wide terrorism, Milnes declared that both companies were "fearless of future punishment, because they know that the courts of Canada will not take cognizance of conditions where they traffic."[11] One of the reasons is to be found in the testimony of the Right Hon. Edward Ellice. Gorged with wealth from the Hudson Bay Company, he stated before a British Parliamentary Committee, in 1857, that when he went to Canada, in 1803, "the whole of Canadian society, every person of eminence and consequence there, was then engaged in the fur-trade, it being the only trade of any consequence in that country." Cumulative proof of murders and other crimes in outlying fur-trading regions was so great that finally, on September 10, 1802, the Grand Jury at Montreal acted, handing in a strong presentment and demanding a remedy.[12] For three years more the murders—at least those caused by the companies—continued; the merging of the companies, in 1805, put an end to their warfare; but the warfare between the now enlarged North West Company and the Hudson Bay Company went on violently.

Collisions between these companies kept increasing, and the methods of both stirred bad feeling among the Indians. Ellice testified that, in 1811, Lord Selkirk brought over a shipload of tenants, founded a settlement, now Winnipeg, on the Red River, and joined the Hudson Bay Company. According to a remonstrance sent by Chief Peguis, of the Saltean Tribe, on the Red River, to the Aborigines Protection Society, London, Lord Selkirk (whom the Indians named the "Silver Chief") obtained 20 to 24 miles of the tribe's land along the Red River by a fraudulent arrangement. He had represented that because of troubles with the North West Company he could pay little then, but would return the next year. Meanwhile, he induced the tribe to take some ammunition and tobacco. Selkirk never returned and, the remonstrance read on, "either his son or the Hudson Bay Company have ever since paid us annually for our lands only the small quantity of ammunition which, in the first instance, we took as a preliminary to a final bargain about our lands." Chief Peguis' remonstrance further declared that for the "proprietary rights" claimed by Selkirk, the Hudson Bay Company had paid Selkirk's executors £84,111, and "now claim all of the lands between the Assiniboin and Lake Winnipeg, a quantity of land nearly double of what was first asked from us." [13]

In the conflicts between the Hudson Bay Company and the North West Company, an action on the Red River, in 1815, between their armed forces, resulted in the killing of sixteen men. Accusing William M'Gillivray, principal partner in the North West Company, of having instigated the trouble, Selkirk seized both him and his property, and other North West Company magnates were arrested. M'Gillivray made counter charges. Powerful as was the Hudson Bay Company in England, the North West Company was all powerful in Montreal. Its members almost completely controlled the acts of the Government and the Governor in Council, and finally secured acquittal of its men. The well-known Judge Reid, says a Canadian historian, had married M'Gillivray's sister, "and this mighty influence had something to do with the final issue." [14]

The inflammatory effect upon the Indian tribes of the war between the fur-trading companies was luridly related in Ellice's testimony. "Rum," he testified, "was given to the various parties acting in competition, to the Indians and half-breeds; the whole country was demoralized; the Indian tribes were in conflict, one against the other. In fact, whatever a particular trader carrying on his business at a particular post thought was likely to ruin his competitor and advance his own interests was done without the least regard to morality and humanity." During this very time the Hudson Bay Company was boasting that its missionaries were "civilizing the heathen." Ellice blamed the American traders for the necessity of using rum; in the contests about trading posts on the frontier, he said, "the universal article used to corrupt the Indians is spirits." [15] In turn, the United States Government was making indignant remonstrances, charging the companies in Canada with responsibility for the rum traffic in the fur trade.

Both the Hudson Bay Company and the North West Company finally concluded that warfare between them was too costly. Ellice testified that it was he who in 1819 or 1820 succeeded in merging the companies, which thereafter figured as the Hudson Bay Company.

Two notable incidents accompanied this merger. Contrary to its previous claims, the Hudson Bay Company now held that its territory extended *west* of the Rocky Mountains. The other incident was the further inflation of the company's capital stock, and later there came still more inflation. Apart from the great, continuing profits of the Hudson Bay Company, those of the North West Company created large fortunes which later were conspicuous in Canadian banks, steamship and railroad lines.

While British critics, neglectful of the scope awaiting their talents in Australia and Canada, were assailing Americans as a money-seeking people, what was the state of trade in their home land?

There high British officials were boasting of Britain's extent of commerce and wealth, and were lauding the integrity of its merchants as the great reason why its manufactures had prospered. Sentiments expressed in a debate in the House of Commons, on March 5, 1802, were an example of this insular satisfaction. Henry Addington, then Premier and Chancellor of the Exchequer—soon to become Viscount Sidmouth—enthusiastically declared Britain "happily a splendid instance" of the "uniting of military excellence with superior wealth." Britain's success in attaining both, he argued, proved how false was the supposition of their incompatibility. On the same day, Lord Hawkesbury extolled the sway of British money. "In capital, Great Britain is rivaled by no country, but still more important," he went on solemnly, "is the confidence to which the honor and punctuality of her merchants entitle her. The only country which has been able to rival us is Holland, who founded her commerce upon a similar honesty and punctuality. But France has never been able to rival us because the French character is not honest, just and punctual." [16]

Neither then nor for decades later did any important member of Parliament lay himself open to the charge of impropriety by even mentioning the conditions under which children were employed. Underpaid and driven labor was the basis of Britain's ability to manufacture cheaply. But by general tacit consent among members of Parliament, this was a barred subject.

Meanwhile, the example of British manufacturers in fast acquiring fortunes had made a deep impression upon American promoters. A meeting of a group proposing to establish woolen, cotton and linen factories was held on March 16, 1775, in Carpenter's Hall, Philadelphia. The chief speaker described Great Britain's factories "as the foundation of her riches and power. They have made her merchants nobles and her nobles princes." Some manufacturing work, he said, could be done in the homes of the poor, but the age of machinery had arrived, and factory buildings were necessary. The American colonies, he further said, were largely of an agricultural character, but in England the greater number of "hands" had been taken from the plow for factory service. The speaker urged the need of imitating the English system of employing women and children.

"A strong objection to factories in America," he acknowledged, "is that we cannot manufacture cloths so cheap as they can be imported from Britain. It has been the misfortune of most of the manufactories which have been set up in this country to afford labor to journeymen only for six or nine months in the year, by which means their wages have necessarily been so high as to support them in intervals of labor. . . . The expense of manufacturing cloth [in America] will be lessened from the great share women and children have in them." Then the speaker argued in a humanitarian tone: Although, because of unwholesome diet, damp houses and other bad conditions, diseases were prevalent among British factory workers, such distressing results could be prevented in America by taking care to supply good living and factory accommodations.[17]

When, in 1791, Samuel Slater established a cotton mill at Providence, Rhode Island, he imitated the English custom of employing whole families, including very young children. This system led to the migration of families from country districts to the city where they were wholly dependent upon the mill; when work was lacking, severe suffering ensued.[18] But factories then and for years later were rarities in America. Commending the introduction of labor-saving machinery, a leading American publication stated in 1789 and 1792 that one great objection to manufacturing in America was the high price of labor. Another obstacle was the absence of hereditary class formations, fixing the station of laborers. "Mechanics in America are of as much consequence as the farmers themselves. . . . In England there is more difference between man and man than there is here between man and beast." Often the American mechanic, it was further pointed out, desired to educate his son in the law, medicine or other professions, and there were no caste barriers to interfere with his so doing.[19]

How sparse America was in factories was shown by the report of Alexander Hamilton, Secretary of the Treasury, in 1792, on manufactures in America. "It is computed in a number of districts," he wrote, "that two-thirds, three-fourths and even four-fifths of all the clothing of the inhabitants are made by themselves." His report then dealt with the efficiency of British cotton mills. Run by water power, they were "attended chiefly by women and children, night and day." Hamilton pleaded the necessity of woman and child labor to operate the factories to be established in America. "Of the number employed in the cotton manufactories of Great Britain," Hamilton's report went on, "it is computed that four-sevenths nearly are women and children, and many of them of a tender age." Machinery would counteract the high price of labor in America, Hamilton argued, and equality of religious rights would promote immigration. Many who came to America to go into factories would, he thought, go into agricultural pursuits.

The phenomenally swift advance both of industrialism and commercialism in Britain caused consternation among the landed gentry there. Long accustomed to the system of political power based upon land ownership, they were intensely alarmed by the encroachments of other groups whose rising economic power imminently threatened a corresponding shift of political sway. The gentry, therefore, now roused themselves to vigorous efforts to defeat any change in the electoral system. Scandalous as that system was, they took the ground that it was venerable, traditional, and therefore should not be disturbed.

The gentry's stand was frankly demonstrated when, in 1793, petitions demanding reforms in the method of electing its members were submitted to Parliament. The majority of the House of Commons, the appeals set forth, was elected by less than 15,000 electors out of at least 3,000,000 male adults in the United Kingdom.[20] One of the petitions, that of the "Friends of the People," denounced the "progressive degree of fraud and corruption" by which, for an expenditure of from £3,000 to £6,000, men could get themselves elected to Parliament. Controlling the election districts, termed boroughs, there were regular manipulators called "borough jobbers" or "borough mongers," disclosures as to the evil operations of which were brought out in the debate.

Bitter complaints were made by the landed gentry of the incursion into Parliament of men with nothing more to recommend them than a commercial stamp. Corrupt previously, the election system was no more corrupt when men who had amassed wealth in the East and in the West India trade scrambled for seats in Parliament. The only difference was a big increase in the prices demanded. Having fixed incomes, the gentry could not compete with a set of men to whom the object was everything and the cost a minor item. And so uprose Sir William Young with his candidly-stated reason why the system in force was the only salvation for men of landed estates. "I will repeat," he said, "that boroughs bought and controlled by men of [landed] property forms the only balance to the commercial influence which is increasing by too rapid strides and ought to be checked." [21]

The thundering of a few members against venality had no effect upon the swarm of immovable men of landed estates in Parliament. Election of members, declared Richard Brinsley Sheridan, was a farce. "Corruption," he brusquely told his colleagues, "is the pivot on which the whole of our public government turns; the collection of taxes is under the direction of wealthy men in Parliamentary interest. The consequence is that the collection of them is neglected; to make up the deficiency excisemen must be added to the excise—this sours the temper of the people." Sheridan told how the Premier in power had metamorphosed into peers a hundred men "who had never rendered the least service to the public in any action of their lives—but merely on account of their Parliamentary influence." [22] By a vote of 282 to 41 the House of Commons overwhelmed electoral reform.

Seeking to impress upon his fellow members "the general feeling in Britain of the corruption in the House of Commons," and with pertinent remarks upon men who "had grown rich upon public money," Lord Cochrane, in 1807, introduced a most displeasing resolution. It called for an inquiry into places, sinecures, emoluments and pensions held by members of Parliament. By a decisive majority the House expeditiously voted down the resolution.[23]

It was probably this incident which caused "The Quarterly Review," for decades a venomous condemner of American venality, to indulge in a homily on Parliamentary corruption.

"Parliaments," it explained in May, 1809, "are seldom, very seldom bribed to injure their country, because it is seldom the interest of ministers to injure it; but the great source of corruption is that they will not serve it for nothing. Men get into Parliament in pursuit of power, honors and preferment, and until they obtain them, determine to obstruct all business and distress government."

At this period the East India Company stood forth as the greatest single example of British commercialism. In 1793 it was looked upon as a colossus with its 81,000 tons of shipping manned by 7,000 men. Its operations, power and revenues were viewed in Britain with mingled awe and admiration. Yearly it exported more than £1,500,000 of British products to India and China. Fortunes acquired by British individuals connected with it in India amounted to an aggregate of at least £1,000,000 a year. The wealth thus drenching England—or at least a considerable range of beneficiaries—gave the company commanding prestige and power there. In India it dominated governors, councilors, judges, generals and chiefs of provinces. From Bengal alone the company or its agents had extracted, it was computed, a total of £150,000,000.[24]

In 1796 the Emperor of China interdicted the importation and use of opium; smuggling was severely punishable, and persons found guilty of smoking the narcotic were liable to beheading. Notwithstanding this decree, the East India Company found ways of pouring into China great quantities of opium. In the north of India a whole province, under the company's direction, was purple with poppy fields. Protests by China's Government against systematic opium smuggling were fruitless. The East India Company's revenues expanded. In the four years 1799–1802 it made (excluding profits from spices and some other goods), a total profit of £6,220,229, of which (to be further exact), it distributed £2,841,644 in dividends. Moreover, so well was the company fortified with cash that it proudly announced its annual surplus as more than £237,000, and with triumphant self-approval pointed to its total surplus, in the four years, of £1,349,125.[25]

In a broader aspect, British sentiment was jubilant over the mounting value of British exports. During the successive Napoleonic wars human life was vastly sacrificed, and governing classes did not relent. But in Britain industrialism rejoiced at seeing exports from England and Scotland rise from £22,-000,000 in 1803 to more than £25,000,000 in 1805. Above the conflicts of sea and land was heard the prosperity chant of the woolen manufacturers—who exported in those years an average of £5,550,000 of woolen goods—and likewise of the cotton manufacturers, with their showing of an annual average export of £6,000,000 of their cloths. Wrought iron manufacturers did exceedingly well with their average annual exports of £900,000; and the proprietors of cotton yarn, hardware, hat, stocking, silk, apparel, wrought brass and many other factories all were suffused by an overweening sense of deserved good fortune.[26]

Women and poor or pauper child toilers were pitilessly overworked in foul factories; miserable wages doomed them to semi-starvation. Disease epidemics in the factory districts of Manchester caused widespread agitation for a regulatory factory law, which Parliament was goaded into passing in 1802. This law prescribed the remedy of ordering all factory walls whitewashed—the legislature imagining that this application would prevent further disease. No corrective recognition was given to the fearful slums in which workers existed.

The census returns of neither Great Britain nor the United States in the first decades of the nineteenth century gave any information as to the number of factories. But how greatly England had transformed itself from an agricultural to a manufacturing nation was shown by the British census of 1800. Of a total population of 8,331,434 in England, 1,524,227 persons were chiefly employed in agriculture, and 1,789,531 chiefly in trade, manufacture or handicraft. Of this latter classification, 595,707 were concentrated in the industrial districts of Lancashire, York and Middlesex.[27]

In the next decade or so the wide introduction of steam-operated machinery in England brought an enormous extension of trade. The outcome of the Napoleonic wars left Britain in command of the seas—a supremacy which was effectively challenged by America alone. But at that time the British, with greater experience and better shipyards, were able to produce more and often superior ships, and the British held a monopoly of the East India, and a firm grip on the West India, trade. In Lancashire handlooms were rapidly supplanted by machines. Manufacturers procured additional needed labor by turning to child-traffickers. These provided great numbers of workhouse pauper children who often were compelled to toil sixteen hours a day in the factories. It was not until 1819 that Parliament passed an act forbidding employment in the cotton mills to children under nine years old, and fixing the hours of employment of those from that age to sixteen years at not more than twelve a day. The story of laborers' riots to destroy machines in Nottingham in 1812 and 1813–1814, and in Lancashire later is not unfamiliar.[28]

As yet few factories had arisen in America. Shoe-making establishments started at Lynn and Haverhill, Mass., in 1812, were only rudiments of factories. The manufacturers cut the stock, and then distributed it to be made up in little country shops where the wives and daughters stitched the uppers. This system lasted until the invention in 1859 of the Blake sole-sewing machine, and soon thereafter of the McKay shoe stitcher. The system of complete manufacture in the factory was not well developed until 1870. Building of the Lowell, Mass., cotton factories dated from 1821 when a farm site was bought, and erection was begun on it the next year.

The landed estate and agricultural interests, which politically ruled America, looked with apprehension upon the prospects of industrialism supplanting them in power. One of many examples of the expression of this dread occurred in the New York State Constitutional Convention of 1821. New York City then had 123,000 population, a small part of that of the entire State. "At present," Chief Justice Spencer, a spokesman for the land interest, declared, "the agricultural interest predominates; but who can foresee that in process of time it will not become the minor body?" Chancellor Kent argued for a measure to ensure political power to men of landed property; he voiced his fear of the evils produced by a commercial and manufacturing population with the ensuing "wealth and luxuries, and the vices and miseries they engender." He pointed as an example to Paris, where one-seventh of the population subsisted on charity.[29]

One of the strangest aspects of criticism of America by the

British was that, while accusing Americans of money-seeking, they at the same time reproached America for its paucity of manufactures. Naturally enough, these critics linked the development of arts and sciences with factories. Rude and rural America, they declared, accordingly, could offer little in the artistic and scientific fields.[30]

Frauds in the manufacture and sale of goods still went on in Britain. Evidence before Parliamentary committees investigating the woolen trade showed that, in 1803 and 1821, manufacturers were making weavers use their homes as what we now call "sweatshops." In these the weavers worked fourteen to sixteen hours a day. When weavers tried to organize to better their lot they were arrested and convicted of criminal conspiracy. On the other hand, woolen manufacturers were using the stamping laws merely as a cloak for fraudulent representation of their wares, and they concealed defects in damaged cloths by the device of flocks and fine drawing.[31] The decay of the framework knitters trade, Parliamentary reports stated, was attributed to the practice of making bad and fraudulent goods; and fraud was practiced in the making of Nottingham lace.[32] Spurious worsted stockings were made and sold.[33] In the manufacture of watches and jewelry base metal was used both in England and in some other European countries; good watchmakers' names were pirated and stamped on watches and clocks; quantities of such inferior watches were smuggled into England, and then, together with fraudulent jewelry, exported by the British traders to North America for use in barter with the Indians for furs.[34] Continued frauds in the making of cutlery were complained of by good cutlers, and finally caused official inquiry into the imitative manufacture of edge tools.[35] There were long-lasting frauds in other lines of British manufacture.

Rich as well as poor were grossly imposed upon by fraudulent measurement and selling of coal. The great majority of bakers' shops were owned by the millers; cheap bakers used only inferior flour, adulterating it to give it whiteness. To shield themselves from prosecution for selling bread shortweight, bakers frequently paid informers a stated sum weekly not to cause

wise disciplining menials was the only treatment conducing to social order and stability. All of Bristed's assertions were, of course, foolish when not ludicrous. But they were believed in England. The strange feature of Bristed's representation of American employers' helplessness was that, at this very period, employers in America were invoking the terrors of old English law to tyrannize over their workers. It was by the force of this transplanted law, supposed to have been incorporated in American common law, that American factory and other industrial owners, while themselves organized in associations, sought to crush every effort of workers to organize for better wages and shorter work hours. Falling back upon precedents of English law, American judges outlawed workers' organizations as criminal conspiracies, and labor union organizers were often fined or imprisoned. Not until nearly the mid-nineteenth century was the first successful effort made in America to efface the incubus of this old law. At the instigation of Massachusetts boot and shoe manufacturers, Boston officials brought an action against the Boston Journeymen Bootmakers' Society, on the ground that it was a conspiracy. The lower court ruled against the union, and the jury returned a verdict of guilty. But on an appeal in the Supreme Court of Massachusetts, Robert Rantoul, by an able plea, caused reversal of the verdict. The law of Queen Elizabeth's time making a criminal offence of the refusal to work for certain wages had not been, he argued, specifically adopted as common law in the United States after the Revolution.[1] The lingering influence of this Elizabethan statute was not obliterated from American jurisprudence until almost 1880.

At the time of Bristed's sojourn in America, general—then styled "universal"—suffrage did not exist in the United States. Only men owning land voted, and only those having prescribed amounts of property could be elected to high offices in various States. Manhood suffrage did not make its advent until 1821–1828. But even the American qualified voting system, necessitating, as it did, a genuine and popular appeal to a partial thinking electorate, upset Bristed and other British critics. They were accustomed to their own smug, compact, easily manipulated system.[2] The idea that "universal" suffrage led to tumults was widespread in Britain,[3] and Bristed's book catered to that fashionable view.

Popular election of judges in America, he wrote, resulted in grievously encouraging litigation among the poorer classes, and "a horrible perversion of justice corrupts the whole body of the commonwealth." As a matter of fact, recourse to law in America was easily had, while in Britain it was one of the most expensive of things. In England the winning of the most trivial cause in court cost £40, and so much more costly was suit in the Court of Equity that it was better to abandon claim for £500 to £1,000 than to contend in an action. Bristed described American laws generally as favoring the debtor at the expense of the creditor, and thereby encouraging dishonesty. Only a few months after Bristed's book was published, a House of Commons Select Committee, submitting its report on Britain's bankruptcy laws, specified various phases of those laws of which, it stated, the public had good cause to complain. One phase was "the ease with which undeserving and even dishonest bankrupts obtain their certificates [of discharge from debt], and the total absence of all discrimination between culpability and misfortune." Under an old law any bankrupt concealing assets to the amount of £20 was still punishable by death—a law so repugnant that in eighty-three years the British courts could bring themselves to sentence only three bankrupts to execution.[4]

"It requires no prophetic inspiration," Bristed oracularly concluded as to America's fate, "to foretell the rapid dissolution of a government planted in the soil of universal suffrage, when once its electors have become deaf to the calls of duty, and when the mere sale of their votes to the highest bidder may be considered as one of the least dark in the long catalogue of their crimes." Seeing in America a complete absence of that alliance of Church and State common in Europe, Bristed decided that Americans had "little religious feeling." And among a list of other charges against Americans he made this pronouncement: "The national vanity of the United States surpasses that of any other country, not excepting France." Despite all of which defects and traits, Bristed, in a conciliatory burst, visioned the American people as possessing "the materials of moral greatness superior to those of any other country." [5]

For attributing this last-named quality to Americans, Bristed was upbraided by "The Quarterly Review" (January, 1819). It criticized him for not telling how the moral greatness was to be accomplished, and reproached him for not having adopted "a more modest tone in vaunting the superior materials for moral greatness possessed by Americans." Then asserting Britain's supereminence in all things, "The Quarterly Review" used the strictures in Bristed's book as the basis of a long tirade against America. It arraigned both American parties as bent on conquest and plunder; said that virtuous England would not buy Louisiana from the robber nation France, as unscrupulous America had bought it, and imputed to America "talk of sending forth fleets to subjugate the world."

At about the same time was published another book on America by Henry Bradshaw Fearon. This book was strongly endorsed by Earl Grey as "full of the most valuable information, distinguished by the marks not only of an inquiring, observing and intelligent mind, but of the greatest fairness and impartiality." Some extracts will show the book's nature:

"The United States are cursed with a population undeserving of their exuberant soil and free government.

"We do not meet in America with even an approach to simplicity and honesty of mind.

"No people are so vain as Americans; their self-estimation and cool-headed bombast, when speaking of themselves or their country, are quite ludicrous.

"There would appear to be placed in the very stamina of the people a coldness, a selfishness, and a spirit of conceit which form strong barriers against improvement.

"The Americans are most remarkable for complete and general coldness of character and disposition—a cold-blooded callousness of disposition.

"Cleanliness is scarcely known on this side of the Atlantic.

"Neither sex [in Philadelphia] possesses the English standard of health—a rosy cheek. The young females are indeed genteel; but their color is produced by art, but for which disgusting practice many of them might pass for beautiful. You will be surprised to hear that in the practice of *rougeing* the cheeks junior branches of the Society of Friends are not at all deficient.

"The dirk is the inseparable companion of all classes in the State of Illinois.

"A cold uniform bigotry seems to pervade all religious sects.

"No species of correction is allowed in the American schools; children even at home are perfectly independent." [6]

In such vein of criticism Fearon had abundantly more to say, not omitting depiction of American officials as ignorant, vulgar, brutal and corrupt. But, in the eyes of British reviewers, Fearon's book was not an artistic performance. He did make one concession to Americans. Fearon informed the emigrant that he would find in America: "A country possessed of the most enlightened civil and political advantages; a people reaping the full reward of their own labors; a people not paying tithes; not subjected to heavy taxation without representation; a people without spies and informers; a people without an enormous standing army."

For his saying this "The Quarterly Review" (January, 1819) assailed Fearon as a renegade Englishman, "evidently a man of limited faculties." Notwithstanding which opinion it devoted *forty-three pages* to a review, seizing greedily upon his disparagements of America and elaborating them with its supplementary comments. Taking the current books on America as its text, "The British Review or London Critical Journal" (May, 1819), described Americans as "hordes of discontented democrats, mad, unnatural, enthusiastic and needy or desperate adventurers." "The North American Republicans are the most vain, egotistical, insolent, rodomontade sort of people that are anywhere to be found. They give themselves airs." "The Americans may overrun a portion of the world but they will never civilize those whom they conquer. . . . The mass of the North Americans are too proud to learn, and too ignorant to teach." "The States of America can never have a native literature any more than they can have a native character." "The government at Washington . . . will one day outstrip all other nations in warlike exploits and commercial wealth, under the auspicious stars of the Union."

Passing over various other British books on America of this particular time, this question obtrudes itself: What was the attitude of American writers toward this stream of ridiculous calumny? With but one exception it was that of a meek acceptance and compliant acquiescence.

Why was the name and work of this lone exception—Robert Walsh, Jr.—long since allowed to sink into utter oblivion? He deserves a living place in American memory. The preface of his book, published in Philadelphia in 1819, avouched as his purpose not merely to assert the merits of calumniated America: "I wish to repel actively, and if possible, to arrest the war which is waged without stint or intermission upon our national reputation." The hope was cherished—but vainly—he wrote, that the spirit of envy and arrogance of English literary censors would be righted. He went on: "It was, too, believed by many that the British writers would assign some bounds to their attacks so long as we forbore to recriminate; and it was thought harsh and uncharitable to touch the sores and blotches of the British nation on account of the malevolence and folly of a few individuals, or of a party within her bosom. The whole is proved to be a mere illusion."

Then, recounting "The Quarterly Review" attacks, Walsh showed how publications representing both British parties had joined in the campaign against America. The Whig journals were railing in the same strain as the Tory; both the Ministerial party and the Opposition had united, even on the floor of Parliament, in denouncing "American ambition and cruelty and in affecting to credit the coarse inventions of Englishmen who have visited us for the express purpose of manufacturing libels, or betaken themselves to this expedient on their return home, as a profitable speculation." The purpose of the British campaign, Walsh asserted, was "to inspire the British farmer and artisan with a horror of republican America, and the nations of the world with a distrust of the spirit of her government." He added: "The British writers and orators never throw out their reproaches against the United States without putting Great Britain in glorious contrast." [7]

Walsh's book was in nine sections dealing with Great Britain's political and mercantile jealousy, its enmity after the American Revolution, the animosity of British periodical writers toward America, their system of derision and obloquy, and data on the state of society in Great Britain. He pointed out the glaring inconsistency of British publications in making occasional strong admissions of the real social conditions in Britain while at the same time virulently attacking American conditions. Thus "The Quarterly Review," speaking in 1816 on British matters: "The great mass of our population is in a state which renders them the easy dupes of every mischievous demagogue." "The English are an uneducated people." "In the road which the English laborer must travel, the poor house is the last stage on the way to the grave." "In some parts of England the paupers average nearly one-fourth of the population."

These admissions, however, gave only a meager idea of the direness of realities in Britain. Into these Walsh should have examined thoroughly; and, above all, he should have given a full, needed contrast by presenting American aims and accomplishments. Perhaps then and later the few American writers who undertook to defend their country were smarting unnecessarily under the staple charge of American boastfulness, and hence refrained from pointing out American deeds. But these were of a character entitling them to the widest publication. American writers could then with complete propriety have done what a noted Englishman—Macaulay—did more than a quarter of a century later in Parliament. As we shall see, Macaulay did not stint giving high praise to groups of settlers in New England and elsewhere for having early established the principle of general education—a principle gradually developed into national proportions.

What was the record in America? While still in an embryo condition, in a circumjacent wilderness, Massachusetts Bay Colony, as early as 1646, had enacted an educational law. This affirmed "the necessity and singular use of good literature," and a law of 1674 compelled every town to establish schools. Further legislation came and similar laws were passed by Plymouth Colony.[8]

"For the encouragement of learning and promotion of public concernments," Connecticut enacted, from 1672 to 1714, a series of school laws requiring every town of thirty families to maintain a school to teach children to read and write; grants of land and money were made, and a free school was established in each of the towns of Hartford and New Haven. Law after law iterated that the upholding and improvement of schools was of great importance to the public weal.[9]

By the third quarter of the seventeenth century all New England, except Rhode Island, was under a compulsory system of education. Tuition fees collected from parents, guardians or apprentice masters were the usual means of sustaining the schools, but the laws did provide that in cases where fees could not be contributed toward paying teachers' wages, the inhabitants in general had to make up the deficiency.

Many laws were passed in New England forever exempting from taxation any lands or house donated for school purposes, or elaborating plans of public taxation to make up for any lack caused by insufficiency of funds derived from tuition fees. The thirteenth article of William Penn's preface to his "Frame of Government" in Pennsylvania provided for "a committee of manners, education and arts." [10] In 1697 Pennsylvania Quakers established a free school; their concern was with elementary education; they attached little value to higher education. South Carolina, 1710, established a free school; likewise New York in 1732. Virginia, in 1748, passed a law requiring that all apprenticed children, boys and girls, should be taught to read and write.

A resolution adopted by the Continental Congress, in 1783, declared that "schools and the means of education shall be forever encouraged." The ordinance of 1785, followed by that of 1789, reserved perpetually for public school support and endowment 640 acres in every township in the territory northwest of the Ohio River. The total of Government grants of public lands for schools, agricultural colleges and universities ultimately reached more than 116,000,000 acres. New York State, in 1805, granted the net proceeds of a half million acres of unappropriated public lands for a school fund. By a Pennsylvania law of 1809 the expense of educating children was made a county charge.

This, a mere résumé, shows the deep concern in America for popular education. In Britain the first serious attempt to provide for the education of the populace was made in 1807. But where in America the opposition of the rich and well-to-do to paying taxes for the education of all children hindered for a time the establishment of the common school system, the resistance in Britain was both on that ground and on many other grounds. At the organization of the Free School Society,[11] in New York, in 1805, DeWitt Clinton pointed out in an address: "The fundamental error of Europe has been to confine the light of knowledge to the wealthy and great. . . . More just and rational views have been entertained on this subject in the United States. Here no privileged orders, no factitious distinctions in society, no hereditary nobility, no established religion, no royal prerogatives exist to interfere barriers between the people and to create distinct classes in society. All men being considered as enjoying equality of rights, the propriety and necessity of dispensing, without distinction, the blessings of education followed as a matter of course." [12]

The Parochial Schools bill in the House of Commons was of simple scope, providing for the establishment in every parish of an elementary school to be supported by taxes and controlled by the taxpayers.

In spurning the measure the House of Commons opponents advanced many arguments. "For," said one of the chief objectors, "however specious in theory the project might be of giving education to the laboring classes of the poor, it would, in effect, be found prejudicial to their morals and happiness; it would teach them to despise their lot in life, instead of making them good servants in agriculture and other laborious employments to which their rank in society has destined them; instead of teaching them subordination, it would render them fractious and refractory . . . it would enable them to read seditious pamphlets, vicious books and publications against

Christianity; it would render them insolent to their superiors," etc., etc.[13] Another antagonist declared that if large schools were established, "immorality was more likely to be imbibed than morality and virtue."

With the clause for compulsory education struck out, the bill was finally passed by the House of Commons. In the House of Lords the Archbishop of Canterbury objected to the bill as leaving little or no control to the minister of the parish. "This," he said, "would go to subvert the first principles of education in this country, which had been, and he trusted would continue to be under the control and auspices of the [Church of England] establishments. . . . Your lordships' prudence will, no doubt, guard against innovations that might shake the foundation of religion." Earl Stanhope then pointed out that the bill had nothing to do with religion. "It is merely to teach its objects spelling, reading, writing and arithmetic for purposes useful in life; and in a manufacturing country like this . . . the superiority of workmen with some education, over those who had none, must sensibly be felt by all the great manufacturers in the country." [14] The House of Lords threw out the bill, and more than sixty years passed before Parliament consented to enact a similar measure.

In Europe generally efforts to prevent popular education were long successful. During the French Revolution educational proposals were drafted, but there was neither the time nor the opportunity to establish any as realities. Giving no attention to primary schools, the first Napoleon concerned himself exclusively with university education, and likewise the succeeding king under whom the preposterously scanty sum of 50,000 francs were granted for popular education. It was not until 1833 that a law was passed in France authorizing elementary schools in all department capitals and in communes; but this law was so devised that the only qualifications demanded from teachers was authorization granted by the bishops. Still powerful, the Church discouraged public schools, and to a large extent the law remained a dead letter. The years 1881–1882 were reached before a free, compulsory and secular system of education was instituted in France.

The practical effect of Holland's law of 1806, decreeing primary schools, was to make them charity schools; while the middle classes, upon whom the greater share of the taxes fell, sent their children to private schools. Furthermore, the provision in Holland's law of 1806 declaring public schools entirely independent of ecclesiastical influence, led to dissatisfaction on the part of Belgium's Catholic population and to the separation of the two countries in 1830. Twelve years later, in deference to the Catholic minority in its boundaries, Holland authorized consideration of the religious faith of teachers, and examination of textbooks by the clergy. A dozen more years passed before Holland enacted a law which, on the whole, proved satisfactory to the conflicting elements.[15]

In Germany serfdom was not abolished until 1807, and, in the elementary schools thereafter established, religious education in accordance with the creed of the commune's majority was the paramount duty; the local clergyman was *ex officio* a member of the school committee and was authorized to censure defects, but final decisions were reserved to the State rulers.[16]

No reliable data of illiteracy in continental Europe can be located. In Britain such portion of elementary education as was popularly given was long dependent entirely upon casual philanthropic endowment, irregular charitable contributions, and was conducted strictly in line with the Church of England doctrine and discipline. Upon these bases the National Society was formed in 1811. By 1817 the National Society had 725 schools and 117,000 scholars, all under the direct control of the parish minister.[17]

But so wholly inadequate were the efforts of this body in a population in England and Wales approaching 12,000,000 that vast numbers of children grew up in densest ignorance. In London alone, a Parliamentary inquiry showed, from 120,000 to 130,000 children were utterly without means of education. A large portion had to drudge long hours; about 4,000 were hired by parents to beggars or were employed as assistants in pilfering. Toil, mendicity, theft, prostitution—this variously was the fate of swarms of London children.[18]

Testifying before a Parliamentary investigating committee in 1818, William Freeman Lloyd, secretary of the Sunday School Society, gave this picture of conditions in London: "There are

an amazing number of children in the metropolis who are prevented from attending any school whatever, from the absolute
want of anything like decent clothing; there are a vast number
of children employed in selling matches, sweeping the streets,
and various low employments. . . . Many of the parents are
likewise so extremely poor, where there are large families, as
to be unable to procure clothing. In Southwark, in one district,
2,000 children were found who could not attend any school
whatever for want of clothing." [19] Conditions similar to those
in London prevailed in all of the large British cities, and more
markedly so in the manufacturing districts. In its report the
Parliamentary Committee on "Education of the Lower Orders" dwelt upon "the neglect and abuse of charitable funds
connected with education," and upon the fact that "equal negli-
gence and malversation appears to have prevailed in all other
charities." [20] Yet for fifty-two years longer Britain allowed the
operations and influence of these charitable societies to control
such scant popular education as was given, and to be supreme in
shaping its spirit and methods.

Robert Walsh's book made but the slightest, most transient
impression in British editorial offices. In a discourse upon the
book "The Edinburgh Review," in May, 1820, admitted that
America had cause for complaint. "Nothing can be more des-
picable and disgusting," it agreed, "than the scurrility with
which she has been assailed by a portion of the press of this
country—and disgraceful as these publications are, they speak
the sense of a powerful and active party in the nation."
Seeking to place the blame upon the Tory Party, which, it
said, was not friendly to liberty and was hostile to all extension
of popular rights, "The Edinburgh Review" went on: "Now it
is quite true that this party dislikes America and is apt enough
to decry and insult her. Its adherents have never forgiven the
success of her war of independence—the loss of a nominal sovereignty, or perhaps of a real power of vexing and oppressing—
her supposed rivalry in trade—and, above all, the happiness
and tranquillity which she enjoys under a republican form of
government. Such a spectacle of democratic prosperity is un-
speakably mortifying to their high monarchical principles, and

is easily imagined to be dangerous to their security." Pursuing this line of partisan differentiation, "The Edinburgh Review" enlarged upon the alarm caused in England by the steady success of American popular government. It then proceeded to rehearse "the undeniable defects of Americans" which it had frequently specified, and "some indefensible absurdities of Americans" which it had often scored.

Only a few months before its comments upon Walsh's book, "The Edinburgh Review" had published a splenetic attack by Sydney Smith upon America, taxing it with having done absolutely nothing for the sciences, arts, literature or the drama. "In the four quarters of the globe," it had sneeringly asked, "who reads an American book? or goes to an American play? or looks at an American picture or statue? . . . Who drinks out of American glasses? or eats from American plates? or wears American coats and gowns? or sleeps in American blankets?" And, as a climax, it had vented the never-failing British denunciation of America for maintaining negro slavery. "Under which of the old tyrannical governments of Europe is every sixth man a slave, whom his fellow-creatures may buy and sell and torture?"

Lord Castlereagh, Foreign Secretary of Britain, had sent out a questionnaire on the subject of negro slavery. According to answers made by the African Society of London, British, Portuguese, French, Dutch, American and Danish vessels all participated in the traffic. During a series of years in the late eighteenth and early nineteenth century, British ships alone annually carried from Africa 55,000 slaves. Defying prohibitory laws of the American Government and those of several European Governments, ships of various nations, including British and American, persisted in the traffic. British condemnations of Americans for enslaving human beings contained no recognition of the outlawing of slavery by various Northern States. But this fact was made a most pregnant point by some speakers in the British Parliament when, in 1833, a bill was considered for paying £20,000,000 to West India slave owners for the freeing of negro slaves there. Opponents to making payment reminded the House of Commons: To be consistent with that body's declared principle that no man could claim property in his fellow man, nothing should be paid, and they held forth the example of a number of American States which, in freeing slaves, had not paid a dollar to the owners.[21] Sir Eardley Wilmot asked why appropriations were not made to relieve the great distress in England itself; he instanced the horrible lot of workers whose earnings did not average two-and-a-half pence a day.[22] Over such protests the £20,000,000 was obligingly voted.

Using Walsh's book as a renewed opportunity for berating America, "The Edinburgh Review" fell back upon previous inimical books. It had the testimony of every traveler who had been in America, it asserted, to justify its branding of Americans as inebriates, rudely inquisitive, absurdly vain, and offensively boastful. Had the practice of critical visiting been reversed, American critics would have found in British public meetings a notorious custom of high-flown boasting. The continuance of this self-congratulatory process drew forth biting comment from at least one noted Englishman, Lord Brougham, then Lord Chancellor, who chaffed at the Pharisaism bedeviling English public speakers. "We are described," he said with fine pungency, "as the people of all other nations, possessing the highest tone of moral and religious feeling. I can only say that I hope this is the case; but this is undoubted—that whether we are the most moral and religious people in the world or not, we, of all people in the world, are the most satisfied that we are so." [23]

John M. Duncan's two volumes on America and Canada were largely an inane description of scenes and places. Such observations as he otherwise made were partly favorable, and in part unfavorable to Americans. Of their literary and religious characteristics, which he esteemed their most important features, he was persuaded that "much misapprehension prevails in my native country." He praised educational conditions in New England; "it is next to impossible to discover in Connecticut a white native who cannot read and write." He credited real religious liberty to America while in England, he pointed out, toleration only existed. Reversely, he saw no merit in American "universal" suffrage, deprecated its democracy as mere popular clamor, and extolled Britain's political system as the nearest to perfection.[24]

"The British Review and London Critical Journal," in May, 1824, used this book as the ground for a long declamation against America. It sermonized on American lack of taste due to the "republican state of discipline which prevails in their schools"; spurted captious remarks on "the evil tendency of universal suffrage"; and ended with this outburst: "Our possession of Canada, we know, is a circumstance very galling to American ambition."

Without exception various important British magazines and other publications were intent upon contrasting the excellencies of an hereditary social order with the grievous defects of the American system. In one way or another these publications lauded an hereditary order as the only kind assuring culture and manners. The sweeping, rapid movement in America for education of the mass aroused increasing antagonism among the British upper classes and their spokesmen.

In large portions of America the introduction of manhood suffrage was taken as, of course, presupposing the need of an enlightened citizenry. Indiana led, in 1824, with a general school law, and Illinois followed in the next year. Widely throughout America articles were published and addresses made at education conventions giving the clearest reasons why education was held a supreme duty.[25] For the first time in its history, the Massachusetts law of 1827 made compulsory the entire support of the schools by taxation; when, in 1820, a Boston primary school committee had discovered that three hundred children were not attending school, it expressed its "great surprise and grief." [26] At another time consternation was felt in the Rhode Island legislature because, in a population of more than 100,000, there had been found 1,600 adults unable to read and write.[27] From 1827 onward Ohio, Michigan, Pennsylvania, Kentucky, New York and other States established public school systems. A typical address of the period was that of S. Lewis before the Education Convention at Columbus, Ohio, in 1836: "Other nations have hereditary sovereigns. . . . These children about your street, who cannot even speak your language, are your future sovereigns. Is it not important that they be well educated? . . . All nations are looking on at our experiment; individuals bid us Godspeed; but every court in Europe would rejoice to see us do as they have long prophesied we must do, Viz. dissolve in anarchy." [28]

Son of Sir James Hall, baronet, Captain Basil Hall, of the Royal Navy, toured America in 1827 and 1828. The result was a couple of volumes, which unmistakably were the quintessence of snobbery. As in the case of various other critical books, his volumes, after their issuance in Europe, were republished in America and widely read.

Jeering at American education was one of Hall's main themes. With a superlative condescension he explained to America how in England families of high station kept their young men at the public (private) schools and universities. "We do not maintain the doctrine of entire independence, according to the American acceptation of the term, to be a good one. Moreover, with us all men are divided into ranks or classes, which although they blend insensibly, and intermix with one another when they meet, are yet very obviously distinguished, while the acknowledged rights and privileges of each are scrupulously preserved. Every one finds out, also, in the long run, that his best chance of success and happiness consists in conforming as nearly as possible to the established habits of that branch of society in which he happens to be born, or which he may reach by dint of extraordinary industry or good fortune. I may even add, that without doing so, no man is considered respectable. Every class has its own particular marks by which it is distinguished from all the rest." And more to the same effect.

Informing his readers that he had been told a hundred times that comparisons should not be made between so old a country as England and so new a country as America, he declared that he "saw not a single reason why not." He compared America and Canada thus: "In the United States places of power and eminence depend entirely upon popular caprice . . . the fluctuating will of a giddy populace. In British provinces all situations of honor and profit are derived from the crown. After all, it is perhaps better to be subservient to a monarch than to a mob." His volume was replete with jibes at "the visionary doctrine of universal equality," and the incapacity of America to produce capable men.[29]

Contrary to Captain Hall's opinion, however, one may well question whether the Irish of his day found their "best chance of success and happiness" in conforming to the habits of their fathers. Aside from the ignorance, destitution and squalor among the "lower classes" in Britain itself, the condition of British-ruled Ireland at this time would seem unbelievable were it not attested by indubitable testimony. This, given in 1825 before a House of Lords committee, showed: One million of seven millions of the Irish existed entirely by charity and plunder. A host of vagrant mendicants infested Ireland. Very rarely did the Irish peasant have money; not one in twenty Irishmen found constant employment; heavy taxes and a tithe, even on potatoes, the chief food, for support of a hostile religious establishment, further beggared the people. To get employment, Irish Catholics had to conform to Protestantism; Catholics were excluded from various offices, including grand juries; unless they took an oath obnoxious to their religious convictions, they were not allowed to qualify for elections and were not even eligible to become guardians for their own children. So severe were the magistrates in penalizing for the least infraction that (such was the testimony of Daniel O'Connell, the noted Irish leader), to influence the magistrates' decisions, it was the common practice of peasant men who could do so to make presents, and of women to yield their chastity, to the magistrates.[30]

Movements in Britain for the repeal of laws decreeing death for numerous transgressions were long stolidly viewed by a Parliament domineered by upper class insensitiveness to any compassion. Prolonged agitation did force the abolition, between 1818 and 1824, of capital punishment for twenty-one offences. Complaining that many ferocious laws remained, humanitarians pressed for their repeal. A typical petition, in 1833, repeated the strong language of previous petitions in denouncing Britain's criminal law as "vindictive and barbarous"; the introducer of the petition held up to Parliament, as an example to be emulated, the case of America where one or two crimes only were punishable by death.[31] Prosecutions in England and elsewhere for criticism (stretched into charge of libel), and on medieval lines for blasphemy, were not infrequent.[32]

No sense of weariness in harping upon the same strain affected British reviewers. Hall's book had an immediate wide circulation and was made the text of a new explosion against America. To give his book special weight "The Quarterly Review," in November, 1829, admitted that most of his predecessors had made "only hasty flights through the republic . . . and then fancied themselves qualified to impart to the European world some information respecting their descendants beyond the Atlantic." Ignoring the clear fact that it had taken seriously each of the previous books, "The Quarterly Review" certified Hall's book as a most genuine, true series of observations.

American democracy, said that publication, lacked stimulus in producing characters of "excellent moral principles," and never, anyway, would use such characters "whilst all power shall depend upon the fluctuating will and coarse passions of an illiterate, conceited, encroaching and sottish populace." Captain Hall, that genteel quarterly further said, "must have collected many instances of American vulgarity, knavery, sottishness and hypocrisy." And still further: "The eager, universal desire of gain is unchecked by any classes of persons or by any considerable numbers of individuals who are so easy in circumstances as not to dwell constantly on subjects connected with profit and loss. This . . . leads, with a great portion of the people, to a species of trickery and deceit. . . . The speculations of land jobbers, bankers, manufacturers, merchants and dealers in funds conduct operations to an extent . . . far beyond anything that can be conceived by those acquainted even with the most gambling marts of Europe." And at about the same time "The Times" of London added, apropos of America: "The worship of the divinity of lucre is withal so universal, we might add, so fanatical throughout this money-making republic."

In the year before Captain Hall betook himself to America there turned up a reverberating scandal implicating various members of Parliament. England, in 1824, was in another vortex of stock speculation, this time in gaslight, railway and mining enterprises of which many members of Parliament were promoters or in which they were financially concerned. General Sir William Congreve and some other members of Parliament acquired the Arigna mines, chiefly iron, in Ireland, for £25,000 and then organized the Arigna Iron and Coal Company, capitalizing it for £300,000, in shares of £50 each.

Two years later the shrill outcry from investors caused the appointment of an investigating committee by the House of Commons. After taking much testimony this committee reported of the company's managing director: "His management in feeding the [stock] market through the medium of brokers, aided by the delusive representations which the prospectus of the company afforded, and the dazzling effect of the names of persons of station and eminence associated in the undertaking, seems to have produced results which, even at that period of epidemic speculation, could scarcely have been anticipated." The committee related how the "insiders" had made large sums from stock-jobbing operations which it termed "a deliberate fraud," "a fraudulent pillage of the public." Specified members of Parliament, the committee found, did pocket money from the sale of shares; in roundabout fashion the committee suggested that until some impartial authority admitted their title to the money, they should return it.[33] No record is available showing that they did.

The practice, or rather the profession, of lobbying has been generally supposed an insidious American conception, the spawn of American corruption. In the British Parliament lobbying had been elevated into a fine art reserving all services and profits to the honorable members themselves. They, and not outsiders, did the lobbying. So malodorous did the scandal become that Parliament could no longer blink it. The debate, on February 26, 1830, brought out undisputed facts. On various House of Commons committees were members whose own financial interests were involved in the bills before them. Canal, gas-light, railway and other companies had their men securely stationed on these committees. In a seeming mood of sudden virtue, the House of Commons passed a resolution forbidding any member to engage, directly or indirectly, in promoting private bills for pecuniary rewards.[34] This rule did not in the least disconcert the implicated M.P.'s; they merely evaded it by transferring their lobbying business to sons or other relatives or to partners.

This ruse caused another lively discussion in the House of Commons, in 1837, but nothing was done.[35]

Various American money lenders found furtive ways of circumventing laws against usury, but in superfine methods on this score they could teach nothing to the British. On the London Stock Exchange laws against usury were almost invariably evaded by bonus and other devices; charges of seven, eight and nine per cent were customary. So testified David Ricardo, the noted political economist, before a Parliamentary Committee. On mortgages many persons were compelled to pay an onerous 9 to 12 per cent—a general condition affirmed by the testimony of bankers and other witnesses. The Committee reported that laws against usury "have been extensively evaded," subjecting the borrowers to "enormous charges." [36]

Industrialism had made further vast strides in England. Manchester was an example; from fifty-four factories there in 1820 the number had risen to seventy-three by 1828. Britain's exports of more than £50,000,000 (including £10,000,000 of foreign and colonial merchandise), were almost five times those of the United States. Nearly one-half of American exports comprised raw cotton, and much of the remainder rice, indigo, pork and other produce. Above 600,000 bales of the more than 1,000,000 bales of cotton raised in America in 1831 were exported to Britain; 127,000 bales to France; and 27,000 to other European countries.[37] In the matter of aggregate factories the best procurable comparison for America and Britain is one for the years 1831 and 1836. Enumeration of factories in the entire extent of America, with a population of 12,850,000 in 1831, showed 666 woolen and cotton factories, mostly small cotton-goods concerns, and a few hundred other kinds of factories, likewise mainly small.[38] Britain in 1836, with a population of about 26,000,000, contained 3,016 cotton, woolen, flax and silk factories. But British returns included only textile mills coming within the provisions of the Factories Regulation Act, and did not, of course, comprehend the additional large number of other kinds of factories.[39] More than half of the employees in British textile factories were under eighteen years of age, and of these a great number were in childhood.

CHAPTER XII

INSULAR SELF-SATISFACTION

A BARRISTER who cared more for learning than for law, Thomas Anthony Trollope had been unsuccessful in his profession and also in a later attempt to run a farm. His wife, Frances Milton Trollope, thought prospects of making money in America were promising. She went from England to the pioneer town of Cincinnati to establish a bazaar, English style. The building which she ordered erected was, according to her countryman Captain Frederick Marryatt who subsequently visited Cincinnati, "composed of every variety of architecture." He described it as altogether "preposterous." Her business was entirely unsuited to the needs of the population which was not concerned in buying dainties. Cincinnati folk, Captain Marryatt wrote, dubbed the venture "Trollope's Folly." He commented: "It is remarkable how a shrewd woman like Mrs. Trollope should have committed such an error."

Returning to England deeply disappointed, Mrs. Trollope wrote her book, "Domestic Manners of the Americans." Not notoriety but revenue was Mrs. Trollope's object. Her subject in general was hackneyed by this time, but European prejudices against America were as strong as ever, and, as repeated experience had shown, were highly profitable if purveyed to with the right animus. Well did Mrs. Trollope do the catering; in Britain her book quickly attained five editions, then rated an extensive sale, and it was translated into French, Italian and German. It netted her some £600 which replenished the desperate family finances. She was flattered and fêted; her reputation as a writer was so puffed and her writings in such demand that thereafter she wrote fifty novels and books of travel, all of a kind palatable to popular fancy.

"Domestic Manners of the Americans" was one of a number of books on America published almost simultaneously in Eng-

138

land. One of the others was James Stuart's "Three Years in North America"—a book that gave a refreshing change from the customary traducing. Stuart had none of Captain Hall's love of the patriciate nor any of Mrs. Trollope's affectation of gentility. He allowed full credit to America for its diffusion of general education, and for its rights of religious equality as distinct from the European vouchsafing of toleration. He warned British travelers not to expect in America the deference given to rank and station in the Old World. Stuart's book made no impression, while Mrs. Trollope's was, with perhaps one exception, effusively hailed in Europe. "The Edinburgh Review" could not stomach the "great smartness" of her style and the pretentious superficiality of her comments. In its review, July, 1832, it accused her of not making a single sensible observation on any important subject. Of her pseudo facts it said: "The adroitness with which they have been doctored, gingered and got up, resembles the skill of a clever horsedealer preparing for a fair."

Mrs. Trollope's book was a prolonged sneer. American educational institutions, she represented, taught thoroughly little else than reading, writing and bookkeeping. "Republican equality was most distressing." Americans were dull; "the total and universal want of good, or even pleasing manners, both in males and females, is remarkable." She emitted floods of words on the essential vulgarity of republics and their disastrous effect upon development of the arts. Rebuking her lack of knowledge, "The Edinburgh Review" felt called upon to inform her of the flourishing state of the arts in the ancient republics of Greece and Rome and in Florence. Mrs. Trollope imputed to Americans "a profound ignorance on the subject of art," and an "utter ignorance respecting pictures to be found among persons of the first standing in society." And finally: "Neither art, science, learning or pleasure can seduce Americans from pursuit of money."

Just so; but what, speaking of art, was the record of Mrs. Trollope's home land in that respect?

The low state of the pictorial arts in Britain was disclosed by the records of Parliament itself. A resolution to appropriate the modest sum of £3,000 for the British Museum had come before the House of Commons in 1777. To the greater number of members the subject of art was new, bewildering and disconcerting. Of the entire membership less than a handful manifested any interest. John Wilkes tried hard to arouse fellow members from their lethargy. "The British Museum possesses few valuable paintings," he told them, "yet we are anxious to have an English school of painters. If we expect to rival the Italian, the Flemish or even the French schools, our artists must have before them the finished works of the greatest masters." Talking against a mass of inertia, Wilkes announced a forthcoming offer to Parliament by Sir Robert Walpole's family to sell its great collection of paintings, Italian and others. "I hope," Wilkes fervently said, "that it will not be dispersed but purchased by Parliament, and added to the British Museum. . . . Such an important acquisition would in some degree alleviate the concern which every man of taste now feels at being deprived of viewing those prodigies of art. . . . At present they are perishing in a late baronet's smoky house at the end of a great smoky town." And now Wilkes reminded his fellow members of a fact which was generally well known but about which Parliament could never be persuaded to take any action. "Those paintings," he said with extra emphasis, "are entirely secreted from the public eye, yet they were purchased with public money before the accession of the Brunswick line." Wilkes did not explain the process by which paintings bought with public funds could have been claimed and held as personal possessions. He asked whether there could be a greater mortification to any English gentleman than to be deprived of viewing fine paintings which, although thus purchased with public funds, were allowed to be stowed in the recesses of a private mansion.

The scant funds appropriated for the British Museum, Wilkes further said, were inadequate to buy paintings and books. "This capital," he went on, "after so many ages, remains without any considerable public library. Rome has the immense collection of the Vatican, and Paris . . . the greatness of the King's Library. They are both open at stated times, with every proper accommodation to all strangers. The best here is the Royal Society's, but even that is inconsiderable, neither is it open to the public, nor are the necessary conveniences afforded strangers for reading and transcribing. The British Museum is . . . rich in manuscripts but it is wretchedly poor in printed books." [1]

Nearly a half century passed before Parliament was persuaded into taking the first steps for the founding of the National Gallery. It was the bequeathing of art and other collections by various individuals which forced the erection of a National Gallery. In 1805 came the Townley collection of ancient sculpture, and, subsequently, his collection of antiquities, medals and coins; the Elgin marbles in 1816; and various other collections of antiquities, manuscripts, books and minerals.[2] Charges were made in "The Edinburgh Review," and repeated in Parliament, that the British Museum's collections—mainly natural history—were in a chaotic condition. Parliamentary friends of the trustees denied these charges, but they did not deny the charge that among the trustees there was not a single scientist.

On the Strand, London, a palace called Somerset House had been built in 1549, later acquired by the Government, demolished in 1775; and subsequently the work of rebuilding it was begun. No refutation was made of John William Croker's statement in the House of Commons that the topmost floor of this building, for thirty years remaining in a half-finished state, was the out-of-the-way, unfavorable place used for exhibiting paintings which were at a disadvantage in such unsuitable rooms.[3]

Such was the lack of facilities for exhibiting works of art and so general had been the absence of interest in art itself, that Parliament's move, in 1824, to create the National Gallery was hailed by the few art lovers in that body as the inception of a new era in the arts of Britain. One of these expressions of satisfaction was mingled with the hope of corresponding money returns flowing into England. Endorsing the prospect of developing a British school of painting by placing before native students first-rate foreign examples, Agar Ellis interested his fellow members by suggesting a result in addition to the advancement of Britain's art as such. He ingenuously asked: "Might it not be productive of emolument, even in a pecuniary point of view? What was it that attracted so many travelers to

Italy, but the numerous works of genius which were contained in it? And if a similar condition was made in London, was it not likely that a similar cause would produce a similar resort of strangers to it?" [4] The building of the National Gallery, Joseph Hume said, would at last "rescue the country from the disgrace which the want of such an establishment had long entailed upon it." [5] A resolution was adopted to expend £60,000 for the purchase of the Angerstein collection of paintings. The building erected for the National Gallery was, it seems, not relished by artists, who declared it "unworthy of the nation." [6]

Among British officialdom generally and the powerful manufacturing class, as also among large groups influenced by factory interests, the outstanding concern in art matters was dominantly utilitarian. Into Parliament flowed petitions vigorously pleading that the establishment of schools of design would aid manufacturers and—this was a secondary consideration—improve public taste. No time was lost by Parliament in giving favorable response; in 1841 a grant of £10,000 was voted for a School of Design.

Quickly, various cities requested an allotment of funds. The memorial of the municipality of Sheffield read: "The proposed institution would greatly improve the talent and skill of the artisans, and the quality of the staple productions of the town; at the same time it would gratify and elevate the public taste in all branches of the fine arts. There are probably few places in England where manufacturers are so likely to be benefited by such an institution. Large sums are yearly paid to distant artists, many of them foreigners, for models and designs of articles. The great population of Sheffield, 110,000, are all interested in the staple trade of the place. Many branches of trade require a knowledge of the arts. The cultivation of taste has been too long neglected, to the disparagement of the wares in foreign markets. A universal opinion pervades the town that nothing could be of more essential service than the immediate establishment of a School of Design." City officials, manufacturers and clergy of Nottingham made a similar appeal for such a school in that city, "as calculated to be of much use in promoting the development and application of the principles, excellence and taste of patterns produced in the fabrication of lace and hosiery which are the staple trades carried on in this vicinity." Other manufacturing cities submitted like applications. These, as the Council of the School of Design—the body in charge of the disbursement of funds—reported, were the considerations influencing its decisions. . . .[7]

But to return to Mrs. Trollope: Her book, said "The Knickerbocker Magazine," a New York publication, in October, 1833, "has been read, we imagine, by greater numbers of people in the United States than any book of travels upon our country that has been published." By now, it would seem, Americans were addicted to the habit of curiosity as to what foreign critics thought of them.

If some American editors did not see the true nature of this attitude, at least one British traveler grasped it. Most travelers, his article said, observed in Americans a solicitude to hear or read the opinions of strangers on American ways and institutions. Seemingly, this anxiety was induced by a thirst for praise. But in such a display, the writer went on, he could not detect any particular weakness or vanity. "The extraordinary progress —the forest converted in the course of a season into a city—are circumstances calculated to cherish a great notion of national superiority; but the chief cause is the readiness with which the inhabitants adopt new inventions. Thus . . . they conceive their knowledge is proportionately advanced in all things. . . ."[8]

The pettiness of foreign criticism was what exasperated Americans. Of the many tourists writing books on America, at least one recognized this fact. He pointed out the widespread American feeling that British travelers did not give attention to the great achievements and results in America; that they caught up and commented upon trifles. "It is the absence of a spirit of philosophy generally in our writers, and this affectation of prating so like waiting-gentlewomen, that stings Americans."[9] But often American magazine editors isolated themselves from the popular currents. To its regret, "The Knickerbocker Magazine" decided, such caricatures as Mrs. Trollope's "were too much to the public taste." And, instead of exhibiting a wholesome belligerence, striking back hard and exposing conditions in Britain, that magazine meekly accepted Mrs. Trollope's strictures: "Her rebukes have already done visible good. May they still do more."

The indignation of James Fenimore Cooper was kindled by the subservient spirit of a number of American editors. To Cooper the subject had long been a rankling one. Such was the fashion prevalent among American fiction writers of laying scenes and atmosphere in Europe, that in 1821, in "The Preface" to his novel, "The Spy," Cooper felt constrained to elaborate "several reasons why an American, who writes a novel, should choose his own country for the scene of his story." While in Venice, in 1828, Cooper had written a book, "The Bravo," defending America from calumnies. For this he had been violently attacked not only in Britain and France but also by some New York City editors.

In the course of these attacks one French publication—"The Revue Encyclopédique"—assuming the "social grossness" of Americans, asked: "But is it not to the mother country that they owe, in a great measure, this coarseness of manners?" It then summed up the situation, in describing the campaign of critics against America: "All the sins which they can accumulate against that detested word—*Republic*—are lavished without rhyme or reason; and all the vices and defects with which they can reproach her are ascribed, without exception, to the equality which reigns there. . . . This war . . . is carried on not so much by a regular attack on the political institutions of the Republic as by a satire on the manners of the people. . . . It is no longer possible to deny that Americans are well governed. . . ."

Now, addressing Americans, Cooper declared that there was no justification for the custom, peculiar to America, "of quoting the opinions of foreign nations, by way of helping to make up its own estimate of the degree of merit that belongs to its public men." Manliness and independence of thought, he urged, were necessary to render a people great or a nation respectable. The habit of fostering deference to foreign opinion "is dangerous to the very institutions under which we live," for the war now was that of democracy against aristocracy. Crediting with such dangerous facility the audacious charges of Europe's hostile agents led to this: "We appear in the eyes of others like a people who do not more than half believe in the evidence of our own facts, and who are not sincere in our professions. This is one of the reasons that Europe fancies we are living under a violent and rude democracy. . . ." [10]

At about the same time Washington Irving also published a remonstrance. It had, he wrote, been America's peculiar lot to be visited by the worst kind of English travelers. While men of cultivated minds had been sent from England to study the manners and customs of barbarous nations, she depended upon scheming adventurers or shallow, biased individuals as oracles respecting America. Although America, he further wrote, was undertaking one of the greatest political experiments in the history of the world, those purblind visitors were capable of judging only the surface of things. The conveniences and comforts which they missed in America were "all-important in the estimation of narrow minds," whose motives in defaming America were often mercenary. "We attach too much importance to these attacks," he went on. "The tissue of misrepresentations attempted to be woven round us are like cobwebs woven round the limbs of an infant giant. Our country continually outgrows them."

Thus Irving, in "The New York Mirror: Devoted to Literature and to the Fine Arts," January 24, 1833. This periodical also commented editorially on English travelers: Americans "still attach undue importance to their expressed opinions. . . . It is, indeed, a strange thing that no man can come to America to write a book, with a mind large enough to think of something more important than fashions of eating, little peculiarities of speech, unbrushed hats, and the arrangements of the toilette or dinner table." (A century later we find a British critic complaining of the opposite—namely, of the too great comforts provided in America, compared with her native land. See, "The Provincial Lady in America" by E. M. Delafield, novelist, in "Harpers Magazine," May, 1934.)

What the American writers should have done then and later was to express themselves in facts, not in sentiments. For Britain furnished in abundance the facts as to its own materialistic corruption.

The system of bribery in borough elections in Britain was

general and inveterate. "All sense of shame was extinguished by its prevalence; the whole caste of freemen deemed it part of their privilege to be bought and sold . . . sunk in the lowest state of venality and corruption." Customers had intimidated tradesmen; "landlords have driven whole streets of their tenantry to their poll, like droves of cattle to the market"; tenants having the hardihood to refuse to vote as directed were evicted by the landlords.[11]

In the House of Commons, in 1831, the great majority of members were owners of landed estates; of the entire membership four were peers, ninety-eight were sons, and one hundred and fifty-five near relatives of peers; sixty-two members were connected in one way or another with the East India Company; fifty-one were engaged in trade and manufactures; and various other groups of members were bankers, lawyers and military and naval officers. A considerable number of the members held the rewards of subserviency by having some profitable office or emolument or the endowment of a pension.

Agitation for the reform of the electoral system was met by the cry that reform meant revolution and a war against property. The story of the chartist riots leading to Parliament's yielding to the reform demands is well known. But the sequel is barely known. Bribery at elections continued; frequently thereafter the outcry made by public-spirited men caused during the next half-century the introduction and passage of a succession of Corrupt Practices Acts.

In America there was and remained strong prejudice, particularly against Catholics, but so far as law was concerned no barriers existed against persons of any religious creed except that in a few States the governor had to be a Protestant. Variously during and after the American Revolution, laws which hitherto disfranchised and disqualified Catholics, Jews and some other faiths had been repealed.

This extension of religious liberty in America, novel at the time, was in marked contrast to the bigotry in Britain, where old discriminatory laws long encumbered the statute books and were enforced. And it was while they were still being enforced that British critics were railing at America's bigotry. Not until 1829 did Parliament consent to admit a Roman Catholic to its membership, and it was only shortly before that time that Parliament could be persuaded to pass an act prescribing a new oath which a Catholic could take with self-respect. Elected to the House of Commons, the Catholic Earl of Surrey took his seat on May 6, 1829, and a note to the "Debates" recorded: "The circumstance occasioned some sensation, and the noble earl was warmly greeted by his many friends." [12] Full rights of citizenship were only grudgingly granted in Britain to dissenters from the established church, to Unitarians and to Catholics. Frequently, in the House of Commons, advocates of religious liberty pointed to examples of America, France and Holland as establishing the perfect competency of Jews to perform functions of civil and military offices. Obstinately did the majority of Parliament refuse to repeal laws denying full rights to Jews. Finally, in 1850, electors of London's financial quarter resolved to wait no longer. They requested their elected member, Baron Rothschild, to present himself in the House of Commons and offer to take his seat. He did so.

Open ways of corruption in America were more than matched by the insidious methods in Britain. When the London & Birmingham Railway was projected, the owners of estates and canal proprietors made common cause against that enterprise as well as against other railways. In all of the counties through which the London Birmingham Railway would pass, public meetings were incited and the project was denounced as chimerical and as destructive to the estates and to the nobility.

In 1832, a bill for granting to the company a charter and a right of way came before a committee of the House of Lords. The railway's promoters were in consternation at finding avowed opponents of the measure filling the committee. The bill was thrown out. It was re-introduced in the next year in a Parliament supposedly pledged to principles of reform. The perplexing sight was then witnessed of the bill smoothly passing both houses and with such slight opposition that the transaction for a time was inexplicable. The mystery was solved by the company's directors issuing a circular. In this it was stated that negotiations of the directors with the most influential of their opponents had thoroughly conciliated the noble lords and other large landed proprietors. The means found to conciliate them was by trebling the estimate of land acquired by the railway company and paying the owners a munificent £750,000 for land originally appraised at £250,000.[13]

In the "reformed" Parliament of 1833 advocates of popular education met with rebuffs and defeat; as a sop intended to express its contempt for the measure, Parliament voted the ridiculously paltry sum of £20,000 for national education. Six years later, when another move was made in Parliament to raise the bounty to £30,000, Lord Ashley, afterward the Earl of Shaftesbury, denounced in the House of Lords the plan of national education as hostile to the Constitution, to the Church, and to revealed religion itself. Most piously did the Bishop of Exeter proclaim that as a class the poor were assigned by Providence to life's laborious occupations, and that it was not to be expected that they should be able largely to cultivate their intellects. There were similar other fervid protests in the House of Lords which voted overwhelmingly against the motion. During this period England was full of absentee clergymen who, while themselves drawing fat salaries, made the curates do their work, most of the curates receiving a stipend less than that paid to a country carpenter or to a servant.[14]

Contemporaneously with the publication of Mrs. Trollope's book and of other books defaming America, British official and other reports were giving glimpses into social and industrial evils in Britain. English and Scotch factories were crowded with children, some six, many seven and eight, and the greater number nine years of age. Hours of labor were from eleven to thirteen. In the small mills of Scotland children were strapped and beaten. The investigating commission thus reporting described the intense effects of labor fatigue upon children in stunting their growth, causing pains in limbs, and so exhausting them that often they were unable to move or eat. Accidents in factories to children and adults were frequent. In the big factories there was but one privy, it filled the place with stinks, was used indiscriminately by men, women and children, and conduced to immorality.[15] America had its child labor and other factory abominations, but not as bad nor as persistent as those in Britain—a fact to which reference was made in a debate in Parliament in 1847 on a Factories Bill discussion which revolved around the high mortality among women and children in British factories.[16]

Investigations by physicians of the Poor Law Commissioners and by other bodies revealed the slum horrors in English cities. In Liverpool, in 1839, an estimated 35,000 to 40,000 persons—one-fifth of the town's whole population—existed in nearly 8,000 damp and dirty cellars. In Manchester and Salford a considerable portion of the population inhabited cellars; and of 37,000 workers' abodes examined, more than 18,000 were shabbily furnished and more than 10,000 altogether destitute of furniture. In Bury, having a population of 20,000, the dwellings of 3,000 workers' families were visited; in 773 of these places three and four members of the family slept in one bed, and in hundreds of other places the number occupying a bed ranged from four to six. In Leeds there was similar congestion. Lack of sewers and other sanitary arrangements in these towns, and the disgustingly filthy state of the streets, were loathsome features.[17]

Frequent epidemics of disease scourged British factory cities; and it was finally the cholera epidemic of 1831 which upset the complacency of the British upper classes, among whose ranks the outspreading disease took its toll. Long stonily indifferent to the terrible living conditions of the submerged poor, the scared higher classes now came to a realization of their own susceptibility to contagion, and were willing to listen to the expedient need of sanitary reforms. But the execution of these was tardy, and in 1849 there came another visitation of cholera which, sweeping from the filthy alleys and crowded lodging houses, encircled the neighboring mansions.

A Parliamentary Select Committee investigating drunkenness in Britain submitted a long report. As a reaction against immoderate drinking, there was now a movement tending to temperance. The committee pointed out that while in the American navy and army the supplying of liquor had been discontinued, "one-sixth of the effective strength of the British navy and a much greater proportion of the British army was as much destroyed by the effects of intoxication as if destroyed in battle." The committee told how seven hundred vessels in the American merchant marine sailed with no liquor aboard except for medicinal purposes; they thus obtained freights in preference to British vessels. Of the inordinate drinking by English ladies and gentlemen—the ladies upon arising began the day by drinking healths in brandied wines, and both sexes pledged healths in liquor all day long—this fact was brought out: "The secret cause of Americans holding faster to temperance obligations . . . is that they have not the hundredth part of the moral temptations of etiquettes and compliments soliciting them at every corner; in Britain there is an unhappy propensity of ladies and gentlemen to interweave courtesy and strong drink." And further: "The practices of the upper ranks have ever been, and are likely to be, the spring from which the fashions and etiquettes of the lower are originally derived." The sum of £20,000,000 it was estimated, was expended annually for liquor in Britain.[18]

The findings of another Parliamentary committee disclosed some appalling results of the demoralized condition of the working class. This committee was investigating combinations (organizations) of workingmen, but the testimony brought out many associated facts.

Archibald Alison, a magistrate, and his brother, a professor of medicine in the University of Edinburgh, had spent a lifetime studying the conditions of the poor. Dr. Alison considered that poverty and consequent recklessness inevitably induced prostitution among many Scotch girls at the age of puberty. "A large proportion of these females," testified Magistrate Alison of Glasgow factory girls, "I should say three-fourths of them after the age of puberty, I do not say become mothers, for they have too much intercourse with men for that, but they lose their virginity before they are twenty." And he went on: "I have observed in the cases that have come before me, and in the judicial declarations of prisoners, that the intercourse of men and women in the manufacturing ranks in Glasgow is coarse and loose to a degree that is indescribable. I find continual cases of separation between husband and wife in consequence of the avowed and open and undisguised living of the husband with another woman, and of the wife with another man. I find the intercourse of the sexes going on almost in an indiscriminate way in rooms, before a number of witnesses. In short, there is a degree of coarseness subsisting between the sexes which no person without practical acquaintance would believe." [19]

Parliament insisted upon its right to prevent the publication of such evidence in newspapers. Reminding the House of Commons, on April 21, 1837, that in 1832 the publisher of "The Dublin Evening Mail" has been arraigned before the bar of the House of Commons for printing testimony, Lord John Russell notified the House of the culpability now of another newspaper. The Select Committee on the Poor Law Amendment complained that portions of the evidence and parts of the documents produced before that committee had been published in "The True Sun." One House of Commons member—D .W. Harvey—ridiculed the secrecy demanded and the composition of the committee which, he said, represented men of aggregated property leagued against "all that is pitiable and miserable in the land sunken alike by ignorance and extreme poverty." All evidence, Harvey urged, should be published in a cheap form and widely disseminated. Joseph Hume told how he had been a member of the Finance Committee which heard the evidence given by the Duke of Wellington on the military expenses of the colonies. Hume expressed his regret that the evidence had been kept secret; he was sure that had it been published an expenditure of £2,000,000 on the canals in Canada would have been prevented. These protests were disregarded. By an overwhelming vote the House of Commons adopted this resolution:

"That, according to the undoubted privileges of this House, and for the due protection of the public interest the evidence taken by any Select Committee of this House, and the documents presented to such Committee, and which have not been reported to the House, ought not to be published by any Member of such Committee, nor by any other person." [20]

CHAPTER XIII

A CONFLICT OF OPINIONS

POSSESSED of qualifications as a student, lawyer and traveler, Alexis de Tocqueville had been sent by the French Government to America in 1831 to study its penitentiary systems. He did not, however, confine his view to this special field; he also applied himself to a survey of America's social and political institutions. His book, "Democracy In America," was published in France and later translated and brought out in other countries.

Tocqueville clearly saw the life-spirit of the American people whose passion, as a whole, was that of aspiration toward equality. "Nothing struck me more forcibly than the general equality of conditions. I readily discovered the prodigious influence which this primary fact exercises on the whole course of society. . . . The more I advanced in the study of American society, the more I perceived that the equality of conditions is the fundamental fact from which all others seem to be derived, and the central point at which all my observations constantly terminated." Aristocracy had been completely disabled. Laws abolishing entail and primogeniture had dispersed the old great estates. The last traces of hereditary ranks and distinctions had been destroyed. Democracy was all-powerful. America's social state presented a most extraordinary phenomenon. In point of fortune and intellect, men were seen there on a greater equality than in any other country or in any age recorded by history.

Thus Tocqueville went on. He might have added that the plane of women was also higher. The radical Frances Wright, evangelist for women's rights, had noted in her book published in 1821, that in a social sense many of the prejudices against women prevailing in Europe had been abandoned in America. "The youth of both sexes here enjoy a freedom of intercourse unknown in the older and more formal nations of Europe. . . . The women are assuming their place as thinking beings, not

in despite of the men, but chiefly in consequence of their enlarged views and exertions as fathers and legislators. . . . The
liberty here enjoyed by the young women often occasions some
surprise to foreigners." [1]

By equality of conditions, Tocqueville explained, he did not
mean that there was any lack of wealthy individuals in America.
At this point he harped upon the customary strain of critics:
"I know of no country, indeed, where the love of money has
taken a stronger hold on the affections of men and where a pro-
founder contempt is expressed for the theory of the permanent
equality of property. But," he hastened to add, "wealth circu-
lates with inconceivable rapidity, and experience shows that
it is rare to find two succeeding generations in the full enjoy-
ment of it." In aristocratic governments, he pointed out in
another part of his book, the heads of affairs were men already
rich, whereas "in democracies statesmen were poor and had to
make their fortunes." As a matter of fact, very few American
statesmen ever made any fortunes; at death they left relatively
little; thus Alexander Hamilton, who made many rich, himself
died poor. Public officials in America were often bribed, but
it was the capitalists bribing them who acquired the corporation charters and the natural resources and reaped great fortunes.

Seeing evidences of corruption in America, Tocqueville did
not attempt to exonerate his own France. Most of the men who
had administered France's public affairs during the forty preceding years, he wrote, had been accused of corruptly making
their fortunes—an accusation not without substantial foundation. But the bribery of voters, he noted, was almost unknown
in France, while in England it was notorious; in the United
States he had never heard of a man charged with spending his
wealth in corrupting the populace.[2] He might have looked
deeper into this phase. The practice, common among British
manufacturers, of intimidating their employes at elections, had
perhaps no equal in the United States or was not so directly
done. It was nevertheless frequent here, in campaigns in which
the tariff was an issue.

Necessarily, Tocqueville's view was of America's social and
political accomplishments—spectacular innovations, when com-

pared to Old World standards and conditions. He was concerned with what he saw, not in foretelling probabilities. But in seeing the pervasive passion for equality he saw profoundly. American democracy, Tocqueville warned Europe, was rapidly transplanting itself to the Old World and rising into power there. This warning was unnecessary; European upper classes well sensed the danger. And now was seen a scurrying to kill the influence of Tocqueville's book by distorting its meaning and point. Taking that book as a text, publication after publication, writer after writer in Europe, mendaciously used it as proof that the reign of mediocrity and vulgarity was ominously beginning; the leveling of society would abolish great souls; it would supplant the beautiful with the useful; practical economy would be substituted for religion; and a democratic age would crush intellect, which was purely aristocratic.

In these assaults the dominant theme was, as usual, the mercenary character of the American people. Thus a titled German visitor on America: "The moveable moneyed aristocracy of our times I consider the greatest enemy of mankind. . . . It enslaves the people . . . introducing everywhere the most sordid principles of selfishness, to the exclusion of every noble and disinterested sentiment. . . ."[3] Another German, Frederick von Raumer, Professor of History in the University of Berlin, also emitted a book on American vulgarity and on other things detested by him, one of them the lack of any class separation of passengers in American railway cars and stage coaches, as in Europe—an outrage, in his estimation, past condoning.[4]

A leading modern German historian, not unrenowned as a eulogist of his own country, has given an account of the state of Prussia at this time. A bureaucracy ruled supreme, says Treitschke. The masses "blindly did what the authorities ordered." Dominant philosophical writers did their utmost, "by the use of an incomprehensible argot," to make themselves appear surpassing prodigies of thought, and "the Berliners were fond of boasting of their town's intellectual brilliancy." The position of men of intellect "was not high in this land of courtly and bureaucratic divisions of caste." Germans with political ideals had to go to America to realize them.[5] Then came the 1848 uprising—called revolution—which, another German historian tells, saw the mob do as it liked, because the people were accustomed to taking orders—and for a time no official dared to command or forbid! [6]

Not long after von Raumer and his compeer had published their attacks on America's sordidness, a great, self-sprung money mania swept Germany. Capitalist development of that country had begun in earnest and in force. After many years of succumbing to the crushing competition of British industrialism which flooded it with goods, Germany now set out to organize its own industries on a large stock-issuing basis. There was seething speculation in shares of cotton mills, sugar refineries, banks, railways and many other enterprises. Such were the attractions of profit from investment or speculation that, between 1853 and 1857, the issue of shares in new banks alone amounted to 200,000,000 thalers; new railway shares reached 140,000,000 thalers; in shares of other concerns there was a similar increase. In the twenty years after 1851 more than two hundred companies, with a total capital of 2,404,000,000 marks, were organized in Germany.[7]

On through the 1830's and '40's the inundation of books on America was such that it would be supererogatory to mention more than a few. Harriet Martineau's "Society in America" was a favorable account, perhaps somewhat too colored by her enthusiasm. But if one is interested in the proportions a writing fashion can assume, it is only necessary to unearth the many examples, long since forgotten and buried, of productions purporting to inform Europeans on America. Some of these books, however, offered a new point or two. To differentiate his book from the common run, and to give it distinctive weight, one British author took pains to assure the public that *he* was no tourist but a person who had actually lived in America for years. American business men, he wrote, sought big stakes in transactions; but, he asked, did this prove them more grasping than the French, who excelled in the minutiæ of frugality and who, of a little money, always managed to hold on to some? [8]

On the other hand, Michael Chevalier saw American trading propensities as an enlargement of the English. Sent to America in 1834 by Thiers, French Minister of the Interior, to inspect public works, Chevalier did not allow himself to miss the oppor-

tunity of writing a book on America. At the outset, to prove
his own impartial judgment, he pronounced almost all English
travelers in America afflicted with obliquity; "they have seen a
great deal that was bad and scarcely anything good; the por-
trait they have drawn of America and the Americans is a carica-
ture, which, like all good caricatures, has some resemblance to
the original." He then relieved himself of this generalization,
by no means unsupported by circumstance: "All English travelers in America have belonged to the aristocracy by their connections or their opinions, or were aspiring to it, or aped its
habits and judgments that they might seem to belong to it." [9]

Chevalier was much impressed by the absence in America
of women laboring in the field. Thus, said he, they escaped "that
hideous ugliness and repulsive coarseness of complexion which
toil and privation everywhere else brings upon them." He
viewed American democracy as imperious and overbearing
toward other nations, its foreign policy as egoistic, and its
aggrandizing pretensions as unbounded. He pronounced Americans absorbed in material pursuits. "It is certain that the
Americans are an exaggeration of the English, whom Napoleon
used to call a nation of shopkeepers. The American is always
bargaining; he always has one bargain afoot, another just
finished and several more in meditation. . . . At the bottom,
then, of all that an American does, is money, beneath every
word money." Chevalier, however, conceded American munifi-
cence.[10]

It was droll that another visitor also, British and a most
severe critic of America, professed to see in American activity
a distinct English trait. Whatever was notable in America was
of English derivation, according to Frederick Marryatt. A captain in the British Navy, Marryatt had left the service in 1830
to devote himself to novel writing. While he was touring
America, the bustle he witnessed everywhere admitted of no
dismissal or denial. In his book he thus treated it: "Now all
this activity is of English origin; and were England expanded
into America, the same results would then be produced. To a
certain degree the English were in former times what the Americans are now; and this is what has raised our country so high
in the scale of nations." [11]

In a slightly different form, Marryatt's characterizations of Americans were the same as those of the prior line of British critics. We hear the old strain of the demoralizing effects of a democratic form of government. And so, too, the parrot-like repetition of the ubiquitous worship of money. Impervious to the plain fact that in Britain many successful business men bought peerages and other honors, Marryatt pictured Americans in this wise: "Honors of every description, which stir up the soul of men to noble deeds—worthy incitements—they have none. The only compensation they can offer for services is money; and the only distinction—the only means of raising himself above his fellows left to the American—is wealth; consequently the acquisition of wealth has become the great spring of action. But it is not sought after with the avarice to hoard, but with the ostentation to spend. . . . The only great avenue open to all . . . is that which leads to the door of Mammon. . . . Having no aristocracy, no honors, no distinctions to look forward to, wealth has become the substitute, and with few exceptions, every man is great in proportion to his riches."

Other condemnations, made trite by many a previous book and article, were repeated by Marryatt and given the color of fresh observations. American educational methods, he declared, caused insubordination and bred national conceit; "monarchy is derided, the equal rights of men declared; all is invective, uncharitableness and falsehood." Frequently, to heighten his accusation of American money lust and the scoundrelly composition of America's foremost financial and commercial city, he took up an old device made popular by refugee loyalists from America in books written during and after the American Revolution. One after another, those refugees had pleased the British and consoled themselves by representing Americans as the scum of the earth.[12] And now, forgetting for the moment the boast of his country's Government that its people were the most law-abiding and its administration of justice was the strictest and most effective to be found anywhere in the world, Marryatt presented this picture: "Every scoundrel who has swindled, forged, or robbed in England, or elsewhere, makes his escape to New York. Every pickpocket who is too well known to the English police, takes refuge here. In this city they all concentrate . . . the criminal inpouring of the Continental dregs . . . outcasts from the society of the Old World." [13]

If many criminals succeeded in fleeing from Britain, the police records there did not show it. In England and Wales alone, in each of the years from 1834 to 1838 inclusive, there was an average of 21,000 commitments for crime. Not until 1832 had capital punishment been abolished in Britain for cattle and sheep stealing, petty larceny in a house, coining and forgery. Until 1833 British law ordered death for housebreaking; until 1835 for sacrilege and letter stealing by post office employes. In 1837 capital punishment was effaced for all offences except murder, burglary with violence, rape, unnatural offences, riot, embezzlement by Bank of England employes, piracy and high treason. After the change in 1837 death sentences were ten times less than in previous times. In 1841 Britain eradicated capital punishment for rape and rioting. Captain Marryatt was not even slightly acquainted with the criminal statistics of his own country. A large number of offenders there were not in any sense intelligent or quick-witted; more than a third sentenced from 1836 to 1838 were unable to read and write.[14]

After Marryatt there came to America a more distinguished visitor—one whose celebrity has lasted. This was the novelist Charles Dickens.

Dickens assailed America's press as lacking respectability and as licentious. Accustomed to the timidity and constraint of English newspapers and to their deference to titles, office and wealth, he was repelled by the unrestrained spirit of criticism in American newspapers. In partisan matters this criticism, it was true, often descended to blackguardly extremes. Nevertheless, in its whole social effect, it was of a probing, beneficial order unknown in Europe: no man's position or riches gave him immunity. But, according to Dickens, this free and full criticism in America incited jealousy and distrust of public men, caused worthy men to shrink from entering legislative life, and produced a disgraceful class of candidates. It resulted

in popular fickleness; American "inconstancy has passed into
a proverb." The charge of volatility, applied by British writers
to the French, now was extended to Americans.

As a former reporter, Dickens had good reason to know the
disdain with which the British Parliament treated representatives of the press. Certainly, the attitude of British newspapers
toward politicians did not win for them any regard. The only
accommodation allowed by Parliament to reporters, when for
one reason or another they had to withdraw from the galleries,
was a tiny apartment, not much larger than a closet, which, by
a Parliamentary fiction, was called a "drawing room." When
the nineteenth century was verging toward midway, every
London morning newspaper employed a staff of short-hand
reporters. Only a few years after Dickens wrote his "Notes"
on American legislators, a newly-established London magazine,
of popular sympathies, related that London newspaper men
reporting Parliament's proceedings were all educated men;
some were lawyers, others authors, and still others of various
professions. "Many of them are vastly superior in every intellectual attainment to the great mob of members whose prosy
speeches they yawn over as they report." [15]

The American Congress was largely composed of lawyers
and farmers, with a sprinkling of tradesmen, manufacturers and
nondescripts. On the whole they were men of ability; or if
some did not have that quality, they had a fair share of common
sense. That spread-eagle speeches were common in Congress;
that, indeed, speeches were printed which were never delivered;
that members took the greatest liberties in punctuating their
published speeches with generous "applause" which nobody
had ever heard—all of this and more did not vitiate the fact
that in caliber and virility Congress compared more than well
with European legislative bodies. If in Congress members were
actuated by partisan policies, Parliamentary members were
not less so, following the motions of leaders like flocks of sheep.

In France hereditary legislative rights had been abolished
in 1831, when, to secure the passage of a bill in the House of
Peers, the Government created thirty-six new peers, thus giving
a sufficient majority for extinguishing purposes. And what was
the state of the British House of Lords in Dickens' time? The

London magazine previously cited told of the difference in atmosphere between the noisy Commons and the somnolent House of Lords, carpeted, cushioned and wax-lighted. "Upon the woolsack, just in front of the throne, sits the Lord Chancellor, seemingly half asleep; at the table, the Earl of Shaftesbury, the chairman of the committees, and general factotum of the House. Half a dozen noble lords, who appeared to be overcome by the influence of the 'land of dropsy-head,' make up the whole audience. . . . There is no excitement at all about it; noble lords address each other across the table as quietly as in a private conversation." "The Duke of Wellington is there in his blue frock, white waistcoat and dandified pantaloons. 'Torpid' is scarcely the word; he seems to be in a deep slumber, his chin resting upon his breast, his arms crossed and his legs crooked together. . . ." Nevertheless he hears everything but when he chooses to reply "cannot speak two sentences without a painfully long pause between them." Of the life and earnestness marking the House of Commons, the description went on, there was none visible in the House of Lords. "What have the peers, in fact, to be earnest about? They have nothing to fight for—nothing to gain—they are generally old men, many of them 'used up.' " [16]

The old refrain of American Mammon-worship was taken up by Dickens. He omitted any acknowledgment to the train of predecessors who, for nearly half a century, had made the same accusation. A prominent American feature, Dickens chimed in, was the love of "smart dealing," which veneered many a swindle and gross breach of trust. In like manner, he went on, all kinds of deficient and impolitic American usages were referred to the national love of trade. In the most incidental way he added: "Though oddly enough it would be a weighty charge against a foreigner that he regarded the Americans as a trading people." With this slight, casual admission he resumed his attack. "The love of trade is the reason why the literature of America is to remain forever unprotected." Then making use of a literary device, he purported to quote the consensus of what Americans said of themselves: " 'For we are a trading people and don't care for poetry, though we do, by the way, profess to be very proud of our poets; while healthful amusements, cheer-

ful means of recreation, and wholesome fancies must fade
before the stern utilitarian joys.' " [17]

The attempt to fathom motives—to go behind the returns—
is a pursuit as deceptive as it is profitless. For the change of
view which Dickens in later years expressed toward America,
various explanations have been made. He was chastened in
spirit, he was better informed, and so on. Passing over these
ascriptions we anchor upon one solid fact: in England itself
his "American Notes" was subjected to criticism. But this did
not come until after an American woman, compelled to remain in London by the delays of a lawsuit she was pressing,
had retaliated to Dickens' criticisms by writing a book—
"Change for the American Notes." [18] This offered some improvement over the usual inadequate tenor of American replies to British critics.

Those replies, whether to Dickens or Marryatt or other
critics, were couched in the form of a general denial. "John
Bull is led to believe that every American eats his dinner in
five minutes; that the good citizens of New York walk about
with bowie knives; that every American is an unregenerate
spitter, and otherwise irretrievably vulgar, presumptuous and
overbearing. Looking at the surface of our society, these English critics conclude that the ways and institutions of their
country are infinitely better. After all, let English authors think
and write what they will about us; we can survive slander and
go on our way as an independent nation." This composite
epitome suffices to give a faithful idea of the replies in American publications.

In London, however, "An American Lady" went a step further. If, was the gist of her book, Mammon was the god of
American worship, pounds sterling were the idol of the English
people. She could claim, and not unjustly, that she was in a
city where the rustle of pound notes was conspicuously audible.
Her accusation had its effect upon one London publication; the
editors of "The Economist" were too well informed on financial
affairs to dismiss it as a vagary. "Nor do we think," said a
comment in that publication on her charge, "that this is simply
a 'You, too.' The reverence paid to wealth in this country is
undoubtedly great but [this saving qualification had to be

slipped in] it is not as great as in the United States. In that country, money is almost the only source of distinction, and therefore is more sought after than here, where it is not the only one. . . . But we are not prepared to assert that this eager desire for wealth is peculiar either to England, or to her American children or to both of them together." [19] An unavoidable admission, this last named, seeing that all along in the columns of the same periodical was regular correspondence from various European capitals showing clearly enough the zealous struggle for wealth there. The periodical agreed with "An American Lady's" opinion of English travelers in America. "Many," it said, "who pretend to give a fair and true picture of men and manners in America do, in fact, produce caricatures of the coarsest kind." But it criticized her for following the same course in England in drawing erroneous conclusions from insufficient data. Her charges of British love of money, boasting, unfeelingness and cruelty, were not, it further said, sustained by specific proof.

This was a valid objection, and gave a most useful hint of a line to be followed in such later American replies as were made to European criticism. Generalizations did not answer the purpose, and were all the more without reason considering that an examination of current British records would have brought out the fullest amount of incriminating data.

Maryatt's book had hardly been published and Dickens' not yet issued when, at the behest and for the benefit of the East India Company the British Government warred with China. Despite the Chinese Government's interdictory decrees, great quantities of opium were surreptitiously poured into China; in 1836 alone more than 27,000 chests of opium had entered the one port of Canton. In and out of the British Parliament the ghastly effects of the opium habit were recognized. But trade was trade, and India was then, all in all, yielding an estimated £6,000,000 a year to Britain.

A heated debate ensued in the House of Commons, in 1840, over the question of the propriety of war. Leading the opposition forces, Gladstone declared war needless. The British Government, he stated, had the fullest power, if it cared to exercise it, to suppress the opium trade. It could, he indicated, stop vessels laden with opium, break up the opium depots in India, check the cultivation of opium there, and put a stigma upon the traffic. None of these simple and effective measures had been taken. Another member—Sidney Herbert—allowed his indignation to transcend the customary bounds of discreet Parliamentary language. He denounced the war with China as a war without just cause; "we are," he set forth, "endeavoring to maintain a trade resting upon unsound principles to justify proceedings which are a disgrace to the British flag." [20]

It was during the course of this war that Lord Palmerston, a member of the Cabinet, took occasion to tell Parliament of the Government's pre-eminent service in advancing British trade interests. With a politic disclaimer that he intended to boast, Palmerston then delivered this encomium upon the Government represented by himself: "I assert it as my opinion that no former Government ever attempted so much to improve the commerce of the country, or ever attempted it with so much success." Sums then rolled from his lordly lips; from 1830 to 1839 British exports had risen from £38,000,000 to £53,000,000, and in the same period imports from £46,000,000 to £62,000,000. To his audience these figures spoke with ingratiating eloquence.

By the war against China the East India Company profited well. The British Government had arranged to recoup the company for its expenses in preparing armament in India for use in the war. The company's bill was £573,442. Under the terms of the peace treaty with China the owners of opium which was confiscated or surrendered in China were, it seems, recognized claimants for compensation amounting to more than £1,281,000. [21]

A banquet was given, on December 20, 1844, by the municipality of Manchester and its merchants and manufacturers, to Sir Henry Pottinger upon his return from treaty negotiation with China. In proposing the toast, Mayor Alexander Kay of Manchester glowingly said:

"I may remind you, gentlemen, that the Empire of China, which has been extensively opened to you by the successful negotiations of Sir Henry Pottinger . . . comprises a population which is now computed to amount to upwards of three hundred and forty millions of souls; and it will be easy for you, gentlemen, all of whom are accustomed to minute calculations, at once to determine what the degree of advantage will be to this manufacturing city by having a market of this extraordinary extent opened out to us. (Loud cheers.) You will recollect, gentlemen, that the population of Great Britain amounts to twenty-seven million of people; and if we consider for a moment that twenty-seven million of people now have the opportunity of free and equal trade with a population exceeding three hundred and fifty million of people, the advantages must be wholly on our side. (Loud cheers.) I heard an exclamation which proceeded from one of our country manufacturers on the subject, which I daresay will convey some idea to the minds of the gentlemen present of the advantages which we are likely to derive from the extension of our intercourse with China: 'Why,' said the worthy manufacturer, 'all the mills we have now will hardly make enough yarn to find them with night caps and socks.' (Laughter.)" [22]

A different note came a little later from "The People's Journal," of London, in February, 1847. Was not the populace told, it growled, that British wars in China and India were righteous and defensive? "But as in the present wars with the Kaffirs, for what has this system of war been so far perpetuated and encouraged? Simply for the aggrandizement of the aristocracy and the capitalists connected with the East India Company."

An estimate authoritatively made at this time computed Britain's average annual accumulation of capital at £60,000,-000, possibly £70,000,000. The greatest share came from the manufacturing, mercantile and trading elements. In less than a quarter of a century Britain's shipping had increased, despite ships worn out or lost at sea, from 2,648,000 to 3,588,000 tons. Since 1820 British cotton factories had so expanded that from 150,000,000 pounds of cotton, they now used more than 700,-000,000 pounds. Where British woolen factories had used 7,691,000 pounds of foreign sheep's wool in 1820, they now consumed 69,493,000 pounds of imported wool, independent of the increase meanwhile in the home growth. In a similar way, silk, linen and other industries had all extended their operations.[23] Britain's yearly exports exceeded America's by more than $100,000,000.

So opulent were the British industrial and commercial classes that, joined by the men of landed estates, they were able to invest enormous sums in railways in Great Britain and in America, Canada and other countries. Up to 1845 Parliament passed four hundred and twelve acts for two hundred and seventy-eight railways, including extensions, in Britain. These acts empowered the raising of a total of more than £154,000,-000 as either capital or loans.[24]

In America railway promoters frequently had to resort to bribery for the passage of acts giving subsidies in grants of public lands or money. The procedure in Britain's Parliament was different. No money corruption was there evident; members of both houses of that body themselves composed many of the leading railway promoters, each group, in reciprocal support for its measures, voting for acts benefiting other groups. In fact, in the advertisements of railway prospectuses, the names of members of Parliament were prominently featured as an inducement for public investing in the stock, and as a guarantee that the railway interests were well conserved in Parliament.

Thus, to take the single year of 1845, we find John Benbow, M.P., chairman of one railway company, and other members of Parliament, together with Lord Forrester, Viscount Duncannon and Lord Alfred Paget on its managing committee. On the committee of a second railway company were Lord Francis Egerton, M.P., other members of Parliament, and the Earl of Sefton, and Lord Lilford. The provisional directing committee of a third projected railway embraced four members of the House of Commons, and the Earl of Denbeigh and Desmond and Lord Leigh. Of a fourth railway company the chairman was John Lewis Ricardo, M.P., and on its board were Viscount Leveson, M.P., the Earl of Macclesfield, the Earl of Shrewsbury and the Earl of Wilton. On the managing committee of a fifth railway company were Lord Sussex Lenox, Viscount Curzon, Lord Dunboyne, Lord Edward Chichester, and two members of the House of Commons. Such examples could be multiplied; the list of promoters of British railways read like a roll-call of Parliament itself.[25] Justifying its action by the plea that the certainty of high profits was necessary to stimulate railway construction, Parliament sanctioned the charging of rates guaranteeing the high returns of ten per cent dividends. But, as the sequel showed, the average dividend on common stock was, for many years, less than three per cent. Vast sums went into the pockets of landowners in the buying of land, into the hands of lawyers in legal arrangements, and into the coffers of contractors. Up to the end of 1850 the construction of British railroads—often "scamped" work, as we shall see,—cost £34,-243 a mile, a clear waste of £24,000 on every mile the construction of which later was done for £10,000.

The great sums put into railway projects came largely from manufacturers and traders all saturated with profits, and from estate owners. From real estate in England the annual income had expanded from more than £49,000,000 in 1815 to more than £80,000,000 in 1843, a sixty-two per cent increase.[26] In praising British capacity to pour funds into railways, without causing a dearth of money in other quarters, a noted British economist reckoned that between 1846 and 1850, the sum of £150,000,000 was invested in railways in Britain. This amount, he specified, came from the middle (capitalist) classes, and so glutted were they with money that this large investment was made "without disorganizing the trade of the country, or hindering our progress in other directions." [27] He, however, gave the figures for only five years; the total amount of money raised in Britain for railroad construction from the inception of railways to the end of 1858 seems to have been more than £325,-000,000. And before 1854 Britain invested £550,000,000 in other countries, its foreign investments thereafter increasing at the rate of £30,000,000 annually.[28]

The London authority on financial and industrial interests gloated over the rapid building of railways, and visioned in this and other mechanical innovations the regeneration of mankind. "It must, we think," declared "The Economist" for August 23, 1851, "be perfectly clear to every man that the growth of an opulent middle class lies at the bottom of all modern improvement in politics."

While one class was reveling in opulency and vaunting itself as the source of all progress, what was the state of the working population? Three-fourths of this in London lived and slept in one room; in nine deaths out of ten among the poor, the body remained in that single room for five or six days. The Parliamentary report relating the prevalence of such conditions made a comparison with some American States with their strict sanitary laws.[29]

Partly because of humanitarian urgings, and in part because the higher classes were badly scared by recurrent epidemics, a movement for public baths and washhouses was begun, in 1844, in many English cities. A memorial of the Governor of the Bank of England and others lamented the high mortality among all classes. Of London's vast population, a large proportion, the memorial set forth, could only on rare occasions find the time to go the necessary distance to obtain a bath. When they tried to get one they were confronted with impediments. Penalties prohibited bathing in the Thames. Only at particular seasons and at certain hours were the Lee and Serpentine rivers open to them. By its costliness the comfort of a warm bath was out of their reach. "In the one close room in which the family is frequently forced to live, even if the wife is lying in, or there are sick and dying persons in it, the whole of its washing must be done. There the fire must be made, the water boiled, and the clothes washed, dried and ironed. Disease is constantly aggravated to a fearful extent, and death itself frequently occasioned." The report went on to say that the poor could not afford to buy soap, and that the dirty condition in which they existed was demoralizing.

At a public meeting in London for the formation of an association to supply the working class with public bathing and washing accommodations, the Bishop of London spoke: ". . . The crowds who line the streets of this great metropolis, and who are surrounded on all sides by the evidence of its wealth and grandeur, are little aware of the fearful masses of human misery and wretchedness masked by the splendor of those streets. They are little aware that perhaps within a few yards of the shops filled with the richest productions of the world, and of those counting houses belonging to men whose fortunes are to be reckoned by millions—that in this very 'city where merchants are princes'—there is a vast amount of human misery masked by the splendid front presented by her great streets." The Bishop went on to tell how only medical men and visiting clergy came in contact with such conditions. The poor "lived in a compulsory state of filthiness"; such were the expense and trouble of going out to fetch water that dirty water was retained in rooms. Another speaker told of one London parish having a population of 50,000 "many of whom are living in hovels not fit for the lower animals," while in another parish of 112,000 population fully 92,000 were destitute; "many of them do not take off their clothes from week to week." [30]

Criticism aroused in continental European countries, over disclosures showing English contrasts of wealth and misery, led to a British reply instancing the same in France. In that country, it was conjecturally and roughly estimated, there were (in terms of francs), 50,000 millionaires; 200,000 rich men; 550,000 in easy circumstances; 4,200,000 in moderate circumstances; and 6,000,000 who earned a decent but uncertain existence. Of the remainder of France's 36,000,000 population, 16,000,000 were subject to the most scanty and uncertain existence; 5,000,000 were in extreme poverty; and 4,000,000 were paupers, thieves and prostitutes.[31] Further to heighten Britain's superior position, the plight of a great number of France's small farm proprietors was brought out. Mortgages in France amounted to more than £300,000,000, and called for an average payment of eight per cent. This exacted a yearly sum of about £25,000,000 in interest; "nearly," commented "the Economist," of London, "the same as the whole interest of our national debt." Much of France's pauperism was attributed to the combined operation of heavy taxes and interest. Official French reporters were cited as showing that of 3,494,666 dwellings, 348,401 did not have a window; 1,817,328 only one window; and 1,328,937 only two windows. "In these huts," the British editor summarized, "live 16,000,000 of the population, or nearly one-half the whole." [32]

The British farmer, however, was loaded with his own troubles, financial and otherwise. He too was weighted with heavy taxes and interest charges. Antiquated game laws, such as the Revolution had abolished in France, still were in force in Britain. Crops there were often destroyed by rabbits and other animals, but the farmer had no remedy. All farm leases or rental terms contained clauses for the preservation of game; in the case of tithes, game was a portion of the produce reserved to the church, and where an individual landlord was the owner, game was reserved for his pleasure. Moreover, anyone without a license who killed game was subject to heavy fine and imprisonment.[33] The British farmer looked upon the poacher as a godsend.

Midway through the nineteenth century, however, assaults upon America were frequent in British publications. "The Edinburgh Review" was still spouting calumny. In its number for January, 1845, it described the Presidents of the United States as demagogues by nature and profession; men who "adopt the language, stiffen the prejudices, inflame the passions, and obey the orders of the people." The article went on: "To the influences which thus corrupt and degrade the person who is both her chief magistrate and her prime minister, we attribute much of the deterioration of the public, and, we fear we must add, the private character of America—the bluster, the vanity, the rapacity, the violence and the fraud which render her a disgrace to democratic institutions, and a disgrace to the Anglo-Saxon race."

CHAPTER XIV

POUNDS STERLING TRIUMPHANT

IT was a British scientist who provided Americans with an effective reply to the scoffs of his own countrymen. Sir Charles Lyell, renowned geologist, visited America for no other purpose than to study its geological formations. Free from any ulterior motive to deride America's people, he was able to see conditions impartially. One thing that greatly impressed him was the American standard of using wealth. In America, he wrote, there was no compulsory law as in France for the equal partition of property among children, nor any law of entail and primogeniture as in Britain. "Not only is it common for rich capitalists," he noted of America, "to leave by will a portion of their fortune towards the endowment of national institutions, but individuals during their lifetime make magnificent grants of money for the same objects."

Lyell was astonished at the large sale of literary works in America, and at the prevalence of popular libraries, especially in Massachusetts. Dealing with America at large he expressed this opinion: "In no subject do the Americans display more earnestness than in their desire to improve their system of education, both elementary and academical." Another American trait that caused him to comment was: "One of the first peculiarities that must strike a foreigner in the United States is the deference paid universally to the sex, without regard to station. Women may travel alone here in stage-coaches, steamboats, railways, with less risk of encountering disagreeable behavior, and of hearing coarse and unpleasant conversation, than in any country I have ever visited. The contrast in this respect between the Americans and the French is quite remarkable. . . ." [1]

Following Lyell's lead, "The North American Review," in October, 1848, made a cutting reply to John Stuart Mill's

170

jibe at America as a land where "the life of one sex is devoted to dollar hunting, and of the other to the breeding of dollar hunters." So well established in America was the custom of liberality, declared that magazine, "that very wealthy people are in a manner constrained to make large bequests for public objects in their wills; and if one occasionally fails to comply with the general expectation in this respect, his memory incurs such obloquy that sometimes his heirs have been shamed into an attempt to atone for his neglect." In England, "The North American Review" further pointed out, the founder of a fortune wished to entail it to his family, to be held inalienably. "But an American is much more likely to covet immediate applause and the transmission of his name with honor to posterity through the endowment of a public institution or the furtherance of some scheme of public utility. . . . We do not tolerate gold lace, nor cocked hats, nor footmen with powdered heads and gold-headed canes. . . . The most natural and sensible way of deriving personal gratification from newly-acquired wealth and by making a show of it in the eyes of the world is to give largely to public charities. The sums which are contributed here by individuals for the support of schools, colleges, churches, missions, hospitals and institutions of science and beneficence, put to shame the official liberality of the oldest and wealthiest governments in Europe."

Philanthropy by rich Americans was, in fact, established by a long line of donors. Stephen Girard was one of the more conspicuous examples. When this Philadelphia money-getter died, in 1831, his fortune of $7,500,000 was the greatest in America at that time. To relatives he left but $140,000, and to friends and former employes $65,000. The remainder was bequeathed to public benefactions, including a college for the education of white orphans.

Among other millionaires who were then giving legacies for public benefit was John McDonough. Originally from Baltimore, he had acquired his fortune from real estate in New Orleans and vicinity. This peculiar personage was supposed to be engrossed in selfishness. To the end of his life he clung to obsolete fashions. His tall figure was clad in an old blue coat with high collar, a white vest, ruffled shirt and voluminous white cravat; his hair was combed back and gathered in a queue; his feet were encased in antiquated round-toed shoes. How would the aged eccentric dispose of his property? Public curiosity was intense.

His will, it developed, had been drawn in 1838, and was unchanged when he died in 1850. It began with this statement: "And for the general diffusing of knowledge and consequent well-being of mankind, convinced as I am that I can make no disposition of those worldly goods which the Most High has been pleased to place under my stewardship that will be so pleasing to Him as that by means of which the poor will be instructed in wisdom and led into the path of virtue and holiness." And of this "general diffusing of knowledge" his will declared: "One thing is certain, it will not take wings and fly away as silver and gold, government and banknotes often do. It is the only thing in this world of ours which approaches to anything like permanency; or in which at least there is less mutation than in things of man's invention. The little riches of this world, therefore, which the Most High has placed in my hands, and over which he has been pleased to place and make me his steward, I have invested therein that it may yield an annual revenue to the purpose I have destined it forever." He bequeathed a slight sum to Baltimore relatives; his millions were given for the establishment of an asylum for poor children, an orphan asylum, and a school farm for destitute children. He further explained in his will that had he children, "I would bequeath, after a virtuous education (to effect which nothing would be spared), a very small amount to each, merely sufficient to excite them to habits of industry and frugality." [2]

Even John Jacob Astor, who combined the extremes of avariciousness with notorious parsimony, felt obliged to leave at least $400,000 of his $20,000,000 fortune for the establishment of the public library in New York City.

Ineffectual attempts again were made in Britain, in 1843 and in 1847, to have Parliament pass acts for general education. The House of Lords could not on these occasions be charged with sole responsibility for opposition. It was in 1847 that Macaulay, in the House of Commons, delivered a long speech exposing the widespread illiteracy in Britain. Apart from other facts that he gave, he cited the reports of inspectors of marriages. Of nearly 130,000 couples wedded in the year 1844, more than 40,000 of the bridegrooms, and more than 60,000 of the brides, could not sign their names but made their marks. Macaulay then directed attention to acts of the Massachusetts settlers "illustrious forever in history," in establishing popular education, and to William Penn's advocacy of such education as a policy. Macaulay referred to Washington's last legacy to the American Republic, "Educate the people," and to the same unceasing exhortation from Jefferson. Taking up the antagonism in Britain to popular education, Macaulay concluded: "A future age will look back with astonishment to the opposition which the introduction of that system encountered, and will be still more astonished that such resistance was offered in the name of civil and religious freedom." [3]

A factor that now intensified feeling against America among important classes in Britain was American mercantile competition. Largely as a means of warding off the incoming steamship competition, the clipper was created; and American shipyards excelled in the building of this type of ship. The prime quality of the clipper was speed; in cargo carrying she was not as fully serviceable as other classes of ships. The progenitor of the clipper was built at Baltimore in 1832. The first real clipper —"The Rainbow"—was designed in 1843 at New York City. "The Dreadnought," otherwise called "The Flying Dutchman," built at Newburyport, Massachusetts, was one of the largest and fleetest clippers; and on one occasion, it was reported, she made the run from Sandy Hook to Queenstown in thirteen days, nine hours. The charge for cargoes to distant ports was then in a measure determined by the speed with which cargoes were delivered. The earnings of a single voyage would often amount to more than the original cost of the clipper ship.

With the repeal of British navigation laws, British merchants began to buy or charter speedy American clippers each of which could make five voyages while a British ship made four of equal distances. American ship tonnage did not exceed British. And Britain had built many iron ships, selling some to France which had built none. Yet in Britain America's merchant marine was looked upon as a perilously close rival. In 1850 America's total merchant marine, including steam vessels, was 3,535,454 tons, and American ships carried nearly three-fourths of America's imports and exports. In the same year Britain had a merchant marine totaling, in the home and foreign trade, 3,565,133 net tons, of which 168,474 net tons were steam vessels. The shipping of the entire British Empire totalled 4,232,-692 tons.

Referring to the rapid progress of America's merchant marine, "The Economist," of London, on June 21, 1851, took occasion to point to Britain's superior trade as proof of "how ill-founded are those unworthy jealousies and apprehensions which are so often expressed in relation to United States rivalry with this country." American government returns showed, "The Economist" stated, exports in 1850 of $136,946,912, or about £27,000,000, while in the same year exports of British produce and manufacturers from Britain amounted to £70,000,000.[4] Computing the value of British imports against that of exports, there was an apparent balance against Britain of perhaps £22,-000,000. But this, "The Economist" stated, was overcome or nearly so by the more than £10,000,000 of exports of foreign and colonial produce not included in the official figures, by the profits on all exported goods, by profits from ship freights, and by returns from enormous investments abroad. With Britain in so flourishing a condition, "The Economist" advised, symptoms of increasing prosperity in the United States "should not be viewed with that narrow jealousy which we regret to observe has become too much the fashion among a class of antiquated, but not altogether uninfluential politicians of the day."

Some accurate idea of the huge amount of British capital employed in various parts of the world had been given by "The Economist" in a previous issue (January 11, 1851). It stated that British India annually yielded nearly £4,000,000 in dividend payments. In addition, India yearly remitted a further large sum, estimated at about £5,000,000, for interest on British capital used in banking establishments, sugar and indigo cultivation, and in internal commerce in India. Furthermore, there were constant remittances of money to Britain from British officials in India, and profits which British merchants in India sent home for investment.

From every British colony revenues from investment flowed into Britain. Most of the banks in Australia, Canada and the West Indies, "The Economist" enumerated, were conducted with British capital, the dividends from which were sent to Britain. To the same point were sent the profits from British colonial land-cultivation enterprises, a considerable part of which were operated on British capital. Still further, "The Economist" went on, British investors had a large investment in foreign railways and canals, and owned great blocks of American, French, Dutch, Russian, Spanish, Mexican, South American and other foreign bonds, payments upon which likewise streamed into Britain.

In selecting a British company as an example of the dimensions of profits reaped, we need only turn to the testimony regarding the Hudson Bay Company. Its general profits at this period averaged 12 per cent upon its capital; the total profits acquired during its existence from the fur trade alone were estimated at £20,000,000. Supplementing this amount were great profits from its vast land holdings, parts of which it kept selling to settlers at high prices. Also, it drew continuous profits from other lines of business. On the list of Hudson Bay Company stockholders, in or about 1856, were the Earl of Selkirk, Countess Lydia Cavan, Baron Wynford, Viscount Folkestone, Sir George Sinclair, Sir Edmund Antrobus, Bishop John Banks Jenkinson, the Rev. Oswald Littleton, and scores of other notables in the aristocracy and the church, in politics and business.[5]

This, in America, was a period in which bribing was lavishly done by railway promoters to obtain from Congress or some legislatures great areas of public domain—and frequently Government, State or municipal financial aid as well.[6] The process of corruption was different and highly surreptitious in France and Britain. In France railway promoters, by methods of which there is no formal record, were able to requisition the Government itself into acting as agent for extracting from the public and collecting much of the capital needed. Until this arrangement was made, French financiers declined to advance any capital for railway construction. Only after securing extraordinary privileges did French railway promoters consent to begin railway construction in France, almost a decade after Belgium had built its State-owned railway lines. The French people were taxed to supply four-tenths of the required capital, the stockholders contributing the remainder. Nine great lines (seven radiating from Paris, the other two provincial) were built, after stipulation by the Government that each should have a monopoly in its district and a guarantee of high profits. Under the régime of Napoleon III, the complaisance of which cloaked the worst forms of gilded corruption, the duration of railway franchises was extended to ninety-nine years, interest on railway bonds was guaranteed, and the lines were consolidated under a government regulation which allowed stockholders great dividends. Except in the case of one company paying 10 per cent, dividends from French railways were 15 and 16 per cent—very high returns compared to those in either America or Britain.

The lords and other members of Parliament so considerably comprising the boards of directors of British railways had the necessary influence and finesse to obviate official disclosures and hush private contention. But one scandal implicating the management of the Eastern County Railway broke through the bounds of secrecy by being taken into the courts. The case involved two groups of contending stockholders, each side charging the other with fraud. The episode induced "The Economist," of London (on February 2, 1856), to draw a parallel in which it did some plain talking. It editorialized: "The English and Americans resemble each other very closely in their eagerness to grasp wealth. We know there has been great jobbery and great fraud in connection with the American [railway] lines, as there have been in connection with the English lines. . . . In the [United] States, however, the check of public opinion over unusual rapacity is more prompt and more powerful in its operations than here, and we may expect that jobbery, corruption and fraud are on the whole less there than here, where the check of public opinion is more mixed with and weakened by a reliance upon the action of Government." This last reference was an obscure and complacent assumption that for the rectification of abuses the British public depended upon the action of the Government, including Parliament. But, as we have seen, Parliament was reluctant to open up scandals in which its own members were often implicated.

The editorial then fully acknowledged the profit-making capacity of French railway promoters, but made a distinction in the case of the French people at large "simply because here [in Britain] the whole community is more exclusively bent on acquiring wealth than there [in France]."

In England, then, and in some other European countries, American railway jobbery was given loud publicity. Damnation of American corruption was blared in many an article and editorial. But that moralizing was never tempered by any admission that European financiers and investors hastened to seek their benefits from the proceeds of that corruption. Not with the means but with the results were European men of capital concerned; bribe-giving assured great grants of public domain and subsidies of public funds, thus making railways a luciously attractive investment.

But while the evil deeds of American railway promoters were widely heralded abroad, hardly any mention was published of the operations of railway promoters in Canada. To Europeans, and, in fact, to the population of contiguous America itself, affairs in Canada were effectively screened from attention. Unlike America, Canada was not a cynosure, and no group or country was interested in making it an object of attack. Little news of Canadian happenings filtered into America, and, except of course through investment accounts in English financial journals, still less into Europe.

Consequently, Canada eluded scrutiny, and so escaped the reputation of a venality and jobbery which, in one signal respect, outstripped anything America could show. Nothing like the rapacity of Canadian legislators and executive officials was known in America. In dispensing charters, railway and other, the Canadian Parliament followed the British model. There was hardly a member of the Parliament of the Province of Canada (then composed of Ontario and Quebec), or of other legislative or executive bodies, who was not boldly pushing projects in which he was a paramount beneficiary. The men having the power to enact laws did not, as often was the case in America, make them to give booty to outsiders. Canadian legislators made and used the powers of their law for their own individual enrichment.

From this point, the Canadian system differed from the British, and ran parallel to that in America. Like the United States, Canada had its vast areas of vacant public lands ready for spoliation. As a country with immense unsettled sections, and with such parts as were settled sparsely inhabited, Canada afforded railway promoters the opportunity of making the same plea so generally effective in America. This was the argument that construction of railways could not be undertaken without public aid. Of this assistance, the granting of public lands was one kind and of public funds another. But in Canada solicitude for railway owners was extended to the point of Government guarantee of railway bonds.

A history of Canadian railways might fill a volume; an informative sketch will here suffice. At the outset of railways in Canada, eminent politicians hurried to pre-empt the charters. One of the most industrious of those politicians was Allan N. MacNab, long a notable member, then Speaker of the Canadian Parliament, and later Prime Minister of Canada. He made the cynical declaration, famous in the Canada of his time, that "railroads are my politics." Amassing wealth, he was created a knight, then a baronet, and his daughters married British titles.

Associated with MacNab as railway promoters was a large contingent of prominent fellow-members of Parliament or high office holders. As a member of Parliament, MacNab held the pivotal position, for a considerable time, of chairman of the Standing Committee on Railways. On this committee were Sir Francis Hincks and other men who, at the same time, were engaged in promoting their own railway projects. Many other members of Parliament—some of whom became Cabinet and Prime Ministers—busily co-ordinated their functions as legislators with their activities as railway promoters.

Lord Sydenham, Governor-General of Canada, was highly vexed at the uncouth conduct and too open rapacity of the men in the Canadian Parliament. He was accustomed to the show of gentlemanly detachment with which the British Parliament consummated the most flagrant jobbery; long experience had made the executing of such transactions a fine art. "You can form no idea," wrote Sydenham in a private letter, in 1840, to Lord John Russell, British Secretary for War and the Colonies, "of the manner in which a Colonial Parliament transacts its business. I got them into comparative order and decency by having measures brought forward by the Government, and well and steadily worked through. But when they came to their own affairs, and, above all, to the money matters, there was a scene of confusion and riot, of which no one in England can have any idea. Every man proposes a vote for his own job; and bills are introduced without notice, and carried through *all* their stages in a quarter of an hour! . . ." [7]

Frequent and continuous was the jobbery in Parliament for the benefit of members. A group of these, headed by MacNab, were the incorporators of the London & Gore Railway Company. Foremost among the incorporators of the St. Lawrence & Atlantic Railway Company were A. T. Galt, for many years an influential member of Parliament, and Peter McGill of the Legislative Council of Canada, for years president of the Bank of Montreal.[8] The array of incorporators of the Canada, New Brunswick & Nova Scotia Railway Company was largely a roster of legislators, with MacNab at the front of the list.[9] Hincks and other politicians obtained the charter for the Woodstock & Lake Erie Railway Company which later developed into the Great Southern Railway Company, the line of which traversed Southern Ontario.[10] The ubiquitous MacNab was one of the incorporators of the London & Port Sarnia Railway Company; almost immediately after the charter for this was granted, lease was transferred to the Great Western Railway Company of which MacNab was the head.[11] A crowd of members of Parliament comprised the incorporators of the Grand Trunk Railway Company.[12] Likewise of the Strathroy & Port Frank Railway Company, and of three other railway corporations chartered in 1857.[13]

Well fortified, also, with the needed influence was the North Shore Railway Company (later the Quebec, Montreal, Ottawa

& Occidental Railway Company). Sir George Simpson of the
Hudson Bay Company was an early president, and various
members of Parliament were directors. The chief promoter of
this railway was J. Cauchon, a prominent Quebec politician;
he was Crown Commissioner of Lands and a member of the
Canadian Government Ministry in 1857, and later became the
company's president.[14] As in the case of various other railways,
the influence worked with perfect precision in securing boun-
teous gifts; a total of 2,700,000 acres of land was granted to
the North Shore Railway Company by the Quebec Legislature.
The company also received $752,000 in cash bonuses, and
$1,948,600 in loans from the Provincial Government and from
various municipalities.

The incorporators of the European & North American Railway Company embraced almost the whole personnel of the
Government of the Province of New Brunswick.[15] Part of this
railway later became the Government-owned Intercolonial Railway, and another portion was merged, in 1872, into the St. John
& Maine Railway Company, which received from the New
Brunswick Government and from certain municipalities $1,240,-
000 cash subsidies—a sum equaling nearly one-half of the railway's cost.

These instances are merely indicative of the prodigal business done in Canada by legislators bestowing charters upon
themselves. But railway charters were only one phase of Parliament's industry. At the same time coteries of members presented
themselves and associates with a miscellany of charters for the
establishment of banks and of insurance, gas lighting, water,
canal and other companies. MacNab, Hincks, Malcolm Cameron and various other notables in Parliament or occupying
high office were incorporators.[16]

At a later period, members of the Canadian Parliament
adopted evasive tactics, hiding their connection with corporations by substituting names of relatives, friends or go-betweens.
But at this particular stage subterfuge was deemed wholly
unnecessary. Aside from the brazenness with which members
voted charters and other vested rights to themselves, they
boldly used their names and positions in prospectuses which
often were decoys for stock-jobbing purposes.

Within a few years after the initiating of some of the railway projects, the promoters succeeded in transferring to their corporate selves an aggregate of nearly $22,000,000 from Canada's central Government treasury, and $10,000,000 from the poorly-populated counties and municipalities. The process of draining public treasuries was continued until, in the course of decades, the cash subventions for privately-owned railways reached more than $244,000,000, and Government guarantee of railway bonds covered more than $245,000,000. These were not the only features of Government aid. Many of the railway charters specifically authorized the free appropriation of timber, stone and other construction material from the public domain. Municipalities were influenced to make extensive gifts of land for railway approaches, terminals and stations. And land grants to railways were extended, ultimately rising to a total of more than 56,000,000 acres.

With members of Parliament acting as both legislators and as principals in corporations, there was obviously no need of money corruption. But as to railway construction contracts and the influencing of officials, charges of corruption were frequent. One ugly scandal broke forth in 1854. In his capacity of Inspector-General or Finance Minister of Canada, Hincks was sent to England to negotiate with the British Minister concerning the building of the Grand Trunk Railway.

The English contracting firm of Peto, Brassey, Betts & Jackson had amassed wealth by railroad construction in England and France. (If any curious investigator seeks to learn the methods by which railways in England were built, he need only consult Samuel Smiles' "Life of George Stephenson," written not long after the inception of railways. Stephenson was the perfector of the locomotive. That book supplies informative details of how those railways were "scamped" by improper ballasting and other inefficient construction.) The banking house of Rothschild owned an eighth interest in the Grand Trunk Railway's capital stock; and the Grand Trunk Railway construction contract was awarded to Peto, Brassey, Betts & Jackson, who agreed to take two-thirds of their pay in the railway's stocks and bonds.

According to Thomas C. Keefer, perhaps the most eminent

Canadian civil engineer of his time, the general assumption was
that this firm had obtained the contract by exercising its own
powerful influence, without need of any intermediary. Subsequently, however, disclosures showed that Hincks' name had
been inscribed in the contractors' books as the proposed recipient of a "douceur" (a present or an intended bribe). The
gratuity was £50,400 of paid-up Grand Trunk Railway stock.
Hincks made a public announcement repudiating the transaction.[17] Unfortunately for Hincks, the books did show that the
amount was credited to him. The Speaker of the Canadian
Legislative Council or Parliament at the time was John Ross,
head of the Grand Trunk Railway Company. The scandal
could not be suppressed, and the leaders of Parliament re-
luctantly consented to the appointment of an investigating
committee.

A principal witness, George Brown, a member of Parliament,
definitely charged: That Hincks had made a bargain with the
English contractors by which they were to get exorbitant sums
in stocks, bonds and money, and that they obtained, by means
of Hincks' influence in the Canadian Parliament, contracts
for building two other railways, and authority to amalgamate
these and other lines. For these services, Brown further testified,
the English contractors, it was believed, had placed in Hincks'
name the £50,400 of stock, and that of this amount £10,080
had been paid on account to Hincks' credit when public disclosures of the affair caused stoppage of further installment
payments.

Rejecting the plea that admission of circumstantial evidence
was customary, the majority of the investigating committee
voted against accepting Brown's testimony, upon the ground
that only matters within his personal knowledge would be considered. Publication of his testimony in the records was allowed,
however. Hincks' own explanation was that the stock credited
to him was merely "held in trust for allotment in Canada to
parties who might be desirous to take an interest in the company." This explanation was generally ridiculed, but it was
given full credence by the committee, which even went further
in its accommodating exoneration. The stock, it reported, had
been put in Hincks' name "without his knowledge," and he was

cleared from having any personal interest in it. With the offhand remark that everyone else who could do so was doing
likewise, that report was frankly cynical in excusing stock
speculations by Cabinet Ministers.[18]

In addition to Ross and Hincks, the directorate of the Grand
Trunk Railway Company comprised E. P. Tache, James Morris, Malcolm Cameron, Peter McGill, George E. Cartier and
other Parliamentary notables. "At this identical time," wrote
Keefer, "the contractors wielding a gigantic scheme which
traversed every county in the Province, virtually controlled the
Government and the Legislature while the expenditure continued." [19] With equal accuracy he might have added that they
controlled the policy of certain influential newspapers. After
having been manipulated wildly upward, the market price of
Grand Trunk Railway stocks and bonds began to decline. Notwithstanding the 50 per cent discount at which its stock was
selling, the St. Lawrence & Atlantic Railway, controlled by
Sir A. T. Galt and others, was "unloaded" upon the Grand
Trunk Railway Company. After it had paid an exorbitant
price upon the representation that the purchased railway was
complete, the Grand Trunk Railway Company had to spend
$1,000,000 to put the line between Montreal and Portland in
some fair degree of condition.[20] Finance Minister Hincks now
had to meet the charge that he had obtained secret advance
information of this amalgamation, and had speculated in the
stock. That he did get a telegram from Galt and did buy stock
was admitted, as likewise the fact that after the amalgamation
the market value of the stock rose. But the generous Legislative
Council Committee reporting on this charge palliated the transaction, on the ground that Hincks did not buy the stock until
several weeks after the amalgamation.[21]

As the value of Grand Trunk Railway stocks and bonds kept
on depreciating, the agents or sub-contractors of Peto, Brassey,
Betts & Jackson resorted more and more to "scamping" construction work. For, in addition to their two-thirds payment
in securities, they were paid by the mile for work performed.
On the section east of Toronto, where the work was carried on
by the English contractors, the rails were of such poor quality,
and the placing of sleepers so badly done, as to lead later

"to a destruction of property . . . which is unprecedented in the history of railways." [22] The entire scheme of construction was manifestly inefficient. In level country the roadbed was not raised to keep out snow and water. The gradients in hilly regions were poorly arranged and flagrantly defective. Everywhere "the contractors kept the road as near the surface as the contract permitted, no matter how much it might be smothered in winter and flooded in spring, or how frequent and severe the gradients became." Irrespective of railroad considerations, stations were placed where land was cheapest; this was done to obtain political support, or to benefit from a speculation in building lots. [23]

High members of the Canadian Government saw no impropriety in making fortunes by having contracts themselves for railroad construction. The firm of Gzowski & Company, which constructed the western part of the Grand Trunk Railway, from Toronto to Sarnia, comprised such members of Parliament as A. T. Galt, L. H. Holton and D. L. Macpherson. Gzowski later was knighted; Holton subsequently became a Cabinet Minister in various administrations, and was twice Minister of Finance.

The agreement of the British contractors to take the bulk of their payment in Grand Trunk Railway stocks and bonds led presently to the ruin of all the partners except Brassey, who shrewdly edged out of the mess. He left a fortune estimated at £7,000,000. This was largely inherited by his son, who became a British Cabinet Minister and, in 1886, was created a lord.

The Grand Trunk Railway jobbery, of which only parts have been here set forth, was typical of many railroad scandals in Canada. The promoters of the Great Western Railway were later accused of having at this time illegally appropriated $4,000,000 of its capital for the building of an American line— the Detroit & Milwaukee Railway—and for other unauthorized purposes. [24] The Northern Railway Company was enmeshed in a heinous scandal that uncovered its methods in obtaining municipal subsidies. [25] Another malodorous scandal unearthed corrupt transactions of the Great Southern Railway Company directors in awarding construction contracts and in procuring subsidies from cities and towns. [26] Still another sensational scandal concerned the illegal loaning of public funds to the Coburg & Peterboro Railway Company.[27] These scandals were but outcroppings of a mass of other dealings common enough yet never exposed by any public investigation.

Only a glimpse of the enormities in Canada has been here presented. And they continued, although with somewhat changed visage. "Corruption taints the majority of railway enterprises from their inception to completion," wrote David Mills in 1872; he was a member of the Dominion Parliament, and later Minister of the Interior. "Charters are sought, not infrequently for purposes of speculation. Sometimes, they are used to blackmail existing lines. However much a railroad is needed, a charter is seldom obtained without difficulty, and stock is bestowed for Parliamentary support." [28] But railway jobbery up to the time at which Mills wrote was only a preliminary to the ensuing great jobbery, as exemplified in the case of the Canadian Pacific Railway and other lines in developing the western regions of Canada. Yet intermittently down to recent times Canadian editorial writers and Canadian speakers made a practice of harping upon "Yankee corruption."

The only professed European critic of America at this period who evinced anything like discrimination was Adam G. de Gurowski. But, in his book, even he felt that he had to comply with the existent convention. "Undoubtedly," he wrote, "money-making has eaten itself deep into the American character." He then provided a qualification and an acknowledgment: "Neither is the love of money less violent, less intense, among the majority of Europeans than among Americans." Elsewhere in his volume, however, by declaring that great numbers of Europeans emigrated to America expressly to make money,[29] he insinuated—perhaps unintentionally by his mode of expression—that America stood out as nothing but a money-making country. If, Gurowsky wrote, European aristocracies did not make money in the same commercial way as Americans, they acquired it by oppressing millions in extortion of taxes and other dues. This was too sweeping a generalization, as we have amply shown.

It need hardly be said that while some immigrants came with

the expansive idea of making fortunes, the motive of the greater number was the simple one of improving their economic welfare. A living wage in America, the opportunity of obtaining farming lands in the West and Northwest, the aim to escape from military conscription—these were impelling reasons enough for emigration from Europe to America.

PART FOUR

AN UNABATED CAMPAIGN

CHAPTER XV

A CHANGE OF TACTICS

THE mischief done to a country by antagonistic criticism is not alarmingly evident in times of peace. A people may be irritated or indignant at abuse, or they may look upon it as accustomed treatment carrying no threat of danger to themselves. But when a nation thus assailed is embroiled in war, the cumulative power of prolonged misrepresentation becomes formidably manifest.

Such was the situation with which the North found itself confronted during the Civil War in America. Before that event European critics descending upon America made no regional distinctions in their condemnation of the mercenary character of all Americans. Inhabitants of North and South were alike depicted as wholly absorbed in money-making—the North from its varied industries, its shipping and finance, the South from its cotton, and both sections from land speculation. The Civil War caused a sudden critical shift and an abrupt differentiation. Favoring the South and viewing the conflict as one which was disrupting democratic America, European aristocracies concentrated calumny upon the North.

One of the British writers who quickly recognized this new mode and hastened to pander to it was Anthony Trollope, a son of Frances Milton Trollope. Family impecuniosity in his youth had inflicted upon him privations the memory of which had implanted a keen desire for money. Trollope made of writing a methodical business. Rising punctually at 5.30 A. M., he steadily poured forth words at the rate of 250 every quarter of an hour. Each book he regarded as the output of a prescribed number of days' work, and, with a factory-like supervision over himself, he carefully measured the quantity as he proceeded. He had seen the family rescued from penury by the returns from his mother's book caricaturing Americans, and he judged the time now propitious for him to repeat the performance. The expense of a trip to America, he reckoned, would well repay him, and it did; his book, opportunely entitled "North America," and dealing with the Northern States only, was published in London in 1862 and republished in America in the same year.

Trollope followed his mother and nearly all previous critics in his lines of attack. "New York," he wrote, appears to me infinitely more American than Boston, Chicago or Washington. . . . Free institutions and the ascendency of dollars are the words written on every paving stone along Fifth Avenue, down Broadway and up Wall Street. Every man can vote, and values the privilege. Every man worships the dollar, and is down before his shrine from morning to night." [1] Trollope had established his major premise with fine abandon. If there was any fact particularly notorious it was the un-American character of New York City with its hordes of immigrants; from 1847 to 1861 a total of 2,671,745 immigrants, largely Irish and Germans, had landed at New York,[2] and a large proportion had remained in that city. To such a marked extent was New York of foreign composition that the number of alien naturalized voters almost equaled the native, and the power of the foreign vote was so great that Tammany Hall politicians made a system of catering to it. With reckless certitude, however, Trollope went on:

"It is generally conceded that the inhabitants of New England, the Yankees properly so-called, have the American characteristics of physiognomy in the fullest degree. The lantern jaws, the thin and lithe body, the dry face on which there has been no tint of the rose since the baby's clothes were first abandoned, the harsh, thick hair, the intelligent eyes, the sharp voice and the nasal twang . . . all these traits are supposed to belong to the Yankee. . . . But at present, they are, I think, more universally common in New York than in any other part of the States. . . . No man has a type of face more clearly national as [sic] the American. . . . I think it comes from the hot-air pipes and from dollar worship." By "hot-air pipes," he explained, he meant "hot-air chamber heated houses." [3] Facetious as this observation seems, Trollope made it seriously. He had been in a mansion or two heated by hot-air furnaces, and forthwith rushed to the conclusion that all American houses must be so equipped.

Coursing hastily through the Middle West, Trollope remarked: "No men love money with more eager love than these western men, but they bear the loss of it as an Indian bears his torture at the stake." [4] "Mushroom" fortunes were a feature of the times, it is true. Often made rapidly, their sudden loss was usually tempered by the ardent hope of regaining riches. Because of war conditions in America and famine in Europe, beneficiaries in the North and West at this period were reaping wealth. Profits of railroads, and of woolen, cotton, munition and other factories were enormous. In the three years 1860–1862 the harvests of Great Britain were a failure, and in one of those years the harvests of all Europe failed. From an export to foreign countries of 20,000,000 bushels of wheat annually for the ten preceding years, America's export of wheat in 1862 reached 60,000,000 bushels.[5] Oil wells had been struck in Pennsylvania, and there followed wild, pervading speculation in petroleum stocks; a speculative "get-rich-quick" mania in stocks of gold mines became a craze in East and West alike.

This was one aspect of American activity at that time. It was perhaps the one aspect visible to a novelist who, like Trollope, preferred to view the whole of the Union, during the Civil War years, as the scene of an ill-natured social comedy.

Trollope pictured the men of the West as beginning to drink early in the morning and taking their liquor "in a solemn, sullen, ugly manner, always standing at a bar." Of the Western women: "They are as sharp as nails, but they are also as hard. They know, doubtless, all that they ought to know, but then they know so much more than they ought to know. They are tyrants to their parents, and never practice the virtue of obedience till they have half-grown-up daughters of their own." He bemoaned the fate of Englishmen in America. "Men and women will sometimes be impudent to him; the better his coat the greater the impudence. The corns of his Old World conservatism will be trampled on hourly by the purposely vicious herd of uncouth democracy." Trollope raged at "the continued appliance of the irritating ointment of American braggadocio."

However, he did have sense enough to see that he had to vary his long plaint by yielding some slight concession, which he made thus: "For myself I do not like the Americans of the lower orders. I am not comfortable among them. They tread on my corns and offend me. They make my daily life unpleasant. But I do respect them. I acknowledge their intelligence and personal dignity. . . . I see they are living as human beings in possession of their faculties; and I perceive that they owe this to the progress that education has made among them." [6] He predicted that if the negro slaves were set free it would "make such a hell upon earth as has never yet come from the uncontrolled passions and unsatisfied wants of men."

Every representation in Trollope's book was eagerly accepted by European reviewers; not one questioned his assertions, many of which were obvious absurdities or sheer distortions. In France a defence of the North was published in a book written by Count Agenor de Gasparin. He told of the prevalence of erroneous ideas throughout Europe about the North, and urged the need of distinguishing between "a few corrupt cities in which immigrants from our Europe flow unceasingly and that which is met in the whole country." He reminded Europe of its attitude toward the North: "Where we have unceasingly (even yesterday again) predicted excesses, acts of violence, disasters, lack of discipline, impotence, anarchy and bankruptcy, it has known how to place order, firmness, the organization of armies, the creation of a fleet, confidence in the public funds." [7]

Trollope's book was abundantly used by the powerful aristocratic party in Britain in its aim to turn the whole of British opinion against the North and thus to bring about recognition of the Confederacy. In an article purporting to be a review of Trollope's book, "The Quarterly Review," in October, 1862, affirmed that undoubtedly democratic institutions had failed; they had been unsuccessful in repressing rebellion and in upholding liberty. America, the article prated on, was "governed by the irresponsible ruler of a mob's choice" and the South had produced the stronger leaders; "the aristocracy that was decried as enervated and demoralized, has borne the powerful and braggart democracy to the ground." For nearly fifty years "The Edinburgh Review" had thundered against enslavement of negroes as a mockery of America's boasted equality. Now that periodical uttered its grave doubts whether slavery would be suppressed by what it termed the conquest of the South. If the slaves were freed, it argued, would not Northern capitalists take them over and work them under compulsion? Many Englishmen, "The Edinburgh Review" further stated, felt undoubted satisfaction at the breaking up of the great democratic government in America, but "if the restoration of the Union is possible, it can take place only under Jefferson Davis, not under Lincoln."

Trollope had incidentally mentioned in his book that £60,-000,000 of British capital was invested in American railways and other enterprises. Under the circumstances this admission was regarded as of minor importance, and was obscured by the mass of his furious invective against American money-making proclivities. But at about the same time other British authors, engaged in glorifying their country, were bringing Britain's foreign investments to the foreground to demonstrate how that nation far outclassed any other country or combination of countries in its possession of money. Meagerly concerned with any British intellectual or scientific achievements were many of the exaltations of England at this period. Britain's command of stupendous financial resources was the fact most conspicuously blazoned; and Britishers were infused with the assurance that, whatever the flag of a country, British capital had penetrated there, yielding torrents of profits.

The laudations of Charles Knight, an English publisher noted in his era, were but one example. In a series of volumes descriptive of London he devoted a chapter to the mighty resources and far-reaching ramifications of the London banks. Raptly and reverentially did he write: "The power here alluded to of great accumulated wealth is one of the most remarkable characteristics of England. . . . There is not any circumstance which so much distinguishes a young country like the United States, wonderful as may be its latent resources for future opulence, as the absence of masses of capital, ready at any moment to be moved hither and thither, wherever a profit is to be realized. The railroads, canals, roads and most of the great improvements of the [United] States could not have been

completed without English capital. There is, indeed, scarcely an
important enterprise in any quarter of the globe which is not
in some degree sustained by the 'money power' of England."
He then gave figures showing the magnitude of the daily money
operations of the London banks with their mountains of gold.[8]

An article in "Blackwood's Edinburgh Magazine," in 1864,
gorgeously styling London "The City of Gold," set forth: "As
a nation we have grown very rich. It is computed that the annual savings of the nation amount to the enormous sum of
£80,000,000. Like thrifty men, we desire to employ that sum,
our spare money, in the most profitable manner. Now-a-days,
too, we have the whole world open to us as a field of commercial
enterprise." The "savings" here referred to were not savings
in the American sense, but comprised surplus profits; and the
amount stated was an underestimate. According to the foremost
British financial authority, annual surplus profits exceeded
£100,000,000.[9] The bankers and big capitalists, complained the
"Blackwood's" article, took advantage of every monetary crisis
by charging the usurious rate of nine or ten per cent for money,
sweeping into their own coffers the profits of trade. "Parliament
inflicts misery upon the country out of an antiquated deference
to some bits of yellow dross [the gold supply in the banks]. Is
this wisdom, is this humanity, is it civilization? It is barbarism
and folly, preached up by the moneyed interest, the high priests
of Mammon, at the expense of the community."

So great were swiftly accumulating profits that the sums
which British capitalists and financiers had at their disposal
for investment were augmented yearly at an astounding ratio.
By the end of 1865 the amount invested in British railways
alone totaled more than £455,000,000,[10] a great part of which
came from moneyed men and concerns. And such, too, was the
further acceleration of British capital that in 1860 British investments abroad mounted to what was then esteemed the huge
height of about £750,000,000, an increase of £200,000,000 since
before 1854.[11] Many a native publication and speaker proudly
pointed to this fact as incontrovertible proof of British super-
eminent acumen and of Britain's invincible financial power.

Within two years after the outbreak of the Civil War, the
American merchant marine had shrunk to one-half its former

tonnage, and the decline continued. Simultaneously, English publications exultingly contrasted Britain's superior trade fleet with the poor or lesser fleets of other countries. "The Spectator" of London, on October 25, 1862, contained a typical eulogy of British mercantile leadership. France, that periodical pointed out, had spent great sums in the ambitious endeavor to encourage its commerce; it had subsidized steamship lines to various parts of the world, yet it had not been able to stem the deterioration of its commercial fleet. Germany's exertions had produced better results in creating a merchant marine, but Britain's fleet surpassed that of all countries.[12] Further, while the Civil War was disrupting America's foreign trade, the British Board of Trade was glorying in the fast-increasing volume of its country's exports, which rose from more than £146,000,000 in 1863 to nearly £166,000,000 in 1865.

Now, too, the greed and inhumanity of British railway owners were displayed in a way peculiar to a thickly-settled country. Disclosures in Parliament brought out the methods pursued, and showed anew the revolting conditions in which the poor of London existed.

Railway companies in London had utilized the legal power conferred upon them by taking over land in crowded districts for approaches and terminals, and peremptorily turning out the inhabitants of entire neighborhoods. The Earl of Shaftesbury, in 1853, had tried, but in vain, to get an act passed compelling every railway company to provide lodging accommodation for a number of people equal to those displaced. In Parliament again, in 1861, he scored the rapacity of the companies: "While they seek to make a profit from a proceeding which spreads devastation through the whole neighborhood, it is not right that gain should be all on one side and all loss on the other." Generally, he stated, the people ordered out of their abodes were poor working people who had not time to look about for new lodgings, or could not find a place elsewhere, and were in a state of consternation.

"The consequence is," he went on, "these hundreds or thousands rush in vast crowds into already overcrowded dwellings of the neighborhood. . . . I will give your Lordships the result of an examination that was instituted only last week. A great demolition of houses took place a few years since in the neighborhood of Field Lane, City. A thousand homes were pulled down, four thousand families, comprising twelve thousand individuals, were turned out and driven into surrounding tenements. The result of an inquiry made a few days ago is as follows: I took forty-five courts, within a compass of a few minutes' walk; twenty of these courts contained in the aggregate two hundred and fifty houses, in which were one thousand and thirty-three families, each occupying one room. . . . The total number of inhabitants in these rooms is five thousand, six hundred and sixty-five. . . . These rooms were, in all instances, low, dark, dismal and dirty; and it was with difficulty that I could stand upright in them. Some were so narrow that, by stretching out my arms, I could touch both walls at the same time."

Shaftesbury's exposé was, as we see, duly reported in the proceedings; but of the noble lords present none, except the Earl of Derby and perhaps a few others, gave it any serious attention. Yet Shaftesbury continued:

"I would not for the world mention all the details of what I have heard, or even of what I have seen, in these scenes of wretchedness. But there are to be found adults of both sexes living and sleeping in the same room, every social and domestic necessity being performed there; grown-up sons sleeping with their mothers, brothers and sisters sleeping very often, not only in the same apartment, but in the same bed. My Lords, I am stating that which I know to be the truth, when I state that incestuous crime is frightfully common in various parts of this Metropolis—common to the greatest extent in the range of these courts. Can anybody doubt that anything can be more prejudicial to the human system than the filthy squalor, the fetid air, and depressing influences of these dwellings? When you ask why so many workingmen betake themselves to the alehouse and the gin palace the answer lies in the detestable state of their homes."

As a climax Shaftesbury gave this information:

"Poor children having no other ground accessible to them, trundle their hoops and play at 'cat' in the thoroughfares . . . and I learn that no fewer than fifteen young boys were sent to

Coldbath Fields Prison for no other offence than indulging in these amusements." [13]

The Earl of Derby told how he was informed by a resident of one parish or district that, "The aristocracy of my parish consists of families who are able to indulge in the luxury of two rooms." Derby cited from a report made by a London Sanitary Committee physician, who described how husband, wife and often four or five children existed in one room. "Adults of both sexes—sometimes of the same, sometimes of different families —lodge in the same room, men and women herding together like savages, and where the slightest regard to the ordinary rules of common decency is impossible." [14]

While Trollope and others were inveighing against American susceptibility to speculative manias, in England a multitude, seduced by hopes of quick gain, had been lured by the stock schemes of several British promoters. And France, periodically responsive to the operations of plausible financial buccaneers, had produced another of the type in the person of M. Mires.

The son of a poor Marseilles watch-maker, Mires somehow obtained money to begin his climb. He bought a leading railway journal, then other periodicals, flowered into a promoter of railway, and coal-mining enterprises, and established a company which was partly a bank and partly a stockbroking concern. By skilful propaganda he coaxed from the recesses of many a French household a stream of savings from which he purloined sums for payment of dividends. The diffusion of this bait influenced an increasing swarm of investors, excited by the prospects, to intrust their money to his magical handling. For years Mires was looked up to as a marvelous financier; on his part he was meanwhile successful in cloaking his wild-cat and pyramiding methods and his thievery.

But the day inevitably came when his great fraudulent edifice collapsed. The crash entailed the loss of a vast aggregate sum by many sections of the French people, as infuriated now as they were trusting before. The Mires scandal was a sensational event in 1861. He and a chief accomplice were convicted of embezzlement, swindling and distributing false dividends, and were sentenced to tolerably long terms in prison. The British press found itself in the embarrassing position of not being able to moralize on French public credulity and French financial scoundrelism. Mires, it was acknowledged, had but taken British promoters as his model and adapted their methods to native conditions.[15]

In the aim to dazzle the public, England's commercial classes, with their overloaded stock corporations, made a policy of annexing titled aristocrats. To gratify and entice a title-loving people, schooled in the tradition that peers were men of honor, companies induced titled men to serve as directors or even as executives. Both in pursuit of trade and in the race to attach to themselves the éclat of lofty names, companies sharply competed. There was no lack of admonition to the public that these personages were, in a business sense, complete ignoramuses. "Only too often they [the companies] bestow head positions on mere aristocratic or high-sounding names—on men who can supply no one desideratum of a large business undertaking— men who have never had personal experience of a single function essential to business." [16] Later came sharper warnings, cautioning the public to view with "infinite discredit any concern which boasts titled names, merely as such, among the directors." [17]

Opportunities to speculators to promote any flimsy enterprise and wheedle the public were not less easy in Britain than in America. Contrary to erroneous ideas held in America of strict British regulation, English laws afforded wide license. Any crowd of promoters could form a company at a minute's notice and issue a roseate prospectus doctored with statements based upon falsehoods. The period was rated by British promoters ripe enough for another projection of stock-jobbing. In every conceivable line of finance, industry, utility and trade, hundreds of new companies were forthwith organized. Some were bonafide; many in reality were mere "bubble" concerns. The stock issued mounted to enormous proportions, and the capital subscribed by throngs scrambling to make money rose to large sums. In the year 1863 alone 263 companies—banking, manufacturing, railway, steam, gas, shipping, mining and others— were formed, and there was subscribed £78,000,000, of which a considerable part was paid in. The results of the speculative excesses of 1847 and even those of 1857 had become dulled in the public mind.

When apprehension was expressed as to whether the strain of the huge capitalization required would not ruin the country, monetary experts came forward with a soothing assurance. Essentially, British investors were informed, there was nothing to cause alarm; so much money were Britain's commercial classes making that "we have capital for a vast number more [of companies] if they will prove profitable." [18] If, indeed! Within two years many of the companies had exploded with detonations of fraud; England had again proved itself "a paradise for dishonest speculators," with consequent "great swindling of the public." [19]

Up to the Civil War period, America had but a sprinkling of millionaire, and not many multimillionaire, fortunes. England, however, had produced a notable showing of both, each year witnessing fresh accessions. The factor conducing to bring them strongly to general attention was not the fortunes themselves. It was the sight of possessors openly and boldly using their wealth to bribe their way into Parliament. In America the millionaire cared nothing for personal incumbency in political office. Wealth conferred upon him all of the distinction he wanted; and whatever legislation was necessary to his projects of expansion he could often accomplish by purchase. But the ambitious scope of British millionaires included their own direct wielding of political power with its coveted social opportunities. As we have seen, groups of rich commercial and financial men had long been potent in Parliament. Yet Britain had never quite beheld anything to equal the spectacular rush that it now saw of millionaires reaching for seats in that body and attaining their goal by crude wholesale corruption.

The glaring turpitude of this spectacle aroused growing comment and agitation. Elucidating the circumstances and the reasons why business millionaires sought political power, one London publication editorialized at length. There was no doubt whatever, it declared, that if bribery had not increased, the extension of money influence over elections had. The tendency of English affairs was toward a great increase of wealth, and to the agglomeration of wealth in many hands, as compared with the total in previous epochs. When, during the Napoleonic wars, Pitt introduced the income tax, he thought it useless to frame a scale for properties of more than £1,000,000, yet it was probable that many hundred persons had now reached that position.

"Year by year," the editorial flowed on, "traders of all kinds —contractors, builders, linen drapers, cotton dealers, money lenders, metal founders, miners [mine owners] and importers [of goods] from the East—deposit on the soil some three or four men with that amount and more.

"The men who have made these fortunes are generally active-minded, pushing persons, ambitious either for themselves, or more frequently for their sons, and the quickest road for an ambitious man with any brains at all is Parliamentary life. . . . English society is aristocratic with reservations, and one of the reservations is this: if a really wealthy man, and we mean by that anybody worth more than [an income of £] 10,000 a year clear, displays political ability, all barriers disappear, and the greatest in the land *admit* one who, as they think, may be greater still. Nobody who may be a Minister of State is allowed to feel any social distinction. This exemption is what men who have achieved wealth really crave for, and year by year, the wealthy candidates who present themselves to the boroughs seem to increase. . . . Sometimes they bribe and bribe heavily, buying not the score or two score of men who once held the balance of power, but an entire majority. . . . A more indirect form of corruption is the purchase of the borough [vote] under cover of public-spirited benefactions. . . . So the new man with a full purse is duly returned with little opposition." [20]

Much truth as there was in this explanation of the individual ambitions of British business millionaires, it did not by any means supply a full diagnosis. The direct sway of political power for the protecting and economic benefit of their corporations was a large determining motive. It was for this end that rival companies furiously competed at elections to get candidates elected to Parliament.[21]

British standards of estimating millionaires differed greatly from American. In America there ordinarily was a certain well-defined existent admiration of the millionaire as "smart" and enterprising, and if not a condoning of his freebooting, a recognition of his shrewd ability in "getting away with" the proceeds. But during the Civil War widespread and intense popular indignation was manifested at the sight of profiteers gorging themselves with wealth while the battle-fields were taking heavy toll. Whether, however, times were those of peace or war, illicit methods of acquiring wealth did not escape uncovering in America. More or less regularly, as occasion demanded, Congressional and other penetrating investigations unearthed some of the means by which huge fortunes, such as those of Astor, Vanderbilt, J. Pierpont Morgan and others, were originally acquired or were enlarged.

But in Britain not a sign of any spirit of inquiry was evinced; the ways by which fortunes were amassed was a subject not explored either by Parliamentary examination or private scrutiny. Facts might be brought out fortuitously in the course of some proceeding or other. But there was no urgent curiosity as to the underlying means whence came great business wealth— no disposition even to institute inquiry, which was considered unwonted and unwarranted. Once anybody attained wealth, he passed into a sphere of immunity; and if he munificently and discreetly maneuvered his ascendant way, the bestowal of a title might well be his crowning reward.

In keeping with the exclusiveness of a caste code, pretentious sections of the old-established British aristocracy professed disdain for the moneyed business man. But this asserted aloofness was not allowed to interfere with the cherishing of a precious regard for their money. Any attempt to keep aspiring rich men in "their place" was a futile undertaking; the assigned bounds were constantly broken by the resistless force of money's encroaching power. Aristocratic purpose was directed toward the feasible policy of ensuring the complete submissiveness of the mass of poor. An ironical article in "The Saturday Review," at this time, described the ideas instilled. Over the poor was set an aristocracy "which, it is supposed, Heaven intended to guide them, to care for them, and to own them." The lordly landowner, the clergyman, all benevolent laymen were an aristocracy ordained by God's will over the poor. "It is the duty of the poor to be obedient, industrious, humble and contented. . . . Other people may try to get on, but the poor must be content with the station to which God has been pleased to place them. . . . And almost all modern literature which attempts to inculcate the duties of respectable readers through the medium of fiction, repeats and dilates on this theory in every aspect. . . ."

While men as voracious for political power as they had been for wealth were corrupting voters *en masse,*—while this corruption was a matter of common usage, and soon to call forth Parliamentary action,—British publications were denouncing the state of American politics. One magazine self-righteously discovered that—at least in the American northern States—public men were generally held in disrepute: "To be a member of Congress and an influential leader of parties by no means proves a man to be honest or respectable. . . . The mob—indeed the lowest portion of the mob—has got the whole political power in its hands; and the tendency of each year's immigration is to swell the numbers and power of the mob." [22] Another British magazine jeered at Americans as "tactless, rustic and childish," and declared that the American Union was "going nigh to ruin." [23] Editorializing upon a letter written by Abraham Lincoln to the unconditional Union men of Illinois, the leading London newspaper thus stigmatized it: "It has a dash of Yankee slang and terms of expression which remind us alternately of Ossian, of the incoherent utterances of the Maori chiefs, and of schoolboy translations of corrupt choruses in Greek tragedies"; yet it was "tempered by a lawyer-like smartness." [24] Another London newspaper heralded the fate of American democracy: "Beyond controversy, the form of government and the institutions which were held up as models of perfection, have failed, fallen to pieces, and become a wreck." [25]

An especially flagrant election scandal in Lancaster caused such commotion that Parliament could not withhold ordering an inquiry. The report of its Investigating Commission showed that in the Lancaster election £14,000 had been spent in bribery and treating; of 1,408 voters, 843 had been bribed.[26] Benjamin Disraeli expediently introduced a bill aimed at election corruption. Editorial comments in some British publications emphasized the difference between the former "rotten borough" system of buying a few then having votes, and the newer system, as disclosed at Lancaster, of purchasing a majority of the enlarged electorate.

"A new class of millionaires," observed the outspoken "Economist," "is rising up among us, who regard money as mere counters in a great game, and the greatest game they can in our society play is the Parliamentary one. A safe seat confers at least as much social status, particularly in London, as two or three thousand acres of land, and they would cost from £80,-000 to £100,000. These men can afford £50 and £100 a vote, and the great sums tempt electors. . . . Hitherto, an absurd idea that bribery was a check upon democracy had immense secret weight with the House [of Commons]. . . ."

In Parliament at that time there happened to be a few members who bluntly expressed the truth. John Stuart Mill who, as we have seen, had taunted Americans with dollar chasing, now had to admit and deplore the power of moneyed men in England. As a member of Parliament he felt that he had won his way by mental ability, and he resented the incoming of purse-proud, unlearned men battering their way solely by force of money. "There is in this country," he complained, "a large and growing class of persons who have suddenly and rapidly acquired wealth, and to whom it is worth any sacrifice of money to obtain social position. The less they have to recommend them in any other respect—esteem, either by qualities useful and ornamental— the more they are sure to resort, if they can, to the only infallible means of gaining their end, the obtaining of a seat in this House." [27]

But the onslaught most disconcerting to Parliament's equanimity was that made by R. B. Osborne, representing Nottingham. Dispensing with indirection he delivered what was substantially an indictment of the membership of Parliament itself. It was very pleasant, he sarcastically began, to hear those little ebullitions of indignation in which most members of the House indulged whenever there was discussion of bribery. Yet, he pointedly stated, there were not thirty members who obtained their seats by fair means; where bribery was not used, appeals to the prejudices and passions of voters were, and such appeals were as bad as bribery.

Most of Osborne's fellow members showed mingled anger and dismay at this arraignment of hypocrisy, venality and demagoguery. Not confining his strictures to the branch in which he sat, Osborne proceeded: "Is it not a fact that two-thirds of the members of the Upper House [the House of Lords] have obtained their peerages because they had freely spent their money in contested elections? Who is looked upon as a worthy member of a party? A man who has contested a county [election] and spent some thousands [of pounds] in the undertaking. Why are baronets made? It is very easy to get up in the House and make fine speeches. I do not believe that half of those whom I address are sincere in their endeavors to put down bribery. The fact is that one half of the House [of Commons] would not have entered it at all had they not happened to have long purses, and had they not been prepared to spend the contents of those purses."

Venomous glances shot from many of Osborne's auditors. He undauntedly went on: "Bribery will continue to exist until it comes to be looked upon as infamous, and what is termed ungentlemanly. At present, it is the fashion, and no man happens to think the worse of another because he happens to have bribed. . . . Bribery will continue. Loyal adherents will be made peers, and obsequious followers baronets." [28] Disraeli succeeded in passing his bill; but of course corruption at elections was not uprooted.

Accompanying the rush of moneyed magnates into Parliament came constant exaltations of London's greatness, measured solely by its money-making capacity. Commercial or other self-puffery was professedly viewed in Europe as an atrocious American vice. Many American communities had vied with one another in each proclaiming its remarkable growth in population, industry and commerce. But this elation was not unnatural and without reason in a country which in a short time saw settlements go through quick, expanding stages and become transformed into bustling cities. At the end of the Civil War, however, there were not many evidences of this glorifying spirit, except in the far West, distant from the arenas of war. Prostrate and impoverished, the South had its pressing problems, and likewise had the North with the war's aftermath.

An old, stable city such as London with its recognized eminence could not plead the same justification for excesses of self-booming as could, let us say, upcoming cities of the grade of

Chicago, Cincinnati or San Francisco. Yet, dealing with proposals for an improved system of taxation in 1866, one publication jubilated: "There is a real wish to make London worthy of its position as the greatest, richest and most populous city in the world. . . . The richest persons in the Empire throng her; her scale of living is most magnificent; her rents highest; her opportunities of money-making widest." [29] So ceaseless was the chorus of self-praise that another London publication was driven to make protest. "London," it impatiently declared, "is never tired of admiring its own vastness and wealth; its population, greater than that of many kingdoms; its trade, larger than that of India; the annual addition of a new city to its extent and resources. It is well before the next hymn is sung to Mammon and his glory to remember this little fact: The number of London paupers relieved by legal alms on the last day of February in this year [1868] was 156,650. Add the professional beggars, the tramps, and the people who do not beg but remain dinnerless, and we shall find that London contains a population as great as that of Leeds with nothing to eat. The social cohesion must be strong which stands that strain." [30]

But pauperism was only one dark phase of the abysmal contrasts to wealth. When, in 1870, W. E. Forster introduced in Parliament his bill for elementary education, disclosures showed the widespread illiteracy. In England more than a million children between six and ten years old, and half that number between the ages of ten and twelve, Forster stated, were utterly without education. A million and a half other children were nominally "on the registers," but their attendance was irregular in such schools as received Government grants of funds. [31]

The contrast with Saxony, Switzerland or Prussia, attested A. J. Mundella, representing Sheffield, "is enough to make an Englishman blush for his country." Citing recent Parliamentary reports on education, Mundella ominously went on: "When the future historian writes the history of his country some of its blackest pages would be found to be based upon those reports. According to them, the estimated population of Birmingham, Leeds, Liverpool and Manchester is 1,500,000; the average attendance in all the schools 124,000, or allowing for the children of the middle classes, for whom one shilling and upwards was paid, 150,000. And what a class of schools some of these are! Cellar schools, garret schools, and all sorts of miserable and pestiferous places." [32] Mundella's figures were substantially confirmed by another speaker, J. T. Hibbert. The vast illiteracy in London was indicated by T. Salt, still another proponent of the bill. London with its population of three millions, Salt bade his hearers note, contained about half a million children of school age; an estimate made in a single square mile denoted that 23,000 children were "growing up in more or less entire ignorance." [33] Despite emasculations in the House of Lords, Forster's bill was passed. But not until twenty-one years later was payment of fees in elementary schools abolished.

CHAPTER XVI

"WANT OF SOUL AND DELICACY"

"BEFORE I ever went to America, and when I had no expectation of going there, I published under the title 'A Word About America' . . . a few modest remarks on what I thought civilization in the United States might probably be like. I had before me a Boston newspaper article . . . and taking this article for my text, I observed that from all I had read and could judge I should for my part expect to find the rather such and such other things, which I mentioned." [1]

That British authors were swayed by preconceived ideas of America was consistently shown by the tenor of their productions. But it was left to Matthew Arnold, as cited above, to reveal in so many words how perhaps the foremost English literary critic of his time could pass judgment upon a country without ever seeing it.

What, it is pertinent to ask, would have been the reception in England of a plague of books written by Americans on the people there? Especially of books grounded on preconceptions and lacking in first-hand knowledge? Without doubt, the authors would have been hooted and their work impugned as competent exhibits of Yankee effrontery. Yet when that course was pursued by Arnold and other British writers professing to deal with American life, it was accepted in Britain as entirely proper and commendable.

Fixed ideas had long dominated Arnold. When young he had developed an enormous respect for the British aristocracy's manners, reticence and governing capacity, while at the same time he deplored its lack of culture and intelligence. Sorrowfully, he viewed power as slipping from the cherished aristocracy into the hands of the multitude which, he was convinced, could never regulate its affairs or govern properly unless it discarded individualism and centered power in a tran-

207

scending, all-powerful State. He attacked the middle class in particular as Philistine—that is, antagonistic to culture.[2] As he grew older, no English class seemed to have his approval. He criticized the upper class as materialized, the middle class as vulgarized, and the lower class as brutalized—notwithstanding which general disapprobation he retained a deep-seated respect for the aristocracy and gentry, and fervently pleaded their cause.

Some years before he visited America, he delivered an address on "Equality." Social equality he condemned as demoralizing; and he warmly supported views expressed by various noted Englishmen on the fallacies of that doctrine, and on the superior leadership and splendor of the British upper classes. Arnold had slight patience with any advocate of equality, political or other. George Sand's pronouncement, that the human as well as the social ideal was achievement of equality, was dismissed by Arnold as the persiflage of "an enthusiast." [3]

Filled with such views Arnold made two visits to America, one in 1883 and the other in 1886. He held then an official position as inspector of English schools; and his literary reputation, both in his own right and as professor of poetry at Oxford, had long since preceded him. In person Arnold was impressive, with his broad-shouldered, almost burly, figure; but as a lecturer he was not forceful, so poor was his delivery. His manner of speech, however, was no impediment to the spread of his influence. Every word he uttered was so highly esteemed by his following as to be published and republished in books that reached wide audiences.

Before Arnold's advent, foreign critics on tour of America had condescended to give talks or interviews. But he virtually started the fashion for exotic critics who, as a formal undertaking, lectured down to Americans on the ugliness, greed and vulgarity of American life. The supine willingness of some Americans to pay for the privilege of hearing their national customs derided has been one of the oddest phenomena of our cultural history. In a European country the mere suggestion of handing over money to listen to visiting lecturers berate and affront the people they addressed would have been deemed sheer lunacy. How much of this American patronage of alien critic-lecturers has been financed by tolerant curiosity is, of course, a question which need not be discussed. The point worth noting here is that, while European critics have attacked every conceivable aspect of American rapacity, they have preserved a confederation of discreet silence, from Arnold's time till now,[4] on the workings of this lecture industry so agreeable to their patriotic impulses—and often so satisfactory to their individual pockets.

All along—so Arnold admitted without a trace of apology or compunction—he had criticized Americans on intangible grounds. In the past, he conceded, he had perhaps speculated too much about America in the abstract. Then, apparently to prepare his hearers for something more specific, he plunged into a series of suppositions. But, taking these in turn as granted premises, he launched into denunciation. He "supposed" that in a democratic country such as America, the newness, the magnitude, the press of business, and sheer freedom and equality must, perforce, produce a danger. Treating this imagined danger as a demonstrated fact, he proceeded in the most positive terms to define it. The danger threatening Americans, so Arnold told them, lay "in the absence of the discipline of respect; in hardness and materialism, exaggeration and boastfulness; in a false smartness, a false audacity, a want of soul and delicacy." Further, he arraigned Americans as afflicted "with tall talk and self-glorification," and designated more particularly that "the new West promises to beat in the game of brag." [5]

Had Arnold even partially understood American conditions, one further count of his indictment—that of political corruption—could have been made definite and strong. In this respect his case would not have been open to challenge. It would not have presented itself as a shadowy reliance upon glimpses or gossip. Political corruption in America was a glaring, ugly commonplace. Investigation after investigation had disclosed proofs of it; and these were matters of the most ordinary knowledge. But the best that Arnold could do was to characterize as "thick-and-thin-skin American patriots" any who advanced against his prejudices the opinion that political corruption was no more inveterate in America than in England.

A few years before Arnold visited America a notable scandal in England had again shown the great difference between the American policy of openly, frankly uncovering its corruption, and the British method of stifling disclosures.

Parliament had long since progressed to the point of investigating factory and social conditions. But it had assiduously withheld from any investigation of high finance, which was looked upon as an inviolate region. However, in 1875, Parliament found that it could no longer provide this immunity. The reasons were:

In 1867–1873 bonds totaling about £10,000,000 of loans sought by Honduras and other foreign countries had been floated by London bankers. These secretly employed a corps of stockbrokers who deftly manipulated the market, juggling prices to high quotations, whereupon the bonds were unloaded upon the British public. Later, news leaked out that the Honduras loan was based upon insufficient, or rather upon well-nigh worthless, security. There ensued a financial collapse enmeshing investors, including influential persons, in large losses. Parliament could not resist the outcry, and ordered investigation. Herran, the Honduran Minister to Great Britain, wrote a sensational letter to the Select Parliamentary Committee. First, he informed the Committee that before the 1867 loan had been put forth, the revenues, domains and forests of Honduras had already been pledged for two previous loans. Next, he stated, he had tried to prevent Captain Bedford Pim, M.P., improperly representing himself as Special Commissioner for Honduras, from floating the new unsecured loan. On his part, Pim had accused Herran of opposition to him because he, Pim, had declined to pay booty—£40,000 to Herran, and £16,000 to the Consul-General of Honduras. Herran denounced Pim's charges as calumny. After this letter had been read before the Committee, reporters for "The Times" and "The Daily News," of London, made formal application to the chairman of the Select Committee to see so startling a communication. He gave permission. They then published it, along with such matters as they could gather of the inquiry.[6]

Urging that this publication of proceedings before the Select Committee was a most serious infraction of House of Commons' dignity, Charles Lewis, member, made stern complaint in Parliament. He called to attention the resolution of 1837 forbidding such publication. "There are," said Lewis, "precedents in the 'Journals of the House' having exercised its plenary authority of imprisonment on those who have offended in this respect." He then moved that the publication in the two newspapers was a breach of the privileges of the House of Commons. His motion was carried by an overwhelming vote. By similar large majorities the arrest of Francis Goodlake and Winking Hales, publishers of the offending newspapers, was ordered.[7]

This plan to terrorize and gag the press caused a commotion in public opinion. The proscriptive majority of Parliament speedily learned that it could not safely attempt the repressive methods of former times. But what perhaps almost equally created surprise was the novel sight of a Parliamentary investigating committee exploring the sinuous channels of financial crookedness. "This Committee has got into a new region," editorialized "The Economist," of London, on April 17, 1875. "It is investigating 'business' and every syllable on business is interesting. Every word which passes before that Committee may, in its effect, take money from some one, or give money to some one. . . . The lying on oath before the Committee must have been enormous, for the contradictions contained in it are so. There are whole sections which read like products of Asiatic mendacity. . . . If the Committee were to stop now, or if its future operations are comparatively inefficient, it will give the gangs of 'operators' who have not been exposed, a pre-eminent advantage over those who have." Then dealing with the measures against the publishers of "The Times" and "The Daily News," the editorial agreed that unquestionably a breach of privilege had been committed: "the proceedings of a Select Committee of Parliament are as sacred as those of Parliament, and those who divulge them may be punished." But, concluded the editorial, to enforce such rules in this case would be tyranny.

The action against the newspaper publishers was ridiculed in the House of Commons by Sir William Vernon Harcourt, a prominent Liberal. The House, he declared, "was becoming the laughing-stock of the nation." Having noted the strength of a public opinion adverse to the House of Commons' course, Premier Disraeli sagaciously made a motion, which was adopted, discharging the order summoning Goodlake and Hales. By this move the proceedings against them were dropped.[8] Those proceedings, stated "The Spectator," of London, on April 24, 1875, were an absurdity, and the Commons had been forced to abandon its "rather silly position." However, the House of Commons' retreat on this occasion did not signify any fundamental change of attitude. One member—Sullivan—proposed the instituting of a reform which should "relieve the public press from the hazards at which it now discharges important and useful functions towards this House and towards this country." The Government, Disraeli replied, had no intention of introducing any such innovation.[9] A few days later, in fact, reporters were ordered excluded from the House of Commons, and during their absence, speaking "amid great excitement," Disraeli relieved his feelings. He deprecated the disturbing tactics of some members of the House, which he eulogized as "an assembly of English gentlemen." It was only, he explained, to foil these tactics of members who favored admitting "strangers" (reporters) that he would move suspending during the session the rule for their exclusion.[10] The adoption of his motion was a notification anew by the House of Commons that solely by the vouchsafing of its grace and pleasure were reporters allowed in its precincts.

We must not at this opportune place, however, overlook the Select Committee's findings after disentangling the web of fraud perpetrated in the floating of the loans. Jay Gould's "Black Friday" operations and some other great American financial marauding transactions were given noisy publicity in Europe. But American newspapers did not provide their public with even a passable idea of the magnitude of the swindles and thefts in England. Nor had any American investigating committee ever more severely scored the acquisitiveness of men of the Gould-Vanderbilt type than did this Parliamentary Select Committee score the cupidity of whole classes of Englishmen who came under its purview. Judged by the customary restraint of British reports, its language was exceptionally strong. A famous report it was; yet literary men like Arnold visiting and chiding America knew or seemed to know nothing of it, or of simultaneous disclosures that showed damaging realities in their own country.

Only a glancing insight into the Select Committee's voluminous report can be given here. Lying statements spread as to the Honduras loan "had the natural effect of deceiving the public . . . tempting them to become purchasers of bonds [at prices] far above their value." These and other operations were carried on secure from inquiry by law enforcement officials and with the connivance of certain newspapers. The means used to influence public investment the Committee branded as "flagrantly deceptive." Grossly false statements were circulated in floating the San Domingo loans. Bought by a London syndicate of bankers at £50 per £100 bond, the Egyptian loan was issued to the public at the price of £80 or £84.

"It is true," the Select Committee commented, "that the credulity and cupidity of certain classes of the community have blinded them to the danger of embarking in speculations such as your Committee have described. They appear to have measured the value of the promises held out to them, not by any rule of experience, but by their own sanguine expectations, and thus they have fallen a prey to those who, by trading on their credulity, have obtained their money, and then betrayed their interests." And appertaining to this betrayal: "Enormous sums have been abstracted from the Honduras Loans and appropriated among those who were entrusted with its management." Finally, the London Stock Exchange was severely criticized for its practices of indiscriminately dealing in all securities, whether good or bad.[11] Unlike reports of American investigating committees, however, this report avoided fixing the responsibility in personal terms.

Another noteworthy example of the equivocal processes in the British Parliament was furnished by exciting disclosures. As a young man Samuel Plimsoll underwent extreme destitution and learned to sympathize with the oppressed poor. Later, upon attaining a competence, he devoted his energies to social reform. He particularly agitated against what were called "coffin ships." These were unseaworthy and overloaded vessels, often heavily insured by the owners, who had the sanction of British law in operating ships which were a constant menace to the lives of the crews.

Shipowners, powerful because members of Parliament, long resisted efforts at remedial legislation. But in 1862 they made an appearance of yielding, and an act was passed giving but the weakest powers of regulation to the Board of Trade. In 1868 Plimsoll was elected to Parliament for Derby, and four years later wrote a book, "Our Seamen," which made a profound impression in Britain.

To settle the ferment of public opinion, a Government bill dealing with the shipping evil was introduced in Parliament in 1875. The measure was flaccid, which Plimsoll well knew; but on the principle that any kind of relief was better than none, he decided to support it. Opposition pressure of shipowners in and out of Parliament was brought to bear, and Disraeli, on July 22, 1875, tersely announced that the Government would abandon the bill.

Deeply enraged, Plimsoll denounced "the shipowners of murderous tendencies outside the House, and who are immediately and amply represented inside the House, and who have frustrated and talked to death every effort to procure a remedy for this state of things." Before his hearers could recover from their consternation at such plain speech, Plimsoll passionately went on: "Continually, every winter, hundreds and hundreds of brave men are sent to death, their wives are made widows and their children are made orphans in order that a few speculative scoundrels may make unhallowed gains. There are shipowners in this country of ours who have never either built a ship, or bought a new one, but who are simply what are called 'ship-knockers.' " The Speaker called Plimsoll to order. The command was not effective. Shaking his fist in the Speaker's face, Plimsoll resumed: "I am determined to unmask the villains who send to death and destruction—" The flustered Speaker again called Plimsoll to order, and remarked that presumably Plimsoll did not apply the epithet of villains to any member of the House. "I did, Sir," Plimsoll said, "and I do not mean to withdraw it." Such language, the Speaker declared, was unparliamentary. Again Plimsoll declined to retract.[12] Disraeli moved that he be reprimanded, but upon Lord Hartington's politic suggestion to allow Plimsoll time for reflection, disciplinary action was delayed for a week.

For his transgression of Parliamentary conventions Plimsoll eventually made due apology, but in no respect did he desist from attacks in the House of Commons upon the diabolism of unscrupulous shipowners. Returning to the subject later he presented specific facts as to the devastation caused: "I can say without exaggeration that since the act of 1862 nearly 20,000 British subjects have been drowned, and nearly £30,000,-000 of British property have gone to the bottom of the sea." His statement went uncontradicted. Shipowners, he said, were well aware of the dangers of plying unserviceable vessels, but every time any attempt was made to get remedial legislation, he charged, they invariably strangled the proposals. Cries of "No! No!" Plimsoll maintained that his charge was true.[13]

Already stirred by Plimsoll's campaign to ameliorate the lot of the seamen of the merchant marine, Britain's pride, public opinion now became heated at the sight of one lone man, a humanitarian, having to battle in Parliament against massed and obdurate self-interest. The subject matter at issue was no intricate affair of abstruse economics, but a very simple one which could be understood by everybody and which appealed to elemental feelings as well as to fairness and sense of justice. Intense popular agitation forced a reluctant Government to change front, and, in 1876, Parliament passed an act vesting in the Board of Trade stringent regulative powers. From Plimsoll's efforts came the term "Plimsoll's mark," denoting the limit to which a ship could be loaded. And so popular was Plimsoll that, after he retired from Parliament in 1880, thirty different constituencies vied in offering him election to a seat in the House of Commons.

Purely in chronological order we shall at this point consider another example of the difference between the American and the British systems. In America municipal common councils in the large cities were composed mainly of professional ward politicians, and not infrequently a considerable number of members were saloon keepers. The tone of these bodies was low, and bribery scandals were numerous. By comparison, British municipal councils were looked upon as highly respectable, filled as they were with staid business men invulnerable to bribery. But the kind of corruption festering among them was shown by a statement in Parliament in 1875. Due largely to a ten-year fight waged by the medical journal, "The Lancet" of London, a series of acts against food and drug adulteration had been grudgingly passed by Parliament. Every one of these acts was emasculated by some provision or other which largely nullified its force. The usage of dealers was to dilute milk with one-fourth part of water. Alum was heavily mixed with flour. Sulphuric acid was put in vinegar, and sand in sugar. Tea, coffee, cocoa, mustard, beer and many other drinks and food were badly adulterated, and drugs and nostrums often contained deleterious or poisonous substances.[14] The same evils abounded in America at the same time, and in both Britain and America considerable, and often large, private fortunes came from the business of adulteration.

Britain much preceded America in arriving at legislation, passed in 1872, to compel honest labeling, so that the buyer should know what he was purchasing. But the gaping defect in British law was the absence of any adequate provision for preventing adulteration and for punishing offenders. On this latter point, G. M. W. Sandford, a member, charged in the House of Commons that analysts or inspectors were appointed by the Government upon the express understanding that they should take no punitive action against adulterators. Sandford went on: "If you consider for a moment of what persons the municipal councils, especially in large towns, are to a great extent composed, you will perceive that they are the very class of persons to be proceeded against." Which statement, thoroughly true, not one of his hearers disputed.[15]

For another and different example of how English local officials ran affairs, let us turn to the municipal council of London, called the London Corporation. In Queen Victoria's speech to Parliament, in 1882, a reference was made to the need of reforming this body. But the London municipal authorities wanted no reforming. They immediately began concocting measures to prevent the change, and to counter the agitation carried on by the Municipal Reform League. After a bill had been introduced in Parliament, in 1884, to reconstitute the London Corporation, the opposition of the politico-business men in this body increased. Charges were made in Parliament of the corrupt use of city funds by the London Corporation in seeking to defeat the reform bill. A Select Committee was ordered to investigate.

Parenthetically, it may here be observed, these were the years in which British authors, editors and speakers were pointing out the great thefts and frauds committed by the Tweed régime, which had for some years governed New York City, as typical of the corruption of American municipalities. But more than a decade before these charges against the London Corporation, the Tweed régime had been overthrown. Tweed died in jail, and his chief accomplices had fled to avoid prosecution. Tammany Hall thereby learned the lesson of refraining from the dangerous business of stealing public funds outright. While in Britain high moralizing was done on American official rascality, the municipal officials of London, to advance their own interests, were using city funds in the manufacture of public opinion and in trying to influence Parliament.

The Select Committee reported: From 1882 to 1888 £19,-550 of city money had been thus taken and expended by the London Corporation. The agents of this had engaged astute politicians and others to organize meetings which passed strong resolutions against the reform proposals, and newspaper reporters had been engaged to write favorable accounts. According to the Select Committee's report, packed meetings were an activity of both sides; "the various associations subsidized by the Corporation, and also the Municipal Reform League, packed their own meetings to a greater or lesser extent." An illuminating insight this report gives into the moulding of British public opinion, represented by the writers of that country as so honest and spontaneous. The Select Committee itemized various other ways in which city funds had been distributed in the campaign. But the sapient Select Committee could not bring itself to see that there was any barefaced looting in the transaction. The charge of malversation had not, "in its opinion," been sustained; but it did find that "improper use" of a portion of the city's funds had been proved.[16]

But for their apparent eagerness to blind themselves to the furious race for wealth within their own spheres of influence, European critics of American materialism could have found in Germany a much nearer exhibition of surging industrialism. There, thanks to the vast indemnity in gold exacted from France after the Franco-Prussian War of 1870, an extraordinary impetus was given to the formation of new enterprises.

Germany was saturated with stock issues between 1871 and 1874; more than 3,000 million marks of paper values were then issued by a legion of new corporations. A delusion of sure riches enveloped countless Germans in a speculative frenzy. Many of them subsequently found themselves wiped out in a crash; but this did not halt the onward sweep of Germany's industrialism, which based itself upon a secure foundation of underselling in competitive markets. In 1886 Germany boasted a grand array of more than a thousand corporations, an outpouring of stock issues exceeding 4,000 million marks, and bond flotations reaching nearly six hundred million marks.

So inveterately bent was German industrialism upon advancing its hold by any means, however discreditable, that in one sense Germany was an outlaw among nations. In all industrial countries fraud in making, stamping and selling merchandise was so common as to be an institution. The decent manufacturer was either hard driven in contesting with it, or else for sheer self-preservation had to abandon scruples and descend to the same level. Certain British manufacturers made inferior goods bearing the names of widely reputed French makers. Belgian foundries exported into Britain itself iron stamped as "best Staffordshire" which was sold at so low a price that Staffordshire mills could not compete. These are but two of a multitude of instances. But now Germany proved that it could not only carry the process of fraud to an unparalleled extreme but could swamp the markets of other countries in a ruinous competition. To lessen the world-wide effects of fraudulent stamping of merchandise, many Governments, including those of Great Britain, America, France, Italy, Norway, Sweden, Switzerland and other nations, had participated in a convention sanctioning the Union for the Protection of Industrial Property. An agreement was made to seize all manufactured goods the origin of which was fraudulently labeled. The German Government refused to accede.

Rivalry in fraud briskly continued. We may give full credence to the evidence before the Parliamentary committee which studied the situation, because there was no attempt to palliate the practices of English manufacturers themselves. A vast number of foreign watches, the testimony showed, were sold in England as native-made, the cases bearing the English hallmark. English cigar manufacturers put their names on boxes or labels which were stamped as of genuine Havana make, and Bremen cigar manufacturers did likewise. In various other lines of manufacture the same fraudulent branding was brazenly persistent. But in the great diversity of frauds, those in the cutlery trade were an uppermost grievance of English manufacturers against German. After having made the name of Sheffield a world-wide trade-mark for cutlery, long-established manufacturers of that city found themselves, to their great ire, undercut by German commercial piracy. The Cutlers' Company, an association of Sheffield, formally and loudly remonstrated, in 1883, against the making in Germany of large quantities of inferior cutlery shipped to Sheffield and there labeled with the name of some mythical concern as of Sheffield manufacture.[17]

By such methods, copied from other countries and improved by ingenious and disciplined proficiency, did German industrialism fast forge ahead and pile up fortunes for the owners. At the same time, the legend of a different Germany was widely spread by professorial writers of that country and even by some English authors. Then and later the world heard much of a romantic Germany of sentiment, and a cultured Germany suffused with philosophy, poetry, music and art. A small truly cultured class there was in Germany, as in differing degrees there was in every country. But the strain dominating German impulse was a combination of intense martial vaingloriousness, and pride in an unprecedented industrial progress. While pedants were flaunting German culture, German manufacturers were flooding their country with the most execrable "art wares" and sending shiploads of these to other countries. In England and America particularly their cheap price won a buying public.

Tawdry bronzes, stained-glass windows, papier-mâché mould-
ings and a conglomeration of other "ornamental" iniquities were
spewed forth in an appalling mass.

In its redoubtable march, materialism in Germany had
greatly shattered the stiff, pompous caste exclusiveness in which
the long-governing landed bureaucracy had incased itself. Officialdom now was subservient to the interests of powerful industrialism. No longer did an official career offer the great
prizes of material success. Increasingly, this was estimated by
possession of industrial, commercial and financial wealth. The
rise of Socialist philosophy and agitation somewhat neutralized
the worship of industrial success. But it did not seriously impair a widespread elation in Germany at the commercial and
industrial status which that country was attaining in the van
of nations. Within a decade or so it sped to fourth rank, and
later challenged still more closely the trade of pre-eminent
England and America.

However, reserving their detractions for America, hostile
British critics had no mind to notice this near-by demonstration
of materialism, portentous to Britain itself. They must needs
cling to the overworn convention of journeying to America. An
English journalist of ephemeral reputation, George Augustus
Sala, now joined the procession. He made of the hospitality
shown him by sundry American hosts the invidious occasion for
showering jibes. In his book, "America Revisited," he contrived
to do this by acknowledging the courtesies of "pork-packing
kings," "railway kings," "silver kings" and divers others. And
from a second English journalist, G. W. Steevens, came a ful-
mination against America. It was a tissue of opinions—the
repetitions of old scribblings—but it was printed as fresh, contemporary correspondence in "The London Daily Mail." Later
it was issued in a book with the title "The Land of the Dollar,"
and was published in London and New York. Steevens condemned Americans "as the most materialistic people in the
world." And then, while seeming to mitigate this sweeping assertion, he returned to the charge: Americans, he said, were
not materialistic "in the sense of being avaricious," but "because they must make something, and there is nothing else to
make" except money. This is a sample of Steevens' judgment

and poise: "No American is fit to talk until he is thirty, and he retains all his life a want of discipline, an incapacity for ordered and corporate effort."

One of the tribe of hostile critics, however, overreached himself by the sheer excess of his acerbity. If Rudyard Kipling had held himself down to routine preconceptions, as had many another before him, he might have escaped attack. But the snarling provincialism of this youthful prodigy proved too much even for the numerous American admirers of his verse and fiction. Despite his unquestionable talent for the turn of a phrase, his "American Notes" were all too plainly dictated by the most hackneyed of preconceptions. He visited Chicago, and found it "inhabited by savages." "The American of wealth," said Kipling, "is owned by his family. They exploit him for bullion. The women get the ha'pence, the kicks are all his own." Before the stranger, he wrote in his "Letters of Travel," American people of the Eastern cities preferred to talk of their mighty continent, "and to call aloud upon Baal of the Dollars —to catalogue their lines, mines, telephones, banks and cities, and all the other shells, buttons and counters that they have made gods over them."

Just so. But, while British critics of America were busying themselves with the supposedly American phenomenon of the millionaire and multimillionaire as significant of "Yankee" worship of money, hardly any attention was given in Britain to the fast-increasing number of millionaire fortunes there. In a long editorial, on May 19, 1883, "The Spectator," of London, discoursed on "that curious and little-studied subject, the History of Property." It related how, ten years previously, it had published a list, compiled from "The Illustrated London News," of all British fortunes exceeding £250,000 personalty at death during the decade. "That list, which was the first of its kind, and excited at the time a preposterous amount of interest," showed: Within the decade ten persons had each left more than £1,000,000; fifty-three more than £500,000; and a hundred and sixty-one more than £250,000 sterling. During the next decade—up to 1883—thirteen men had left more than £1,000,000; fifty-six more than £500,000; and one hundred and ninety-five more than £250,000. The number of fortunes ranging between £100,000 and £250,000 had "increased enormously."

The account in "The Spectator" stated that these returns were based on the payments made for probate duty, and did not include land or houses, or the enormous masses of wealth invested abroad. Although liable to income tax, this wealth held in other countries escaped legacy taxes entirely. "Much of this mass belong to the very rich, who have accurate information, who like a good percentage, and who are in many cases haunted by an idea that distribution is equivalent to insurance. The English holdings in the Rentes [government bonds] of all countries, in railways and banks abroad and in foreign house property, elude this list altogether, as do the immense sources of wealth classed as 'business' with their offices outside Great Britain." But even these partial returns showed an increase of 18 per cent in Britain's multimillionaires and millionaires. Excluding the Rothschild wealth, there was, however, no one in the list with a fortune equivalent to $10,000,000. An annual income of £80,000 denoted the highest sum in the list. No British fortune approached the dimensions of the Vanderbilt or the Gould "mammoth" fortunes in America.

"What a list it is!" commented "The Spectator" on British millionairedom. "The immense majority were quiet traders, bankers, iron masters and the like. . . . They represent the profits of Trade. As to popular hostility to millionaires there is no trace of it. . . . The rising rich men in England have purse-pride, but it is toned down by the social ascendency of an aristocracy which loves money, and despises moneyed men. . . . Wealth, when not too pompous, is liked like any other ornament. . . . Indeed, even opinion hardly presses on the rich; there is no 'feeling,' as in America, that a millionaire should do something for the public. . . . Englishmen lament over a fire all the more, if the person burnt out was rich."

CHAPTER XVII

SPEAKING OF COMPARISONS

In contrast to the long line of caviling critics, it is refreshing to turn now to an expositor who, before writing about America, took pains to acquaint himself with the subject. This distinction can be deservedly accorded to James Bryce, an English practicing lawyer and Regius Professor of Civil Law at Oxford. He had, in 1870, begun the first of a series of visits to America, improving each occasion by making a serious and thorough study of American politics and government. The knowledge thus gained he incorporated in his voluminous book, "The American Commonwealth," published in 1888 after five years of due preparation. Since Tocqueville's, Bryce's book was the first to show real understanding and authentic grasp. "The American Commonwealth" was accorded wide approbation in America. In due time it was pronounced a classic, and it had an exceptional longevity.

But the paradox about Bryce which escaped notice was that, although for one of alien associations he had an excellent understanding of American politics, he did not seem to comprehend the parallel implications and import of the politics of his own country. He exposed himself to this charge of incongruity and strongly invited criticism on this account, for, in dealing with American corruption, he frequently drew comparisons with European conditions, particularly British. These comparisons, all to the great disadvantage of American political morality, were grievously one-sided, in that they failed to distinguish between the workings of two different kinds of corruption. The outright bribery often done in America to procure the passage of laws granting public franchises and other special privileges profoundly impressed Bryce. But the underlying methods used in Britain in achieving precisely the same results were excluded from his observation.

Bryce's training had been of the legalistic order; he saw governmental activity as predicated by political motives; he lacked adequate perception of the powerful infiltration of economic aims, of which political action was often only the expression. In setting forth the comparison with Europe, Bryce made only a few offhand and general references to corrupt conditions there. Some quiet jobbery had been perpetrated by English town councils. Content with that fleeting admission, he followed this phase no further. Instead, he turned his attention to France, where he found that a great deal of jobbery had been committed in Paris when Baron Haussmann renovated the streets of that city during the reign of Napoleon III.

He then became vastly more definite regarding America: "No European city has, however, witnessed scandals approaching those of New York or Philadelphia, where the public till has been robbed on a vast scale, and accounts have been systematically cooked to conceal the thefts." Had Bryce been better grounded in historical knowledge of his own country he would not have made so sweeping an assertion, all-inclusive in its scope and implications. For, as has been fully proved from the British records themselves, great thefts of public funds were being effected in England when American municipalities were in merest embryo. The only difference—and it is not impertinent to regard this distinction as vitally important— was that the robbery in England was done by Government, and not by municipal, officials.

What were the contemporaneous conditions in Britain at the time when Bryce wrote "The American Commonwealth"? Since, as we have said, Bryce professed to make the comparison, the question is strictly in order. Anyone having insight into the extent and power of the moneyed interests personified in the British Parliament would have seen the need of much elaboration. Yet to this more important factor Bryce devoted only a single random observation. The British Parliament, as he pictured it, was composed of an Outer Circle the members of which were not primarily concerned with professional politics but with their avocations, and an Inner Circle the majority of which were professional politicians in a sense only, because politics was the main although not the sole business of their lives.

And in these desultory sentences he compressed the pursuits of the Inner Circle: "A handful hope to get some post, a somewhat larger number find that a seat in Parliament enables them to push their financial undertakings, or gives them at least a better standing in the commercial world. But the making of a livelihood does not come into view of the great majority at all." The only kind of bribery in Britain to which Bryce gave attention was election bribery. English morality, he wrote, regarded (or until very lately had regarded) the corrupting of voters as an offence only when detection followed it.[1]

Bryce need not have gone to much trouble in order to ascertain the real composition of the British Parliament. The simple process of consulting the English "Directory of Directors" would have enlightened him, had he been so inclined. He would have found that the dominating forces in Parliament were the members who were directors in financial, industrial and other corporations. A solid bloc, twenty-three members of the House of Lords, were directors of an array of one hundred and eleven corporations. Apart from that multiplicity of directorships, eighty-seven noble lords were corporation directors. But this was not a complete list. Aside, too, from the holding of corporation directorships by members of the House of Commons in general, a puissant group of twenty-six members alone held directorships in two hundred and eighteen corporations—an average per individual of more than eight directorships. There they sat, alert to watch proceedings, keen to detect any move trenching upon their business interests, zealous in promoting legislation benefiting these, and vigilant in blocking proposals counter to the same. Estimated by formal appearance, all of these members were acting in the capacity of representatives of their voting constituencies, and were untainted by venality. They were garbed in a fine veneer of respectability; and no one, upon pain of prosecution, could impute dishonest motives to them.

Yet, in roundabout fashion, there developed scandal after scandal revolving around their self-interested acts. One typical instance was the report of the House of Commons Select Committee appointed to inquire into the stock-watering operations of four English railway companies. The Select Committee tacitly assented to the plea made in defence of the corporations that watered stock was good for both railway owners and investors, and it definitely recommended the continuance of Parliament's policy of non-intervention in the financial affairs of railway companies [2]—a finding gleefully hailed by every British stock-jobbing promoter. Meanwhile several English newspapers were thundering against the viciousness of American stock-watering, and warned English investors against marauding American stock jobbers. But, with its usual forthrightness, "The Economist," of London, attacked evils at home. On June 28, and July 26, 1890, it expatiated upon the dual-headed crowd of members of both houses of Parliament who were corporation directors, and it earnestly moralized upon the attendant scandals. "No doubt," editorialized this periodical, "the best way of preventing the recurrence of the scandals which have arisen in the past in connection with the question we are discussing would be for members of Parliament to agree, by a self-denying ordinance, either to leave the direction of public companies [private business corporations] to other people or to resign their seats."

At this point two facts stand out. As American industrial "kings" gradually bought their way into seats in the United States Senate, turning it largely into "a rich man's club," British publications pointed to this irruption as damning evidence of the sway of money in America. The other fact was the light way in which the British type of legislative scandal was taken in Britain. American corruption, on the one hand, was viewed there as a great, affrighting and demoralizing evil. A transaction such as the bribing of a majority of the New York City Board of Aldermen, in 1884, with $500,000 cash to grant the Broadway surface railway franchise to Jacob Sharp and associates, was treated in England as downright criminal corruption, while the self-interested actions of many British legislators were viewed at the worst as an impropriety.

Shielded by the subtleties of their system, British legislators were not liable to any penalties for their acts, nor did they even have to experience the discomfort of serious attack. Contrariwise, the cash corruption in America, both by its nature and its trail of consequences, produced shocks upon public opinion.

Exposure itself made sensation enough, but this was supplemented and prolonged by uproar of indictments, arrests, extended trials, and by imprisonment of the convicted. In the case of the Broadway franchise bribery Sharp was sentenced to prison; he obtained a retrial but died in the interim. A number of aldermen were sentenced, and various other aldermen fled to Canada to escape prosecution.[3] Once vested rights were conferred by act of the British Parliament, though, there could not ensue any public demand for abrogation; Parliament's enactments were binding and incontestable.

Governing functionaries in other European countries also had their corrupt systems, but these were surrounded and buttressed with such wily indirection that it was difficult to trace their ramifications. All that can be itemized on this point is that, adroit as was the technique of the traditional French system, it was not proof against the outbreak of successive scandals. Because of the corrupt traffic which his son-in-law Wilson carried on in bestowing offices and decorations, François P. J. Grévy, President of the French Republic since 1879, was compelled to resign in 1887. And in 1888 (the year in which Bryce's book was originally published), the French Parliament was corrupted wholesale by de Lesseps' Panama Canal Company. After spending or squandering an amount equal to nearly $250,000,000 subscribed by the French people, the company had become insolvent. All along, as disclosures later showed, the company had subsidized Cabinet ministers and members of Parliament. Floquet, president of the Chamber of Deputies, admitted that when Prime Minister he had received 50,000 francs from the company for the purposes of his political party, and he stoutly justified the acceptance of the funds as consistent with French political custom.

Unable to raise more funds by the usual investment appeals, the Panama Company induced the French Parliament to authorize a lottery loan. Later came a great commotion when charges were made that one hundred and fifty members of the Chamber of Deputies shared in the distribution of 5,000,000 francs for the purchase of their votes for the passage of the act. Added to direct corruption, several of the Deputies and Sen-

ators participated in the underwriting syndicate floating the
loan. When this surreptitious affiliation was disclosed, they affected much surprise at the denunciations. They had, they contended, as much right to engage in this undertaking as in any
other financial venture, and they upheld their course as not
deviating from the code of official morality.

To French newspapers large—often munificent—subsidies
had been paid by the Panama Company since its inception. En-
dorsements and laudations of its promoters and enthusiastic assurances of its success were spread in many an editorial and
article which were supposed by credulous investors to be disinterested and authoritative. For approving and puffing the
loan of 1888, owners of some Paris journals were paid sums
respectively ranging from 60,000 to 100,000 francs. With the
exposure of these dealings, the owners assumed a bold attitude,
holding that the selling of publicity was their line of business,
and that they had a perfect right to vend it at as high a price as
they could get.

Only twelve Senators and Deputies were actually committed
for trial, but the difficulty of legally proving the actual pocketing of money bribes resulted in acquittals. The solitary instance of conviction was that of a former Cabinet Minister, and
he was regarded by the French public as a scapegoat. Meanwhile, the French Parliament had ostentatiously carried on
the motions of an inquiry into its own conduct. It appointed a
Deputy to summarize the evidence and draw conclusions. His
report was a grand flourish of extenuation. Charges of bribery
were waved aside as pure fiction concocted to divert attention
from the mismanagement of the company's directors, who were
declared the culprits for wasting so great a sum of French investments. Moreover, the bribery charges were indicted by the
report as a campaign of monarchist plotters to discredit republican institutions. But, the report triumphantly proclaimed,
the maneuver did not succeed, and "the calumniators were con-
founded." The complete failure of the Panama Company, the
causes thereof, the abandonment of the canal project, and the
subsequent sale of its rights to the American Government,—
these comprise another story.

Oddly enough, at this juncture there bounded forth a French

critic to discharge his volley against the curse of American mammonism. Writing under the pseudonym of Max O'Rell, Paul Blouet enjoyed—and he did enjoy it—much literary vogue both in America and England. On English life O'Rell wrote books such as "John Bull and His Island" and "Daughters of John Bull"; and he presumed to dissect Americans in a volume "Jonathan and His Continent." The America that he presented in his book was the picture made tediously familiar by many a prior writer. In America the dollar was supreme and omnipresent in thought and action. Overcome by dollar valuation, the ordinary American "looks upon every man as possessing a certain commercial value"; in America "more than anywhere else talent without money is a useless tool."

Presumably Blouet had read somewhere that America led all nations in the importation of diamonds. So it did; but England, France and Germany were also excellent customers, and if relative populations and resources were weighed, they stood high in the rank of diamond buyers. However, suiting the scope of his indictment to the geographical breadth of his subject, Blouet visioned diamonds as worn, not to some extent, but *everywhere* in America; "to the American woman they are objects of prime necessity, not of luxury," and he unleashed his scorn upon the vulgarity of the display. In a page or two more he veered, and, although he still regarded all Americans as money graspers, he acquitted them of the charge that they adored it. "If the American thirsts for money, it is not for the love of money, as a rule, but for the love of that which money can buy. In other words, avarice is a vice wholly unknown in America. . . . In Europe, there is a false notion that Jonathan thinks only of money, that he passes his life in the worship of the almighty dollar. It is an error. He cares little for money at heart, but for the things money buys." [4]

The real America, patent to anyone who cared to see, was entirely different from the fable of a population surfeited with money. At the apex was a plutocracy never satisfied with its already great wealth, and ceaselessly craving more and ever still more. But nearly one-half of America's population— 29,000,000 in all, at that time—toiled in manufactures, mines, trade and transportation, agriculture, domestic and other service. The exceptional working woman might sometimes be presented with a modest diamond engagement ring, but what luxuries could she herself buy on an average weekly wage of $5.24? Such, according to the report of the United States Commissioner of Labor in 1889, was the prevalent woman's wage in the chief American cities. And men working for an average daily wage of $1.69, which was the pay of millions employed in the manufacturing industries,[5] were in no position to think of indulging in adornment. In point of stern fact, many workers in factory towns lacked even decent apparel; they were unable to go to church on Sunday because they had no appropriate clothes.[6]

It ill became critics like Blouet to sneer at diamond-wearing America when the French, German and English capitalists who controlled the diamond mines were exerting themselves to find ever wider markets, and were deriving high gratification and opulent profit from America's increased imports. And the owners of Amsterdam's cutting and polishing factories, the most extensive in the world, were also beneficiaries of the expanding traffic. Diamond finds in British, French and other European colonial possessions had long been going on, but the greatest impetus came with the discovery of the Kimberley diamond deposits in South Africa. There a number of French capitalists, incorporating themselves as the "Compagnie Française des Mines de Diamont du Cap de Bon Esperance," early preempted a block of claims running nearly across the Kimberley mines from north to south. Headed by Cecil Rhodes and other British capitalists, the DeBeers Mining Company was organized in 1880, and within the next ten years had absorbed a group of adjacent companies. These included the French company, for the holdings of which £1,400,000 was paid.[7] To keep up the price of diamonds by regulation of output, the DeBeers Company restricted annual diamond exports to between four and four-and-a-half million carats.

In South Africa there was an intense scramble for wealth—a passion reflected in the stock markets of London and other European capitals. But although the South African situation was news, and was novel in several respects, no European critics journeyed there to write accounts of the rampant money spirit. Profits from diamond mines were so large, and so dazzling were the future prospects, that both in South Africa and Europe there followed crazes of speculation in diamond mine shares.

In the early 1880's, before consolidation had been effected, there sprang up a host of diamond mining companies, some with good, others with dubious claims, and nearly all lacking adequate capital. "But," wrote a resident mining engineer on local conditions, "a speculative mania had taken possession of the public, and mining script was regarded as a sure passport to wealth. . . . Within the space of a few months, the promise of certain fortunes to investors was held out by more than a hundred diamond mining companies, and it rarely happened that any of these failed to be floated, or their shares to be rushed up to a big premium. The eagerness to be 'in the swim' silenced every prompting of prudence; clerks threw up their situations, merchants left their stores, and professional men their duties, to hang about street corners and dabble in stocks, of the real value of which they were profoundly ignorant. . . . So great was the demand for fresh stocks that claims which were known never to have paid for working were floated almost as easily as the richest proved properties." [8]

The bursting of this bubble was no lesson; later came other wild excesses. Great was the popular confidence in anything projected as a diamond mine venture. But in the operations of substantial diamond mine companies there were stupendous profits, which convinced an investing and speculating public that it could not fail in its money-making aims. Take for instance the DeBeers Mining Company. In the span of eight years it had progressively increased its capital from £200,000 to £2,332,170, on which it had paid more than £1,000,000 in dividends. These were equal to a shade less than 72 per cent on the sums at which the capital had successively stood. Moreover, stockholders were further elated by a distribution of 41 per cent in bonus stock.[9] For the period from the discovery of the South African diamond mines, in 1867, to the end of 1892, the value of the diamond export was estimated at £70,000,000. Britain

now possessed its cluster of "diamond mine magnates," to en-
hance its wealth and to radiate luster as "empire builders."
But transports of enthusiasm were not tempered by a sign of
concern, or even thought, for the native negro mine laborers.
The exploitation of these was so destructive that the death
rate regularly, year after year, was excessive—fifty-seven or
thereabouts in every thousand. Profits held sole and charmed
attention. Repeatedly speculative activity in diamond mine
shares on the London Stock Exchange was rampant; prices advanced "by leaps and bounds." And it was the support of
English, French and German capitalists that upheld the force
of this speculation.[10]

Simultaneously an "intoxicating gold mania" swept the British speculating and investing public. It was in 1886 that many
an eye opened wide when "The Times," of London, published
an authentic account of the discovery of the great Rand gold
mines in the Transvaal. The glorious reality of another prodigious source of wealth caused paroxysms of excitement.
Hastening to take advantage of this condition, promoters
rushed forward. Scores of South African mining companies
were organized, stock was issued torrentially, and every device
of manipulation was deftly engineered. Such was the "vast
throng of speculators" that the London Stock Exchange established a section dubbed the "Kaffir Circus" for dealing in South
African mining stock. Stock of some companies was propelled
to a hundred times the original issue price, while stock of other
companies which had not done a stroke of mining work was
pushed to twenty and thirty times its nominal value. In both
England and South Africa crowds were drunk with dreams of
wealth.

The dreams of the many were ruined by the collapse of
prices. But recurrently there came on new aspirants to fortune,
although in much diminished numbers. These could not be dis-
suaded from the hope that, with such vast gold wealth in South
Africa, they would somehow be blessed with luck. And they
were continually deluded by "the rascality which has been connected with many of the mines"—rascality thus defined: "Wire
pullers on the spot treat the mines which they are supposed to
manage as so many gambling vehicles. Capitals have been in-

creased over and over again, amalgamation has been forced on, and all sorts of dodges resorted to in order that a few gamblers might secure large profits." [11]

Phantom or flimsy companies faded away, but the solid gold mining corporations having rich claims and adequate funds and equipment reaped incredibly large profits. "Cabbage patch" locations, bought for trifling sums by English capitalists well informed of the riches underneath, were made the basis for the organization of mining companies which extracted an immensity of gold. After 1888, the first year in which Rand gold mining became of notable proportions, the output rose enormously. A group of grandiose "gold mine magnates" made their entry into British finance, society and politics. How often and caustically British critics expressed themselves about pioneer crudities in America, we have amply seen. South Africa was now undergoing its pioneer stage, with *its* crudities, raw environment, ugly towns, itinerancy, noisy land booms and wild wealth seeking. But in these manifestations no British or other European critic saw anything calling for adverse comment. The most favorable accounts of South African development were spread in England. On the London Stock Exchange, stock of South African land companies was a prime feature. And in publications South Africa was recommended as a place pre-eminently inviting to money-makers. A typical paean this: "Above all, for capitalists, both large and small, there are opportunities for profitable investment such as probably no other country can offer." [12]

The great influx, mostly of British subjects, into the gold districts in the Transvaal brought on a war in 1899 with the Dutch Boers, who had governmental control over the region. A description of that war is not pertinent to this narrative; but a comparison between a share of public opinion in Britain toward an American war a year previously, and the full British opinion toward the Boer War, is here competent. When, in 1898, America warred with Spain, various British newspapers and periodicals denounced America's aims. "The Speaker" condemned the American "lust for empire." "The Saturday Review" sneeringly dealt with "the oil and corn and the iron and pigs" of America, contrasting these with the poetry, art and fiction of Spain; and it told how Englishmen "are all disgusted with these raw, vulgar, blatant Americans who scour Europe in search of their self respect and cannot conduct a mere legal case with decency." The Edinburgh "News" declared that "the Yankee is thirsting for blood." And so on through an assaulting list. Toward Britain's own war, however, the general British position was that of righteous self-justification, and one victory in particular was celebrated in London by an outburst of hooliganism the like of which has seldom been witnessed in any other city of modern times.

The Transvaal was annexed to the British dominions, and with the compliance of the British Government the gold mine owners now had full license to run affairs to suit their interests. Accounts of hellish conditions in the mines reached members of the Labor group in Parliament—a group not yet large but pertinacious and militant. Severely pointed questions were put in 1903 to Cabinet ministers. The subject could not be parried, and Viscount Milner, Governor of the Transvaal, was ordered by the Government to submit information.

A series of exploitation horrors was disclosed by the reports of native inspectors, magistrates and chiefs. In America many and bitter were the contests between mine operators, notably in the coal regions, over wages, hours and other issues. But viciously bad as were conditions in many American mines, they did not begin to equal abominations in the Transvaal Rand gold mines. The bulk of mine labor there was recruited from primitive African tribes. Agents of the mine owners scoured Africa, and by promises of good wages and treatment induced hordes to leave their villages for mine labor. In the Transvaal mines there were employed nearly 75,000 negro natives, of whom 56,000 had been decoyed from Portuguese territory in Africa, and the remainder from Basutoland, British Central Africa, Bechuanaland and other regions. "The laborers proceeding to Johannesburg are packed like grain or coal bags in trucks. They are not regarded as human beings as Europeans are. No shelter of any kind on the line to Johannesburg is provided for them." [13]

Dumped in an exhausted state at the mines, the laborers found themselves under the tyranny of overseers. Some of these

were brutal Europeans; others were Zulus, from the fiercest
and most bloodthirsty tribe in South Africa. To "hustle them
and quicken their movements" negro mine workers were lashed
with cowhide whips. In some mines they were, for the slightest
infractions, put in subterranean cells. They were forced to work
on Sunday as on other days, and their pitiful wages were
drained for the companies' profit in compelling them to buy
necessaries at company stores. The havoc among underground
workers was ghastly; the mortality rates ranged between fifty
and a hundred per thousand, with an average of more than
seventy. The miners' abodes resembled a huge charnel-house;
and, with the realization borne in upon him that it was this
slaughter which was causing agitation in England, Lord Milner
reported: "The high mortality rate is the weakest point in our
armor." He sought to explain the death rate as "primarily due
to the impoverished condition in which the natives generally
arrive from their homes at the mines, and to the sudden change
from semi-tropical regions to the comparatively cold climate
and different altitude of the Witwaterstrand." [14] Under Boer
rule flogging of the native workers had been common, but the
evils under British rule were so much greater that native laborers sighed for the return of Boer government.[15]

Chinese coolie labor, the Rand gold mine owners had urged
meanwhile, was what was most needed, and with it the mines
would run peaceably. From a responsive Government in London they obtained consent; for their benefit a treaty was
quickly made with China, and cargoes of Chinese laborers were
placed at their disposal.[16] Next, the mine owners demanded the
removal of the assessment placed upon the Transvaal on account of the Boer War. It was, they complained, an "overshad-
owing incubus" upon that country's progress—meaning a drag
upon their profits in which, as stockholders, many of England's
notabilities were concerned. "South African financiers," commented "The Economist" (May 28, 1904), "have been so tenderly treated by the present Government that they apparently
imagine there is no limit to the benefits that may be showered
upon them." And there was no limit; the Government soon announced its decision to abandon all claims to a war contribution
from the Transvaal.

The death rate among workers kept mounting. Chinese coolies had not proved a successful speculation after all; and the recruiting of natives from African tropical regions went on constantly. Among the swarms of negroes brought to the mines from these torrid areas the death rate was enormous, running monthly in 1913, for instance, from one hundred and fifteen upwards per thousand. These fatalities were denounced by the Minister of Native Affairs in the Union Parliament of South Africa as "little less than murder." Evidence before the South African Commission showed that the annual death rate among certain classes of mine workers even approximated the extraordinary devastation of three hundred per thousand. Two-thirds of the native mine workers afflicted with phthisis died on the Rand, and those recovering had to travel such long distances that few reached their kraals. In recounting these gruesome facts, several members of the British Parliament sought to have a Committee of Inquiry investigate, but Secretary of State Harcourt would not accept the proposal.[17]

With these essential glimpses into affairs in a distant continent, we now go back to scanning Europe, particularly France. Anyone who had a tolerable acquaintance with life in Paris, the vaunted city of pure devotion to culture and the arts, was well aware that money was as much a lodestar there as anywhere else. In American cities newspapers of popular circulation throve on exploiting antics and scandals among the rich fashionables. To such prying, invasive publicity the wealthy in France were not exposed. But at times a scandal, by reason of its criminality and political connotations, broke through this reserve, and notoriously exemplified the power of money in drawing to its fold men reputed the most illustrious in France.

Such an edifying episode ensued in Paris, in 1892, in the sensational "Humbert Affair." America had its demonstrations of cold-blooded financial swindling, but its politics never saw anything remotely approaching this audacious and vulgar exhibition in the realms of finance and politics. Madame Humbert was the wife of a former Deputy whose father, Gustave Humbert, was Minister of Justice in 1882. She invented a claim that she and her family had inherited an English estate of several million pounds. For years, by sheer arts of persuasion, she succeeded in maintaining the imposture and in convincing even some of the most hard-headed bankers of the truth of her story. On this they loaned her huge sums which she used in sustaining a luxurious establishment, including a political salon. The atmosphere of riches and the blandishments provided were irresistible attractions for an assemblage of the most noted French politicians, who vied in basking in her gracious and golden favor. She had almost succeeded in marrying her daughter as a great heiress to a leading French politician when the thunderbolt of exposure came. A succulent topic this scandal made in Paris, and the flight of the Humberts and their arrest in Spain intensified the excitement and distraction in French politics.

And now, passing to the question of national wealth, we encounter facts jauntily overlooked by America's critics. Representing all kinds of wealth, the estimated figures were: America, eighty-one billion dollars; France, forty-eight billion dollars. In proportion to size and population, France's national wealth was manifestly greater. And the world's supply of money was widely distributed; in 1890 the world's banking resources were computed at nearly sixteen billion dollars, of which America had less than a third. Although, in the fifteen years following, American banking resources increased in greater degree, European banks in 1905 still had the lead by nearly four billion dollars.

Once again, however, in a book brought out by a prominent New York publishing house, one of the French critics depicted the entire American people as swept madly into the current of one common pursuit: "There is no diversity of striving; all are striving for money, money, money. Money here is tyrant, as it is tyrant nowhere else." He did not specify the countries in which money lacked power of command; instead, he went on: "Men will do for money here what men will do nowhere else." Precisely what was the differentiation he did not tell or even hint. This critic then went to the ludicrous extreme of lumping all Americans into one indivisible grouping: "Here all men are in the one colossal class of the money makers." [18]

Not unconscious that he was depending upon mere "impressions," another French critic dexterously turned them into a

tenuous volume of 425 pages. Throughout these emerged the
pain of a fastidious soul exceedingly shocked by America's bar-
barities. America, as Paul Bourget saw it, was a country of
incoherence and haste; its big town streets were crude; its fashionable life went to excess; its culture had an artificial tension;
its business men were ferocious; its politicians and office holders corrupt; and in its pleasures there was an absence of re-
laxation and abandonment. And so went on the list of egregious
deficiencies, some of the charges containing elements of truth
yet ringing false by the way in which they were put. Was there
in his view no worthy thing in America? He did note one feature, long before pointed out, but which he dwelt upon as
though it were his fresh and acute observation. "Great men"
(he meant rich men) acknowledged their civic duty by bequeathing large sums to public benefactions; when a man of
wealth died "without having taken steps of this kind universal
blame overshadows his memory." [19]

As Bryce had properly remarked a few years earlier, the
fault of which Americans were most frequently accused was
worship of wealth. But he had had the fairness to draw a parallel with conditions in Europe. "It may seem a paradox," he
set forth, "to observe that a millionaire has a better and easier
social career open to him in England than in America. Nevertheless, there is a sense in which this is true. In America, if his
private character be bad, if he be mean, or openly immoral, or
personally vulgar, or dishonest, the best society will keep its
doors closed against him." Parenthetically, one assertion here,
that regarding dishonesty, may be questioned as overdrawn;
business and financial dishonesty in America, so long as it did
not entail excessive scandal, conviction and prison sentence,
was no bar to the millionaire's social access, did he seek it—
which the pioneer millionaire usually did not. "In England,"
Bryce went on, "great wealth, skilfully employed, will more
readily force these doors to open. For in England great wealth
can, by using the appropriate methods, practically buy rank
from those who bestow it; or by obliging persons whose position enables them to command fashionable society, can induce
them to stand sponsors for the upstart, and force him into society, a thing which no person in America has the power of

doing." The rich man in England might be distrusted and disliked by the élite of the commercial world, he might be vulgar and uneducated, and have nothing to recommend him except his wealth and willingness to spend it in providing amusement for fashionable people. "All this will not prevent him from becoming a baronet, or possibly a peer, and thereby acquiring a position of assured dignity which he can transmit to his offspring." Bryce declared that less snobbishness was shown toward the rich in America than in England. Except in a few places in America, he noted, the very rich did not make so ostentatious display of wealth as did the rich of England or France.[20]

The difference between the original rich in America and in England was thus editorially explained by "The Economist," of London, on February 16, 1889: "We have very rich men among us, the field of speculators is quite as large as in America, or, if we include the Continent, is larger. . . . The eagerness to make money is just as great. . . . The American who has made a great fortune in business finds nothing else so interesting, and goes on accumulating, just as a whist player goes on playing, because it amuses and distracts him. . . . The English millionaire, when his fortune has become large and solid, turns to other things—takes to collecting, buys estates, founds a family, or interests himself in the much larger game of politics. . . . Great speculation involves great risks, and the Englishman never quite regards his fortune, as the American appears to do, as a mere instrument and weapon with which he plays his part in life, but rather as part of himself, the loss of which would destroy his self-respect and energy. We often hear in this country of men who have lost three fortunes which they have successively inherited, but the men who have made and lost three are rare. In America they are countless. . . ."

CHAPTER XVIII

"THE BITCH-GODDESS SUCCESS"

As the years passed, an increasing number of America's critics were novelists. Many a European purveyor of fiction, on the strength of repute acquired in a totally different field of writing, now turned reporter for the duration of his American visit. It was perhaps natural enough that this should be so. The business of novelists, as they often assert, is to create a self-sustaining world of fancy out of the aspects of real life—in other words, to turn fact into legend. But, as we have seen and shall see again, the Land of the Dollar was a legend already well established in the mind of the European observer. What, then, could be more pleasant than to visit a dream world and report the facts to be seen there—at so much per word? What better recreation could a novelist desire?

Among the more querulous of these transients was Henry James, an English novelist of American birth and antecedents. Most of his boyhood had been spent in England and on the Continent, where he was educated by private tutors. In 1860 he returned to America and studied law at Harvard. However, he remained European in view, cultivated an aloof attitude toward his native land, and resumed European residence in 1869, living thereafter in London or in a rural English retreat. After nearly a quarter of a century thus spent he revisited America, and recorded his impressions in a book, "The American Scene."

Characteristically, Henry James' analysis of American life abounded in fine-drawn aesthetic distinctions. It was couched in the involved style habitual with him, since, even in his proper field, he was a coterie-writer. His tangible statements were infrequent, but a few did emerge here and there. He was affrighted by the "Trusts and the weight of the new remorseless monopolies that operate as no madnesses of ancient personal

240

power . . . ever operated. . . ." He was repelled by "the huge American rattle of gold," the "endless backing of money" that conferred sacrosanct privilege upon wealth-owners. Uneasy in America, Henry James returned to England once more. In 1915 he became a naturalized British subject; and not long afterward he was decorated by King George with the Order of Merit.

Henry James' brother, Professor William James, had also been educated in Europe. Both men, as Henry wrote with a strong tincture of pride in one of his autobiographical volumes, had acquired an attitude of detachment toward America. But William James released himself from this genteel tradition and attached himself to America; or, as a recent commentator expresses it, he "found" America.[1] He became a convert—albeit a "metaphysical" one, whatever that term may convey—to the doctrine of democracy. But on one occasion this deservedly famous philosopher descended to that type of error which makes a partial statement seem a whole truth. He scored as distinctively American "the squalid cash interpretation put on the word success"—"the moral flabbiness born of the exclusive worship of the bitch-goddess success." That last is a telling phrase. On the evidence, however, one must submit that it deserves a wider application than William James intended for it.

And now for the first time, in 1906, came H. G. Wells, whose scientific romances had proved him the possessor of a bold imagination. In writing about America, though, he stressed the point that his book embodied "a search after the realities." As put forth by Wells, these so-called realities turned out to be merely the projection of hackneyed prejudices. For example, he laid down this dictum: "In no other country and in no other age could they [the men of wealth] have risen to such eminence." In the way this was put it was, of course, sheer nonsense; Wells should have consulted history sooner than he did. Evidently unfamiliar with the fact that only a small section of America had been settled by Puritans, Wells went on gravely: "America is still by virtue of its great Puritan tradition and in the older sense of the word an intensely moral land. Most lusts are strongly curbed by public opinion, by training and tradition. But the lust of acquisition has not been curbed but glorified. . . . They [the Americans] have no doubt carried sharpness to the very edge of dishonesty but what else was to be expected from American conditions? Only by doing so and taking risks is pre-eminent success in getting to be attained." [2]

A variation on this theme was supplied by the English novelist Arnold Bennett, described by an editorial interviewer as a "brilliant one-man literary machine." Presumably, he had been solicited for a book on America, and post-haste he did it—192 pages, at the end of which came this burst of honest confession: "On the subject of America, I do not even know enough to be fully aware of my own ignorance. Still I am fully sensible of the enormous imperfection and rashness of this book. When I regard the map and see the trifling extent of the ground that I covered—a scrap tucked away in the northeast corner of the vast multi-colored territory—I marvel at the assurance I displayed in choosing my title. Indeed, I have yet to see your United States." [3] If Bennett had any prankish disposition he must have chuckled over the hoax that he had perpetrated, when, candidly facing his own hot pursuit of money and knowing that of other English fiction writers, he gave the wonted theme of American business men a new cast in his book. Suppose those business men did love money? Did not many money-seeking writers love it too? So Bennett cogitated. He himself later told in "The Journal of Arnold Bennett" that he turned from editorial work to fiction expressly for greater pecuniary returns. And he made money fast from his writings—$80,000 in the year 1912 alone. He drove a keen bargain with American editors, demanding two shillings a word for his articles. At his death in 1931 his estate of $500,000 ranked as one of the largest literary fortunes in English history; Charles Dickens had left $400,000, and Anthony Trollope $350,000.

To critics like Henry James the simple thought of scrutinizing conditions other than American never proposed itself. If, living as he did in an abstract atmosphere, Henry James was unaware of great business combinations in Britain and in continental Europe, the fact of those combinations was nevertheless patent. The divergence between American and European combinations was but one of names used, magnitude of capital, and public status.

In America there had been formed an agglomeration of more than four hundred and forty large industrial, franchise and transportation consolidations with a total capital exceeding $20,000,000,000. Much of the avalanche of stock issued was goodwill or watered stock, usually based upon monopolistic anticipation of earning power from the ability to control production and prices.[4] These massive amalgamations were called Trusts in America, and as fast as they arose they incited bitter public opposition. As economic evolutions of gigantic power, the Trusts developed capital to an unprecedented degree, and it was because of this great concentration of wealth, not to mention their threat to the liberty of individual enterprise, that public sentiment was strongly antagonistic. The Trusts were repeatedly subjected to investigations by legislative committees and to the enactment of drastic laws. The Sherman anti-Trust act passed by Congress in 1890 made Trusts in restraint of trade illegal, and the persons involved liable to prosecution. Many Federal investigations of Trusts followed. To evade law and to place their beneficiaries or retainers in high pivotal political office, various Trusts resorted to corruption whenever the need arose. The Trust issue was long a furious one in American political campaigns, and the resounding excitement centered general attention upon America as the country under the yoke of the Trusts.

Yet at the same time the movement to consolidate industry into great organizations of capital had been proceeding in Europe. Britain had its industrial combinations; but they were termed "pools" or "rings," and their progress was unattended by the inimical clamor of popular agitation. On the contrary, their legal fiat came early. In 1891 British shipowners had formed a combination to extend trade and increase profits. In this leading case—the "Mogul" case—the House of Lords' ruling established the legality of shipping "rings," and, in subsequent years, further sanctioning decisions followed.

When complaints were made about this monopoly, which had raised rates on almost all ocean routes, Parliament stirred and ordered an investigation. The result was wholly palatable to the shipowners. The public, a minority of the investigating committee reported, was bled in higher rates. The committee's majority report admitted existence of a "limited monopoly," raising of rates, payment of secret rebates and other arbitrary acts. But, taking the stand that most shipowners were "public-spirited men," it could see no reason for Government action—or rather "interference." If merchants and shippers had to have a remedy, the committee's majority accommodatingly suggested, they could organize counter combinations.[5]

Year after year the reports of British shipping corporations to stockholders told of great profits, often on progressively watered stock. Equally prolific in returns were other British combinations controlling the iron, coal, textile, dyeing, thread, soap, tobacco, wall-paper, salt and other industries, all heavily overcapitalized on not much more than the intangible item of "good will." So certain of their prospects were many of these combinations that to attract the ordinary investor they held out alluring expectations of seven or eight per cent dividends.[6]

In the course of two decades of consolidations and other paper operations, the great British railway companies had expanded their capital stock to the colossal sum of £1,000,000,-000. The object of this watering was to keep up rates and fares, and to prevent construction of competing lines. And the methods used in stock issues were of such intricacy and so well covered that only by the most arduous labor could an outsider unravel the tangle.[7] As to other combinations, the time was not far distant when English banks were virtually merged into six institutions having huge financial power, and when powerful mergers in the chemical, rubber, tin and other mining industries were consummated. Meanwhile, much British wealth was invested in the securities of American Trusts.

Glancing at continental Europe we find other such great concentrations of capital. Germany was the chief creator of combinations; there, in 1897, three hundred and forty-five openly flourished. Presently, the smaller combinations were swallowed by the larger. German law did not inhibit combinations, and German court decisions dealt gently, and often favorably, with the great syndicates of capital. In France, where the penal code contained severe provisions against private monopoly, existing combinations had to move with the greatest caution and shroud their price control agreements in well-guarded secrecy. Combinations controlled many branches of industry in Austria, and had nothing to fear from officialdom; a Government Commission even recommended their validation and regulation.

Thus the Trust, which in America so impressed Henry James as an appalling, formidable phenomenon, had its counterparts in various European countries—not to speak of South America, Japan, Australia and New Zealand. And the dishonestly acquisitive spirit which Wells construed as peculiar to America was obviously commonplace throughout the world. Wells, the man who could write "Tono Bungay," had occasion enough to know how a spectacular episode in England had recently disclosed the avidity of all classes, from peers down, to make money by following the lead of a man reputed a financial wizard.

Ernest Terah Hooley was a lacemaker, then a stockbroker in Nottingham, before he injected his presence into financial London. He seems not to have been exceptionally able, but he had a conjuring idea. This concerned the applying of methods of consolidation to certain industries which promoters before him had ignored. He also had a naturally shrewd insight into the weaknesses, credulity and trust of the British investing public. His process was the simple one of arranging to buy a company's business for more than its value, obtaining credit for the transaction, watering the stock, and then by a "whirlwind" campaign selling the securities to the public for far more than the business was worth. This was the era when bicycle riding was the vogue; of the twenty-six companies promoted by Hooley between 1894 and 1896, fifteen were bicycle corporations. Well understanding British susceptibility to titled names, he easily secured lords to serve on his boards of directors; other lords deemed it a high privilege to partake of financial dealings with the "Napoleon of Finance"—for so he was acclaimed.

His dealings totaled £25,000,000; he towered a golden colossus in Britain. "Fashionable society, always in a hurry to get richer, hung on his lightest word," editorialized "The Economist" at a later time. "Ancient colleges and venerable deans shed the light of their countenances upon him with a lively sense of benefits to come. Processions knew him clothed in the

magnificence of a High Sheriff. His name connoted millions."
From Lord Ashburton, Hooley bought an estate of nearly
11,000 acres in Wiltshire and paid for it in stock of one of his
companies. He then employed a renowned architect, giving him
carte-blanche to put the entire estate in first-class condition;
£27,000 was expended on buildings alone. Hooley also bought
an estate of 3,244 acres in Essex, spending many thousands of
pounds in its improvement. For a yacht—the Venetia—he paid
Lord Ashburton £50,000. Furthermore, as subsequent disclosures showed, he aspired to the distinction of a title and had
handed in to the proper recipient the sum agreed upon for the
purchase of a baronetcy.

London had its crowd of lesser promoters to whom Hooley
was the idol of superior daring. To pass over the schemes of
other promoting coteries, we need only notice as an example
those then fattening on the public by the flotation of stock of
mine ventures in West Australia—Westralia, as it was called.
Apart from the many mining companies organized in Westralia
itself, hundreds of companies had in a short time been floated
in London. The total capital of these Westralia companies,
£39,000,000, was further watered, bringing it to £55,000,000.
This was approximately the same capitalization as that of all
the Transvaal mines, including those of the Rand, which in a
few months produced as much gold as did the whole of Westralia in a year. Rosy prospectuses gulled a swarm of investors,
and the promoters and stock vendors pocketed on an average
almost three-fourths of the proceeds of Westralia mine stock
sold.[8]

Many of these promoters held on both to their harvest of
loot and to their fair reputations. But Hooley's fate was different. His pyramided system of credit inflation could not with-
stand collapse, and, on June 8, 1898, he filed his petition in
bankruptcy. His failure made a great commotion. Reflecting
upon the event, a leading London periodical noted: "Considering what a great commercial people we have been for centuries,
it is strange how easily a large section of Englishmen can be
deluded." Then, proffering an explanation, it went on: "But it
is safe to say that the average investor is most taken, not by
the business matter, but by the names on the prospectus. Who

ever heard of Lords Albermarle and De La Warr as great financial or business authorities? We say nothing as to the financial transactions which passed between them and Mr. Hooley; but even assuming that they had never received 'gifts,' how strange to the rational mind that any person should have rushed to buy Hooley shares at a considerable premium because these titled names appeared on a prospectus! In America they would have needed the name of a very strong Wall Street magnate or high-placed railway president, an authority in the greater business transactions. But here the names of two Lords of little or no experience are considered to be enough to attract the county clergy, maiden ladies and shopkeepers who are in an especial degree the victims of the company promoter." [9]

Hooley announced that he had not benefited personally by the large sums realized from stock-jobbing operations. Both in interview and in his minute, voluminous and sensational testimony in the bankruptcy proceedings, he asserted that financial journalists had squeezed considerable sums from him, either to assure favorable publicity or by the threat of criticism. He exonerated the owners of any knowledge concerning these transactions, but, so he said, a single article in one financial journal cost him £10,000. The representative of another such publication blackmailed him for £40,000. Every time he organized a new company, he stated, at least twenty of these men besieged him in the corridor of the Midland Grand Hotel where he stayed, and openly demanded of him: "Well, what are we going to get out of this?"

"This," "The Economist," of London, editorially commented on June 11, 1898, "is by no means the first time that charges of gross corruption have been leveled against a section of the financial press, but the charges have been put forward in a concrete form upon very few occasions, although it is notorious that large sums of money are continually being paid away either for newspaper puffs of companies or for the suppression of unfavorable criticism. And if one of the results of Mr. Hooley's failure is the exposure of malpractices of the kind suggested, that failure will be anything but an unmixed evil, for nothing could be more contemptible than for journals professing to guide and protect the investing classes to enter into a lucrative conspiracy with company magnates to defraud those who follow their advice. The system is a gross public scandal."

The testimony by Hooley before the Registrar in Bankruptcy was viewed in England as disgraceful revelations of political corruption. "They leave a bad taste in the mouth," commented "The Times" of London. "The case reeks with moral garbage," declared "The Spectator." Hooley had related that when Sir William Marriott was introduced to him, Marriott informed him: "I do all of the dirty work for the Conservative Party." Hooley told under oath how he had paid £1,000 for admission to the Carlton Club, the Conservative stronghold, and how he had contributed two checks, each for £5,000, to Lord Abergavenny for the Conservative Party's campaign fund. Further, Hooley related his bargaining with Marriott to have himself made a baronet at the distribution of honors at Queen Victoria's jubilee celebration. Hooley unsuccessfully haggled to have the sum fixed at £35,000; he had to pay £50,000, the amount asked. Rumors of Hooley's imminent bankruptcy had already spread, but when the £50,000 check was taken to a prominent London bank for inquiry, the assurance was given that, of course, the check of a man worth at least £1,000,000 would be honored. Perhaps Premier Lord Salisbury knew too much of Hooley's devious methods and hazardous position, and judged the risk of recommending him for a baronetcy too great; whatever the reasons, Hooley's name was not included in the list of honors, and after several months his £50,000 check was returned.[10]

We need not linger upon Hooley's checkered career. After getting out of bankruptcy he continued to speculate in land and to float companies—one a Siberian gold mine. The culmination came in February, 1912, when he was convicted of obtaining £2,000 by fraud, and was sentenced to twelve months' imprisonment. Many a British editor then moralized upon the ignominious end of a man who at one time was credited with a magician's power in creating wealth by the millions and in dispensing fortunes.

Certain phases of the Hooley disclosures, however, remained either to disturb British conscience or vex British complacency. Often had American campaign corruption been made the text of preachments on the integrity of the British system. In America campaign corruption was admitted, and what was not specifically admitted was brought out in Congressional and legislative investigations. Trusts, railroad companies, corporations of all kinds, and rich individuals periodically contributed large amounts for campaign election purposes. Before a special committee of the United States Senate, the president of the Sugar Trust testified that this "politics of business" was the custom of "every individual and corporation and firm, Trust, or whatever you like to call it." [11] He further testified that, in State campaigns, the dominant party always received the contribution. The funds were variously used. Emissaries were employed to influence the trade-unions. Newspapers were bought up or filled with provided editorials or with partisan matter represented as news. Foreign-language newspapers were subsidized. A host of "orators" were sent out to "spellbind." And wherever votes could be bought they were bought.

So much for America. But now English editors were again driven to acknowledge that political corruption was not confined to America—that Britain had its own kind, whereby the patronage of the Government was prostituted in order to fill the campaign fund on the eve of a general election. Unlike the American plan, the English system did not require so crude an expedient as the general conscription of funds for election. In England the party managers recommended to the Prime Minister wealthy candidates for peerages, baronetcies and knighthoods—the aspirants, meanwhile, sending large sums of money to the political clubs. Recalling that the claim of wealth as a title of entrée to the peerage had long since been conceded in England, one London periodical discoursed: "Forty years ago everybody said simple knighthood was contemptible, unworthy even of a Lord Mayor, but today a good many persons are willing to purchase that lowest of titular distinctions for £25,-000. . . . Moreover, the English with all their virtues, and they have many, are plutocrats at heart. They reverence wealth, they like those who lead them to be rich, and if titles were sold in open market, they would purchase them as evidence of riches." And again in the same periodical: "Unfortunately, the multiplied chances to be very rich have not only turned men's heads, but they have weakened their morals. . . . Even in England, in spite of all that legislation has done—and we gladly admit that in this country it has done much—we doubt if, among large classes of the electorate, bribery is looked upon with the severe moral reprobation which one would like to see. . . . While actual gifts of money to voters are very rare, while expenditure is not permitted by law on the great scale of former years, nevertheless the constant checks forwarded to local bodies by Members [of Parliament] on the one hand, and the directorships of companies assumed by Members [of Parliament] who are not especially noted for business gifts on the other hand, appear to show a laxity of view regarding absolute financial honor which at times fills one with a certain misgiving as to the future." [12]

Charges were made that the conferring of titles was but one way in which the British Ministry paid off campaign contributions. Directing attention to grants of public money to special "interests," "The Economist" on August 12, 1899, bluntly declared that the Government had given the impression that it was paying off its election debts to its supporters, and was thereby introducing the worst feature of American politics— "though it might perhaps be better described as reviving the old methods practiced in England in the last century." Then followed this discharge: "It is undeniable that during the Session just ended there has been an atmosphere of money in the lobby and precincts of the House of Commons scarcely noticed before. All manner of 'interests' have gathered there as they gather in Washington and in the various State Legislatures of America. More attempts to influence the votes of members have been made than has been known before, or, at any rate, than members can recollect since the days of railway construction."

A singular disclosure seeming to confirm this charge came out unexpectedly in later years. It was a regular practice of "The Economist" to publish full stenographic accounts of the annual meetings of stockholders of companies. At such a yearly meeting of the London United Tramways, in January, 1912, the chairman reported, among other items, legal expenses incurred. R. F. Parker, a stockholder, arose and drew critical attention to the law charges and Parliamentary expenses. It might have been possible in the course of the past fifteen or sixteen years, he protested, to have saved some of the great amounts spent in Parliamentary matters. Expenses of that kind, he urged, should in future receive the serious consideration of the board of directors. The stenographic account proceeded: "The chairman, in reply, said that there was no desire on the part of the directors to go into more Parliamentary business than was necessary. He wished the stockholders, however, to remember that they had a great many concessions [franchises] and when those concessions were nearly run out, they had to go to Parliament to get them renewed, or allow them to lapse altogether." [13] This was one of the rare leakages occuring in the affairs of British corporations, and was quite accidental; there was a grievous oversight somewhere in not censoring that report.

The sale of titular honors continued a favorite means of raising campaign funds. Denouncing the practice, O. Locker-Lampson, a member of the House of Commons, sought, on May 19, 1914, to obtain leave of that body for the introduction of a bill prohibiting the traffic. Many of the persons recently receiving titles, he pointed out, were astonishingly mediocre, and the amazing size of some of the party funds could not be wholly unrelated. He went on: "Titles, like boots and shoes and even potatoes, have become marketable commodities, and are dealt in as such. There is a division of labor on the Front Treasury Bench, because while the Chancellor of the Exchequer is busy catering for the million, the Chief Whip of the Party is busy catering for the millionaire." Locker-Lampson characterized the House of Lords as "the Mecca of Snobs." A sardonically amusing argument was made by J. M. Hogge in opposing the motion. "Bear in mind," he urged, "that we want to preserve our nobility and that an infusion of fresh blood will prevent it from declining. It improves our stock. . . . Look at the traffic in titles between this country and America. There is no tariff on the importation of American heiresses, and it surely is necessary . . . to secure increased capital from abroad, and that can only be secured by multiplying the present titles that exist in the country." [14]

Parliament still abounded with members who held directorships in corporations. Of the House of Lords, a number were
what were dubbed "guinea pigs"—lords serving in the capacity
of decorative directors. But there were other members who
owned vast corporate holdings, which they secured by their
own influential power. An instance was the British South Africa
Company, the incorporators of which were the Duke of Abercorn, the Duke of Fife, Lord Gifford, Cecil Rhodes, diamond
magnate Alfred Beit, and others. In 1889 this company obtained a sweeping charter, vesting in it an enormous area of
land and the authority to engage in almost any kind of business or undertaking. It was empowered to establish steamship
lines, railways, telegraphs, carry on mining and industries, grant
lands—in brief, to do anything it wanted, even to the making
of laws and the maintaining of a military police force. It was
the greatest chartered company created in modern times, and
its powers were qualified in only one respect. The British Government reserved the right to alter or repeal any of the provisions, or to enact others, at the end of twenty-five years from
the charter's date and every decade thereafter.[15] Grave charges
that company men had knowledge of the Jameson raid in the
Transvaal before the Boer War were doubtless instrumental
in causing the issue, in 1900, of a supplemental charter to de-
prive the company of its law-making and military powers.[16]

The wealth-producing possibilities of this company were
thought to be of such magnitude that there was a rush of European investors to obtain stock. The company's original capital was a million shares at £1 each. There was great speculation in the stock, the price of which was boomed to £8 a share.
A report to the House of Commons, in 1895, showed that of
nearly fifteen thousand stockholders, three thousand were
French holding more than 252,000 shares, and four hundred
and fifty were German with 38,370 shares. But development of
Rhodesia was slow, dividends were matters of gradual future
development, and the price of stock fell below par. The company's heads had to console stockholders with visions of future
profits from its extensive land possessions, its huge power sites,
and its gold and copper mining in the area of 450,000 square
miles over which it held domain. And to the applause of as-

sembled stockholders, the company's spokesman boasted that its land rights "made the British South Africa Company incomparably the greatest land owning company in the world." [17]

Agitation was recurrent over directorships in corporations held by Cabinet Ministers. In 1900 there had been a loud scandal concerning the financial interests controlled by Colonial Secretary Joseph Chamberlain and members of his family in corporations that were securing Government contracts. Chamberlain had signalized his entry into political life by exposing a crooked official in Birmingham. After entering Parliament as a Liberal Unionist, in 1885 Chamberlain had severely attacked Prime Minister Lord Salisbury, Conservative Party leader, because Salisbury and his friends in the House of Lords had insisted upon putting in an Act a clause the effect of which was calculated to give an enormously enhanced value to Salisbury's own property in London. Now, on December 10, 1900, Joseph Chamberlain, his son, J. Austen Chamberlain, Financial Secretary of the Treasury, and Arthur, a brother of Joseph, were criticized in the House of Commons by David Lloyd George. No charge of corruption was made by Lloyd George, who simply stated facts of record.

Joseph Chamberlain, as Colonial Secretary, had issued strict orders to his subordinates forbidding them to have any interest in companies that did business with the Government. Thus beginning, Lloyd George referred to recent cases of Cabinet Ministers, some of whom were directors of companies having Government contracts, and others of whom were stockholders in companies contracting with their own departments. As to the Chamberlain family, Lloyd George specified that: 1) While Colonial Secretary, Joseph Chamberlain was a stockholder (the number of shares was stated) in the Colombo Commercial Company, which was awarded a Government contract to build barracks or huts in Ceylon for Boer prisoners of war. 2) That he was a considerable stockholder in the Birmingham Trust (Company), which in turn was a large stock owner in Tubes, Limited, and in Elliott's Metal Company. Formed to acquire bicycle companies, Tubes had sunk to bad condition, and Arthur Chamberlain was brought in to save it. He did so by converting it into a boiler-tube manufactory; contracts were secured from the British Admiralty, and the company was now making a profit of £10,000 a year as contractors to the British Navy. Joseph Chamberlain transferred his stock in Elliott's Metal Company to his son; practically half of the company's stock was owned by the Chamberlain family; and the company had contracts to supply large quantities of materials to the naval dockyards. 3) In Knoch's, manufacturers of cordite and other munitions of war, another Chamberlain had an interest; likewise the Chamberlain family in another company. Favoritism in the awarding of Government contracts, it was charged, was shown to one company.[18]

During the discussion in the House of Commons, Sir Henry Campbell-Bannerman quoted with approval this rule proposed by "The Economist": If a Cabinet Minister happened to be directly or indirectly connected with any company the dividends of which were affected by his influence, he should sever his directorship before taking office. When Campbell-Bannerman became Prime Minister a few years later he announced, in forming his Administration, that he would consider anyone holding corporation directorship ineligible to serve in his Cabinet. That pronouncement, however, applied to Cabinet Ministers only; and as it had no legal force, never going beyond the plane of an ethical stand and an individual ruling, it had neither permanence nor effectiveness.

So, in the House of Commons, on March 26, 1913, Swift MacNeill asked H. H. Asquith, now Prime Minister, whether the Government would consider introducing legislation to make illegal the holding of corporation directorships by Cabinet Ministers. "I think the rule is a good one," replied Asquith, "but I do not see my way to introduce legislation to make it binding upon future Administrations." MacNeill inquired whether Asquith was not aware that in a prior Administration eleven Cabinet Ministers held seventeen corporation directorships, and fifteen Administration heads held twenty-five directorships among them? Asquith remained silent. Somewhat more than a fortnight later MacNeill resumed the subject, asking Asquith to furnish a report as to corporate directorships held by Cabinet Ministers. "The information sought," said Asquith, "is obtainable without difficulty from other sources." MacNeill pressed:

"I cannot for the life of me ascertain what contracts of Government departments are being executed by companies which have Ministerial directors. Will he [Asquith] make a compromise with me and give me a return [formal report] of the contracts which the Government had with the Royal Mail Company when Lord Selbourne was one of the directors?" Asquith: "I should be very sorry to make any such promise. Neither do I think that for the life of me I could grant the return." [19]

Meanwhile, Lloyd George, now Chancellor of the Exchequer, and Attorney-General Sir Rufus Isaacs were under fire for a transaction which caused much talk out of Parliament and excitement in it. Marconi's invention of wireless telegraphy had been commercialized by newly organized companies. The English Marconi Company was the largest stockholder in the American Marconi Company, and Godfrey Isaacs, a brother of Rufus, was a managing director of the English Marconi Company. A contract with the English Marconi Company was made by Postmaster-General Herbert Samuel for the establishment of a chain of wireless stations throughout the British Empire.

So thick were the rumors regarding the circumstances of this contract that Postmaster-General Samuel forestalled opponents by himself moving in the House of Commons, on October 11, 1912, for a Select Committee to investigate. This motion opened the way for sundry members to express themselves. The contract, said Sir Henry Norman, had been criticized on two grounds—first that it was a bad bargain, and second "that it is a bargain tainted with corruption." He, Norman, believed such criticism preposterous, but, he urged, the persons who had made charges ought to be summoned. "Grave rumors are all over the city," said George Lansbury, Labor member, "that people have made money out of the business who ought not to have made money out of it." Both Lloyd George and Sir Rufus Isaacs demanded to know what the rumors and charges were. "I made no charge," Lansbury replied. "All that I have said is that there has been disgraceful, scandalous gambling in the shares." Rufus Isaacs and Lloyd George had the opportunity then and there to tell of their participation, but neither divulged a word. Postmaster-General Samuel made an explicit statement that, "Neither I myself nor any of my colleagues have had at any time one shilling's worth of shares in this company, directly or indirectly, or have derived one penny profit from the fluctuations in price." [20]

However, as later specifically published, the main facts were: Attorney-General Rufus Isaacs had bought 10,000 American Marconi shares as a speculation, and he had induced Lloyd George and another Ministerial colleague to take 1,000 shares each. All swore that they had lost money in the speculation, for the stock had fallen from a boom to a low price. Here at any rate was the delectable sight of how Rufus Isaacs, one of the cleverest of lawyers, Lloyd George, the cleverest of clever politicians, and an associate who was the cleverest of wire-pullers, had stepped into a pitfall. Differing slightly, the Select Committee's reports exonerated the Cabinet Ministers concerned from any corrupt thought or act. The main report was a complete vindication. That of the Conservative members was likewise, but it did think that unwittingly the Attorney-General had placed himself in a position where private interest might easily have conflicted with public duty.

In the ensuing debate in the House of Commons, on June 13, 1913, Sir Rufus Isaacs and Lloyd George frankly admitted that in making the investments they had been ill-advised. They might have added that the most astute of legal luminaries and politicians could be the worst of amateurs in stock speculation —a fact well attested in many countries. Prime Minister Asquith spoke at length upon the move to prohibit Cabinet Ministers from owning stock in any company with which the Government had or might have a contract. He declared the proposal an absurdity. But, he concluded, a stock-owning Minister should disclose his holdings, and stand aside while the contract was being made. And, furthermore, no Cabinet Ministers should enter into any transaction whereby their private pecuniary interests might conflict with public duty. Asquith put these principles upon the ground of ethics, but he failed to see that they should also apply to stock-owning members of Parliament while voting on legislation that affected their individual financial interests.

Finally, after considering various motions, accompanied by maneuvers and by "conversations" behind the scenes, the

House of Commons found a self-satisfying solution as to the disposition of the Rufus Isaacs-Lloyd George matter. Commons adopted a resolution which accepted expressions of regret made by these men for not having mentioned their stock purchases in the debate of October 11; acquitted them of acting otherwise than in good faith; and, "reprobates the charges against Ministers which have proved to be wholly false." [21]

Sir Rufus Isaacs was later created Lord Reading, and for a time was British Ambassador at Washington.

CHAPTER XIX

RUBBER MADNESS AND WORLD TRADE

In his purely literary productions Maurice Maeterlinck, Belgian poet, playwright and essayist, showed penetrating individuality. In his attitude toward America, however, he aligned himself with a fashion when he stigmatized the American people as exhibiting "the most pitiless commercialism in the world." At the time of Maeterlinck's statement his own country, headed by King Leopold II, had recently been exposed as responsible for a commercialism so murderous as to make all other exposures elsewhere tame in comparison, and to shock a world grown callous to revelations of inhumanity in pursuit of trade.

The invention of rubber-tired vehicles, first the bicycle and then the automobile, created an ever-mounting demand for rubber. There was a concerted rush in several European countries to form corporations for the acquiring and exploiting of rubber-producing regions. These lay in the tropics where a variety of trees yielded a sap which was worked into rubber. In the Congo district of Africa, Belgium possessed an estimated 900,000 square miles of territory, equal to nearly one-third of the expanse of the United States of America. This vast domain had been constituted the Congo Independent State by a Congress of European powers, which decreed King Leopold sovereign. Under his supervision, bureaus at Brussels administered the Congo colony's affairs, with a proconsular representative at Boma, recently no more than an inland post, but now styled the Congo's capital.

As in other parts of Africa, the tribes in the Congo had collectively owned the land. This communal system was abolished by the Belgian Government, and the entire territory was claimed as the private property of the Belgian State, which parceled out huge areas to great corporations called concessionaires. A native population of 30,000,000 was put under the direct domination of exploiters whose every order and movement was backed by armed troops. At first the corporations applied themselves to the trade in ivory, palm oil, nuts and some other commodities, but with the swelling demand for rubber they turned their chief efforts to that product.

Presently the British Government received memorials from English philanthropic societies whose missionaries were in the Congo, and like reports from British consuls there. These communications all told of systematic atrocities, seemingly incredible but vouched for as absolutely true. Upon every Congo village was laid a rubber-collecting imposition, and, if villages failed to gather and deliver the required amount, the troops of concession companies destroyed them, made the men prisoners, and gave away or sold their wives. The shooting of natives for slight reason or none at all was tragically frequent, and as proof that the soldiers had fully done their merciless duty, there was general mutilation of the dead. Mutilation of the living was a prevalent cruelty inflicted as "punishment" at the arbitrary will of commanders. Such were some of the charges; and, independently of memorials and reports, the British press published accounts which fired even the most phlegmatic temperaments.

The British Government was stirred to action. In 1903 Lord Lansdowne, Secretary of State for Foreign Affairs, wrote to British Ambassadors at the various European capitals. There was, he stated, a wide and grave suspicion in England that many of the charges were founded upon truth. The time had come, he declared, when the British Government had to consider whether the Powers signatory to the Treaty of Berlin regarded the system in the Congo consonant with the Treaty's provisions. Furthermore, it was competent to question whether the granting to concession companies of vast areas of territory with complete monopolies of trade was permissible.[1]

Driven now to take notice of the charges, the Belgian Government denied the existence of any systematic régime of cruelty and oppression in the Congo. It put the Aborigines' Protection Society in the category of irresponsible accusers. The term "Congo atrocities," it asserted, was invented by English and other adventurers who, it more than hinted, were motivated by commercial jealousy. As tending to support this imputation, the Belgian official statement pointed to circumstantial facts. In 1887 the Congo Independent State had exported hardly thirty tons of rubber, but after 1895 the Congo rubber trade had developed remarkably, exports rising from 10,000,-000 francs in 1895 to 50,000,000 francs in 1902. The annual collection of rubber in the Congo now amounted to five thousand tons which were sold at Antwerp. It was after this great increase began, the Belgian statement held, that the campaign atrocity charges was started.

Passing to another line of defence, Belgium claimed for itself the credit of having civilized the Congo. Then, expressing surprise at England's stand, the Belgian statement declared: "She certainly has not escaped criticism in regard to her numerous and bloody wars against native populations, nor the reproach of oppressing natives and invading their liberty." [2] With full grounds Belgium might have accused some other European nations whose inroads in Africa were marked by slaughter; at that very time the Germans in German Southwest Africa were butchering the resisting Herreros, and had established a system closely resembling slavery among tribes in their power.

The British Government ordered Sir Roger Casement, Consul at Boma, to investigate Congo conditions. His elaborate report, giving full evidence, confirmed most of the charges. The infamies practised on helpless natives to instil terror and ensure obedience were set forth in detail. Women were held as prisoners to compel their husbands to bring in the prescribed amount of rubber on each market day. Under armed guards natives were marched to the company agency, each native carrying his fortnightly supply of rubber. Many natives had been killed for not having turned in the required amount of rubber, and mutilation by cutting off of hands was one of the lesser punishments. "The Concession Companies, I believe," Casement reported, "account for the armed men in their service on the ground that their factories [agencies] and agents must be protected against the possible violence of the rude forest dwellers with whom they must deal; but this legitimate need for safeguarding European establishments does not suffice to account for the presence, far from these establishments, of large numbers of armed men quartered throughout the native villages." [3]

In effect, the Belgian Government admitted the truth of a number of these charges when, in 1906, it promulgated a series of reform decrees. These prohibited collection of taxes by men armed with guns; abolished punitive expeditions against villages; and ordered the punishing of any State functionary making exactions from natives. But although systematic atrocities were now formally forbidden, systematic exploitation remained.

The Belgian Minister to England might, as he did in 1911, represent Congo conditions as further improved by the abolition of forced labor for public works, and by curtailment of the concession companies' power in the reducing of holdings of two of them from 30,000,000 to 220,000 acres. Only a few days after this statement had been made, Vandervelde, a Socialist leader, produced in the Belgian Chamber of Deputies a batch of official documents. These evidenced that many natives, said to be "volunteers" employed in Congo posts and stations, were brought there by force and held by force. Despite proclaimed law, the documents also showed, liquors were widely sold to the natives. Another Belgian Socialist leader, Coppoierters, denounced what he called the continuing ruthless exploitation of the Congo on the most vicious of capitalist lines, and he assailed the concession companies as "making huge profits." Early in the next year—1912—the Reverend J. Harris, after traveling five thousand miles of Congo territory, arrived at Boma where he reported to British Consul Lamont: "On the rubber plantations the contract labor is today very largely impressed labor, or, as the director of one commercial company humorously termed it, 'volunteers by the rope,' i.e., recruited and then sent to the plantations roped neck to neck." [4]

The Belgian Government, remonstrated a memorial of the Congo Reform Association to the British Government in 1912, had "by an unparalleled act of spoliation" expropriated all of the natives' land in the Congo and had never repealed its act. The memorial went on: "In many parts of the British, French and German dependencies [in Africa] the native population is allowed to cultivate for its own use cocoa, rubber and other products. The population of the Congo is debarred from such enterprises." [5]

Nevertheless, British as well as other European capitalists were concerned about their own profits and heedless of the natives' rights and welfare. In Ashanti, on the west coast of Africa, the British had introduced themselves by burning its main place or capital in 1874, and had formally annexed the country in 1896. The adjacent Gold Coast, stretching three hundred and fifty miles along the Gulf of Guinea, was likewise under British mastery. When the palm oil, petroleum, mineral and other resources of these colonies first attracted European capitalists, they had taken immediate steps to vest land ownership in themselves. They bribed the tribal chiefs who were the trustees for the tribes' communal lands. In a report describing how large land concessions were thus made, an investigator sent by the British Government could see no greed on the part of interloping corporations. He saw only the rapacity of the chiefs, "whose sense of obligation to the tribe in respect of their trusteeship was frequently obscured by their greed for money." [6]

The unmitigated demoralization of an entire people went on in Nigeria, another African territory under British control. Nigeria contained by estimate more than 300,000 square miles. It had a population of about 25,000,000, and for administrative purposes was divided into Northern Nigeria and Southern Nigeria. For more than a century Nigeria's main staples of palm oil and palm kernels had been monopolized by powerful British chartered corporations. The old practice of drenching aborigines with liquor was methodically carried on by British traders, who so habituated natives to the use of gin that to them it became both a means of barter and a sign of wealth.

A series of complaints by missionaries caused the appointment of a Parliamentary investigating committee. Evidence showed the regular annual importation into Southern Nigeria alone of 3,000,000 gallons of gin. "Traffic in spirits practically dominates trade," testified Bishop Tugwell, whose diocese covered the whole of Nigeria and who had resided in that country for sixteen years.[7] At the same time, the head of the Nigeria

Investment Company, at a stockholders' meeting in London, was glorifying the marvelous and profitable growth of Southern Nigeria's trade. He gave figures to show the increase; and directors and stockholders were in a mood of mutual congratulation.[8] Some great trading and industrial fortunes in England came either wholly or in part from Nigeria's palm oil.

The discovery of tin in Northern Nigeria opened up a new source of wealth to British mining companies, caused a boom in tin-mining company shares on the London Stock Exchange, and stimulated the launching of sundry swindling projects. On the strength of showings made by sound companies, promoters who held nothing more than imaginary claims poured forth stock issues and honeyed prospectuses. "All sorts of schemes are being propounded for the exploiting of the public interest in these mines," warned "The Economist," of London, on March 2, 1912. "The shares of new companies are introduced almost every day to the Stock Exchange, and at prices arbitrarily fixed by the sellers, who hope to unload on the public. . . . It may be mentioned that the majority of prices in the Nigerian tin [stock] market appearing in some newspapers are paid for by those interested." Fraudulent companies pocketed their loot and then nimbly vanished. But the substantial Nigerian tin-mining companies were a source of continuing wealth to British investors, and paid dividends reaching 30 per cent.

Now came Britain's turn to face charges of atrocities committed by one of its corporations, the Peruvian Amazon Company, on Indians in the Putumayo Region in the upper Amazon River basin in South America. The great basin of the Amazon provided nearly one-half of the world's supply of rubber. In South American countries many corporations, largely British, had entrenched themselves, drawing immense wealth not only from rubber, oil, minerals and other abounding resources, but from utility and merchandising enterprises in the cities.[9] Profit possibilities in the respective fields were carefully calculated. Imports and exports of South American republics exceeded $1,200,000,000 in 1905.

In the rubber industry, in South America and elsewhere, a huge amount of British capital was invested. Speculative crazes in stocks of rubber companies ran epidemic in Britain. "The whole of society, from one end of the scale to the other, has gone rubber mad," recounted an editorial in "The Economist," on April 23, 1910. "The needy peer, who is known to have buttressed his family misfortunes since the end of February, has engaged in the game with the same zest as the commissaire who made fourteen pounds out of nothing in a week. . . . We cannot be sure that the rubber gamble is by any means over. A craze it may be, but people on the whole have made money and want to make more. New [stock] issues continue to pour out at a rapid rate, and are accorded favorable receptions by the public."

An outgrowth of a Peru firm, the Peruvian Amazon Company was registered in 1908 as a British corporation with headquarters in London. It was run by a composite board of directors of whom four were British, and it had a nominal capital of £1,000,000. Its area in the Putumayo district was about 10,000 to 12,000 square miles, somewhat larger than the size of Massachusetts and Rhode Island. Three South American newspapers in 1907 exposed the company's treatment of the Indians, and in the same year an American Consul in Peru sent to Washington a report, "Slavery in Peru," which, however, was not printed until six years later when the House of Representatives published it as a document. In England the facts were first made public by a series of articles in 1909, in the weekly journal "Truth."

The resulting great commotion caused the British Foreign Office, in 1910, to send Sir Roger Casement to the Putumayo district to make inquiry. His report fully supported the charges. In the next year the Peruvian Government commissioned Judge Romolo Paredes to investigate; his report confirmed the atrocities. The House of Commons then appointed a Select Committee, which, after collating a mass of evidence, reported in March, 1913, these findings:

The company had a force of 1,500 whites (whom it termed "armed vigilantes") equipped with Winchester guns which were fast being replaced by modern automatic guns. "Commissions" or patrols of these men searched a region and collected Indians. Natives who ran away were ruthlessly shot down, while those seized were listed as "conquered," and were put to the task of gathering the wild rubber of the forest. "These man-hunts are simple slave raiding," the Committee commented. Of 60,000 or 70,000 Indians in the Putumayo district, more than half were reduced to slavery. Torturing and the burning of men and women alive with kerosene oil were two of the terrorizing methods. "However great," the Committee stated, "may be the reluctance to credit the possibility of diabolical brutalities of this kind, the truth of the burning alive of Indians is too well established by the evidence of eye witnesses."

At the same time, to give the slavery of Indians the color of legality, an accompanying system was enforced. "Advances ('pagos') of European goods were made to them, and they were then regarded as debtors to the company, and forced under pain of merciless flogging to work off their debts in rubber. Thenceforth they were held under the chain of peonage, a system of debt bondage from which they never got free. . . . If they ran away, they were hunted down by bodies of armed men and brought back; and it appears that the Peruvian law would sanction the handing over of such debtors to their employers." Elsewhere in the report the company's armed force was described as "in fact, a gang of ruffians and murderers, who shot from mere lust of blood, or burnt, tortured and violated in a spirit of wanton deviltry . . . for which each was paid £5 a month. The outrages on the Putumayo were carried to an inhuman extreme, which, if it had not been proved up to the hilt, would have seemed incredible."

The Committee related how a board of directors in London nominally professed to supervise the operations of rubber production thousands of miles away in the depths of the Amazon forest. One of the British directors, H. M. Read, was manager of the London Bank of Mexico, and also a director of the Peruvian Corporation, Limited, a concern with large nitrate, railway and land interests in Peru. Read had never been in the Putumayo district, but he admitted having seen Indians shot down in the city of Lima, and that he had done nothing; "it never crossed Read's mind to inquire into the treatment of Indians at all." A second British director was J. Russell Gubbins, who sold goods in Peru but had never seen the Putumayo.

Another of the directors was Sir John Lister Kaye; he knew nothing of Peru or rubber, and he "repudiated the duty of inquiring into labor conditions." This picture of the directors' room in London was drawn by the Committee: "A photograph of the wild, naked forest Indians whom they employed hung on the walls of their Board room, and there was a list hanging in the room of the Indians working in the sections. But no dicussion ever took place at Board meetings about the labor question or the treatment of labor."

In conclusion, the Committee declared that the brutal and murderous treatment of Indians was not confined to the Putumayo district. "It appears, rather, that the Putumayo case is but a shockingly bad instance of conditions of treatment that are liable to be found over a wide area in South America." The same statement, based upon the evidence, was made in the course of ensuing debates in Parliament. And apart from the treatment of Indians, rival rubber companies in the Amazon basin carried on backwoods fighting in which even white nonparticipants were killed.[10]

After these disclosures, the British High Court compelled the dissolving of the Peruvian Amazon Company.

The stenographic reports of the annual meetings of stockholders in London rubber companies do not show a solitary instance where any question was raised as to conditions of labor. Profits engrossed attention. Enormous were the dividends distributed by British rubber companies operating in various parts of the world. After the first three years of its existence, which was a preparatory period, the Consolidated Malay Rubber Estates, Limited, paid annual dividends averaging 89 per cent for the three succeeding years.[11] At the stockholders' yearly meeting in London, in 1913, the chairman announced—as though a considerable sacrifice were being imposed—that the dividend would have to be lowered to 75 per cent, one reason for which step was the increase in capital stock.[12] An audience of delighted stockholders of the Pataling Rubber Estates Syndicate, Limited, at a meeting in London, shouted a heartfelt "Hear, hear" when the chairman congratulated them on their highly satisfactory profits, justifying for the year 1912 a munificent dividend of 275 per cent, less income tax. During eight years, the assemblage was reminded, the Pataling Syndicate had proved itself a peerless money-maker by its distribution of 1,115 per cent in dividends—an average of 140 per cent a year. "I think," the chairman crowed, "that you will agree with me that this is a record of which we may well be proud." The stockholders demonstrated their approval by applause.[13]

These, but a few of many instances, show why the British public was so eager to buy rubber company stocks. Seeing which opportunity, squads of American promoters of dubious rubber companies in Mexico (where cultivation of the product had not been any too successful, financially), shifted their stock-selling activities to London. A further reason was that the American Government had prohibited them the use of the mails.

Wherever money was to be made, at the turn of the present century, companies were busy developing, exploiting and oppressing. The scope of the great American corporations lay mainly in America, which in general afforded them sufficient resources and adequate outlet. Of the world's copper production in 1904, approximately 1,200,000 pounds, American copper companies produced less than half. The most formidable rival of American copper producers was a British company headed by the Rothschilds, that owned the Rio Tinto Mines in Spain—the largest and richest group of mineral properties in the world.[14] The American Sugar Refining Company (the Sugar Trust) was originally content with its American plants, only later establishing itself in Cuba. Much the same was the status of the congeries of corporations embraced in the Tobacco Trust. The Standard Oil Company derived its supplies chiefly from American fields. Most of the plants of the American Smelting and Refining Company were in America, supplemented by holdings of large mining and smelting interests in Mexico and South America.

Considerable as they were in other countries, American investments were far outdistanced by British. Great Britain's invested capital abroad was so gigantic that, of Britain's total national income of about £2,000,000,000, the minimum known yearly net income from foreign investments and businesses in other lands was estimated at £140,000,000, and it was impossible to measure the full sum with any exactitude. The English financial authorities, Professor A. L. Bowley and Sir Josiah Stamp, figured the return at a higher amount.

As an example of the wealth drained from the world supply by some other European countries, Holland's Asiatic possessions will serve. The Dutch East Indies (officially termed Netherland Indies since 1934), comprised Java, Madura, Borneo, Celebes, part of New Guinea and the Molucca Islands. The area of the whole was 733,642 square miles, or about one-fourth that of the United States of America, and the population 40,000,000. Holland's people were heavily taxed for naval and military forces in the Dutch East Indies; but the many corporations—Dutch, British and other—thriving in those colonies waxed fat on the profitable returns of heavy capitalization. The Trading Company of Amsterdam, owning thirty-six, or one-fifth, of the sugar plantations in the Dutch East Indies, reached the point where in the variety of its operations it employed more than 1,000 Europeans and 150,000 Asiatics, and enriched stockholders by a 30 per cent dividend on its common stock.

In Dutch East Indies' rubber plantations the amount of Dutch, British and other capital invested was computed at an amount equal to perhaps $200,000,000. Only the mining of tin, of which one-fourth of the world's supply came from the Dutch East Indies, was reserved as a Government monopoly. Nearly the whole of the world consumption of pepper and quinine, and large supplies of tea and copra, came from the Dutch East Indies. Exports of petroleum became important. Coal deposits in Sumatra produced increasingly heavy outputs —there were undeveloped resources of gold, silver and copper, and rich iron mines in the Celebes. The production of palm oil increased to an extent threatening close rivalry with Africa. But this situation was later met by the fraternizing of British and Dutch interests in a colossal octopus interlocking of soap and margarine companies that controlled all stages of production from raw material to the retailing of manufactured goods. For a puny country about the size of Massachusetts and Connecticut, and with a population of less than 5,000,000, Holland was—or at least its possessing classes were—well fortified with wealth, the estimated total of which (in 1906) was $4,400,000,-000.

Materialism of the most strenuous type was now being exhibited in another part of the world. In general, the people of Occidental countries had an illusory idea of Japan. Superficial and sentimental writers of other nations, visiting that country, went to find a colorful atmosphere. They confined their gaze to the surviving quaintness of dress, queer customs and unique ceremonies, the whole of which made an interesting contrast with the drab industrialism of Western countries. On this representation they lavished an artistry of words. But all of this was an idyl of the old Japan, and not a portrayal of the new.

Influenced by the progress and power of Western materialism, Japan, before the advent of the nineteenth century's last quarter, had emerged from its centuries-old seclusion. Once it had determined upon its course, Japan pursued it with a fervor verging upon fanaticism. From America and Europe it copied industrial, financial and transportation systems. While exotic writers were absorbed in romanticizing over bits of antique Japan, the practical Japanese leaders were exulting over the nascent Japan of factories, banks and transportation lines. Japan's government applied itself as a business to co-operating with capitalists in promoting industrialization. Officials concentrated upon the imbuing of an industrial temper among the people; and to provide a plenitude of factory labor, the State conducted training courses for women. Japan's factory owners then had at their disposal a submissive army of workers, toiling variously from eleven to seventeen hours a day; twelve hours were the standard in cotton mills. The wages were scant, men textile workers receiving thirty sen (thirty cents), and women twenty sen a day. In match and other factories women were paid twelve to twenty sen a day. The daily pay of skilled machinists was somewhat more than one yen (about fifty cents).[15]

The wealth rapidly amassed by Japanese industrialists from cheap labor was augmented by their piratical methods in appropriating trade-marks of European and American manufacturers. Almost every well-known foreign label was closely imitated on Japanese goods, which were sold throughout the Far East as the genuine make of European or American manufacturers. The owners of the trade-marks found themselves virtually helpless. When they sought redress in the Japanese courts, it was repeatedly decided there that no suit could be maintained unless the imitation were identical, in every dot and dash, with the original: complete identity and not similarity was juridically declared the one and only proof of piracy. In his "Conclusions" in the book compiled by him on Japan, Count Shigenobu Okuma, for a time Japan's Prime Minister and Minister for Foreign Affairs, could not avoid confessing: "It must be admitted that [the Japanese] people in general are neither over-particular nor profound in their ideas of business morality." [16] Evidently swayed by the continued protests of foreign manufacturers and by storms of foreign denunciation, the Japanese Vice-Minister of Agriculture and Commerce made a circular appeal to chambers of commerce in Japan. Ascribing the theft of inventions and trade-marks by Japanese manufacturers and merchants to the growing intensity of competition, he hoped the practice would be supplanted by the use of "honorable means." [17]

Speculative crazes of the most approved Western type were enacted in Japan. One such occasion was after Japan's victory in the war with China in 1894, when the receipt of a large indemnity and the glamor of triumph caused a general intoxication which quickly transmitted itself to the business and financial fields. The desire for wealth, already strong among certain classes, now became widespread, and groups of optimistic or unscrupulous promoters lost no time in purveying to the passion. Many projects were put forward, reckless in themselves but made plausible by misrepresentation. "The people in general," wrote a high Japanese financier, "thinking that to form a company, whatever its object might be, meant to realize an enormous profit, competed to subscribe to shares of new companies, and numbers of bubble concerns, whose accounts of profit and loss were never reliable, saw the light." A similar phantasmagoria followed the Russo-Japanese war in 1906, when the Japanese, heady with victory, plunged into the wildest speculative excesses. "The mania," related the same authority, "was indescribable, for it is shown by aggregate statistics that the aggregate capital of the new companies, together with the increased capital of the old ones, was in that year estimated at over 1,600,000,000 yen." The inescapable crash caused wide wreckage, shattering a string of weak banks.[18]

The political morality of Japan was as low as its commercial and financial practices. Elections were corrupt and so was the Diet, Japan's Parliament. The worst of American election methods were borrowed and exceeded. Through political machines and bosses, corporations in America, as we have noted, regularly corrupted; but the American Government did not itself bribe voters to perpetuate partisan power or to ensure a majority in Congress for its measures. In Japan the Government itself resorted to wholesale corruption, notably in 1898–1899, when it took this means for securing in the House of Representatives a majority for its bill to increase taxes. The resultant agitation caused the enacting, two years later, of a drastic Corrupt Practices Act, but despite this law corruption went on, although covertly engineered. Political "rings" and bosses became rooted in Japan; the word politician was in disrepute among many of its people; and distrust of elective officials was reflected in the growing indifference or apathy of large bodies of voters in Parliamentary elections.[19] Again and again came exposures of the corruption of leading Government officials, or their implication in shady financial transactions—a line of sensational exposures that extends practically to the time of this writing.[20]

In the deceptive years, with their peace illusions, immediately preceding the World War, American materialism was as much as ever the object of attack by European writers. Among them were Germans like Professor Hugo Münsterberg who, while drawing a salary from an American university, wrote caustic articles on America for German papers.

By the instructive lessons of competition, however, Britain's business men had been taught the true character of modern Germany. Commercially, Germany had grown so fast that, beginning in 1870 with an unimportant merchant marine, its steamship fleets had increased to millions of tonnage, exceeded only by that of Britain and America. (In point of tonnage engaged in overseas trade, Germany far outranked America, the bulk of whose shipping was in the coasting trade and on the Great Lakes.) Co-ordinating its system, Germany had organized shipping, industries and trade to work in efficient unison, and each contributed to the development of the others. The volume of Germany's industrial production was subordinate only to that of America and Britain. To such an extent had German business prospered that before the World War Germany was clustered with millionaires, some 15,000, each of several hundred of whom could boast of possessing 10,000,000 marks. If, compared to the American dollar millionaire, the German mark millionaire seemed on a lower financial plane, his status was proportionately high when measured by German standards.

One of the few British writers to gauge the significance of Germany's position was William Harbutt Dawson. He had written many books on that country and understood the force of events there. Recognizing the sway of the legend that represented Germany as an ideological nation of thinkers, poets and dreamers, he sought to show the actualities of Germany's modern development. His book was not, he wrote, intended as either a glorification or a disparagement. It aimed, rather, to present the Germans in their real character as an avid trading nation. "The *furor Teutonicus* of old has its modern counterpart in an *ardor Teutonicus* whose object is material wealth." He proceeded with his exposition of Germany's intense materialism as shown not only by "its exaltation of machinery and systems" but also by its "force worship" and by its "fondness for massiveness, its reckless hankering after great effects." [21]

If Germany's industrialism was to be thus exposed as the acme of materialism, how were Britain's own conditions to be described? Perhaps in Dawson's eyes British industrialism, by reason of its much longer existence, had become a thing of usage and respectability. Certainly, were cold figures consulted, Britain outclassed Germany. The gross value of Germany's industrial production (estimated in dollars) was computed at less than $3,000,000,000, exceeding France's by $650,000,000.

Britain's industrial output reached $4,100,000,000, secondary only to the $7,000,000,000 of expansive America. England's financial and commercial organs rejoiced over the increase in Britain's trade. To that country, so dependent upon the revenues from goods sold abroad, figures were not arid. And in a country, too, whose statesmen, publicists and business men were not prone to rhetorical flights, figures were closely studied and effectively cited. From 1909 to the end of 1913 the volume of exports had risen from £377,000,000 to £525,000,000, a gain of £148,000,000. "Trade throughout the country has enjoyed the greatest boom in recent English history; profits have been high," recounted "The Economist," of London, on January 17, 1914. A few months later it estimated Britain's annual income from trade, investments and other sources at the magnificent sum of more than £2,000,000,000.

Yet notoriously formal and reserved as were the English, they —or at least the extensive groups of stockholders—were electrified into emotional response whenever they heard the announcement of high dividends. To this manifestation we have already referred, and unavoidably we shall have to do so again. High dividends were so much the custom that any lapse here or there caused pained astonishment. American boasting was still made a matter of reproach by British writers, yet it is doubtful whether the head of any American corporation could have contrived to beat the solemn flaunting common in England. For example, pointing to the forty-two year money-making career of the company bearing his name, Sir John Barker addressed stockholders: "To sum up, it is no little satisfaction to share in an enterprise which has such a record of upward growth—it is, indeed, a pleasure to be associated with a business whose elasticity and management ensure a safe dividend of eleven and a half per cent on the ordinary shares." At which there was a salvo of applause.[22] Examples more or less similar abounded. As for the multitude of British companies operating in other countries, their large annual dividends were a commonplace, yet each time declared they drew fresh applause. Two of many instances of these dividends were the National Bank of India paying its regular dividend of 12 per cent (on increased stock to boot), and the Chartered Bank of

India, Australia and China with its 15 per cent dividend, free of income tax.[23]

In a powerful letter published in "The Saturday Review," of London, on September 22, 1917, W. R. Lawson, a prominent English financial writer, concluded: "What not only the Bank of England but our whole banking system needs is more daylight both from within and without." To which "The Saturday Review" responded editorially: "We quite agree." But, of course, no investigation was made.

Meanwhile, there had been made in America an unsparing investigation into the power and acts of the great financial magnates, and of the powerful banks and other interests controlled by them. A House of Representatives resolution introduced by Congressman Pujo in 1912 directed the Committee on Banking and Currency in that body to investigate banking and currency conditions in the United States as a basis for remedial legislation. There was reason to believe, the resolution set forth, that a few groups of financiers in New York and elsewhere concentrated in their hold the management and resources of the great industrial and railroad corporations of the country. Leading bankers and other multimillionaires such as J. Pierpont Morgan, Jacob H. Schiff, George F. Baker, and Thomas F. Ryan were summoned before the Pujo Committee and rigorously interrogated. The dictatorial power of a small group of mighty banks in controlling the arteries of money and determining credit; the interlocking of a maze of corporation directorates; the domineering power of clearing house associations; subtle stock exchange operations and practices,—all these were exposed to the glare of publicity. In its report the committee gave the credit usually bestowed upon these inner groups of bankers for their function in building up America's huge industries. But these considerations, it adjudged, did not justify those bankers in taking control of the resources of America's financial institutions, or of the people's savings, or levying tribute upon every large enterprise, or dictating commercial credits and dominating stock exchange values.[24]

A little later came the equally sensational report of an investigation by the Interstate Commerce Commission into the financial transactions of the New York, New Haven & Hartford Railroad Company, controlled mainly by J. Pierpont Morgan and by John D. Rockefeller. In the process of securing a monopoly by acquisition of other lines, this company had paid exorbitant sums—in one case double the real value. It manipulated its securities in the stock market, and unloaded stock upon the public. "A corrupt monopoly," the report termed the company; and its directors were branded as "criminally negligent." [25] American magnates, however they might escape law's penalties, could not shield themselves from probing as could their European compeers.

CHAPTER XX

ARMAMENTS AND PROFITEERING

BEFORE America entered the World War in 1917, European criticisms were twofold. British and French critics bitterly reproached America for making money from Europe's tragedy; and the German Government formally protested to Washington against American corporations supplying war material to the Allies. When had European corporations, including the German, not profited from selling material to nations at war? That time never was.

Manifestly, American corporations were making extraordinary profits. High in the list was the United States Steel Corporation. Profits, called earnings, on its $500,000,000 of common stock rose from 11 per cent in 1913 to 48.46 per cent in 1916 and to 39.15 per cent in 1917. During the same time its profits on preferred stock increased from 22.54 to 75.37 per cent. Even after payment of Federal income and excess profit taxes, the United States Steel Corporation had, in 1917, a net income of $244,738,908 remaining from its total revenue of more than $478,000,000. But were the beneficiaries Americans only? By no means. Before the World War $70,000,000 of the stock had been owned by Europeans, mainly in England and Holland. At the war's outbreak $20,000,000 of this stock had been sold. But in 1916 there was still owned abroad nearly 700,000 shares, 355,000 of which were held in England and 238,000 in Holland.

The Bethlehem Steel Company's profits were such that in 1916 a dividend of $22.50 a share was declared on its common stock, and in 1917, $23.50, supplemented by a grand distribution of a 200 per cent stock dividend. The effect upon speculation was seen in the soaring of Bethlehem Steel Company stock from a point considered high at 46⅝ in 1914 to a climax of 700 in 1916, when the company's earnings towered to 286 per cent. From the World War's start American manufacturers of explosives made such great profits that the regular and extra dividends of I. E. du Pont de Nemours Company jumped from $30 per share of common stock to $100 in 1916, sagging to $51 in 1917. In four years of peace time the du Ponts had made $4,000,000 in profits, but during an equal number of war years their profits ascended to $24,000,000. Thus, in 1934, declared Senator Gerald P. Nye, chairman of the United States Senate Special Committee investigating the munitions industry.

Testimony before that committee showed that du Pont World War dividends totaled 458 per cent of the par value of the company's original stock. At the request of Senator Nye, Lammot du Pont, president of the I. E. du Pont de Nemours Company, submitted, on November 18, 1934, a series of recommendations as to the conduct of the munitions industry. Senator Nye had advocated a 96 to 98 per cent wartime tax on all incomes exceeding $10,000 a year. Du Pont agreed that excess war profits should be eliminated, and he favored immediate action by America in the initiation of its own policy in placing the international munitions trade under strict Governmental control. Whether or not these unexceptionable sentiments will be converted into action we shall have to wait and see.

Confident predictions about how the martial spirit may be curbed are notoriously subject to correction by events. In the mid-nineteenth century there was published "The History of Civilization in England," by Henry Thomas Buckle. This book made a sensation in Europe and America, and raised Buckle to literary fame. It was his avowed belief that the possibility of wars had been greatly lessened by: New gunpowder inventions; modern locomotion; and improved knowledge of political economy. Confident of his premises, he went so far as to maintain that he did not think his conclusion could be impugned. Intervening wars apart, need it be said that by the year 1914 warfare's weapons had been perfected into a mechanism of destructiveness undreamt of by Buckle? Not that factor, nor accelerated transportation, nor any understanding of greater economic interdependence prevented the holocaust of the World War. At the very time when Buckle was penning his speculations, a new and more deadly type of cannon had been invented and was being manufactured in England itself.

In all European countries, belligerent and neutral, the World War was an event ensuring to the business classes extraordinary money-making opportunities. While Governments involved in the war were appealing to their peoples for the highest display of patriotism and were invoking the utmost spirit of sacrifice, the owners of industries in general, of banks and shipping, were heaping up profits that often surpassed those of peace times. Yearly dividends ran from 15 to 35 and 40 per cent. Even these returns, high if estimated by European standards, did not denote the full influx of profits in many business lines. Commonly, liberal portions of profits were set aside for cash reserves, for depreciation charges, or were spent in plant enlargements.

But the activities of industry in general never reached the depths of infamy that characterized concerns engaged in making and marketing armament, munitions and other war material. Industries which did not expressly benefit from supplying naval and military equipment were in nowise concerned in peace times with engendering war fears. Not infrequently, however, some armament and munition manufacturers fomented war alarms to stimulate sales of their death-dealing wares. From the time of Napoleon I the British people were perturbed by a series of invasion scares. After the exhaustive Napoleonic wars the Duke of Wellington assured his country of the improbability of war for a long time; Europe's devout yearning, he declared, was for peace. Nevertheless, from time to time, war scares were disseminated. In a quarter of a century following the Napoleonic wars, Britain spent at least £160,000,000 on fortifications and warships. Perhaps half of this sum represented useful and unavoidable services. But the fact did remain that many of the ships ordered in hysteria were left to rot or were soon pronounced obsolete, to be displaced by others. What proportions of these older scares were spontaneous, and what artfully fostered, cannot be measured or guessed. But certain it is that the war scares of more recent decades were instigated by particular armament and munition interests.

Manifestly the creators of these scares took every precaution to envelop their operations in hermetic secrecy. But disclosures did occasionally come. Two instances occurred shortly before the World War. "Marz," the leading South German weekly review, prominently featured in April, 1912, an attack by Conrad Haussman, a Progressive member of the Reichstag, on the methods used by Admiral von Tirpitz, head of the German navy, in furtherance of propaganda for a still larger navy. Scares against England, Haussman charged, had been spread, and the money for systematic propaganda had come from allied shipbuilding and armament manufacturers. Similar charges against a German gun and cartridge company were made a year later in the Reichstag by Karl Liebknecht, Socialist leader, who charged that attempts had been made to put propaganda in a French paper for the purpose of stirring up the German Government, and thereby increasing the company's business. "If," editorially declared "The Economist," of London, on March 11, 1911, "the history of our naval and military scares be carefully examined, it would be found that they are largely engineered from the dockyard and armament constituencies. . . . Certainly, the members ought not to be allowed to tout for contracts in Parliament for their own constituencies." As a matter of record, a sizable number of members of Parliament were directors or important stockholders in armament companies. In that very year the Chamber of Deputies in France had acted to end a long-prevailing scandal. To a bill for building two large battleships it had tacked an amendment providing that no Government order be given to any firm or company which included among its directors or managers any Deputy or Senator.

The second count against the armament makers was that they imposed defective or otherwise inferior material upon their own armies and navies, as well as upon those of other countries. How ancient were these practices has been seen by facts given in earlier parts of this book. In modern times certain persons in Southern European countries were suspected of spoliation on an enormous scale in war contracts, which often additionally brought the delivery of bad material. But the protection officially afforded to those men and the power they wielded gave them security.

Throughout Europe no scandal touching defective equipment was allowed to be publicly aired. In America facts were occasionally pried out. At the outbreak of the Civil War European manufacturers dumped refuse guns in America. A Congressional Committee, in 1894, had reported of the Carnegie Steel Company that: "The company was hired to make the best possible armor plate, and was paid an enormous price. Resting under these obligations, the company or its servants perpetrated manifold frauds, the natural tendency of which was to palm off upon the Government an inferior armor whose inferiority might perhaps appear only in the shock of battle and with incalculable damage to the country." And according to an official report, the Carnegie Steel Company was making armor plate at a cost of less than $200 a ton, which plate it sold to the Russian Government at $249 a ton, while charging the United States Government from $520 to $700 a ton for precisely the same plate.[1] The complaint said to have been made by the Spanish Admiral Cervera after the American squadron had destroyed his fleet at Santiago de Cuba, in 1898, was by no means proved, yet it had a strain familiar to all acquainted with ways in Southern European countries. Cervera, it was reported, uttered a grievance to the effect that the guns he should have had were in the pockets of Spanish contractors. In the German Reichstag Deputy Erzberger, at a later time, exposed the profiteering operations of German armament makers. If honest prices were charged, he declared, the cost to the German Government would be 50 per cent less, and on that reduction the manufacturers would still make a large profit.

What may ironically be described as a cosmopolitanism of interests existed among munitions and armament manufacturers. Alfred Nobel, the Swedish manufacturer of dynamite, had founded in England, in 1871, a branch called the Nobel Explosives Company. In 1887 there was organized in England the Nobel Dynamite Trust, Limited, which combined in itself the Nobel Explosives Company and four companies in Germany exchanging shares for those in the Nobel Dynamite Trust, which further acquired large interests in South Africa, Canada and other parts of the world.

During the World War, the Nobel Dynamite Trust found

itself under mandatory need of detachment from German interests. At the stockholders' meeting in 1915, at which this
move was announced, Sir Ralph William Anstruther, the company's chairman, reviewed its origin and went on: "That is
twenty-eight years ago, and during that period the German
and British interests have worked harmoniously side by side
for the common good of the shareholders." [2] And at the stockholders' meeting in 1916, Anstruther told how the company had
sold its German assets and bought all interests formerly held
by Germans. In Britain the company was now resolved back
into the Nobel Explosives Company. "It may be interesting
here to recall," Anstruther informed stockholders, "that an
original investment of £100 in the 1872 company now represents a capital interest in this company of £3,000 in ordinary
shares, and that the dividends on that capital investment during
the forty-five years have amounted in all to upwards of £8,500."
Because of the secrecy imposed by war's demands, Anstruther
said, he could not give details of the company's present and
prospective activity, but he did announce a 10 per cent dividend
and a bonus of 5 per cent on the common stock, both free from
income tax. Upon which J. R. Richmond, a large stockholder,
feelingly said: "We should accept our case with more or less
silent gratitude." [3] In the next year the dividend was 20 per
cent, inclusive of a 5 per cent bonus, both free from income
tax.[4]

The career of the Krupp armament company in Germany is
fairly well known. Beginning early in the nineteenth century
with a mere shed, the machinery in which was run by water-
power (unreliable because the dam froze in winter), the Krupp
concern gradually evolved into a huge cannon manufactory. At
a time when war between Germany and France seemed inevitable, Krupp's works were delivering the newest models in
cannon to the Government of Emperor Napoleon III, and those
cannon were used to mow down German soldiers. While armament companies of each country were extolling themselves as
the great sources of supply for patriotic protection, all of the important companies in many countries took steps to form a communion of interest. In the United Harvey Steel Company,
registered in Britain in 1901, were Krupp's and another Ger-

man firm, and large Austrian, British, French and American armament manufacturers. This organization afforded a central meeting ground for the world's armament makers. But as it was too open to the dangers of attack, it later voluntarily dissolved.[5] Many of the Krupp patents, especially for armor plate, were bought by British armament firms, and were constantly used in the making of battleships for the British navy.

Sensational disclosures were made in the German Reichstag on April 18, 1913, by Dr. Liebknecht whose constituency was Essen, where the Krupp works were located. The Krupp company, he charged, had maintained in Berlin an agent (the name was given), whose business it was to bribe officials in the War and Navy Departments to communicate to him documents containing military secrets. "Armament contractors," Liebknecht said, "systematically supply goods to foreign countries, indifferent as to whether they will later be used for the purpose of killing Germans." Although accusing Liebknecht of exaggeration, General von Heeringen, Minister of War, had to admit that some truth lay in his charges. Later in the "Grenzboten," an old-fashioned, conservative German weekly review, Herr Cleinow, the editor, wrote that it was foolish to dismiss the charges as mere Socialist agitation; corruption in political circles was well known, and there could be no denial of the corruption of certain army officers. Repeatedly, though, the Krupp company watered its stock, and on this paid large dividends.

Armament profits in Germany may be judged from the reports of the Deutsche Waffen- und Munitionsfabriken, which had an ammunition factory at Karlsruhe and armament works at Martinikenfeld. Before the World War this company was affiliated with similar companies in Belgium, France and Italy. Starting with a capital in marks equivalent to $1,500,000, the company doubled its capital in 1896, and raised it in 1899 to a sum in marks equal to $3,750,000. This was doubled again in 1912. From 1893 onwards dividends steadily rose from 15 per cent to the point where they reached 32 per cent in the years before the World War. But even these high dividends on masses of watered stock gave no proper idea of the full profits, for large amounts of these were deposited in the company's treasury as reserves.

The Armstrong works in England had been founded by William George Armstrong, an attorney by profession but actually interested in mechanical and scientific matters. He originally built the works for the marketing of a hydraulic crane of his invention. Then, turning his attention to artillery, in 1855 he produced the modern rifled gun that we have already referred to. For a time the British Government slighted the importance of this new implement, but other Governments gave large orders to Armstrong. He was knighted in 1859. Twenty-seven years later he was raised to the peerage, as was, in 1903, his grand-nephew and heir of the same surname.

Branching to a foreign country, the Armstrong works established a cannon factory at Puzzuoli, Italy. At a time when Italy was rated by Britain in the class of its naval competitors, this was the situation as authoritatively set forth: "The Italian Government has no gun or torpedo factory of its own for the Navy. Both guns and torpedoes of every description or service are furnished by two private concerns. Lord Armstrong's gun factory at Puzzuoli, near Naples, provides the fleet with large guns, as well as with secondary and quick-firing ordnance. The torpedoes (called in Italian *siluri*), are made in Swarzkopf's torpedo factory at Venice." [6]

An incident embarrassing to British naval officials occurred in the House of Commons in April, 1911. One of the House members—Kellaway—drew attention to the official statement that the Armstrong works (the exact name was Armstrong, Whitworth and Company), had bid a price of £51 a ton for the building of two dreadnaught battleships for Turkey, whereas the price to be paid by the British Government for the same class of ships was £63 a ton. The Secretary to the Admiralty glided over the issue by replying that the figure for the British dreadnaught was considerably less than £63 per ton, but he would not say it was less than £51 per ton, as he did not know on what basis the Turkish figures were calculated. Shortly after, Sir William Bull inquired whether "the difference is due to a combine amongst the English makers of armored plate?" This question brought the vague but significant enough answer that the navy's policy "restricted the area of competition." But, the Secretary to the Admiralty claimed, "the Navy had been able to make substantial reductions in armor plate within a few years." [7] He was not asked what they were, nor what were the sums formerly paid. As for the armament companies, no information could be wrested from them; on their dealings with their own Government or with any other they were obdurately mute.

There was frequent public agitation in Britain over high Government dignitaries who left posts in the naval, ordnance and construction departments to join the board of directors of armament companies. When, on December 31, 1912, it was announced that Sir William E. Smith, long a Government Director of Naval Construction and also Superintendent of Construction Accounts and Contracts, had consented to join the Armstrong company, "The Daily Chronicle" of London took critical notice. Giving a list of such Government officials who had gone over to the armament companies, it observed: "The drain of State officials into the service of armament companies has of late attracted considerable attention." More expressive was "The Economist." "Public officials," it objected editorially, on January 4, 1913, "ought not to join private firms with a view to securing public contracts; officials intimate with the secrets of the Admiralty, War Office and Imperial Defence Committee ought not to be allowed to place their knowledge at the disposal of private firms which manufacture battleships for the Governments of foreign nations with which we might some day be unhappily at war." In two months came another announcement. Sir George H. Murray who, for nineteen years had been Secretary to the Treasury, retiring in 1911, and Rear-Admiral Sir Charles Ottley, serving in the highly confidential office of Secretary to the Imperial Council of Defence, were elected directors of the Armstrong company. "The Morning Post," of London admonished all concerned that to hold public confidence the Treasury should be above any color of personal connection with Government contractors. These shifts of officials to armament companies, other London newspapers stated, caused general public uneasiness.

Another big British armament company, Vickers, Limited, constantly enlarged its sphere. A circular, issued by it to stockholders, on March 8, 1913, gave notification of an increase of capital by 740,000 shares, an action, it was explained, necessitated by the great expansion of the company's business. The company, stockholders were informed, had acquired a large interest in ordnance works in Japan and in other countries.

Less than a year later there burst a great scandal in Japan over battle-cruiser contracts. When, in 1913, Admiral Count Gombei Yamamoto was called on to form a Cabinet, a leading Japanese newspaper editorially made the sardonic prognosis: "Now that Gombei is Premier we shall see some big Navy contracts." Popular feeling ran high against heavy expenditures already incurred for armaments. Attacks upon the Government in the Diet, in January, 1914, were soon followed by disclosures of widespread bribery associated with the contract for the battle-cruiser Kongo, built by the large Mitsui shipbuilding company in which Vickers was powerful. Anger over these and other bribery charges led to popular demonstrations in several cities. In Hibiya Park, in the center of Tokio, 40,000 persons assembled to denounce navy corruption. The police were powerless to quell the disorder, and regular troops were ordered out to disperse the crowds. Yamamoto and his Cabinet resigned in March, 1914, and two months later a navy court martial swiftly acted. For his part in the transactions attending the building of the Kongo, Vice-Admiral Matsumoto was weighted with a fine of 409,800 yen (about $200,000) and was sentenced to three years in prison. Captain Sawasaki was mulcted 11,500 yen and received a one-year prison term. Quickly followed judgment by the civil courts which decreed punishment of fines and prison for certain Mitsui company directors and other officials convicted of having bribed naval officers to obtain the Kongo contract. The heaviest sentence meted was that to Admiral Terugoro Fujii—four years in prison and a fine of 368,360.05 yen. Fines imposed, it was thought, represented the exact amount of loot individually pocketed.

An account of this episode, by Oland D. Russell, was published in "The New York Times" on September 30, 1929, and was thus retrospectively called forth by a current scandal implicating several American shipbuilding companies. With the aim to limit armaments, a convocation of representatives of leading nations had deliberated at Geneva, Switzerland. At this conference William B. Shearer, an American propagandist, was active in seeking to prevent a reduction of American war vessels, and if possible, to bring about an enlargement of the American fleet. Disclosures showed that his salary and expenses were paid by three large shipbuilding companies, all of which held contracts to build new cruisers. These companies became dissatisfied with his services. He brought suit in the Supreme Court, in New York City, against the Bethlehem Steel Company, the Newport News Shipbuilding & Dry Dock Company, and the American Brown Boveri Electric Corporation. His action was for sums alleged to be due for services at Washington, Geneva and New York City. The agreed and reasonable value of his services, he contended, was $250,000; he had spent $58,885 in his mission; and he complained of having been paid only $51,230.

The Naval Committee of the United States Senate at once set about investigating. Before its sub-committee Shearer repeated these claims, and officials of shipbuilding companies admitted that he had received $50,000 or thereabouts. In Shearer's own testimony there was one part which was mentioned incidentally, but which had an ominous significance. According to his statement, the Council of American Shipbuilders considered that the pacifist influence in America had become too great, and so had hired Ivy L. Lee to counteract it, paying him $150,000 for services in spreading publicity.[8] Lee had begun his career as a press agent many years previously under the patronage of the Rockefellers and various large American corporations. His business was to prepare and send to newspapers and other publications and to a large list of public persons matter favorable to his clients. In time, several foreign Governments used his services. Strong is the temptation to give here some adequate treatment of the systematic campaigns carried on in America by multimillionaires and corporations to modify and otherwise shape public opinion. Enormous sums were thus spent in issuing for consumption a miscellany of skilful publicity the sources of which were generally unsuspected. But we must not be deflected to a monograph on this subject, which would require whole chapters. Suffice it here to say that Lee's connections were once thoroughly investigated by a Federal investigating Commission, and he who is curious may find ample particulars in its report.[9]

But to return to the purview of British armament companies: All—Vickers one of the foremost—were large exporters of war implements. These, irrespective of the possible outbreak of international complications, were sold indiscriminately wherever payment was tendered. A striking instance of this widespread traffic was bruited in the House of Commons in 1913. Captain A. C. Murray, a member, asked Colonel J. E. B. Seely, Secretary of War, whether he had any information pertaining to the adoption by any of the great European Powers of the new Vickers rifle-calibre machine gun. Seely replied that he understood that this pattern of gun had been, or was being, supplied to certain of these Powers. Captain Murray: "What are those Powers?" Seely took refuge in the reply that he thought he knew, but would rather not say without notice. Again, a few days later, Murray importuned for the names of the customer Powers. Seely thus disposed of the query: "There is no official information at my disposal which I can publish on the subject." [10] The stark way in which questions on this momentous matter were put and answered in the British Parliament exposed either the disinclination or the inability to vision the consequences of arming a nation which tomorrow might be an enemy. And this eventuality is precisely what overtook Britain when British guns bought by Turkey were turned against British forces.

The World War did impress some British public men with the need of arranging a measure of international control over the manufacture and sale of arms. When Stanley Baldwin became Prime Minister he broached a proposal for a treaty establishing such a control, but he could not muster acceptance of his plan. And now, many years later, that plan with amplification is (at this writing) being formulated by the American Government.

Bishops, peers and politicians, an eminent assortment, some revered as paragons of piety, others of worldly note, and all ranking illustriously as "pillars of society," were in the concourse of armament company stockholders.[11] Highly did they prize shares yielding them "handsome dividends." The military outlook for Britain in the opening years of the war was dark, and its manhood was being annihilated by the myriads. But if reports to stockholders are any criterion, the generality of leading industrialists were intent upon thoughts of profits.

On a larger capital, Knoch's was soon able to pay a dividend and bonus equaling 20 per cent, free of income tax. From a 2½ per cent dividend before the War, Thornycroft's, a moderate-size plant, increased its distributed profits 200 per cent. The Birmingham Small Arms Company, makers of rifles and Lewis guns, wallowed in profits; these (and they were net) rose from £190,000 in 1914 to £408,000 in 1915, and to somewhat more in each of the years up to 1918; besides which, the company transferred large profit sums to its reserve funds.[12] Frequently, both during and after the war, complaints were made in London financial publications of the sketchiness of information in the Armstrong company's reports. But such figures as the company deigned to give showed a greatly ascending scale of profits, from not quite £600,000 in 1910 to £1,055,620 in 1915, and £4,053,-605 in the three years 1916–1919. The Armstrong company's 12½ per cent dividends did not betoken full profits; out of these £1,300,000 was lodged in reserves, and plant extensions were also built. With the cessation of war, Armstrong dividends dropped to 10, then to 5 per cent.[13] A statement issued to stockholders by Vickers after the war admitted profits during four years of £8,417,612 ($42,000,000). This sum included dividends, income tax paid on these for the stockholders, and an amount put in the company's reserve funds.[14] Embraced in the roster of Vickers' stockholders was a constellation of four dukes and marquesses, seventy other titled personages, three members of the House of Commons, and a group of officials and journalists. Meantime, while lavishing these profits, Vickers had acquired control of other concerns which had proved themselves most attractive money-makers. Such facts regarding profits as came to public knowledge excited rushing speculation in armament and munition stocks—a speculation as intense on the London Stock Exchange as on the Berlin Bourse or on the New York Stock Exchange.

There was in England an old company, the activities of which were denoted by its name—the Metropolitan Carriage, Wagon & Finance Company, commonly abbreviated as the Metro-

politan Wagon Company. Midway in the war, strong indica-
tions of its great profits came to public attention when a few
but telling lines in the chairman's report showed an increase of
its capital stock from £1,000,000 to £3,675,000, and the use of
£1,424,712 as *part* of the plethora of undistributed profits and
reserve funds for this expanded capitalization.[15] A year later
came further impressive news. From American interests the
company had bought control of the British Westinghouse Company for entry into the electrical business; it had embarked
in partnership with the Birmingham Small Arms Company; it
had made an alliance with Vickers; and it had increased its
capital to £10,675,000 by the creation of seven million new
shares at £1 each.[16] A later announcement by the Vickers concern showed that the Metropolitan Wagon Company had passed
under its control.

During the War no questions were asked in Parliament. But
in 1919, in the House of Commons, one of the members—Rose
—prodded the Government official in charge of munitions as
to the contracts which this company had obtained. The information was now elicited that it had been awarded orders for 2,752
armored battlefield tanks. Rose thereupon pointed out how
profits from the company's "fat contracts" had enabled it to
multiply its capitalization and soon to dispose of its properties
for no less a sum than £15,000,000.[17] Military tanks henceforth became a part of the output of the two largest armament
concerns, subsequently combined in Vickers-Armstrong, Limited. Under rules formulated by the Convention for International Trade in Arms, at Geneva, in 1925, a license was required
from the Government of the country in which munitions were
made for their sale and shipment to another Government, and
the transaction had to be reported to the Secretariat of the
League of Nations. Such a license was issued by the British
Government to Armstrong-Vickers, in 1931, for the making
and shipment to the Soviet Government of Russia of one hundred military tanks. The reported cost was $3,000,000.

Although during the World War critical discussion of armament matters was stilled in British, French and other European
newspapers, periodicals and representative bodies, there had
been, as we have seen, some share previously. Yet in all of

it the name and deeds of an individual who had amassed wealth from international traffic in armament was not mentioned, so well did he screen his movements. Basil Zaharoff, born a Greek, naturalized as a Frenchman, and making England his adopted country, had long been a prime character behind the scenes. Warships were his stock-in-trade. So successful was he in his ramification of operations that before the World War he became a masterful power in Vickers, as he later did in Armstrong's. "At the outbreak of the World War," asserts Lehmann-Russbüldt in his book "Die Blutige International" published at Hamburg in 1929, "he was master of the combined armament industries of the Entente." Zaharoff was knighted by the King of England, decorated by France with the Grand Cross of the Legion of Honor for "special services," and in 1924 married a Spanish duchess. "He is," commented Lehmann-Russbüldt, "one of the wealthiest men in the world; but what seems almost incredible is that up to a year or so ago, Europe was utterly ignorant of the machinations and maneuvers of this man. . . ." To those seeking a clarification of the career of this "Man of Mystery," we recommend the vivid account in Lehmann-Russbüldt's book of which an English translation, "War for Profits," was brought out in New York in 1930.[18]

Since that volume was published, supplementary material was disclosed by the testimony, in 1934, before the United States Special Senate Committee investigating the munitions industry. From 1919 to 1930, Zaharoff, the facts showed, received as world agent more than $2,000,000 in commissions from the Electric Boat Company, of Groton, Connecticut, for sales of submarines. Further, a close agreement was shown between the Electric Boat Company and Vickers to dominate the submarine business of the world. Zaharoff, the Electric Boat Company's president testified, had told him that he was a stockholder, although not under his own name, in that American corporation. When his testimony was cabled to England, the need of a Royal Commission to inquire there into the private manufacture and sale of arms was agitated by the Labor Party, with Liberals joining. A Royal Commission was appointed, and at this writing is still taking testimony. At a hearing in London on June 20, 1935, Dr. Christopher Addison, a wartime

Minister of Munitions, stated that nine months after the war had begun the only plant that delivered according to its promises was the national arsenal at Woolwich. "So meagre was the allowance of ammunition for the armies in France," he said, "that it probably is no exaggeration to say that defeat was only narrowly averted by the heroism of our soldiers who were at a great disadvantage and by the success of our national arsenal. I know of no case in history where a great industry was so disastrous a failure in time of need." Previously, however, Lloyd George's "War Memoirs" had exposed these conditions.

The spectacle of a spending class, surfeited with money, was seen in British and other European cities as well as in America during the World War. In both America and Britain capitalist or conservative elements sought to put much of the onus of squandering upon the well-paid skilled working class. Ignoring the fact that the rising scale of living costs had greatly neutralized the benefits of higher wages, these commentators made it appear that workers were reveling in extravagance.

In America, however, conditions differed from those in Britain. The American worker was used to a better standard of living, and things deemed luxuries in Europe did not seem so to him. Also, beginning in 1902, American corporations had systematically set out to dispose of a considerable segment of their stock issues by selling shares to workers. And during the war Liberty Bonds were sold direct to the public. A great deal of American savings went into these channels. But in Britain the old "lofty contempt for the small investor" remained and national finances there were administered with a "superciliousness of small things." The British editor expressing this censure contrasted such an attitude with the situation in France. "While every scullion and chambermaid knew all about Rentes, few British workmen ever penetrated into the arcana of Consols and Local Loans." Consequently, the effects of neglecting the British small investor were seen in his using his money in the only way open to him, that of buying goods.[19]

It was from employers and stockholders and their families that the splurging in Britain came. London shops catering largely to luxurious tastes did an immense business and made large profits.[20] Store owners were in a state of "bursting opulence"; despite scarcity of gasoline and the difficulty of getting an automobile license, "so many ladies are still gliding about the town in large motor cars"; old habitués of fashionable seaside resorts "complain bitterly of being pushed out by the 'new rich' who are spending freely the spoils of war."[21]

The enormous number of rich in Britain was convincingly shown by the Report of the Inland Revenue Commission for the fiscal year 1918–1919. Notwithstanding four years of devastating war and the stupendous financial drain, 5,750,000 persons, in a total population of 47,000,000, reported their taxable income as exceeding the vast total of £2,000,000,000. More than two million persons in this class were relieved, by abatements and exemptions, from income tax payments. The war resulted in the trebling of American millionaires; possessors of annual incomes of more than $100,000 rose from above two thousand to nearly seven thousand a few years later; the number of ultra rich having annual incomes in excess of $1,000,000 increased from sixty in 1914 to more than two hundred. But proportionate to its area and population, Britain could claim for itself a remarkable showing of millionaires and multimillionaires.

In Britain an income tantamount to $50,000 attested a solid millionaire fortune, on the basis of the equivalence of that sum to a five per cent return on a million dollars. And in actual cash-terms Britain's millionairedom was of the sterling breed. Outstanding in the list were two hundred and five notabilities each with a yearly income above £75,000 ($375,000 at par exchange), a rate of income classed in Britain as quite regal. Ranged below that superior group was a class of forty-eight thousand other persons whose income graduated from £75,000 to £2,500 a year. The fruits of more than one-tenth of the national production was taken over by a compact group of 48,205 super income-recipients whose aggregate share was £350,000,000. The portion of the remaining three and a half million income taxpayers amounted only to £937,000,000. Giving a glance at Germany, there we note a plenitude of mark millionaires, the number of whom was reduced by post-war inflation to four thousand, but (so it was estimated) was doubled in later years. For the "Fatherland" whole armies had perished; the big German land-owners, bankers and industrialists experienced the least affliction from war's havoc and inflation's ravages.

Because of laws decreeing heavy taxation in Britain, the legend was spread that there had been compelled a great disgorging of profits. There, however, as in America and in other countries, income-tax and excess-profit tax statutes were much circumvented. Many British corporations seized the opportunity to water their stock and also, as in America, they diverted funds to uses that placed them beyond the reach of profit taxation.

In every country the most outrageous after-war profiteering followed that of the war itself. Many American industrialists added greater sums to their already steep profits. According to the United States Bureau of Labor Statistics, the general increased cost of living between 1914 and 1920 ran from 95 to 100 per cent. Wage increases usually lagged far behind price increases. In some American industries profits in 1919 fell below those of 1918, but in the textile, clothing and dry goods, sugar, food products, petroleum, building material and sundry other lines, the 1919 profits were sensationally more. Public resentment at the extortions provoked a buyers' strike in America. Great complaint in France led to stormy protests in the Chamber of Deputies, on July 18, 1919, and subsequently to a law increasing penalties. To prevent profiteering in food supplies, Britain had created a Food Controller. His regulations were evaded.

Scandal over high prices and large profits caused the House of Commons to order a Select Committee investigation. "Of course," Food Controller G. H. Roberts testified, "we have had experience that speculation does occur as soon as there is a shortage, and undue profits have been made in that way." [22] The offhand and generalizing manner in which this statement was made was typical of the superficial character of the investigation. This did not expose the identity of many big profiteers, although the names of some of these were available, having been noted in British publications. When an anti-profiteering bill was being steered through the House of Commons, the prediction was there made that its provisions would fall upon the little profiteer, but would not deter the big profiteer, who was easily able to pay a heavy fine and continue on his course.[23] British estate owners whose income, derived wholly from land holdings, was stationary or had diminished, bemoaned their fate. They had to meet an onerous taxation which they could not escape, while profiteering cut heavily into their narrowing budget. Bitter were their complaints of the prodigality with which some classes were able to indulge in spending.

Six months after the World War's end, Alfred Shortt, a Labor member of the House of Commons, thus pictured British conditions: "The war has brought to the notice of the people of this country extraordinary manifestations of wealth of which they had little knowledge. Great reservoirs of apparently hidden wealth have been disclosed, and, in addition, we are satisfied that the war itself has led to a vast increase in the private fortunes of individuals. . . . No matter where one turns one finds there has been as a result of the war a great increase in the wealth of the wealthy classes of our community." In contrast, he pointed out, great masses of the British people were forced to subsist on an average pittance of £1 a week.[24]

PART FIVE

THE BUSINESS OF SCOFFING

CHAPTER XXI

A SERIES OF EXHIBITS

"WE have been too often supposed to have been devoted chiefly, if not entirely, to material enterprises. We have been supposed, in the common phrase, to worship the almighty dollar. We have accumulated wealth, sir, we have devoted ourselves to material enterprises with extraordinary success, but there has underlain all that, all the time, a common sense of humanity and a common sympathy with the high principles of justice. . . ." The world-wide and deep-seated effects of the steady campaigning against America were thus acknowledged by President Woodrow Wilson, in an address to the French Academy of Moral and Political Sciences, on May 10, 1919. President Wilson could well have dispensed with admissions and extenuations in discoursing to a Europe large sections of which had long been and were then surcharged with materialism.

True, there had been an interval during the World War when America had enjoyed the unprecedented experience of hearing all sorts of compliments from British and French statesmen. To Americans this ingratiating propaganda was a novelty; but it proved to have been only a preliminary to the business of inducing good will and war support. With America's entry into the war, the Allies received from the American Government more than ten billions of dollars in loans, and at their disposal was placed a powerful navy and an army exceeding two million men. Then, while French statesmen glorified America's humanity and its unbroken and traditional friendship for France, British statesmen effusively deplored the stupidity of George III in alienating the American colonies—which after all, they said, had been composed of Englishmen fighting for a just cause.

But after the war America's longanimity was soon subjected to a resumption of the old attacks, now made in greater force than ever by one group after another of European writers. Philip Gibbs, for example, who attained note as a novelist and war correspondent, ridiculed America as "a nation of nobodies." Americans were never so unpopular in Britain as at this time, Sir H. Perry Robinson, of "The London Times," graciously told the Council of Foreign Relations at a dinner in New York City, on May 11, 1920. One reason for this antagonistic feeling, said he, was because, "You are beastly rich." [1] And Margot Asquith, wife of the former Premier, pertly wrote of Americans, "They would rather hear themselves abused than undiscussed: which inclines one to imagine that they are suffering from the uneasiness of the *nouveaux riches*." She added that they willingly paid their dollars to hear a lecture criticizing them, but balked at being bored.[2] And now came the Earl of Birkenhead. "Twenty-five years ago," he recounted, "the average [American] man of business was conceived of, and not altogether with injustice, as one who left home early and returned late, employing the long day in the feverish interests of Wall Street; he became dyspeptic at forty, he very often died at fifty." But Birkenhead professed to make the great discovery that American dollar madness had been somewhat modified by—what? The game of golf! "And, at last, as I have already pointed out, the United States are beginning to realize that life is short, health vital, dollars incapable of transfer to the next world." [3]

Every era contributes its serio-comic performers to the world stage, in literature as in politics. Thus George Bernard Shaw had contrived to win an international and long-continuing prestige as a great intellect and wit. Shaw had never acquainted himself with America, but for decades he lost no occasion to scoff at its people. Finally, he came to the point where he boasted of his consistent policy of ridicule. "I myself," he wrote in a leading New York newspaper, "have been particularly careful never to say a civil word to the United States. I have scoffed at their inhabitants as a nation of villagers. I have defined the 100 per cent American as an idiot. And they just adore me. . . ." Charles Dickens, he went on to assert, had won America's people "to him forever by merciless projections of Americans as windbags, swindlers and assassins." [4]

When Shaw did at last briefly visit America, in 1933, he effectively exposed himself. The occasion was a long address in the Metropolitan Opera House in New York City, on April 11 of that year. It was Shaw's habit to deny the accuracy of interviews imputed to him. But he could not deny the accuracy of this address, which was stenographically reported in full. In his harangue at the Metropolitan Opera House, he described the American Constitution as "a charter of anarchism," and went on: "You put up in New York a monstrous idol which you call 'Liberty.' And there it is, and the only thing that remains to complete that statue is to put on its pedestal the inscription, 'All hope abandon, ye who enter here.' "

Two days later, under the caption "A Tragic Comedian," "The New York Times" suggested editorially: "Mr. Bernard Shaw really ought to write a play about himself. . . . Did he not in 'John Bull's Other Island' give us a character something like his own—a man discoursing ignorantly but with amazing confidence and cocksureness about everything in the heavens above and the earth beneath? . . ." In London "The Morning Post" editorialized: "He put himself on as a farce at the Metropolitan Opera House, revitalizing that building as the home of opera bouffe."

In England, meanwhile, Frank Harris had written a biography of Shaw, which was published after Harris' death. London newspaper editors were shocked when, in 1931, came the disclosure that Shaw had read and revised the proofs—although, he declared, he had left intact all the jibes at himself. The news of Shaw's collaboration made the front page of nearly all the London newspapers. "The most unpalatable literary sensation of the year," commented "The Daily Mail," which expressed surprise that a man of Shaw's age and "eminence" should have chosen so cheap a path to greater notoriety. In his book Harris appraised the greatly exaggerated importance in which Shaw was held by the world and by himself. "I only wish," Harris wrote, "he had gone to jail for some big idea." He "insulted his times and was well paid for it." Evidently Shaw was proud of this attribution. In a letter of 5,000 words, published in 1933 as a Foreword to G. H. Thring's book, "The Marketing of Literary Property," he related how he "liked bargaining for its own sake," and told what an extraordinarily good bargainer he had been in dealing with publishers.

While Shaw made a profession of mockery, another critic of the day, William Ralph Inge, Dean of St. Paul's Cathedral, London, contrived to draw upon himself the appellation of "the Gloomy Dean." Inge's book "Outspoken Essays" and his lectures in America were a series of croakings; democracy was marked "by the reckless plunder of the national wealth," and was impotent against "revolutionary and predatory wealth." He did not seem to know of the long course of plundering done by or under royal and caste rulers—nor how incompetent those rulers had shown themselves to contend with revolutionary movements.

With variations of phrase, the Gloomy Dean was only repeating the stock indictments of democracy made in the days of his great-great grandfather. However, many American editors overlooked that simple fact. For example, an editorial in "The New York World" of May 3, 1925, timorously took exception to Inge's attacks but accepted the major part of his assertions. For more than a quarter of a century, the editorial sought to explain, Americans had been increasingly aware of defects in the practical workings of democracy; "a critical temper has arisen with regard to the abuses it permits—economic injustice, monopoly, official corruption, vulgarity, intellectual mediocrity, materialism." That pronouncement, too, as we have already seen, is in keeping with a hoary tradition. The brashness of America's foreign critics has been matched only by the encouragement it has received from timid—or perhaps half-informed—American intellectuals.

Inge was one of the leaders among Europeans in assailing America as a Shylock because it expected payment of interest and principal on its war loans. Often in past eras had British newspapers, writers and public men bitterly denounced as dishonest any country which could not pay or failed to pay interest and principal due to British lenders. There still rankles in England a burning survival of resentment from the time of the Civil War when Confederate bonds, bought as prospective rich investments, turned out to be worthless. And to this day, when Britain and other leading European countries are in default to

America, an American hears Englishmen indignantly ask why the Government of the United States does not redeem Confederate paper.

Thus, in his book "England," did Inge deal with America: "If the British flag were hauled down on the North American continent, it is more than probable that the nations of Europe, enraged by the bloated prosperity and airs of superiority of 'the man who won the war' would combine to draw Shylock's teeth. Great Britain, after losing Canada, would no longer have any motive to help a nation which in the circumstances would have finally forfeited its friendship." Irresponsible as it seemed, this utterance had an alarming effect, as was shown by the seriousness with which it was taken by United States Senator Frederick H. Gillett of Massachusetts, one of the most influential of Republican Party leaders. Citing in the United States Senate an excerpt from Inge's statement, Gillett used it as an argument for the passage of a bill providing for more battle cruisers.

"I confess," he said, "to more sympathy and good will toward the British Empire than toward any other nation." But the import of such a statement, he held, must be recognized. "When a high dignitary of the English Church and a professional follower of the Prince of Peace parades such provocative and belligerent sentiments, we can hardly rely upon the pacific and friendly attitude of the rest of the European people." [5] Inge was not an exception among English prelates, however. There had been published a report of a sermon delivered on October 11, 1925, by the Bishop of Durham. "The United States," he was reported as saying, "is at once the most criminal and wealthiest community in the whole civilized world. America is a conspicuous illustration of the folly of neglecting the moral factor in human life." [6]

After Inge's statement had made the stir in the United States Senate, thirteen bishops and leading clergymen of the Church of England, realizing the mischief, issued a disclaimer stating that Inge's sentiments did not represent the views of any considerable number of Englishmen. Unaffected by this rebuke, Inge continued to pour out articles in his accustomed manner and to market them to influential magazines.

In agreeable contrast, there were at this time two British writers who left at home whatever preconceptions they may have had and set out to judge America fairly. Both John Buchan and J. A. Spender were discriminative. Temperate in tone and contents, Spender's book in particular did not occupy itself with minutiae or superficialities. In "Through English Eyes" he tried to include the whole sweep of American conditions; and he made an honest effort to view American life as he thought an American might do. He deprecated the assurance, recklessness and snap judgments of prejudiced British critics; "it follows that an Englishman who goes to that country [America] with the idea of interpreting its life in terms of politics is in danger of going very much astray." He might advisedly have extended his remark to include critics from the Continent as well.

Spender was one of but two or three in the long critical line to admit that America did not need the services of foreign detractors. As an impressive proof of this, he remarked upon "the stream of criticism which is being poured out by the most distinguished American writers on the American way of life."

Observant as he was, Spender failed to distinguish between the groups applying constructive criticism and those whose barkings embodied old attitudes. In this latter group Henry L. Mencken was a leader; he was the Joseph Dennie of the 1920's. He had a crowd of imitators, and the "American Mercury" magazine, as then edited by him, found a considerable and highly vocal audience. Although some articles contributed to this magazine had value in calling attention to matters needing criticism, the general tenor of his expositions was characterized by jeering at democratic society and the influences it created. His contention then was that the average man in a democratic state was a yokel; he was most happy in a mob. Mencken's "Notes on Democracy" was advertised as "a devastating polemic on democratic government and an illuminating analysis of its practice in America." "Such is the price we pay for the great boon of democracy; the man of native integrity is either banned from the public service altogether, or subjected to irresistible temptations after he gets in . . . Democratic man hates the fellow who is having a better time of it in this world.

Such, indeed, is the origin of democracy, and such is the origin of its twin, Puritanism." These were a few of Mencken's many passages.

But here, in view of the fact that Spender's judiciousness has seldom been matched, it might be well to suggest that among European critics the habit has become indurated of regarding American vices as indigenous and American virtues as imported. In general, those critics have shown themselves unable to recognize American self-criticism when they see it. In economics and politics, for example, they have chosen to interpret our frank and open inquiries into corruption as so many shameless confessions of what—so they think—must be the approved, general and daily American practice. And what, then, of the arts? There the European critic, who has imbibed his first ideas of America from the disparaging books written by other Europeans, is prepared to accept the work of our native satirists as full and rounded representations of life in the United States.

A significant instance of this attitude may be seen in some of the critical responses on the Continent to the judgment of the Swedish gentleman who, in 1930, gave the Nobel Prize for literature to Sinclair Lewis. In common with most of their American brethren, European littérateurs in general approved of the award—but for what reason? "Babbitt,"—thus wrote André Levison in "Candide," a Paris literary journal—"Babbitt is a symbol of the average American—100 per cent. . . . Mr. Lewis shows the vacuity, the triviality, the flatness of American middle-class life in America. He puts to shame the agitated sterility of dollar chasing." And Carlo Linati, an Italian critic of some repute, was moved to ask why Americans were so anxious to adopt Europe's scientific discoveries and systems of philosophy: "Is it not that they themselves, in spite of all their materialism, feel that they cannot live without an appearance of culture, even when it is borrowed?"

However, in spite of all their culture, the peoples of postwar Europe could not live without the fact of materialism, whether borrowed or not. While the operations of that materialism were apparently successful, it was the habit of most foreign and many native social critics to lament that the pressure of

American competition had corrupted the business practices of the world. Only when the ventures of European materialism conspicuously failed did it become clear that ingenious American capitalism had devised no process of control through holding companies, no promotion scheme, no system of opening foreign markets to increased production at home, that Europe had not given a new twist to in the borrowing.

Some crowned kings in that continent had been dethroned; but in their stead had arisen industrial kings whose sway, not limited to one nation, was outstretched into a business sovereignty over whole groups of countries. Manifestly, we are not here referring to corporations and Trusts of a purely national character, but to the mammoth international cartels, combines and Trusts of which there were thirty-six. Constructed largely by Fritz Thyssen, a German steel manufacturer, the International Steel Entente included the chief producers in that line in eight European countries. In nine lands in Europe the Bottle Manufacturers' Cartel lodged itself. Through ten European countries spread the Electric Bulb Cartel, with its hold in Japan also. The Superphosphate Cartel was implanted in eleven European, and two African, countries, and the Glue Syndicate's domain comprehended eighteen European countries. These were some of the huge industrial creations variously intent upon harmony of interests, price-fixing agreements and control of raw material and finished production.[7]

In the list of these international organizations was the Match Trust directed from Sweden, and as an outgrowth it was in Sweden itself that the most colossal business swindler of centuries developed. In that country the backwardness of its business men had been made the frequent occasion of self-reproach. Although Sweden, so it was said there, possessed many good technical business administrators, they were routine and plodding compared to the daring, masterful business leaders in other lands, notably America. Sweden had a wide range of manufactures, but timber, matches, iron and pulp were its great staple industries. The corporations that controlled these fattened on good or high profits, while periodically their dissatisfied workers rebelled in bitter and often prolonged strikes. Waiving account of such conditions, we shall restrict ourselves to a sketch of the kind of outstanding business leader Sweden did finally spawn in the person of Ivar Kreuger, the exposure of whose world-wide plundering came only two years after the Swedish award of the Nobel Prize to Sinclair Lewis.

A small-town man born in 1880, Kreuger had been supplied with school opportunities, and had studied at the Technical University in Stockholm until he was twenty years of age. The next seven years he spent as a drifter employed in other countries; he worked for a New York City real estate firm, and had jobs on railway construction in Illinois and on bridge building in Mexico. Next he located in Johannesburg in South Africa, where he made enough money from hotel construction to enable him to spend several years in travel.

Returning to Stockholm in 1907, he went into partnership with Paul Toll in a constructional and engineering enterprise. Shortly before the World War the firm of Kreuger & Toll wedged its way into the Swedish match industry. Within four years, by applying lessons of combination he had learned in America, Kreuger became the dominating force. It was related that, holding a box of matches in his hand, he enchanted directors by showing how, with Sweden controlling two-thirds of the world's match production, the apparently slight increase of one-eighth of a cent per box in the factory price would yield tens of millions of dollars more in yearly net profits. Kreuger was looked up to as a scintillating business genius, and he developed his plans with a swiftness that astonished the Swedish business world.

Kreuger soon outdid his American exemplars. He amalgamated Swedish match manufacturers into the Swedish Match Company, a giant holding company, and, by a series of moves, linked this with Kreuger & Toll. Perhaps nobody but he had any clear understanding of the complicated network and the involved finances of the ever-expanding Kreuger group of corporations. These included match factories not only in Sweden and Norway but also in Poland, San Domingo, Peru and other countries—two hundred and sixty plants in all. Under Kreuger's control were eight large iron-ore, pulp and other natural-resource corporations in Sweden; farm mortgage companies in Sweden, France and Germany; more than fourteen telephone and telegraph companies in six European and in various South American countries; and banking concerns in Sweden, Amsterdam, Paris and other cities. Excepting Socialists, the Swedes in general regarded Kreuger with awe; and at the same time he stood out to fourteen European Governments and one South American Government as the grand lord bountiful whose inexhaustible supplies of cash could conveniently be tapped. The arrangement was simple. In most cases, those Governments created match monopolies which they leased to the Swedish Match Company, or to some affiliated corporation, for a stated period. Kreuger's known loans to those countries totaled $330,000,000.

A chart detailing the intricate inter-relationships of the many Kreuger enterprises would arouse wonder that any mind could keep track of the bewildering maze of ramifications. But Kreuger was gifted with a phenomenal grasp of facts—a memory able to master details which would have staggered most men. He was a convincing talker and a perfect actor, who thoroughly understood the power of apparent guilelessness to radiate confidence among bankers. It was in 1922 that he began the sale of his company's securities to English financiers. With equally conspicuous success he palmed off great batches of securities upon the bankers of other countries, both European and American.

A partner in the conservative banking house of Lee, Higginson & Company, of Boston, narrated in later court proceedings how Kreuger exercised an hypnotic spell over supposedly hardheaded bankers in Europe and America. On a visit to Stockholm, this witness told, he found that in business circles Kreuger was the uppermost subject. "He dominated everything. I never heard a man more beautifully spoken of." Without asking Kreuger any questions whatever about the affairs of his companies, that Boston banking firm readily consented, with a child-like trust, to sponsor his stock issues in America. "Such implicit faith" had they in Kreuger that they "never even thought," as the partner testified, of obtaining verification of his claims to the possession of asserted national match monopolies. From 1915 onward the firm marketed $150,000,000 of his securities to the American public, and members of the firm themselves so greatly prized Kreuger's stock that they bought millions of dollars of it for their personal holdings. They made, as a firm, more than six million dollars in gross profits on commissions in underwriting the Kreuger stock issues and distributing them among six hundred American banks and brokerage houses, which disposed of them at high prices to investors assured of their "gilt-edged" quality.

Kreuger's sway over minds reputedly adamantine in their resistance to the surrendering of cash without due pledges was shown by the action of a group of American bankers in loaning him $15,000,000 upon no other security than his bare word. From descriptions furnished later by some Swedish acquaintances, Kreuger became, it would seem, intoxicated with the idea of his incomparable rank as the world's super business man. In his rôle of international financier he was overcome, it was also said, by a boundless delusion of grandeur. If this were so, the probability was that he measured himself only by his successes and took lightly the fraudulent practices used in achieving them. Some of these practices were not uncommon among certain types of business men in other countries; and if Kreuger did bestow serious thought upon his own frauds, he could feel that he excelled all others in effectual audacity.

He had due opportunity to note the methods which had been employed by one of Britain's leading business characters. A winged rumor in London of the issuance of a warrant against "a world-famous business man" was officially denied, but it soon turned out to be true. For a quarter of a century Lord Kylsant had been a notability as chairman of the Royal Mail Steam Packet Company. The prosecution charged that the prospectus issued by him to float £2,000,000 debentures for the erection of a new company building—the Royal Mail House—and for general purposes was so drawn as to carry the conviction that, during the previous ten years, the company had made an annual profit in the vicinity of £500,000 a year. During some of these years, however, the company had incurred heavy losses. By manipulating figures and raiding reserves of subsidiary companies, Kylsant produced a fictitious showing. In June, 1931, he was convicted of having made false statements in his 1926 and 1927 reports with intent to deceive stockholders. As his remuneration was based upon commissions paid on volume of gross profits Kylsant was not without personal motive for his frauds. In 1927 he drew a sum almost equaling $130,000 as his salary and commission. No less a personage than the Duke of Abercorn, records of the stockholders' annual meeting in that year showed, seconded, as a matter of form, the motion to adopt his report.[8] The ire of influential stockholders overflowed at finding out how the trusted Kylsant had imposed upon their confidence.

Of "strict British justice" much had been professed. But it had been a justice rigorously visited upon the poor. Penalizing for financial buccaneering was a comparatively new development. With such indifference did generations of British law-makers regard false financial statements prepared for public consumption that there was no specific inhibiting statute. Incredible as this fact may seem, it was demonstrated only two decades or so before Kylsant's acts.

After a group of companies fraudulently promoted by Whitaker Wright had collapsed, the Attorney-General (Sir Robert Finlay), in the House of Commons, had scouted the notion that punishment could be meted for the making of a false balance sheet for public deception. Section 84 of the Larceny Act of 1861, he explained, provided for particular cases of stockholders and creditors only, and "does not provide at all for the case of misrepresentations made with the general intent to defraud the public." In support of his elucidation he cited a charge made, in 1880, by Chief Justice Cockburn to a jury in a case that involved the defrauding of the public by intentional misrepresentation of worthless assets as having a value between £1,000,000 and £2,000,000.[9]

When Wright fled to America, some angry House of Commons members raised a tempest. Remissness was charged to the legal authorities for having given him opportunity to decamp. "The circumstances under which Wright was allowed to escape," one member—Swift MacNeill—exclaimed, "looked as if there was one law for the rich and another for the poor." [10] Wright was extradited to England, where a judge did manage to find grounds under some law or other to fix legal responsibility upon him for having issued prospectuses juridically described as "fascinat-

ing," "cunning" and "tricky." Upon receiving a prison sentence
of seven years, Wright killed himself. Comment was made in
some journals on the position of Lord Dufferin who, it was
openly stated, had read at the stockholders' meetings addresses
practically written by Wright.

Lord Kylsant was undone and weighted with a sentence of
twelve months in prison, but Kreuger could contemplate
Kylsant's fate with the superior feeling that, more astute or
fortunate, he himself had long continued to surmount any question of his acts. Subsequently, Percy A. Rockefeller, one of
America's leading capitalists and a director of the International
Match Corporation, gave his testimony on this point. Admitting
that he had never tried to verify Kreuger's statements, Rockefeller told how he had "relied implicitly" upon Kreuger's word,
accepting it without question. In parts of his operations, at least,
Kreuger had no reason to think of himself as committing any
unusual criminality.

The shaky situation in Britain, with its consequent tremors
among some prominent business men over the putative penal
consequences of their frauds, was thus set forth by "The Economist," of London (November 7, 1931), after Kylsant's appeal
had been dismissed by the Criminal Court of Appeals: "Many
of the promoters of the more highly speculative issues of the
1928–1929 boom must needs have scrutinized the reports of the
trial with the painful reflection that a slight turn of fate might
well have found them playing a central rôle in the drama."

In the desolating sweep of the world depression, the market
value of Kreuger & Toll and Swedish Match Company stock
shrank at a terrific pace in 1930–1931. No suspicions were held
of Kreuger insolvency. Suddenly, early in March, 1932, flashed
the startling news of Kreuger's suicide in Paris. The immediate cause of this act was, it seems, a polite but firm inquiry by
certain bankers reminding him of a debt of $11,000,000 due
to the International Telephone & Telegraph Company. Now,
following his suicide, came a hurricane of trepidation in hyper-
sensitive stock markets. Investors everywhere were terror-
stricken, for into his securities had gone three-quarters of a
billion dollars. At least $250,000,000 (some estimates made out
a much larger sum) was contributed by Americans; and hun-

dreds of millions of dollars had been exchanged by Swedish, British, French, Dutch and Swiss investors for his bits of paper.

An investigating committee quickly appointed by financial interests in Stockholm began finding the grisly truth. Accountants had hardly got below the surface before they discovered that the Kreuger ledgers were "grossly wrong"; falsification had been done on a huge scale. Some assets were imaginary, others were listed in duplicate. Accounts had been manipulated by fictitious entries so as to conceal debts. For at least eight years these frauds had been going on. "We know now," fumed the editor of the "Social Demokraten," a Stockholm newspaper, "that the Kreuger company broke down not because of bad luck or bad conditions but because of dishonesty." But these revelations were only a prelude. To get the money to pay dividends to American stockholders, Kreuger had juggled funds. From banks he had twice borrowed $50,000,000 on the same block of German bonds, stealing them from the International Match Corporation of which he was president, and depositing them to his own credit in a Stockholm bank.

Forthwith came evidence of his forging on an amazing scale. In his private room at the Match Trust offices the Stockholm police found an assortment of rubber stamps giving facsimile signatures of public officials and prominent persons. Seemingly, whenever there came into his possession any signature he thought might prove useful, he caused a rubber stamp to be made. World astonishment, already great, grew greater when Italy's Government declared a brazen forgery the alleged Italian match monopoly inventoried by Kreuger as worth more than $52,000,000. Spain's Government likewise announced that Kreuger's claim to a Spanish monopoly, which he valued at nearly $28,000,000, was a myth.

These were some of the tangle of his enormities. In addition, he had secretly speculated in his own securities, with resultant heavy losses. His personal debts, an inventory of his estate showed, reached $179,000,000, while his assets (many of doubtful value) amounted to less than $18,000,000. Proofs were found of his having paid blackmail to many women, and of payments to European public men. Among Kreuger's correspondence was found a letter showing a donation of 50,000 kronor to the Swedish Prime Minister Carl Gustav Ekman, whose resignation was now forced by public outcry. "What has happened," moaned the Stockholm newspaper "Dagen Nyheter," "is heart breaking for Sweden's reputation." And the Swedish administrators of bankruptcy, seeking to make a demarcation relieving the Swedish business men of disrepute, reported their finding: "It is not as a business man but as a criminal that Kreuger was distinguished from his fellow men." A brief while ago statesmen had courted Kreuger, and sovereigns had been glad to claim his friendship. Now he was represented by the European press as the blackest of figures. A "prince among swindlers," "the arch impostor of the ages," "a devil in human guise." These were some of the expressions, oft mingled with the melancholy reflection that the world at large had shown itself a great fool by accepting Kreuger at his own valuation for eight years.

Hordes of investors everywhere were plunged into partial or complete ruin. From all quarters came pitiful tales of destitution following losses. In Sweden itself, where large sections of the middle class had confided their money to Kreuger, the result was calamitous. The rise in the number of suicides and sudden deaths in Stockholm was affrighting, and great proportions of the middling population found themselves precipitated from affluence or ease to penury. The final filing, in 1935, of claims against the Kreuger estate and his concerns brought the total to 2,842,704,000 kronor (about $700,000,000).

Americans were familiar with the names and activities of few other big European industrial leaders and promoters. To Thyssen and to Stinnes in Germany considerable notice was given in American newspapers, and a large share of attention to André Citroën, chiefly because he was designated "the Henry Ford of France." Citroën was credited with having adopted American business methods, which he had studied while visiting America in 1912 and in later years. He led thereby in revolutionizing the European motor-car industry; his extensive automobile factories in France employed 20,000 workers. That there was in Belgium a man whose wealth supposedly approximated that of Ford or of the Rockefellers the generality of

Americans did not know, until American newspapers featured the singular and tragic death of Captain Alfred Lowenstein.

In addition to his European reputation of "Belgian Santa Claus" and "Croesus," Lowenstein was also viewed as "the mystery man of Europe." And there *was* mystery as to how, in the course of thirty years, he had stepped from nothingness to a commanding position of great wealth. Such information as was supplied about Lowenstein's career was scanty,—of the conventionally eulogistic European kind,—and was marked by large and important omissions of explanatory facts.

His father, a small Brussels banker, died in debt, it was related; and Alfred worked to pay off family creditors. The goodness of this act was stressed in all accounts, which further told how he then set out to make his own fortune by selling in Brussels the securities of hydro-electric companies promoted in South America and elsewhere by the British Dr. Pearson. A great gap in the accounts ensued, and the next fact learned was that Lowenstein had accumulated enough wealth to make a much-needed loan to the British Cellulose & Chemical Company, later the British Celanese, Limited. It was after the World War that he spread out hugely, organized a holding company which successively obtained control of Belgian, Dutch, French, German, Polish and American artificial silk companies. Another holding company was created by him to take over his electric-light plant interests in many countries, powerful British and Canadian financiers joining in the enterprise. He became owner of manganese iron mines in Silesia, steel furnaces in northern Spain, vast Congo rubber plantations, and in other ways expanded proprietorship.

Lowenstein's mode of life was that of a magnifico. He had a castle in Brussels, a house in London, maintained a racing stud in Leicestershire, England, and, so it was recorded, owned eight villas in Biarritz alone. On his trips between European centers he was accompanied by a corps of secretaries and typists. Voyaging to America his entourage was even larger, including also a private detective, a masseur and an airplane pilot. Along with him were conveyed two automobiles. So profusely did he use the ship radio that on a single trip his bill amounted to $3,500. In an interview he expressed his high admiration for

American business methods of which, said he, "I have always made use." Both in Europe and America he traveled in one of his twenty-passenger planes, and it was while crossing the English Channel, returning from London to Brussels, that, on July 4, 1928, he disappeared. The assumption given out was that he had opened the wrong door from his compartment and had fallen into the sea. At any rate, the episode remained encased in mystery; almost equally in the dark was his financial status at the time. One fact and one only was generally known in European financial centers. His ambitions had gone far beyond the point where he could be content with mere investments, and he had aimed at nothing less than big amalgamations absolutely controlled by himself. This aim had led to violent conflicts with owners of various companies, especially with British Celanese, Limited. Disposing of his holdings in this company, he sought, by warring upon it, to make it yield to him or be ruined, and this conflict, at the time when he dropped out of sight, had reached a critical stage.

Americans had no such acute interest in foreign financial happenings as did, for instance, British security holders. In 1924 they were drawing a computed £156,000,000 (another estimate stated £208,000,000) of net income from investments abroad. In general, American small investments were in native securities, and such scandals of corporate plundering as occupied American attention at large were almost wholly those in America itself. American popular investments in a foreign concern like Kreuger's were among the exceptions. Americans had little or no adequate knowledge of the facts or methods of groups of industrial leaders in Britain or in other lands. Consequently, Americans were led to imagine crooked finance an American institution; and Kreuger's knavery seemed to stand out all the more sharply in contrast to what Americans supposed were the staid, conservative and correct methods in Europe.

Recurrent financial scandals in France were looked upon by Americans as something outside the orbit and regularities of established French finance. Those scandals, however, were not exceptional but were the sequel to operations commonplace in France. Large groups of the French people, though frugal and parsimonious, were easily induced to hand over the fruit of their hoarding to promoters who would hold out the irresistible lure of unusually large dividends.

One of a number of promoters in post-war Paris was Mme. Marthe Hanau. From the ownership of a lingerie shop in Montmartre, she began, in 1920, ballooning into high finance. How she obtained the funds needed to embark in her extensive operations remained a riddle. Aided by her divorced husband, she organized a group of finance and banking companies, and promised investors the grand possibility of as much as 40 per cent returns from her speculations. She imitated British methods in giving éclat and an aristocratic air to her companies by having as directors titled Frenchmen of the "old nobility." One of these personages was the Duc d'Ayen who, as he later testified, allowed the use of his name for a consideration of 1,800,-000 francs (about $70,380) in shares of the General Financial Company. To push her companies she ran a financial newspaper, the "Gazette de France," the directors of which included prominent French politicians.

There was not an open-eyed French promoter who, in a vaguely general way, did not know of the great sums of money in hiding throughout France. But even fraudulent promoters, with their predacious sixth sense, had no adequate knowledge of how immense was the amount. Eagerly did they imbibe information which came out in 1925, in the Budget Bill discussion in the Chamber of Deputies. The tax on acquired wealth had augmented hoarding, so that now nearly eight milliards (eight billions) of francs were concealed "in sterile safety throughout the country." This complaint was amplified in the Senate by Henri Bérenger. "These milliards," he stated, "are being hoarded in strong boxes and woolen stockings, which has reduced our real note circulation to thirty-three milliards." The mentality of the millions of small French investors was, he added, "perhaps the most sensitive and easily alarmed mind in the world." Some of their money had also been sent to Switzerland, Holland, Belgium and other countries where it would be sheltered from the reach of French taxation.

But much as they sought to hug their money, large numbers of French town and village investors were no match for wily promoters. The amount taken in by Mme. Hanau's companies was estimated all the way from 100,000,000 to 500,000,000 francs—her liabilities, in fact, were 110,000,000 francs. During nearly nine years she had done a flourishing business selling stock in her companies. When she and they went into bankruptcy in 1928, piercing was the outcry from a multitude of investors. The Madame and her ex-husband were arrested. Ugly charges were now forthcoming: some newspaper publishers were accused of having received either money or shares for furnishing her with lists of subscribers; members of the French Parliament were accused of connivance with her, and there was a squall in the Chamber of Deputies. After several months in jail Mme. Hanau sent forth tidings that she could pay creditors. This claim was of no effect; her later trial resulted in a sentence of three years in prison, where, in July, 1935, she ended her career by an overdose of narcotics.

"An enterprise for the exploitation of French savings," the "Journal des Débats" of Paris called her operations. But hers was only one of many. Under the broad generosity of French law there was nothing to prevent an undischarged bankrupt or a person with a criminal record from going into business as a private banker or as a promoter. There was no protective regulation to cover the issuing or advertising of stocks and bonds. Yet, even had there been strict laws, it would have been difficult to shield the public from its own gullibility and greed.

How easily the decoying was done may be shown by two typical cases. In the first a professor of law, tired of eking out his modest salary, started company promoting, and, since he was versed in every turn and loophole of legal procedure, he knew perfectly how to chart his course. Assurances of extra high dividends brought in loads of money. As fast as a million francs came to one of his companies, that company vanished, and there was promptly organized another which repeated the performance. Under different guises he formed many companies, all of which were himself; for the loot, as subsequent evidence showed, went entirely into his pockets. The second swindle was a pork company which excited many French villagers by the pictured wonders of its pig-rearing farm and by the promise of 16 per cent dividends. Further to attract share buyers, the company declared that each stockholder was entitled to a suckling pig which the company would benevolently fatten and hold for his ownership. This inducement had a strong practical appeal to France's agricultural class—that is, to between one-third and one-half of the entire population. Money rained upon the company, and still more would have come in, had it not been for the bursting curiosity of some investors. They went to see their pigs, only to be informed that unfortunately theirs had died. Upon tallying experiences investors learned that the situation was general, and public disclosures followed.

But, since this is not a history of French financial scandals, we shall pass over other notorious instances. In 1929 a Paris newspaper estimated that, from the Humbert embezzlement thirty years before down to date, more than 300,000,000,000 francs—a sum equal to France's internal and foreign debts—had been taken by the sale of worthless shares. This estimate might have been exaggerated; but unquestionably the amount sunk in speculation was enormous, for apart from bogus enterprises there were many valid companies turning out quantities of watered stock. Corps of unctuous stock salesmen thronged public places in Paris to inveigle prospects—a condition paralleled, it is worth noting, in Italy. There speculative mania in the avalanche of new stock issues caused the Committee of the Milan Stock Exchange, in 1925, to restrict the crowd by establishing admission by ticket—an unprecedented action in that country. Yet these were years in which cartoons in French and Italian papers were universally depicting America as a huge money ogre.

The World War was the opportune occasion seized by existent British Trusts greatly to enlarge their power. This expansion, as the official Committee on Trusts reported early in 1918, had been enormously strengthened by the Government's war policy of rationalizing trade.[11] Then, and in the years immediately following, huge mergers were effected along American lines but without American safeguards for investigation. Complaining of the absence of these, the Departmental Committee on Trusts, in its report of April, 1919, recommended:

"We are unanimously of the opinion that it would be desirable to institute in the United Kingdom machinery for the investigation of monopolies, Trusts and combines, similar to the commissions and tribunals created for that purpose in the United States of America and British Colonies [Canada]." Five years later, though, we find the leading London financial journal protesting because the Committee's unanimous opinion had gone unheeded.[12]

Industrial magnates continued doing as they pleased with no fear of investigation. Although legally invalid, great holding companies (shaped after the American) were organized; not until 1928 did these British companies have behind them the authority of definite legal recognition. Parliament, full of corporation directors or stockholders, took no steps to regulate these giant concerns in the interest of the community. In America and in some European countries the reporting of a consolidated balance sheet for the whole group of companies in a holding company was a general requirement. Holding companies, by 1931, had penetrated every branch of British industry, but the supplying of a consolidated balance sheet was not compulsory in Britain, and accordingly there was no enlightenment as to the financial state of such commercial agglomerations. Some of these companies were international in scope, as for example the "Unilever" colossus, embodying more than six hundred companies in Britain, Holland and in eastern and central Europe, and having complete control there of soap, oil-seed crushing and margarine from the raw-material stage to retail distribution. One of the constituents of this huge company was the firm of Lever Brothers (productive of Lord Leverhulme). This firm in itself was an enormous holding concern, and one of its subsidiaries was the Niger Company which had merged with other African palm oil companies.

Side by side with widespread joblessness, extreme poverty, and the distribution of the dole by the Government, it now appeared that Britain's possessing classes had a greater income flow than ever before. The total in 1924 was £4,213,000,000, two thousand million pounds more than the amount thirteen years previously. The bulk of this income—above four thousand million pounds—came from within Britain itself, £205,-

000,000 representing corporation income and undivided profits. Such were the findings of the financial authorities, Professor A. L. Bowley and Sir Josiah Stamp,[13] although the figures should be qualified by allowance for an inflationary period.

This abundance of money provided company promoters of all shades with an urgent reason for speeding from the printing presses great quantities of watered stock. In an article published on May 31, 1928, Thomas Shaw, who had been Minister of Labor in the MacDonald Cabinet, grouped a number of complaints. He protested because British capital had been "watered to an enormous extent," which obviously was true. But as to another condition he was not so well informed. He complained of the backwardness of British corporation directors in not adopting new methods. Those directors, he wrote, drew huge salaries and "appear to be gilded spongers on industry." In point of fact many British business leaders had already adopted every available American money-making device. The American plan of selling goods on installment payments had been transplanted, and was known there as "hire purchase." One result was a 300 per cent increase in automobile sales in Europe in the eight years after 1920.[14] Expanding sales were plausibly cited by corporations as a sound reason for showering stock issues. To sell these, British business financiers zealously followed the American corporation system of ministering to what was called popular stock ownership. No longer was the moderate investor ignored, or the small investor scorned. The mass of purchasers in big, excessively-capitalized industrial corporations had no suspicion that the ratio of profits was grossly insufficient to justify a basis for the high prices asked for the stock. There came febrile London Stock Market booms with manipulated ascending prices to fire the eagerness of an overwrought public.

How widely British corporations succeeded in disseminating their stock was shown by a private financial investigation in 1926. There were in Britain 95,000 companies with a total paid up capital of £4,500,000,000. The vast majority of stockholders, records of eighteen of the large corporations evidenced, had individually less than £500 invested. The claim now made was that stock ownership had become "a truly democratic business." The balance of that democracy seems, however, to have been weighted rather heavily in favor of the corporation heads. For, so we learn, "provided that the mass of stockholders receive their dividends, the directors may hold their power indefinitely . . ." nor is that an exaggeration, since it takes "considerable expenditure of time and money to organize the thousands of small stockholders whose votes are, in the last resort, the controlling factor." [15]

Vulpine promoters of a large miscellany of new companies overlooked no possibility of loot. "The speculative promoter or issuing house, as a rule," stated "The Economist," "regards business from the angle of salesmanship. He is concerned to discover new enterprises which will 'go well' when offered to the public, and after making an issue is anxious to 'get out' as quickly as possible." Some American "high-pressure" methods of stock selling were closely copied. Traveling in automobiles, glib, sprucely-dressed, keen-eyed salesmen scoured the countryside in England and Scotland. They were equipped with lists of persons known to have money, and carried sheaves of alluring "literature." Among the force were American adepts whose services were doubtless requisitioned to coach the rest. Another and also effective method was the inducing of corporation clerks to supply great lists of existent stockholders. These were "intensively" circularized, and enticing personal visits followed. In hotels and restaurants there was so much buttonholing and badgering by stock vendors that measures were moved in Parliament to check the nuisance.

High in the ranks of the more venturesome and spectacular promoters was James White, popularly and even endearingly called Jimmy White. After he had achieved what seemed phenomenal success, the story of his career appealed to numbers of his countrymen with the captivating charm of a fairy-tale enacted in life. As a youth he had been a bricklayer's apprentice, and when eighteen years old had shown initiative and resourcefulness by contracting for cottage building. His capital was so tiny that, to continue, he had to mortgage the houses room by room. He went into ambitious real estate dealing which whelmed him in bankruptcy. From this he gradually and buoyantly emerged. Resuming the real estate business, he found a powerful backer and associate in Sir Joseph Beecham of pill-making fame. The Beecham Trust was organized; White became its chairman and managing director; and through it he handled a succession of bold deals in stock flotations of rubber, cotton, brewery, department-store and other syndicates. He had no knowledge of industrial affairs, but fortune was blindly with him, and "Jimmy White luck" became a popular fetich.

When White reached out to buy control of British Controlled Oilfields, a corporation with £9,000,000 capital, his many followers heeded his generously given advice to invest in its preferred stock. Of the oil business White knew nothing, but it was later recorded that his secret purpose after obtaining control of the stock was to sell it to the Standard Oil Company for perhaps five times the amount he had paid. Most unexpectedly, however, revelations of the position of British Controlled Oilfields became public. In November, 1925, the board of directors was replaced by a new body which, under the direction of Lord Buckmaster, disclosed nearly a year later the startling fact that of the company's $45,000,000 capital $30,000,000 had been lost in payments for worthless concessions. Following its incorporation in 1919, the company in the next year had bought, by the issue of $4,375,000 of preferred and $15,000,000 of common stock, certain rights represented as of great value in Ecuador and Costa Rica. Those concessions turned out to be invalid. For other concessions in Central and South American countries the company had paid $5,000,000 in preferred shares, only to discover that in but one case was the property of any value.

For months the market price of the company's stock had been crumbling. But White had heavily committed himself to purchases of the stock, and, when faced by a London Stock Exchange settlement rule, he could not raise an immediate £750,000. On a July day in 1927 he locked himself in a room in his suburban home, left a pathetic adieu, and chloroformed himself to death—one more sudden extinction from the ranks of financial "wizards" whose operations had brought disastrous losses to investors. Following the stock-watering monomania some corporations were confronted with the necessity of earning dividends—a problem which they set about solving by wage reductions. In several leading industries there ensued great strikes or, when employes refused to take a cut in wages, great lockouts.

But such troubled industries contained only a few of the tens of thousands of British companies. As a whole these, irrespective of the volume of their stock issues, had proved themselves proficient money makers. Analysis of the returns of some seventeen hundred companies showed, for pre-depression times, yearly net profits of some £200,000,000 and average dividends on common stock of more than 10 per cent.[16] The emphasis here is on *average;* the profits of many particular corporations much exceeded that goodly amount.

The dividends of leading London banks ran from 16 to 20 per cent; "distinctly gratifying," a London financier remarked. There was, for instance, Bass, Ratcliffe & Gretton, Limited, whose chairman, "Colonel the Right Honorable John Gretton, P.C., M.P.," announced in 1928 a total yearly dividend of 25 per cent, free of tax, and received a stockholders' resolution of congratulations.[17] And there was the Burmah Oil Company, Limited, of which Sir John T. Cargill was chairman; his father had started it in 1886 with a capital of £60,000 which had now expanded to nearly £11,000,000, with a market value almost five times that sum. When Cargill informed stockholders of a declared dividend for the year of 40 per cent subject to tax, or 30 per cent not so subject, they voted thanks. To which Cargill replied: "Really in a way I have earned a vote of thanks for sending so many of you away from this meeting in such a happy and contented—I won't go the length of saying optimistic frame of mind." [18] Ears heard the words, some clear, some ambiguous, but it was the cash that spoke loudest of all. Again, there was the Kamunting Tin Dredging [Company] Limited, with Sir Ernest Birch, chairman, telling stockholders that on the company's actual capital, as it stood from time to time, they had received 251 per cent.[19] We note, too, the Castlefield (Klang) Rubber Estate [Company] Limited, with the stockholders' enthusiasm kindled by the chairman's report that the original capital subscription had yielded annual dividends of 34½ per cent; or a total benefaction of 727½ per cent in twenty-one years.[20] Further, we exhibit the British India Steam Navigation Company, the nominal annual profits of which, according to an analysis of its structure, had been 20 per cent but actual profits, it was asserted, were 63 per cent.[21]

These were but a few instances from the long list of large money-makers. Even after the onset of the world depression there were corporations operating in and out of Britain to such profit that they could pay 12 and 16 per cent dividends. If a striking instance be desired of how perpetually money poured into Britain, it is supplied by the record of our old acquaintance, the Hudson Bay Company. In the eighteen years prior to 1927, the net profits of this venerable concern from land sales and fur and from trading business in Canada amounted to a sum equaling more than $41,000,000. From all directions converged the golden streams. And now Britain could view a parade, in print at least, of its "Kings of Commerce," a numerous list of whom was published in 1828, all fortified with large fortunes and many ornamented with conferred titles.[22]

CHAPTER XXII

UNCLE SHYLOCK

A NEW cause for feeling against America was now fomented in Europe. Less than a decade after the finish of the World War came outcries against the American "economic invasion" which, it was represented, was undermining Europe's hold upon its own industries. For centuries, as we have seen, European capital had been heavily invested in America and in many other lands. To Europe that was a natural and even a highly laudable mission of money. European financiers had often boasted of the civilizing power of their capital in developing the resources of unsettled or backward countries. But now that American money was flowing for investment into Europe the process was viewed there as fraught with the terrors of an "invasion," and as proving the world-conquering aims of American money domination.

This transfusion of American capital to Europe began after 1910 and quickened rapidly in post-war years. The World War had changed America's status from a debtor to a creditor nation. In addition to the vast sums loaned by the American Government, large amounts of American money were siphoned into Europe from private sources. Profits of interlocked American banks and Trusts were so great that huge amounts of investment capital had accumulated. Many former native outlets for the placing of such surplus had begun to shrivel, railroad building had ended, mine working had reached the limit of consuming capacity, factory production was nearing a saturation point, and utilities had been pushed to the stage of over-extension. Consequently, for an opportune field of investment, American capitalists turned to Europe, disorganized and crippled by the war.

For years, American purchases of European stocks had to be made in Europe's stock markets. It was not until October,

1927, that the New York Stock Exchange adopted regulations to facilitate the buying of British securities. As American investments in Europe kept on mounting, a widespread fear broke forth there at this "economic penetration," and from many sources came outbursts against the ominous "new peril," to wit, that American money would buy up the world. This campaign had its multi-voiced array of periodicals and newspapers, which often featured cartoons symbolizing America as Uncle Shylock and which profusely used the dollar sign as typifying America.

To judge by the vituperative contents of many European papers at the time, the subject engrossed nearly all discussion. Some of the French papers were especially abusive in denunciations of America as a merciless creditor. In the more responsible precincts of the French Chamber of Deputies, several speakers professed to see in American private investments a crafty, iniquitous plot to dominate European industry. These declarations were made in the debate, in 1929, over the debt France owed to the American Government. Amid much talk of American "financial penetration," speakers invidiously pointed out that if America could not actually be classed as an imperialist country, its gigantic capital funds were able to achieve and were adroitly achieving a much more subtle and dangerous kind of domination than ever force would accomplish. And when, in Germany, the great Oppel automobile works came under American capitalist control, various German newspapers joined with those elsewhere in Europe in arraigning America as deliberately planning to "Americanize" Europe. An Italian Fascist official added his voice, stridently protesting against the American "imperialist economic invasion" of Europe.

If the entry of American investment capital into Europe constituted an "invasion," then what name was to be applied to the far greater amount of European capital invested in America? This was a point which Europe did not even consider. European critics had often depicted Americans as a volatile people, blown hither and thither by waves of sheer hysteria. But American conduct was composure itself, alongside the childish gusts of hysteria that swept Europe on the theme of "Americanization" and "dollar domination."

What was Europe's pother about? Here, again, money talks with overwhelming eloquence. For, in comparison with Europe's foreign investments, America's were in the lesser grade. Including American private loans, the total American investment in Europe reached an estimated six and a half billion dollars,[1] and American private loans throughout the world perhaps fourteen billion dollars. On the other hand, according to a statement by Dr. Julius Klein, U. S. Assistant Secretary of Commerce, investments by foreigners in American securities aggregated seven billion dollars.

No estimate was prepared of Europe's investments in the world at large. But the computations of English economists give some accurate idea of the magnitude of British investments. These, at this period, were placed at the colossal amount of twenty-five billion dollars, of which roughly one-third was in America, another third in Latin America and China, and the remainder in countries within the fold of the British Empire. Data set forth in 1931 by Sir George Paish, noted British economist, showed that Britain owed the world about $750,-000,000, while the world owed Britain approximately twenty billion dollars. There was a world-burdening yoke which lost none of its weight even through the computations of Sir Robert Kindersley, as published in "The Economic Journal" for June, 1932. British capital abroad in 1929, Kindersley calculated, was an amount almost equaling seventeen billion dollars, from which was derived a yearly income of nearly a billion dollars. The returns, of course, fell off with the spread of the great world depression.

The scare racking various European countries over American economic conquest was grounded upon the assumption that those inroads were wholly aggressive. But in some cases American planning and capital were either welcomed or eagerly sought. For instance Italy, lacking coal deposits, had pressing need to develop its hydro-electric resources; and so, with its own industrialists unable or unwilling to do the work, the services of American capitalists were enlisted. More than one-half of American direct investments in Italy were in public utilities.

Can anyone doubt that if American corporations had ever

abridged or negatived the rights of foreign stockholders there would have arisen loud condemnations of American chicanery? What floods of revilement would then have broken forth! But now, in one European country after another, measures were taken to nullify or curtail powers of American stockholders. American direct investments in France, largely in industries, amounted to $145,000,000. Under the plea of patriotic solicitude a number of companies in France peremptorily altered their by-laws so as to give plural voting to certain kinds of shares, and incorporated provisions to confine ownership of these favored shares to Frenchmen. Most of the sum of $139,000,000 of American direct investments in Germany was in industries. Some corporations there quickly set about relieving the panicky general state of mind over American "invasion" by adopting omnibus restrictions. One hundred times the voting power of common shares was vested in certain preferred shares which were held by the management or by persons closely affiliated. In Britain, which had attracted one-third of the direct American investments in Europe, drastic measures were taken in a number of cases. The General Electric Company, in 1928, divested all foreign stockholders of voting rights; two other British companies inserted clauses in their by-laws restricting foreign stock holdings to 25 per cent; three other such companies disfranchised foreign shareholders or limited voting rights to British stockholders; no foreigners were allowed to hold shares in Imperial Airways.[2]

Yet in the frenzy of denunciation of American industrialists a few temporizing voices sought to make themselves heard. Viscount Rothermere, a wealthy British publisher-editor, burst out with "Will Wall Street Swallow Europe?"—an article published in "The Sunday Pictorial" of London. Wall Street he pictured as another world power, wielding more authority than the League of Nations and having "more subtlety than bolshevism [has]." But, with profound reverence for the financial might demonstrated by Wall Street, he sagaciously counseled making terms with it instead of giving vent to purposeless resentment. British industrialists were in business to make money, and they might as well recognize the ability of American industrialists to remedy the slackness of British methods: "When the present glut of capital in America produces a surplus we should do everything possible to attract it, together with American technical skill and experience to the task of revitalizing and developing depressed British industries. This is Britain's shortest road to industrial recovery. . . ." Then, after repeating the old assertion, "Work and money-making are almost the sole interests of the entire American nation," he went on with silky persuasiveness to convince his readers that American industrialists made a passion of business, and that their methods were worthy of note.

Commonly, as we have seen, British critics scored American industrialists as being shackled to business. But in Rothermere's view their concentration was the one thing needed to pull British business out of its slump. "They have few hobbies, no leisure class, and rarely retire from business. And the president of any one of a score of American corporations is a greater figure than any political president or Prime Minister in Europe." To strengthen his panegyric of American business methods, Rothermere stretched a particle into a sweeping fact. "Statistics and salesmanship are the scientific hobbies of the nation." Should not Britain, Rothermere intimated, prudently turn to the rising golden sun and conform its policies thereto? America, he proclaimed, was attaining the "financial empire of the world." Did not Britain's supreme interest require the cultivating of good relations with that financial giant? So, advocating the need of affinity with big money, Rothermere advised: "By closer co-operation with the United States, by copying their modern methods, and securing their friendly aid, we shall be using the best means to extricate an older and hardly-tried economic organization from the difficulties which so perilously beset it." Specifying the disqualification of American stockholders from voting, Rothermere pleaded for the removal of all handicaps on the investment of American capital in Britain.

The extent of the "American invasion" in Britain had been greatly overestimated, stated "The Economist" on June 22, 1929. And, it warned, the fettering of American stockholders

was an impolitic course likely to provoke reprisals which, if
successful, would deal a damaging blow to the whole British
economic structure.

We must linger a moment on another aspect of America's
over-seas "invasion." There long had been, and through the
1920's there continued in growing volume, an American influx
which European countries viewed as an invasion of their
privacy, while at the same time they took every possible step
to augment it. This incursion was the American tourist traffic—
"tourism," as it was termed in Europe. The Governments of
nearly all European countries took official measures to encourage and drum up the traffic, each aiming to get for its
country as much of the American tourist visitation as it could.
In New York alone, tourist information offices were maintained
by the travel bureaus or State railways of thirteen European
nations.

While European critics were deriding Americans as money-
loving, Europe through a series of years was gladly pocketing
a total of hundreds of millions of American tourist money.
The year 1929, though not the best, will be offered as exhibit.
American tourists, it was estimated, expended in that year
$839,000,000 on travel outside their own continent. Of that
sum France battened on an estimated $137,000,000, Italy
$30,433,000, Germany $44,676,000 and Britain almost $42,-
000,000.[3]

Above all countries France had a thrifty, most astute sense
of how to exploit its "touristic capital"—its antiquities, art
treasures, and so on. France spent large sums in official publicity to attract tourists. These, however, were only part of the
American influx. A United States Government report in 1928
gave American consular figures vouched for as "fairly accurate," indicating that 77,063 Americans lived abroad in permanent or semi-permanent residence in France, Great Britain
and Italy. An arbitrary net estimate of the amounts spent
mainly in those countries by wealthy American residents, by
American heiresses married to foreigners, and by American
students, was $32,000,000.[4] At the precise time when "The
Osservatore Romano" and other Italian newspapers were de-

nouncing American "dollar superiority" and "materialistic leadership," Mussolini's Italian Government was bending every effort to attract more American tourists, or rather the money they brought to Italy. These funds, together with the large total of remittances sent to relatives by a mass of Italian immigrants in America, were an important consideration in Italy's finances.

When, in the years following 1929, the American tourist traffic to various European countries abruptly dropped, much perturbation ensued there. During the same time, too, when the dollar was devalued and Americans resident in Europe were allowed less native currency in exchange, many of these domiciled visitors, unable to afford the difference, returned to America. Under the lamenting caption of "The Fall of Our National Wealth," the Paris journal "Figaro," early in 1935, showed to what a serious extent that wealth had been impaired by the decline in the number of visitors. Of all European nations the French seem to have experienced the keenest pocket grief from the tourist slump. In their anxiety to retain American customers, French hotel keepers made a belated concession: they agreed to forego the prevailing rate of 15 francs for the dollar and make exchange at the old rate of 20 francs. From Britain, in the dawn of 1935, came an official Home Office expression of satisfaction at the first increase of American tourists there since the depression began—an entry of 56,000 of them in 1934. These, together with Dominion, Continental and week-end visitors to Britain, called forth the jubilant statement that "Britain can add the personal expenditures of 400,000 guests to her invisible revenue for 1934."

Meanwhile, the raiding of America by European critics had continued, but in greater force than ever before. "The trouble with most Americans is that they honestly believe they are better than the man of other lands because they have more worldly goods." Thus did André Tardieu, a noted French political figure, express himself in 1927. Never had there been such a procession of critics as now fluttered in America for a brief span and then launched their attacks. Added to these were squibs by European writers who had not even skimmed any part of America; they followed the short-cut process of remaining at home and taking their conclusions from books at hand.

One of the most notable contributions to the library of abuse was by Georges Duhamel, a Parisian journalist. His book, a rabid indictment of American life, brought out in France with the title "Scenes Out of the Future," accorded so thoroughly with the prepossessions of academic pundits in Paris that Duhamel was awarded the Grand Prix du Roman by the French Academy. Well-informed Frenchmen know how many a prize has been given to fugacious authors, or for books of no intrinsic worth. But the announcement of the conferring of this token upon Duhamel was exploited in America as the granting of an illustrious honor. Forthwith, in 1931, a prominent Boston publishing house put out an American edition of Duhamel's book, under the lurid main title "America the Menace."

Some American reviewers of this book happened to be sophisticates, who had served as newspaper correspondents abroad, and so had joined to their knowledge of America a fair understanding of conditions in Europe. They severely criticized Duhamel's production as superficial and tawdry. They could well had added that it was in essence only a modernized imitation of the long series of derogatory books stretching back for more than a century. The menace which Duhamel saw coming out of America was only a variation of the "American invasion" vagary then overrunning Europe. Instead of construing the invasion in economic terms, he transposed it to the cultural field. He pictured the spread to France and to other European countries of a noxious type of civilization, of which America seemed to him the archetype and the malignant promoter.

Duhamel's personal acquaintance with America was nothing more than that afforded by the brief sojourn of a "flying trip." He had followed the routine performance of scanning some exterior evidences—stockyards, skyscrapers, and the fluff and froth of life in a few cities. Over these sights he moralized in lugubrious mood. American moving pictures filled him with sadness. They were "a pastime for slaves, an amusement for the illiterate,[5] for poor creatures stupefied by work and anxiety." They were "the skilfully poisoned nourishment of a multitude that the powers of Moloch have judged and condemned, and whose degradation they are finally accomplishing." These are fair specimens of his diatribe throughout the book. Most rabid of all his onslaughts was his invective against the automobile in America. It had spoiled and ruined space; "there is no longer any solitude, any silence, any place of refuge."

Automobiles, had he cared to recall it, were made in France before they were made in America; and France, as we have heretofore noted, had its big automobile works striving to make mass sales to the French people. At the date when Duhamel was preparing his book, the French Government, to provide wider facilities for automobile traffic, was planning a progressive four-year road development in its colony in Algeria. Not only there but in Dahomey and Senegal, largely or wholly French possessions, the names of which had long signified little other than tales of primitive travel and colorful adventure, roads were constructed for the speeding automobile.

There arose an informed French critic who ridiculed Duhamel's book. He was a man who had a proper understanding of America—Professor Bernard Faÿ, holder of the chair of American Civilization in the Collège de France. To André Siegfried alone of all current French writers on America, Faÿ credited an effort at fairness, but he criticized even Siegfried as failing to grasp the personality or life of the American people. Faÿ explained how groups of French writers had been influenced by the translations of American books published in France. Those written by Sinclair Lewis, Henry L. Mencken, Upton Sinclair and like authors had sunk readily into the mentality of the French literati. "Outstanding French writers felt impelled to interpret in a pungent and brilliant book" the ideas set forth by American satirists and reformers, and so there came "a veritable deluge of French books on America." Faÿ injected a dash of irony: In answer to accusations that he did not know America, Duhamel could have offered the defence that even though he had been in America but a few weeks "he knew American civilization as the best-known [American] writers had described it. Mencken, Lewis et al were his sources." Faÿ went on: "As a matter of fact, M. Duhamel, in his short stay in America, had been impressed with a few things that were new to him, and he was all the more impressed because they were unexpected. He was slightly ill, he was tired and nervous, and so he hated them all, largely because they were so different from what he was accustomed to seeing. . . . Everything that differed from what he saw every day in Paris he called 'American civilization'." There we have the pivotal point; Duhamel judged America by Paris, and not probably the whole of Paris, but only by that elect section of it in which he lived. So swayed, Faÿ further noted of Duhamel, "with the help of Mencken, Frank, Lewis, and Sinclair, he was able to define 'American civilization' in a surprisingly clear and satisfactory manner." [6]

The furious French vogue of attacking America propagated a variety of freak books. One of these, by two downy Frenchmen, was entitled "La Cadavre Americain" (The American Corpse). Its point was simple: After a European had visited America, the fact that he had suffered that tribulation could be read instanter from his sad expression! To Americans this belonged in the realm of farce, but there were Frenchmen who accepted it as more weighty evidence in a pile of accusation.

Any Frenchman who did not read books could find fearsome articles on America in his newspapers and magazines. Paul Morand was considered a leading French writer of travel books. His qualifications were evinced by his volume "New York." Taking "America, the land of speed" as his text, Morand spread his jeremiad in "La Nouvelle Revue Français" of Paris. He saw no distinction between speed in the pursuit of recreation and enforced speed in the industrial domain; all speed was alike. He did not seem to comprehend America as a country of vast distances where speed for business or other reasons was both a need and a saving of time and energy. To him speed was a horror. Yet it had not always been so; once, he admitted, he had loved speed, but "later not so much." Now the spectacle of twenty million automobiles in America appalled him. A man's philosophy of life, one would think, may admit pros and cons on the question of speed. But for Morand there was no middle ground. He vaulted into bygone times, and became merely one more romancer mooning over the sup-

posed glories of the past. "Speed is overturning all our old
customs. We are throwing overboard, one after another, the
slow tools of the past—horses, cooking over a slow fire, polite-
ness. . . . Speed is disjointing our old world." Morand implied
that America was clearly responsible for this decadence.

It was in America, where the speeding-up system in factories
originated, that mitigations for it were devised. In America
itself this system, called the efficiency or scientific system, was
scathingly denounced by labor leaders and humanitarians as a
cruel means of exploitation. While foreign critics still thought
that this system functioned as when first operated, it had meanwhile undergone one notable change. Agitation and capitalist
concession had brought measurable mitigation by securing the
five-day week in industry.[7]

Among the American phenomena that evoked the scorn of
satirical native writers were the business men's organizations—
the "rotarians" sleek with stuffy self-importance and prosy
with office cant. Yet France, whither the American intellectual
fled—when he could afford it—for a change of atmosphere,
could show a fine array of specimens to whom also "business
was business." Although their veneer was different, their core
was the same. France's one hundred and forty-three Chambers
of Commerce were so many sanctums consecrated to the high
god of trade. France's network of twenty-six large employers'
groups, welded in a single all-potent national organization,
embraced the leading figures in French industry and commerce. Various of these factory owners had installed the speeding-up system, but, unlike a considerable number of American
industrialists, they in the main resisted every plea and defeated
every effort to modify its exactions. From the National Congress of the French Confederation of Labor came denunciations. "As regards scientific management," one resolution declared, "the Congress protests against the growing abuses
resulting from the application of the new methods by the employers in a selfish and inhuman spirit." Recounting how the
system mercilessly overworked men, women and children,
plunged workers into greater hardships by wage-cuts, and
spread despair by throwing many others out of employment,
the resolution went on: "The employers in most cases per-

sistently reject all suggestions made by the trade unions with a view to reducing or averting the dangerous consequences likely to result from such measures"; (the speeding-up system).[8]

Here was furnished a picture of an industrial France unrelieved by even such palliative measures as had been extensively adopted in America. Objectors to American standardization, Morand himself later conceded, failed to realize that Europe now had all of the drawbacks and none of the advantages. Like those of other countries, French industrialists had long enriched themselves from the labor of women and children. Thirty years back more than a million of the three million employes in French industry were women and children,[9] and the pace at which continuing numbers were worked grew ever more fatiguing. Repeatedly did the women protest, but without redress. "Women's wages are unfairly low, and many women workers are subjected to the intense and abnormal overwork resulting from a combination of maternal, domestic and industrial life. . . . Men, women and children are ranged in a competitive battle in the factory. There must be an effective transformation in the social conditions of men and women workers." Thus was voiced a resolution of the women workers at the annual convention of the French General Confederation of Labor in Paris, in 1929.[10]

Exaltations of France aimed to give it a distinctive éclat of artistic excellence, and all things not fitting in with this purpose were, of course, suppressed as non-existent. The discouragements and privations often suffered by French painters was a familiar story to all who knew the undercurrents of French art. Recognition brought its posthumous evils. The higher the standing attained by artists, the more certain the prospects after their death of outrages committed in the name of their art. That excellence for which they had toiled was made the ground for obtaining large sums, a fraction of which would have joyously lightened the burden of the artist during his lifetime. From time to time, scandals had unmasked the forgery in France of paintings that purported to be the work of renowned artists. This counterfeiting of modern art was an industry peculiarly flourishing in France, because its prestige as a productive art country enabled the perpetrators to impose upon confiding buyers. Only recently (in 1935) has come another and large disclosure, with the arrest and conviction of two principals accused of running an "art factory" from which had gone hundreds of pictures bearing the names of Millet, Corot, Manet, Monet and other well-known artists. Quantities of these paintings, the prosecution charged, had been bought by art museums and private art collectors mainly in England and America; nearly five years of investigation had been required to trace the ramifications of the swindle. One of the accused was Jean Charles Millet, grandson of the painter. Specifically proved guilty of having sold paintings falsely represented as those of the famous Millet, he and an accomplice were sentenced to six months in prison, subjected to a fine, and, together with the former wife of one of them, were condemned to pay 120,000 francs damages to the dealer who originally made complaint.

But one more instance will be cited of the post-war French reviling of America. Indeed, the only reason for giving any attention to Lucien Lehman's extravaganza of abuse, "The American Illusion," is because it supplies a particularly conspicuous example of the use that was made of old accusations. Unlike virtually all of his French fellow-authors, Lehman had lived five years in an American city—New York—where he had been correspondent for a Paris newspaper. Yet the opportunities he had thus had for studying and understanding American life were in no iota evidenced in his book. A translation was put forth in 1931 by a New York publishing house, and was advertised as the fresh and timely observations of a knowing and acute critic.

Lehman painted Americans as a race of "bigots," a people "ignorant of its own history" and "drunk with pride and chauvinism." The American man was "ignorant and brutal"; he "fought on the slightest provocation." American children were "the most ill-mannered and disagreeable on the face of the earth." As a race Americans were "vain" and insufferable "egoists." They were a "young *nouveau riche* nation," a "victim of the grandeur mania," governed by "sharp and sordid Shylocks."

Lehman emphasized: "Money, I repeat, is the only thing in

America that will assure one a great name and lasting glory."
To the progressive American political movements which, with
but temporary intermissions, had for years attacked the powers
and privileges of great wealth, Lehman paid no attention.
Apparently he was intentionally ignorant of the continuing line
of investigations, and of the books elucidating the frauds and
thefts by which great American fortunes had been amassed.
This exploration into the genesis of fortunes was a strictly
American accomplishment. No European country had any
literature even faintly resembling that which, in America, ex-
humed and set forth the truth as to sources of plutocratic
wealth from its beginnings to its zenith. Yet with preposterous
certitude Lehman went on: "A permanent halo can come only
to the founder of fortunes so huge that they make one dizzy
to think of them—and the origins of which are never discussed." He descried a lack of "moral excellence" in American
men and women; sporadic corruption in America he stretched
into corruption rooted as "a general usage"; and in the same
style he ladled much more of his accumulated vilification.[11]

At this identical time, however, large sections of the French
public were intensely wrought up over charges of venality on
the part of their public men; French taxpayers were complaining of official inefficiency and malfeasance; and in the
memory of many French investors the fraudulent depredations
of the Oustric bank were poignantly fresh. All of these grievances came to a climax with the disclosure, in 1933, of the
great swindle consummated by Serge Alexandre Stavisky upon
small French investors. The circumstances of this scandal over-
shadowing France are matters of too current knowledge to call
for detailed narrative. Nevertheless, it is essential to point out
a few significant features which in the accounts were either
obscured or unnoticed.

America had its constant swindling by successions of
sharpers; billions of dollars had been filched from investors
by sundry corporations and investment bankers in selling
worthless securities.[12] This had been done not by favor of law
but despite many drastic Federal and State laws. And no
official corruption was involved. Yet the American habit of
viewing conditions in Europe as blissfully "different" was again

shown by the report of the United States Senate Committee on Banking and Currency dealing with the sale of worthless stocks. "England, France, Belgium, Germany and other countries," the report idealized, "have long had comprehensive statutes to meet precisely the same problem with which we are confronted." Such a statement was not only grossly untrue both in substance and implication, but it happened to be published at the precise time (in 1933) when the Stavisky frauds became public.

But what was the spectacle in France? There again, in the person of Stavisky, was an instance of one long known to officials as a slippery, suave and audacious crook, yet nonetheless allowed to perpetrate the enormities of his prime without the slightest hindrance. In all probability there was not an important government functionary in Paris who did not know of Stavisky's criminal career, his past jail sentences, and the appellation "king of the crooks" fixed upon him by at least one Paris newspaper. Certainly police officials had his record. Yet he was authorized to embark in a business which had been peculiarly costly to French investors—that of selling bonds. His wares were municipal pawnshop bonds, of which he forged great quantities. His ascertainable receipts from a mass of victims amounted to 259,000,000 francs.

Prevalent suspicions of official connivance and corruption intensified popular fury, and on February 6, 1934, a great and raging demonstration overflowed in Paris streets. On the defensive, the French Cabinet now resorted to a plea which was not immediately recognized by the public, either in France or elsewhere, for what it was—an old ruse of cornered French officials. Although conservatives and radicals alike had joined in the demonstration, Government spokesmen declared it to be of royalist instigation. The same charge of royalist conspiracy was made by officialdom many years previously when the Panama corruption was exposed. Now in the 1934 upheaval, upon the ground that "the security of the State was menaced" by "foes of the Republic," the French Premier ordered out troops to reinforce the police in overcoming the angry crowds. Sabreing and shooting killed nineteen, and injured more than eight hundred, persons. Public wrath forced the resignation of the Cabinet.

Was any moral to be drawn from the Stavisky frauds? The "Mercure de France," of Paris (December 15, 1933), had published a comprehensive article by G. Welter on the French character and French propensity for taking financial risks that offered prospects of inordinate gain: "Billions [of francs]," he wrote "are thrown every year into the abyss of gambling, stock exchange speculations, horse racing, et cetera. . . . Nothing will stop the perpetual movement . . . only sometimes the movement slows down under the influence of a new crash or financial scandal. Soon, however, the woolen stocking gets tired of being filled without profit and empties itself, whereupon the game begins afresh. No lesson, be it ever so painful, is of any avail. The Frenchman sighs over his losses and begins again."

CHAPTER XXIII

REVAMPING THE OLD THEME

THE rounding of this narrative requires a final dealing with more of the swarm of America's assailants. That many of these enjoyed but a fleeting reputation is all the more reason why they should be noticed here. For they were the popularly-read and much-quoted writers; and however little known or unknown some or all of them may be in receding time, their pronouncements received wide publicity in their own day. It was the total effect of their writings (often translated into other languages) which supplemented and further solidified the mass of older adverse criticisms. Hear the "Commercio" of Lima, Peru, stating the case early in 1929:

"It is generally assumed in South America that the Yankees are grim, commercialized, all of a piece. . . . In the Southern continent of the Western Hemisphere a Yankee is conceived to be a creature who swaggers, a husky being, florid of complexion as of speech, his mouth conspicuous through a pipe too big, his brow frowning, his vocabulary limited, peremptory in his talk, asking much, giving little, intolerant, mechanical in his movement as in his ideas, plenty of money in his purse . . . his sole watchword and motive summed up in the familiar slogan that business is business." These ideas, the "Commercio" pleaded, were absurdly erroneous. But its attempts to correct a grounded conviction were futile in a continent which long had absorbed its fantasies from a host of writings either in the original or in translations.

At this time there went to South America one of America's most voluminous critics, there to add to the force of the prevailing attitude by a series of lectures on the American people. He was Count Hermann Keyserling, who had already revealed his posture and his literary methods in his book "Europe," a translation of which had been brought out in New York. "A more accurate title," commented Professor Paul Monroe of Columbia University, "would be 'Count Keyserling and his Europe.' For this Europe is probably the Europe of no other observer. . . . Count Keyserling includes, with many absurd generalizations about European peoples, much that is probably apt and true about individual nationals of the countries concerned, creating an illusion of comprehensive intimacy out of the minutiæ of character criticism." [1] Keyserling represented himself in this book as the aristocrat censoriously viewing the ineptitudes of democracy; he chanted the glories of aristocracy and extolled "the truly superior persons" as the only possessors of wisdom and culture.

Not for more than fifteen years had Keyserling visited America. This long absence did not stop him from profusely writing about it—though he did indeed begin one long article with an apology for doing so despite his long absence. But with this preliminary to ward off criticism, he set about giving his "vision of America's future," and he passed judgment as though he had the most intimate knowledge of America's present and a crystalline prescience of its future. In sermonic style he directed how America should act. "America will have to learn that if equality is good, quality is better." "It will have to spend leisure nobly." Such were exhibitions of his high-sounding preachments, all revolving around his concept of an America debased by materialism. What especially emerged from this jungle of words? He foresaw "the dawning" of a new Dark Age.[2]

When later he did illumine America with his presence, he quickly gave proof of his masterly divination in a massive book and in various articles on America. The most cursory analysis disclosed his process. He took mere strands of plausible weight and upon them wove a huge cobweb of assumptions. America lacked "spirituality"; its institutionalism looked upon man "in the light of an animal"; material prepossessions dominated its philosophy and psychology. One of his magazine articles was benignly entitled "The Animal Ideal in America." At this time, when European labor organizations were looking emulously to the American standard of living and cultural opportunities, and were passionately demanding an improvement of their own scale, what did Keyserling see? "Almost all the typical manifestations of present day American life are not only the expressions of a higher standard of living—*they really start from the assumption that man is nothing else than an animal* and must be dealt with accordingly." (The italics are his.) [3]

Keyserling, of course, was simply carrying on his part of an old-established business. Out from his stock-in-trade came the sneer at "the American habit of appraising everything in terms of the dollar." There is a fair probability that not one of his hearers knew he was repeating, paraphrasing or modernizing old criticisms applied by his predecessors to other times. Yet he evidently did know that Americans were accustomed to the kind of "truth" he had to deliver, and were willing to pay for the habit. But when he went to South America and lectured there, he nicely adjusted his tactics to the place and temperament. "Count Keyserling's observations on Argentine character," wrote a Buenos Aires correspondent, "are more flattering than the things he told North American audiences. Moreover, at every lecture he flays the American character in a way that confirms the Argentinian's own estimate of himself that he is infinitely more civilized and more cultured than the crude North American he despises." The special cable dispatch from which this extract is taken was a long account quoting from Keyserling's lectures. He discerned that Argentinians were "the most exaggeratedly touchy people on earth," and he tenderly ministered to their susceptibilities; they were "interested only in that I say nothing that will offend them." Among the clumps of information he conveyed was his statement "that the social system of the United States is more nearly Russian than anything else." [4]

While the clairvoyant Keyserling was whitewashing Latin America at the Yankees' expense, what actually was to be seen there? Not only the touchy Argentinians but the governing classes in all Latin-American countries were deeply perturbed later by rude disclosures before the United States Senate Committee investigating sales of munitions. One of the issues which brought about the revolutionary uprising in Brazil in 1930 was the glaring prevalence of graft on the part of the régime in power. But the charges then made, serious as they were, furnished but a slight insight into the general and fixed corrupt combination of politics and business throughout South and Central America and in Mexico. In America bribery was plain bribery but in Latin America it became a euphemism; Latin-American officials merely received "commissions" for influence in the awarding of contracts. American business men described the process as "greasing."

This operation was repeatedly referred to or detailed by heads or officials of American munition concerns in testimony before the Senate Committee. His company, Lammot du Pont admitted, had been told on a number of occasions that it was the general practice in certain foreign countries to give so-called "commissions" to government officials or their relatives, although he never "to his knowledge" included such cost items in price quotations.[5] Much testimony on "greasing" and dealing with officials in Argentina, Brazil, Bolivia, Peru and other South American as well as Central American countries and Mexico was brought out by the persistent questioning.[6] "The real foundation of all South American business is graft." Thus Lawrence Y. Spear, vice-president of the Electric Boat Company, had written to Sir Charles Craven, managing director of Vickers, advising Craven that "at the last minute something extra is always needed to grease the ways." Craven, in London, angrily denied having any knowledge of Spear's letter.

One official in Buenos Aires, it was indicated, had received $50,000 for influence in the granting of a submarine contract, and a group of high Brazilian naval officials had demanded $180,000 "commissions," should certain contracts be signed. To one individual in Peru $253,000 in "commissions" had been paid in eleven years. Senator Bone asked: "Mr. Spear, can you inform us whether or not French and Italian and English munition concerns and submarine builders and shipbuilders paid commissions on business acquired in South America?" "I think they all did," replied Spear. Senator Bone queried further: "They all pursued the same course in getting business?" "Yes," the witness answered. "You will find it impossible to do business in those countries without enlisting the local people."[7] Indignant remonstrance from Latin-American countries when news of the hearings was cabled there did not alter the fact that it was sworn testimony, much of it specific and cumulative.

But what, meanwhile, of Keyserling? When, after visiting South America, he lectured in Paris more than a year later, his pronouncement was of entirely different import than the dictum he had applied to the United States. He had declared of this country that "no real culture will ever develop if America continues to pursue her course along the lines of efficiency." Yet in Paris on March 13, 1931, he advised European nations that they *must* accept American mechanization, and *must* steadily develop it to a certain extent. As usual, he subjoined a series of precepts which, as propounded by him, were the cloudiest formulas: "Intelligence should be restored as a servant of man's spiritual nature by a real understanding of the significance of life"; and more of the like.

During these years the rush of British literati to America went on as of old. Parrotwise, one English writer after another dwelt upon this or that horrendous aspect of American standardization. American small-town women were made automata by mechanical household appliances, a servitude proved by their "mastering the intricacies of electrical washers and dryers and cookers and cleaners." This was the wail (published in America) of Mrs. Rosita Forbes who, after earning a reputation as an explorer of Africa, had now turned "explorer" of America. All the while in her own Britain, had she cared to go exploring there, Mrs. Forbes could have found that millions of European housewives and servants were still in bondage to antiquated, cumbrous, exhausting hand utensils. Yet in this condition, subsisting for ages,—a standardization that imposed the most onerous burdens,—the critic of American modernization could see no evil. The reluctance of England to change old ways was shown again; only recently had that country arrived at the stage of abolishing, by the Law of Property act, the last vestiges of feudal tenure under which archaic household and other customs survived down to the first quarter of the twentieth century.

In this connection, it is interesting to note that the backward condition of British hotels in many districts, and the consequent deterring of tourist travel, was one of the points raised by

J. T. Walton Newbold, a member of a Parliamentary Committee reporting in 1931 on means to improve finance and industry. "The Tourist Industry," he wrote, "has great potentialities, having regard to the romantic as well as the more nearly sentimental appeal of Great Britain and Ireland to the more prosperous as well as the more cultured of the emigrant nations. But until much has been done to modernize hotel accommodations. to improve the transport in the more picturesque parts and generally to cater to people who are accustomed to superior plumbing and a more rational system of interior lighting and heating—just to mention a few deficiencies —a revenue running into tens of millions sterling will continue to be lost to this country." [8]

Be that as it may, the exploring Mrs. Forbes had at least seen something of America. But now C. E. M. Joad spun forth a book in which he freely admitted that he had never put foot on American soil. Joad's production was entitled "The Babbit Warren," and in the prefatory Note to this volume he announced: "The author has not had the privilege of visiting the United States, and has no means, therefore, of judging the accuracy of these reports. His acquaintance with Americans and those who have been to America forces him, however, to the conclusion that the stories given in the text, even if they are not in all respects literally true, possess at least the inventions of that distinguished author, Mr. Benjamin Trovato, that is to say, if they are not true they ought to be."

Joad's sources of information about America were almost entirely English, chosen to enable him to present America's civilization as coarse and otherwise repellent. By his definition, a real civilization was a way of life that promoted truth, beauty, goodness and happiness. While he was thus abstracted in drawing the material for social criticisms out of thin air, a quarter of a million of British miners, together with three times that many women and children dependents, were progressively being reduced to destitution at his very elbow.

Not until 1929, after five years of this harrowing condition, did various British editors show any realization of it. They were galvanized into recognition only when the Prince of Wales, in a broadcast appeal for funds, drew attention to the huge tragedy. When Royal Highness spoke, these editors harkened. The miners had exhausted savings, sold furniture and other effects, and now with all resources gone were "at last in helpless distress, staring starvation face to face—nothing—and few places to go for help." In tattered clothes gaunt men, women and children shivered in the raw cold; rows of houses in the mining villages showed windows plugged with rags; utter desolation reigned.

It was at this time, also, that a firm of London publishers with much commendatory splash brought out "The American Illusion," a book detailing a multitude of things which its author, Collinson Owen, found grievously wrong in America. In a foreword, this critic sought to convince readers that, until his volume appeared, English writers had ignored "the darker side of American civilization." Pluming himself as a fearless truth-teller, Owen proclaimed: "Things have been made too smooth for America. A little roughage, as the dietetic experts call it, should be all to the good for her moral and spiritual digestion." He felt supremely equipped to administer the dose; had he not spent two or three months as a member of a British journalistic party roaming in America? He had discovered in America "an astonishing background"; in this "crime, corruption and politics are mixed in a fantastic manner which apparently the simple English mind is unable to understand."

When we turn to actualities in Britain, we see that no trace of that fine simplicity was to be found, either as a quality of mind or of its politics. There everyone who followed affairs knew well the means and indirection by which political parties obtained their large finances. American politics could present nothing comparable to this clandestine deviousness. Yet because funds got by the disposal of titles were for party use and not (so far as was known) for personal benefit, the complacent attitude was taken that no taint of gross corruption could possibly adhere to them.

If title granting had not been done on too large a scale, perhaps members of the House of Lords would have remained quiescent under a practice that had the sanction of long use. But the peers were restive. From a membership of 126 at a period not too remote, the roster of the House of Lords had swollen to more than 700, and, although only a small proportion could boast of noble lineage, nearly all were united in sentiments of opposition to further accessions. As a body, the Lords were vested with sacred privileges. Within the exalted confines they were superior to common procedure. No member ever had to face the indignity of being called to order, no matter how disturbing the interruption; any number of members could, if they so wished, speak at one and the same time, and they often did so. Their Lordships never lowered themselves by voting "Aye" or "No"; their distinguishing mode was to say "Content" or "Not Content"; and when they gave what was recorded as "applause," it was a queer grunt-like sound. "An interesting and picturesque relic," fit for relegation to the British Museum. So a Labor Member of the House of Commons characterized the House of Lords, and he was severely rebuked by the Speaker for his irreverence.

Moreover, there was agitation to abolish a body so anachronistic. Among other assailants William T. Stead, a noted London editor who at times employed sensational methods to arouse public opinion, had come out with his statement "Why the Lords Must Go." "The majority of men who are made peers," he had written, "are men who have made money and can afford to buy their coronets directly or indirectly." How much was the cost, he stated, could not be learned. "But it is perfectly well known that peerages are never bestowed upon poor men. [There was occasionally an exception.] A title is the fancy trimming of a plutocrat. A big brewer has not achieved the climax of his social ambition until he has scrambled over his beer barrels into the Gilded Chamber." Similarly, Stead wrote, most of the other peers were either active plutocrats or rich men who had harnessed themselves to partisan timeserving. This list was varied by the "thin stream of lawyers that trickles into the House" [of Lords].

To make his "black list" appear doubly black, Stead stretched his indictment to the point of declaring that some recruits to the House of Lords were men who, if just deserts had been meted out to them, would have been in prison. He excepted possibly some other of these new hereditary legislators as having an immediate virtuous ancestry. "But," he forcefully went on, "the progenitors of so many others were scamps and scoundrels that it is impossible to say, without looking up Debrett, whether a man is a hereditary legislator because his father was pre-eminent for rascality or for public spirit. Probably, as a rule, he belonged to the majority—he was pre-eminent for nothing, but belonged to the great army of wealthy, respectable mediocrities who have rendered yeomen's service to their party, and who received the partisan's reward." And Stead hammered away at the viciousness of a system which not only gave such men legislative power for life but also transmitted it to "their sons and their sons' sons after them till the crack of doom." [9] The extraordinary outspokenness of Stead's language reflected the intensity of feeling against the institution of the House of Lords—an intensity by no means confined to him, and one which impressed peers as a formidable threat.

With poised nicety of phrase, Lord Selbourne, in 1914, had sought to have the House of Lords apprise the Government that they disapproved the exchange of titles for money given to political parties. In the House of Lords' opinion, his motion declared, a contribution to party funds should not be a consideration influencing a Prime Minister to recommend anyone for honors. Three years later the issue stirred more commotion in the House of Lords. Earl Loreburn complained of the hidden circumstances surrounding the giving of honors (titles); in the transactions "the actual parties have a profound interest in keeping the matter secret." In the august House of Lords that was a day of revelations—not of generalizations but of specifications—although no names were mentioned. The word of the Lords was taken implicitly. Loreburn instanced one of his friends who three times was accosted with proposals to pay £25,000 for a baronetcy or £15,000 for a knighthood. Selbourne divulged similar cases. Particularizing a case of which he likewise had positive personal knowledge, the Earl of Dartmouth detailed: "He was very wealthy, and he was generous—which all wealthy people are not. He sat in the House of Commons for some time. He was one of those ideal Members who rarely, if ever, spoke, and who was always there when wanted. . . ."[10] When it became known that he was not going to run for Parlia-

ment again, a peerage was offered him, and he accepted it. . . .
Soon afterward, the 'go-between' or the 'tout' or whatever you
like to call him, came to my friend and said, 'How about that
£30,000?' [No Tammany Hall demand was ever more brusque
and business-like.] My friend was very indignant. He said he
had heard nothing of the kind, but he was informed that it was
quite customary. My friend then replied: 'I do not know
whether it is customary or not. You will get no £30,000 out of
me.' " And they did not. But, it turned out, the powers above
concluded that his long partisan subservience deserved reward,
if only to encourage others in the same course, and he was
granted the peerage.

The open support by two London newspapers of the conferring of titles was wryly described by Lord Stuart of Wortley.
Of the large roll of bankers, ship-owners, brewers, railway magnates, manufacturers, newspaper owners and other amassers
of wealth who had been burnished with peerage trappings not
many were present to hear Lord Stuart and the other com-
plainants. The newspapers in question, said Stuart, justified the
practice of title distribution as necessary to get the big balances
needed by the political parties. Stuart reviewed the arguments
of one of these newspapers, "The Westminster Gazette." Yes, it
agreed, titled honors did create and intensify class division,
they did encourage snobbism, and they did stamp and perpetuate inequality; yet without the funds derived from such a
source political parties could not finance themselves, nor could
staunch partisan services be requited.

During these proceedings in the House of Lords we behold
none other than Lord Bryce—the same James Bryce who saw
so much corruption in America—informing his fellow peers of
an additional fact. Bryce said that he did not know whether
money passed when Privy Councillorships were awarded.
"But," he significantly commented, "of recent years the honor
of Privy Councillor, with the title which it carries, has been
sown broadcast in the House of Commons." Submitting the
Government's case, Earl Curzon (Lord President of the Council) felt obliged to admit "the almost complete unanimity
of opinion" in the House of Lords in opposition to barter of
titles.[11]

Within a few years there had been created eighty-seven peerages, numerous baronetcies and knighthoods, and a host of lesser dignities. The mortals so elevated did not have to seek; they were sought. For the methods used we have the authority of Sir Charles Mallet. An assiduous search was made for men able to pay richly for titles; possession of wealth was the prime qualification. As a formality it was easy to credit these persons with some kind or show of public service as a nominal reason for conferment of the honor. "Names," Mallet related, "were collected of men known to have made fortunes in war time; in most busy industrial centers there were such men to be found. Relations were gradually established with them through friends or acquaintances or local lawyers, or by visits from the travelers [agents] of the Ministerial firm." If—and there has been no refutation of Mallet's statements—this were the process, it showed a combination of business system and diplomatic adroitness operating as furtively as it did effectively. The schedule of prices was flexible, varyingly adjusted to individual cases. According to Mallet, from £5,000 to double or more was asked for a knighthood; for baronetcies from £20,000 to £40,000; peerages fetched more. From somewhere, it was certain, came a massive political fund proving, if nothing else, what a canny art British politicians made of collecting and storing a great campaign treasury. Before the Coalition Ministry (formed to pilot Britain through the World War) had dispersed, £1,500,-000 had been compactly gathered and thriftily safeguarded. For, it was further revealed, this amount by fortunate investment increased to nearly £3,000,000 of which Premier Lloyd George, Liberal Party leader, had full control for some time.[12] On viewing such an accomplishment, there was not an American political boss who would not have confessed himself a novice and who would not have contemplated the feat with wonder strongly tinctured with envy.

Such a political party campaign fund, whether $7,210,000 or $14,550,000, was unmistakably mighty for a country of Britain's small area. Even though it was not disbursed in any single campaign and formed a fund to be drawn upon, its size nevertheless rivaled many of the campaign funds used for the whole extent of America in Presidential elections. Yet American politics was constantly condemned in England for its lavish and corrupt use of money. American politics had never reached the stage of having on deposit or in investment a large permanent fund; the money needed was raised in each campaign. During a series of Presidential campaigns from 1896 to 1916 onward, the ascertainable amounts spent in each election by the Republican and Democratic parties together varied from four to six or seven million dollars, the amount depending upon the closeness of the contest. To these sums could be added a part of those spent by local organizations for their own success but contributing to that of one or the other party nationally.

The preliminary to Presidential campaigns was, of course, the competition of candidates for the nomination by the old parties. In 1920 fifteen aspirants spent a total of $2,980,033; of this amount General Leonard Wood expended the bulk— $1,773,303—the publicity as to which was effective in defeating his aim to bag the Republican nomination. The sum spent in the Presidential campaign itself was much greater than in any previous campaign. Expenditures by national and State organizations of the Republican and Democratic parties together totaled a computed $10,338,509, which did not include auxiliary sums supplied by local organizations.[13] The expenditures of all candidates for Presidential nominations in 1928 were $894,000; the total net receipts of the Republican and Democratic parties together during the campaign were $17,-282,000, and the expenditures $16,586,000. A long list of capitalists and other rich men contributed funds to both parties. Seeking out and disclosing every gatherable fact, and listing names and amounts, the United States Senate Special Committee Investigating Presidential Campaign Expenses unearthed no evidence of corruption. "The Committee," it reported, "finds almost uniformly that all those persons engaged in handling campaign funds strictly complied with the Corrupt Practices acts of the several States, and abstained from any ascertainable impropriety." [14]

It was in some Senatorial primaries and elections that corruption was found. Very different were the ways of the American Congress from those in the British Parliament. In Congress no member could charge corruption without being pressed for names or other details. He was expected to give them, and if he did not, methods were put into effect to compel him. Corruption charges by non-members or by newspapers immediately, as a rule, led to the appointment of an investigating committee. There was no slighting of any charge, and seldom was there whitewashing.

Following two of its investigations which proved that there had been improper use of money in electing William Lorimer a Senator from Illinois, the United States Senate, in 1912, by a vote of 55 to 28, declared his seat vacant. Another exclusion was that of William S. Vare, Republican boss of Philadelphia, who had claimed election in a three-cornered Republican candidacy in a Pennsylvania contest in which the rival candidates had spent a total of $2,777,942. A Senate Investigating Committee found "numerous and various instances of fraud" in behalf of Vare's candidacy. For his election $785,000 had been expended in the primaries; one of his unsuccessful competitors, however, had spent $1,804,979.[15] A third case of exclusion was that of Frank L. Smith, presenting his credentials as an elected Senator from Illinois. His contributions and expenditures in the primary election were estimated at a provisional total of $458,782.[16] By the overwhelming vote of 61 to 23, in 1928, the United States Senate, acting upon the committee's report that his methods were tainted "with fraud and corruption," refused to admit him. And there were other cases. No longer was the United States Senate dominated, as it once had been, by multimillionaires and corporation lawyers; of the branches of Congress it had become the militant and radical body.

In contrast, the Parliamentary method in England of dealing with campaign funds and expenditures required a punctilious abstention from damaging inquiry. The sale of titles was again discussed in the House of Lords in 1922. "We are too fond," said Lord Carson, "of carrying on public life in the atmosphere of sham. We are down today, for the first time, on this question with a stern reality. . . . I have had more than once in my chambers to advise on cases in which I have examined long correspondence which showed that there was a regular brokerage, however conducted, for the purpose of carrying out and obtaining honors. What was the connection between broker and the

Government I, of course, do not know. That is the one thing we are all clever enough to know will never be known and will always be kept in the background." [17] No serious attempt was made, he should have added, to find out. As member after member of the House of Lords told of negotiations carried on with friends, not a single question was asked regarding names. There was no curiosity to learn of definite clues which, if pursued, would somewhat have opened up the way to explore the sources and depths of the business.

This session was marked by a steaming time over the Government's recommendation of a peerage for Sir Joseph B. Robinson. He had heaped together a fortune from gold and diamond mining in South Africa, and had been created a baronet in 1908. Among other South African corporation posts, he had been chairman of a mining concern, the Randfontein Estates Company. Citing the records of the Appellate Division of the Supreme Court of South Africa, Lord Harris described one of Robinson's deals. The company's other directors were Robinson's tools, and in 1906 they approved his move to acquire certain valuable mining rights for the company. He then used a dummy company, which he entirely controlled, to buy the rights, subsequently reselling them to the Randfontein Estates Company and pocketing a personal profit of £210,000. Nine years later, when S. B. Joel bought Robinson's interests in the Randfontein corporation, the facts were discovered and suit was brought. The court denounced the dummy company as "a device to camouflage the transaction," and in a scathing decision condemned Robinson to pay a sum, including costs, of more than £500,000. Robinson petitioned the Judicial Committee of the Privy Council for permission to appeal; his plea was considered and dismissed in November, 1921.[18]

These activities of Robinson were familiar enough to the Government—the court findings had been published in the newspapers—yet one of the chief grounds on which he had been formally listed for a peerage was for "National and Imperial services." Referring to his own eight years' intimate association with South Africa, Earl Buxton said that he had never heard Robinson's name connected with any public service; Robinson had been nothing more than a mining magnate. The Earl of Selbourne, who had been Governor in South Africa, declared that when he went there Robinson was known everywhere as a pro-Boer. Selbourne also read extracts from the court's judgment, and went on: "Hitherto there has been no personal corruption in connection with the honors—when money has been taken it has been taken for the benefit of a political party, be it Conservative or Liberal or Coalition—but I do not believe that these immense sums can continue to pass in complete secrecy, with no publicity, no responsibility, and personal corruption not ensue. . . . Peerages are conferred upon individuals about whom nothing is known except their exceeding wealth. . . . Surely this amounts to something like a farce. If the public, if the Press and Parliament, sit down under this without any further protest or effort to clean this Augean stable, is it wonderful that foreigners accuse us of being hypocritical?" [19]

"Complete secrecy, no publicity, no responsibility." When Selbourne thus protested, not one of his hearers took this pertinent occasion to point out how American law required the fullest publicity and responsibility as to campaign contributions and expenditures. The large body of American law was the result of the aim to do away with secrecy and the illicit use of money. In America reports were regularly made giving specific lists of all contributors to campaign funds and the purposes for which those funds were spent.

Also veiling names, the Duke of Northumberland described two letters he had seen from persons purporting to be intermediaries between Downing Street (the Cabinet meeting place) and rich men, friends of his, slated as prospects for honors. These letters asked for confidential interviews, and Northumberland told of the results of his talks with both of the men approached. In one case an intimation of £40,000 for a baronetcy went unheeded; the other man was told he was considered "eminently worthy" of an honor, but that he could not expect it unless he paid according to the scale, which ran from £10,000 to £12,000 for a knighthood, and £35,000 to £40,000 for a baronetcy.[20]

After the attacks upon himself, Robinson made a quick and convenient exit. He sent a letter to the Prime Minister with-

drawing his name; he had not, he wrote, cared much at his age
(he was past sixty) about the projected honor. As a concession
to the opposition, Lloyd George, still Prime Minister, caused
the appointment of a Royal Commission to advise on future
procedure in making recommendations of persons deserving
special honor. This Commission was composed of titled dignitaries—the Duke of Devonshire, Baron Dunedin, Baron Den-
man and various baronets. The only untitled member among
the seven was Arthur Henderson, who later became, from 1929
to 1931, Foreign Secretary in the Labor Ministry governing
Britain. In December, 1922, came the Royal Commission's
feeble report signed by all members except Henderson.

That its report was an index to British political morality—
or rather to the lack of it—the Royal Commission evinced no
realization. Through heavy sentences the report lumbered on,
first falling back upon the sanction, based on long usage, that
justified the conferring of honors for political service. This, it
pointed out, had been continuous since the inception of the
party system. In the practice it could find nothing to condemn.
"Nearly all witnesses that we have examined have proffered
the opinion that such a system is right and ought to prevail."
The report admitted the notorious existence of political party
funds, but affirmed their necessity in modern elections. "Indeed, two of the Party managers with great frankness informed
us [of the funds], giving actual figures as to the sources of
supply" but those managers "were emphatic that so far as they
were concerned" there was no bargain.

Like previous Royal Commissions, this body was most com-
plaisant in accepting testimony at its face value and in refraining from deep inquiry. However, it did manage to see one set
of villains: "Nevertheless there is no doubt that there has been
for some time, and recently in increasing numbers, persons,
who, for want of a better name, we may stigmatize as touts who
have been going about asserting that they were in a position
to secure honors in return for specified payments." These touts,
the Commission urged, should be dealt with by the passage of
a penalizing act. And now came the grand remedy evolved by
the Commission. As a supervising agency over honor-giving, it
recommended the appointment by the Prime Minister of a

small committee to scrutinize names selected for titles. To each name was to be appended a statement by the Patronage Secretary or Party Organizer, certifying that no payment or expectation of payment to any political party or political fund was directly or indirectly associated with the recommendation.

In Henderson the other members of the Royal Commission encountered a severe critic. The Commission, his separate report set forth, might have made a much more searching inquiry; it had the names of "touts" but none of these had been summoned to give evidence. Henderson continued: "The omission of evidence from those who are alleged to have asserted that they were in a position to secure honors for money payments, and from those who have been approached by such persons, has left unexplored one of the gravest abuses concerning the nomination for honors. . . . This system whereby the financial assistance rendered to a party is recognized by the conferment of an honor by the State is, in my judgment, deplorable and discredits the honors system." [21] Henderson could appropriately have gone further. Why, he could have asked, did not the Commission make public such important data as the "actual figures" of contributions and the sources of those funds?

A bill to prevent abuses connected with grants of honors was passed by Parliament in 1923, and the proposed supervising committee was instituted. But did its functioning make any difference? With brief effectiveness E. Thurtle, M.P., on November 10, 1927, put these questions to Prime Minister Stanley Baldwin; Had the Prime Minister's attention been called to "The Daily Mail's" statement that the old abuses in the dispensing of titles were being continued? Did the Government contemplate taking any action against that newspaper? To both queries Baldwin answered in the negative. Four days later, Thurtle denounced the title transactions as a "peculiarly nauseating form of political corruption." [22] Of the peerages granted in that year, one had gone to Sir Charles Greenway, then seventy years old, who had been created Lord Greenway; he was styled in the British press and known in the public mind as the "oil king." At the time, there were 740 members of the House of Lords.

Lloyd George, says Mallet, had often been questioned about the political party fund in his custody but refused to give information concerning its management, "although on its origin he could hardly be expected to dilate." But, in fairness, Lloyd George's attitude was open to a somewhat different interpretation. Early in 1927 Lord Rosebery, himself formerly a Liberal Party Prime Minister, wrote to "The Times," of London, demanding an investigation of the origin of titles of ninety peers and of the source of Lloyd George's political fund. To these proposals one of Lloyd George's spokesmen raised no objections. "Every party," said he, "is so deeply involved that we should not suffer in the least. The same charge can be made against every [British party] Government, including Lord Rosebery's." Questioned as to whether this retort was an admission of the giving of honors in exchange for services in cash or in kind, he replied: "Certainly, but every other Government has done the same." Which undeniably was so. And Lloyd George himself could and did plumply remind Rosebery how he, Rosebery, had financed his own general election in 1895. Any real investigation would have brought discomfiture to both parties.

The size of the political fund wielded by Lloyd George was definitely shown in 1927, when he arranged to sell 610,000 shares in United Newspapers, Limited, to the Daily Chronicle Investment Corporation, a new company organized to acquire a chain of newspapers. The purchase price was £2,888,000, and, Mallet recounts, Lloyd George was treated as the sole seller of the stock; no mention was made of him as trustee. Critical of this former Prime Minister as he was—even referring to the fund as "loot"—Mallet nevertheless fully acknowledged Lloyd George as above any personal misuse of the money. That he would use such a fund for any other than what he deemed political objects nobody supposed, so Mallet wrote. But, in Mallet's appraisal, Lloyd George was too prone to assume the identity of these objects with his political ambitions. Persons fearing money influence in politics and alive to the danger of political corruption felt deep concern in the fact "that a fund of two or three million pounds should be attached to the fortunes of a single politician, used steadily to advance his personal interests and employed to bring into the House of Commons candidates who depend upon his support." After negotiations the National Liberal Federation obtained a substantial part of the fund for immediate needs, and for the time Lloyd George was made the Liberal Party's paymaster.[23]

CHAPTER XXIV

THE TRUE CONTRAST

THE sentencing of Lord Kylsant to prison has frequently been cited as evidence of the workings of "impartial British justice." In America this imprisonment of a peer made a stir out of all proportion to its significance. It provoked not a few editorials in American publications, which unfavorably contrasted America's administration of justice with Great Britain's, and dilated upon the immunity enjoyed by powerful law violators in the United States.

The reality in both countries was much the same, but with the advantage on America's side. Of the large number of British peers, many from time to time had been involved and often openly associated with dubious financial schemes. None of them was ever molested. It should, however, be borne in mind that the company of which Kylsant was the head was reputable and long-established. Had that not been true, his story might well have had a different and—for him—a happier ending. In America, on the other hand, it was by no means uncommon to see multimillionaires indicted on charges of conspiracy in restraint of trade, bribery and similar offences. Those indictments usually followed after Congressional or legislative investigations. As a rule the multimillionaire defendants, surrounded by every legal and financial resource, contrived to escape conviction. Occasionally, though, their prosecution was not without some result.

One partial instance was the outcome of a persistent investigation made by a United States Senate Committee into the leasing of naval oil lands. Testimony showed that, in 1921, $100,000 had been handed to Albert B. Fall, Secretary of the Interior under President Harding, by a son of Edward L. Doheny, multimillionaire oil operator. To Edward L. Doheny was granted a lease of naval oil lands in California. Doheny admitted having "lent" Fall the $100,000. Harry F. Sinclair, another oil operator of the same stamp, obtained from Fall in 1922 a lease of similar areas in Wyoming. Within a month thereafter, it was disclosed, Fall had received from Sinclair a total of $269,000 in Liberty bonds and cash,—an amount subsequently increased to total advances of $304,100. Refusing to answer a question put by the Senate Committee, Sinclair was pronounced in contempt. Fall and Edward L. Doheny were finally acquitted on the conspiracy charges, and, in 1930, there followed Doheny's acquittal on the charge of having bribed Fall. Doheny's defence was that the money handed to Fall was an innocent and sentimental loan. Meanwhile, however, Fall was tried on a charge of bribery, convicted in 1929, and sentenced to a year in prison and a fine of $100,000. Hard but unsuccessfully did he fight to keep out of prison, whither he was taken in 1931 and where he served more than nine months.

In the end, the force of agile lawyers at Sinclair's command could not save him from going to a cell—that jowled magnate, of whom it had cynically been said: "You can't put a hundred million dollars in jail." When, in 1927, in the District of Columbia Supreme Court, Sinclair was sentenced to three months' imprisonment and a fine, he had sanguinely exclaimed: "I do not expect to spend a day in jail or pay a dollar fine." But two years later he was stowed in jail, kept there six and a half months, part of which sentence was for contempt of court in causing the jury to be shadowed in his first trial. More than one American cartoonist, with gleeful captions such as "It Can Be Done," "It's A Reality," pictured a bloated bag of dollars sitting behind prison bars. Both oil land properties were regained by the Government when the Supreme Court of the United States declared the leases void.

In Britain, however, where there could be no deep-searching investigations like those in America, millionaires could consider themselves privileged characters—though more especially, of course, when the aureole of nobility was conferred upon them. Even the routine publicity required in America of corporation holdings and accounts had no serious analogy in Britain, although the mistaken tendency in America was to hold up British laws as models. For example, of a reviewed list of one hundred and eleven British investment trusts, only fifty-two published their holdings at the end of 1933. British corporation executives could well congratulate themselves, when they saw the open way in which the Federal Trade Commission exposed the huge bonuses and other extra amounts—millions or hundreds of thousands of dollars—which, in addition to salaries, had been paid to officers and directors by many of the nine hundred American corporations investigated at that time.

American commentators on Kylsant's fate have overlooked the fact that the case of Joseph W. Harriman was a fair equivalent. In all probability, if Harriman had been a British banker with a position corresponding to that which he held in the flush of his career in New York City (at one time his personal fortune was $14,000,000), he would have been expedited into the peerage. In his domain he assuredly had greater financial power than had Kylsant in his. For long a money overlord and a shining light in society, Harriman, in 1934, was convicted in New York City of misapplication of bank funds and falsification of records. His sentence of four and a half years in prison was more than quadruple that given to Kylsant.

For his frauds in England, Clarence Hatry was sentenced in 1930 to serve fourteen years in prison. But Hatry was an ordinary individual, a business adventurer; and in his case, joined with the cases of his associates, the vigor of prosecution was stimulated by the determination of several big British banks which had been duped and swindled. A few words about Hatry. Neither he nor his partners had expert knowledge of steel production. Yet—and without questioning from anywhere—they confidently attempted an imitation of American mergers by undertaking the reorganization of Britain's steel industry. By pledging steel stock, and in other ways, they were able to raise £4,800,000 of which £1,500,000, so later developments showed, was used partly to pay off the liabilities of a constituent company and partly in a campaign of stock-market rigging to support their shares. Huge was the surprise of the bankers concerned when the revelation came that securities on which £789,000 had been obtained were fraudulent. All of the Hatry quartet pleaded guilty; the prison sentences of his confederates ran respectively seven, five and three years.

As a result of the Hatry operations, some English financial institutions were in immediate need of fund replenishment. Quantities of American stocks were dumped on the New York Stock Exchange, thus giving the initial push to the decline which, late in 1929, became a convulsive stock-market panic. In the preceding "mad-era" speculative boom in America, shoals of European speculators and investors had been madly bent upon money-making in that boiling stock-market ascension. From London alone flashed daily orders for the purchase of scores of thousands of American shares; and likewise, in varying degrees, came the rush of buying messages from Berlin, Brussels and Amsterdam. "Nearly all of the surplus wealth on this side of the Atlantic," complained Lord Rothermere in "The Sunday Pictorial" of London, in the summer of 1929, "is being changed immediately into American stock certificates."

Why, before complying with Hatry's loan application, did not those British bankers acquaint themselves fully with the condition of his group's companies? After the Hatry collapse, Sir Gilbert Garnsey, appointed to examine the wreck, had no difficulty in ascertaining this cardinal fact: From the start of the Hatry venture the central corporation in it, the hub of the merger itself, had been insolvent! Always shielded from cursory, not to say penetrating, Parliamentary investigation, powerful British bankers remained sheltered, their arcana sealed. Thus came about the widespread belief, especially active in America, that, both individually and as a class, British bankers were as much paragons of careful management as they were profound in financial acumen.

Long, as we have seen, had big bankers sat in Parliament. They still did so. The members of the American firm of J. P. Morgan & Co. were, in 1933, as evidence gathered by United States Senate investigators showed, directors of eighty-nine corporations and banks, with total assets of more than twenty billion dollars. Whatever the reach of his indirect influence upon legislation in America, J. Pierpont Morgan had no voice or vote in Congress; he was a private citizen. But the entrenchment of bankers in Parliament was a regular feature of English politics. Such a fixture was E. C. Grenfell, Morgan's partner in his London firm. Question by Senator Gore: "How does he get elected?" Answer by J. Pierpont Morgan: "He is the senior member of the City of London [the financial district]. He gets elected right along." This was a bit of testimony in a Stock Exchange investigation made in 1933 by the United States Senate Committee on Banking and Currency.[1]

This Committee's sweeping investigation supplies another notable example of the difference between the American way of thoroughly exposing business evils and the perfunctory scope of British and other European methods. The series of great disclosures brought out by the Committee (with merited credit to Ferdinand Pecora, its counsel), are matters of recent information. The spectacle before this Senate Committee was unlike any witnessed in Britain or elsewhere. The enormous money power commanded, and the lofty standing assumed, by a procession of American ultra-conspicuous bankers were not of the slightest avail to save them from merciless questioning. Some of these men would have been lordly personages in England. Attempts to take refuge in the plea that certain relations with customers were "confidential" met with stern orders to answer questions. With the recent jailing of Sinclair acutely in memory, the squirming witnesses well knew the penalty awaiting them if they refused. As the truth was wrenched out of them, one after another were proved by their own admissions to have been greedily intent upon enhancing their own interests and those of their cliques at the expense of the investing public.

The speculative fever, the surging, unbounded optimism of this era infecting multitudes were such that costly but honest mistakes of judgment were widely made. But numerous leading bankers could not plead this excuse for their juggling operations. Pools were organized backed by campaigns of systematic stealthy publicity to create activity in certain stocks, and fictitious sales were engineered to give the impression of public trading in those stocks. "The hearings disclosed on the part of many bankers," the Senate Committee reported, "a woeful lack of regard for the public interest and a proper conception of fiduciary responsibility. . . . These custodians of funds gambled and speculated for their own account in the stock of the banking institutions which they dominated; participated in speculative transactions in the capital stock of those institutions which they were paid to serve; participated in and were beneficiaries of pool operations . . . bestowed benefits of 'preferred lists' upon individuals who were in a position to aid and abet their plans. . . ." And, capping these enormities, they "restored to devious means to avoid the payment of their just Government taxes." [2]

All of which and much more impelled the Senate Committee to say: "The record is a severe indictment of many bankers." In relating J. P. Morgan & Company's dealings, the Committee might well have placed in juxtaposition the high-souled claims made by the elder J. P. Morgan before a House of Representatives Committee (the "Pujo Committee") more than twenty years previously. "The first thing is character," he had affirmed as to the factor influencing his firm's dealings. Character, and not primarily money or property, he had maintained, was the basis upon which commercial credit was given. Wondering if he had heard aright, the committee's counsel repeated: "Before money or property"? Morgan: "Before money or anything else." [3]

Testimony in 1933 threw another flood of light upon the character of J. P. Morgan & Company. In flotations of stock issues that firm and an allied banking house had in previous years obligingly allowed "ground-floor" or secret advantageous purchase of those stocks to a "preferred list" of individauls. "This 'preferred list,' " the Senate Committee reported, "included personages who at the time of the private offering held prominent governmental, political and corporate positions." [4] Confidentially permitted to buy the stocks at a much lower price than that demanded in the stock market, these select groups obviously made their easy gougings of profit. The banking house of Kuhn, Loeb & Company also had its "preferred list."

From 1926 to 1930 prominent banking firms had sold nearly eight billion dollars of foreign bonds to the American public which, by reason of the default—in interest at least—of many of those bonds, the Senate Committee reported, had been the victims of a "colossal loss." Thickly coated with respectability, the banking house of Dillon, Read & Company had sold to

American investors $186,000,000 of Brazilian bonds, of which in 1933 a net total of $144,000,000 were in default.[5] Other leading bankers had disposed of large bond issues of like character. "A glaring instance" was the sale of $90,000,000 bonds of the Republic of Peru, and another heinous instance the floating of a similar amount in Chilean bonds, both of which issues fell into default.[6]

"Commercial banks," the Senate Committee reported, "found a fertile field for purchases of security issues which their [the banks'] investment affiliates were sponsoring. These banks, violating their fiduciary duty to depositors seeking disinterested investment counsel from these bankers, referred these depositors to affiliates for advice. These depositors were then sold securities in which the affiliates had a pecuniary interest." But this "circumventing of the law" was not the only result. There, for example, was the mighty Chase National Bank of New York City. The Chairman of its executive committee was Albert H. Wiggin, who had been reputed one of the country's ablest financiers. Through his private corporations he sold $10,596,000 of Chase National Bank "short." Yet, reported the Senate Committee, Wiggin had sanctioned a pool of the bank's affiliates "allegedly formed to stabilize the market [for the bank's stock] and obtain a wider distribution among the investing public when he knew that the bank stock was selling at a 'ridiculously high price.' " [7]

Here again, for the thousandth time, was proof of the American practice of sparing neither person nor name. To pursue Wiggin's activities one step further: In 1933 he had retired as the bank's chairman. In the four-and-a-half years preceding, he had received about $1,500,000 in salaries and bonuses from the bank. Upon his retirement the executive board munificently voted him a pension of $100,000 a year for life. Only after the general scathing criticism that followed this disclosure was Wiggin prompted to request stoppage of the pension.

And what of the acts of the bankers heading the equally mighty National City Bank? One will be mentioned. In 1927 that bank's employes were "permitted" to subscribe to its stock, the amounts to be deductible from their salaries. After the stock-market collapse late in 1929, a particular batch of sixty thousand shares, at $200–$220 a share, was allotted to these employes. At the time of the Senate Committee's bearings on the subject, 1933, the market price of the stock had dropped to $40 a share, but employes were held to payment of the price specified in their subscription contracts. "Most of the employes after paying the installments from December, 1929, still owed more on the stock than it was worth in the market at the time of the hearing." [8] A high official of this bank was selling its stock "short" at the very time when employes were being induced or expected to buy.

In many American cities bankers helped the speculative excesses by making large bank loans. These were disastrously impaired by the collapse of security prices that gutted bank resources and, in various sections, forced the closing of group bank-holding companies. Such were some of the multitude of practices resulting in the passage of the stringent and comprehensive Securities and Exchange laws.

The fullness with which the facts were brought out and the frankness with which they were spread broadcast had their infuriating effect upon the American public, many millions of whom were impoverished by loss of money or jobs. Too often, the common man was convinced, were the banker's pretensions but a mask for the infamies of a financial buccaneer. One candid stock trader did express this reality. In racy American terms he told the Senate Committee that Stock-Exchange manipulators were racketeers on a scale which made the most outstanding underworld racketeer "look like a piker." Not to be gainsaid was this comparison. A dazed investing population, lost in wonder as to how its money had vanished (forty-three billion dollars or more, estimated in shrinkage of values), now had an opportunity to see behind the scenes and learn much of the inside working of a system cunningly organized to ensnare, waylay and plunder.

By no abuse of the imagination could the British Parliament be visualized as undertaking even a similitude of such a vital probing as that made by the United States Senate Committee on Banking and Currency. In the onset of the great depression the Labor Government of Britain, late in 1929, found itself compelled to make some move. It appointed a committee "to inquire into banking, finance and credit." Further, in empowering the committee to "make investigation calculated to enable those agencies to promote the development of trade and commerce," it meant inquiries, not investigations as construed in the American sense.

There were not wanting causes for an inquisition patterned after American lines. Except the bankers themselves, no one really knew of the underlying facts of management and how the power of massed money was used. All that was conveyed to the public were the formal reports of the bank heads, and these documents were taken at their face value with rarely a question. The general attitude was that one should never impugn the honor and disinterestedness of bankers; although why they should be robed in a character beyond doubt or query no one ever explained. This view of the Moguls of the banking world had become traditional—so much so that, when an occasional voice suggested a look below the surface, the proposal was regarded as subversive of the proprieties. The criticism made at this time in Britain was not of the conduct but of the policies of many of that country's banks.

In this respect there was a marked difference between British and American banks. In America banks had taken the lead in financing great industrial corporations and combinations. Many British banks clung to old ways of restricting their financing to the routine avenues of commerce. At a stage when there was much agitation in Britain over the obsolescence of many of its industrial plants and methods, blame was cast upon banks for the backwardness of British industry in not modernizing—or as the phrase went, "rationalizing"—itself.

However, a number of joint-stock banks did deviate from a purely banking business and, for one reason or another, become involved in control of industries. This of itself furnished a provocation for inquiry. A greater and pressing field for severe investigation was the stock-promotion business which had channeled its way into the pockets of investors. Of the hundreds upon hundreds of companies organized in the boom years, many had become defunct; and hordes of embittered people could now ruefully ponder upon the visions held out to them and the losses incurred. Americans did at least want to know *how* they were duped and swindled. Nor was this mere curiosity. By knowing the men who did the "skull-duggery" and the processes by which it was done, there was ground provided for punitive action and for tightening laws. But in Britain there was no such spirit. A characteristic showing of the spinelessness prevailing there was contained in an address at Edinburgh, early in 1930, by a high financial authority, R. O. Hobson, Editor-in-Chief of "The Financial News." The investor, he urged, should be protected against the notorious evils of boom-company promotion, reckless stock flotations, group finance methods, and concealment of unfavorable developments. He could have simplified the case by saying trickery and lying. But what was his grand remedy? He proposed the co-operation of Press, Law and Stock Exchange in overcoming these evils. (In America the first and most natural move was to call for an investigation that would bore deep and supply facts to the public through the medium of newspapers and otherwise.) Where the British press was to get the basic facts, Hobson did not explain. He expected the London Stock Exchange to help purify itself! Never a miracle had come from that body, although on past occasions it had made great pretensions to regeneration. As for the Law, the omnipotent Law, he certainly must have known of the succession of stock jugglery which under it had been easily accomplished, leaving the manipulators in full and honored possession of booty.

Editorializing upon J. P. Morgan's testimony before the United States Senate Committee, "The Economist," of London, on June 10, 1933, made this acknowledgment of the ravages of financial wolves in its own land:

"There is no reason to suppose from anything that has so far emerged, that Morgan's acted in 1929 in any other way than was standard practice both in England and America during the boom period. Indeed, when the whole truth is told—if it ever is—it will probably be found that the Morgan partners were far more cautious and conservative than most people at a time when it was general to act as if the era of prosperity would last forever." Criticizing, nevertheless, the "preferred list" favoritism, the editorial went on: "Now if shares could be rushed up to fancy prices almost immediately the issue is floated—and there are countless similar instances in our own country as in America—the investment banker has an opportunity of enormous profits in addition to his commission."

Here was an obvious need and an opportunity of real investigation of the ways and means by which these schemes had been operated and of the individuals or firms responsible. But who composed the committee appointed by the Labor Government? Headed by Lord Macmillan, it comprised bankers, business men and some labor representatives. Its report, submitted in 1931, was a digest of a subject, not an investigation. The first part was a historical and descriptive view of the gold standard, and dealt with Britain's special post-war problems. Recommendations formed the second part. Two members did urge the transformation of the Bank of England from a private corporation to a public institution. Apart, however, from calling attention to a bank having such vast powers run for private profit, there was no scintilla of suggestion that the way in which those powers had been used should be thoroughly investigated.

As a whole the report was a highly technical document.[9] The point considered by the Committee as of supreme importance was its opinion that immediate efforts should be made to check the violent decline in prices that they thought was endangering political and social stability. The report thus took its worthy place with many a past report, in its adherence to instructions and its consequent avoidance of a course which might induce a different kind of examination.

And here this narrative may properly be brought to an end. The historical record set forth has shown with informative sufficiency the true contrast of American conditions with the practices and pretensions of countries from which so many criticisms of America have come. Further evidence is not wanting; on the contrary, our record closes in the face of an embarrassing wealth of it. This, if it had been incorporated, would have added mass but not more weight to the volume of telling facts herein detailed. Surely, no further evidence is needed to dispose of the legend that America has been the one and great exemplar of materialism. In view of the authentic record here given, the fact that America has been so long and so pertinaciously represented as such is certain to arouse some, if not considerable astonishment. And, what is more to the point, the contrast here presented will serve to supply a much-needed enlightening perspective of American practices, activities and standards as measured by those prevalent in various other countries.

NOTES AND INDEX

NOTES

CHAPTER I

FROM LEGEND TO FACT

[1] "Words to the Deaf: An Historian Contemplates His Age."

[2] Act of 28 Edward I and Act of 37 Edward III. Statutes at Large, Great Britain Parliament. Vol. I, pp. 146 and 302. Edition of 1786.

[3] Act of 5 Henry IV, *Ibid.*, p. 420.

[4] Act of 37 Edward III, *Ibid.*, Vol. 1, p. 302.

[5] Act of 4 Edward IV, *Ibid.*, Vol. 2, pp. 11–12.

[6] Act of 4 Henry VII, *Ibid.*, Vol. 2, p. 65.

[7] Act of 13 Elizabeth, *Ibid.*, Vol. 2, p. 610.

[8] Act of 12 George II, *Ibid.*, Vol. 6, pp. 99–105.

[9] Act of 30 George II, *Ibid.*, Vol. 7, p. 239. My italics.

[10] Act of 13 George III, *Ibid.*, Cap. 59.

[11] Act of 9 and 10 William III, *Ibid.*, Vol. 3, pp. 687–688.

[12] Act of 27 George II, *Ibid.*, Vol. 7, pp. 54–56.

[13] Act of 14 and 15 Henry VIII, *Ibid.*, Vol. 2, p. 137, repeated and amplified in 1529 by Star Chamber decree.

[14] Act of 25 Henry VIII, *Ibid.*, p. 172.

[15] Act of 33 Henry VIII, *Ibid.*, p. 293.

[16] "The Creative Impulse in Industry," by Helen Marot, p. 2. (E. P. Dutton & Co.)

[17] "Prospects of Industrial Civilization," by Bertrand and Dora Russell, p. 171. (The Century Co.)

[18] Syndicated article by Glenn Frank, President of the University of Wisconsin.

[19] It is unnecessary to give the laws of all the colonies seeking to restrain these frauds. Laws of New York will suffice as an instance. See "Laws of the Colony of New York," Vol. III, pp. 788–793; Vol. IV, pp. 926–927, and Vol. V, pp. 65, 67, 71–73, 193, 266–268, 292, etc., covering years from 1750 to 1773.

[20] Acts of 51 Henry III, "Statutes at Large, Great Britain Parliament," Vol. 1, pp. 186–187.

[21] Act of 9 Henry VI, *Ibid.*, Vol. 1, pp. 497–498.

[22] Act of 14 Charles II, *Ibid.*, Vol. 3, p. 240.

[23] Act of 4 William and Mary, *Ibid.*, pp. 484–486.

[24] Act of 2 and 3 Edward VI, *Ibid.*, Vol. 2, p. 223.

[25] Act of 27 Elizabeth, *Ibid.*, p. 634.

[26] Act of 1 James I, *Ibid.*, Vol. 3, p. 15.

[27] Act of 12 Charles II, *Ibid.*, pp. 182–184.

[28] Act of 8 Queen Anne, *Ibid.*, Vol. 4, p. 398.

[29] Act of 13 Elizabeth, *Ibid.*, Vol. 2, pp. 616–617.

[30] Act of 1 George I, *Ibid.*, Vol. 5, pp. 55–56 and 5 George I, Cap. II.

[31] Act of 21 George III, *Ibid.*, Vol. 9, p. 179.

CHAPTER II

"AN ESSAY UPON NATIONAL CHARACTER"

[1] Act of 9 Henry IV, "Statutes at Large, Great Britain Parliament," Vol. 1, p. 424.

[2] Act of 2 and 3 Edward VI, *Ibid.*, Vol. 2, p. 411.

[3] Act of 21 Henry VIII, *Ibid.*, p. 132.

[4] Act of 33 Elizabeth, *Ibid.*, Vol. 2, pp. 666–667.

[5] Act of 1 James I, *Ibid.*, Vol. 3, p. 27.

[6] Acts of 9 George II, Cap. 37, and act of 24 George II, Cap. 32.

[7] Acts of 11 and 18 Henry VI, Vol. I, pp. 510 and 527.

[8] Act of 4 Edward IV, *Ibid.*, Vol. 2, pp. 11–12.

[9] Act of 1 Richard III, *Ibid.*, p. 49.

[10] These laws were passed in 1513, 1514, and 1534. Acts of 5, 6 and 23 Henry VIII, *Ibid.*, pp. 109 and 164.

[11] Act of 27 Henry VIII, *Ibid.*, p. 220.

[12] Acts of 5 and 6 Edward VI, *Ibid.*, pp. 427–432. The stricter regulations prescribed by this law covered five pages of fine type.

[13] Act of 27 Elizabeth, *Ibid.*, p. 636.

[14] Act of 27 Elizabeth, *Ibid.*, pp. 680–682.

[15] Act of 2 James I, *Ibid.*, Vol. 3, p. 63.

[16] Act of 20 James I, *Ibid.*, pp. 101–104.

[17] Acts of 13 and 14 Charles II, Vol. 3, pp. 210–212; 7 and 10 Anne, *Ibid.*, Vol. 4, p. 349 and 509–510; 6, 10, 11 and 13 George I, *Ibid.*, Vol. 5, pp. 191–193, 354, 451; and various acts of George II.

[18] Act of 6 George III, *Ibid.*, Vol. 7, p. 581.

CHAPTER III

ACANADA

[1] DeMeulles, a French official in Canada, to the King of France, 1684, "Report on Canadian Archives," 1899, p. 43. The volumes of these archives containing the original records are not numbered, but bear the date of the year in which they were issued by the Archives Bureau of the Dominion Government.

[2] Biggar's "Early Trading Companies of New France," Vol. 1, pp. 15, 41–42.

[3] Thus, in his Memoirs concerning Canada, wrote De la Chesnaye, who had gone to Canada to represent the interests of the Company of Rouen. "Report on Canadian Archives," 1899, Supplement, p. 39.

[4] "Report on Canadian Archives," 1889, p. 54.

[5] *Ibid.*, p. 55.

[6] *Ibid.*, p. 56.

[7] De Brumath's "Bishop Laval," p. 113.

[8] Duchesenau's correspondence and memoir are published in "Documents Relating to the Colonial History of New York, Paris Documents," Vol. IX, pp. 68, 120, 131, 135, 142, 150, etc.

[9] "Report on Canadian Archives," 1899, pp. 42–43.

[10] *Ibid.*, 1900, p. 71.

[11] De Brumath's "Bishop Laval," p. 173.

[12] "Documents Relating to the Colonial History of the State of New York, Paris Documents," Vol. IX, pp. 441–442.

[13] "Report on Canadian Archives," 1889, pp. 290–291.

[14] "Report on Canadian Archives," 1899, Supplement, p. 227. "Memorial on Affairs in Canada at the Present Time and the Settlement of Cape Breton."

[15] "Report on Canadian Archives," 1899, p. 227.

CHAPTER IV

THE LORDS OF TRADE

[1] The many volumes of "Documents Relating to the Colonial History of the State of New York, London Documents," are replete with reproductions of the correspondence, reports and orders of the Board of Trade. For the list see Vol. III, p. 357; Vol. IV, p. 101; Vol. V, pp. 5, 471, 501, 522; Vol. VI, pp. 17, 24, 32, 35, 160, etc., etc.

[2] *Ibid.*, Vol. IV, pp. 39, 463, 535 and 582. Bellomont had originally been sent to New England on the special mission of suppressing piracy. With others he fitted out the ship *Adventure* for Captain Kidd who was given special powers to arrest pirates. Kidd's own piratical acts led Bellomont to arrest him at Boston, where he had come under a promise of safety, and send him to England. Bellomont died in New York in 1701.

[3] *Ibid.*, Vol. IV, p. 816.

[4] *Ibid.*, Vol. VII, p. 564.

[5] Failure to fulfill this requirement was made a ground, in 1746, by Arthur Dobbs and others to petition Parliament to declare the Charter void and forfeited, and to give similar powers and privileges to himself and associates. The petition was rejected on August 10, 1748. Parliamentary Report, House of Commons of that date on the Hudson Bay Company.

[6] "Report from the Select Committee on the Hudson Bay Company, etc. House of Commons," 1857, p. 398, and *Ibid.*, Appendix No. 411, p. 435.

[7] Only an epitome of this remarkable charter has been here given. The full text is spread in *Ibid.*, Appendix No. XI, Enclosure A, pp. 411–413.

[8] "Report from the Committee Appointed to Inquire into the State and Condition of the Countries Adjoining Hudson Bay, and the State of Trading Carried on There, 1749," House of Commons Reports of Committees, Vol. 2, No. 215. This report was further incorporated in "Imperial Blue Books on Affairs Relating to Canada." Also Pelley's testimony in "Report from the Select Committee on the Hudson Bay Company, House of Commons, 1857," Appendix No. XIII, p. 344.

[9] "Report from the Select Committee on the Hudson Bay Company, etc. House of Commons," 1857, Appendix No. XIII, pp. 427–428.

[10] "An Account of Six Years' Residence in Hudson's Bay, from 1733 to 1736 and 1744 to 1747," by Joseph Robson, Late Surveyor of the Buildings to the Hudson Bay Company (London, 1752), pp. 55–56.

[11] These and an abundance of other facts are set forth in the "Report from the Committee Appointed to Inquire into the State and Conditions of the Countries Adjoining Hudson's Bay and the State of Trade Carried on There," 1749, incorporated in Vol. 40 of "Imperial Blue Books Relating to Canada."

[12] The full report is published in "Documents Relating to the Colonial History of the State of New York, London Documents," Vol. V, pp. 614–617.

[13] *Ibid.*, Vol. IV, pp. 1051–1052.

[14] *Ibid.*, p. 825.

[15] *Ibid.*, pp. 597–629.

[16] "Laws of the Colony of New York," Vol. 1, pp. 428–430. The notion in the colonies that Catholics were seditious was derived from English laws of which colonial laws were copies or paraphrases. A law from Queen Elizabeth's reign indicted all Catholics as "wicked and seditious" and secret stirrers of rebellion. Later English laws followed the same line. See "Statutes at Large, Great Britain Parliament," Vol. 2, pp. 660–662; Vol. 3, pp. 38–41, 44–50, etc. (years 1593, 1604, 1605, etc.).

[17] "Report on Canadian Archives," 1899, p. 414.

[18] "Documents Relating to the Colonial History of the State of New York, London Documents," Vol. V, pp. 727–730, and Vol. VI, p. 527.

[19] *Ibid.*, "Paris Documents," Vol. IX, p. 953.

[20] *Ibid.*, "London Documents," Vol. VII, p. 613.

CHAPTER V

RAGING SPECULATION

[1] "Journal of the House of Commons," Vol. XI, p. 595.

[2] Act of 8 and 9 William III, "Statutes at Large, Great Britain Parliament," Vol. 3, p. 657.

[3] Act of 6 Anne, *Ibid.*, Vol. 3, p. 280.

[4] Act of 10 Anne, *Ibid.*, Vol. 4, p. 542.

[5] Act of 9 Anne, *Ibid.*, Vol. 3, pp. 457–468.

CHAPTER VI

MONEY MANIA IN FRANCE AND ENGLAND

[1] "A Full and Impartial Account of the Company of Mississippi, Otherwise Called The French East India Company" (London, 1720), pp. 11, 13, etc.

[2] "The Chimera: or the French Way of Paying National Debts Laid Open" (London, 1720), pp. 6, 29, 30, 65 and 76.

[3] "The Case of the Borrowers on South Sea Loans Stated" (London, 1721), p. 5.

[4] *Ibid.*, p. 7.

[5] "The Works of James Houstoun, M.D., Containing Memoirs, of His Life and Travels in Asia, America, and Most Parts of Europe," etc. (London, 1735), pp. 120–121.

[6] "The Case of the Borrowers on the South Sea Loans Stated," p. 8.

[7] "A Collection of the Parliamentary Debates in England" (London, 1741), Vol. 7, pp. 330–340. The declaration of the Lords Justices did not include the South Sea Company and other chartered corporations with enormous capitalizations.

[8] *Ibid.*, pp. 349–350.

[9] So Luke Owen Pike wrote in his "History of Crime in England" (London, 1873), Vol. 2, p. 304. Pike asserted that the company was the Welsh Copper Company but the official records cited show differently.

[10] "A Collection of the Parliamentary Debates in England," Vol. 7, p. 351. Inserted in the debates is an historical account of various phases of the South Sea Company's stock operations.

[11] *Ibid.*, p. 353.

[12] *Ibid.*, Vol. 7, p. 355, containing an account of this meeting and subsequent developments.

[13] *Ibid.*, p. 361.

CHAPTER VII

WHEN BUBBLES BURST

[1] These figures are taken from Professor George Tucker's "The Theory of Money and Banks Investigated." This book, published in 1839, embodied the best account written of the Mississippi Company's financial operations.

[2] These are typical extracts from "The South Sea Management Detected," etc., and "The Case of the Borrowers on the South Sea Loans Stated," pp. 4, 5, 9, and 7 and 8 respectively.

[3] "Memoirs"; Preface and pp. 105 and 117.

[4] *Ibid.*, p. 126.

[5] "A Collection of Parliamentary Debates in England," Vol. 7, p. 372.

[6] *Ibid.*, p. 384.

[7] *Ibid.*, Vol. 8, p. 9.

[8] *Ibid.*, p. 11.

[9] *Ibid.*, p. 13.

[10] *Ibid.*, pp. 14–15.

[11] *Ibid.*, pp. 27–28.

[12] *Ibid.*, p. 29.

[13] *Ibid.*, pp. 38–40.

[14] The seven reports were published as an Appendix to *Ibid.*, Vol. 8. See pp. 70, 95–96, etc. These reports showed that, aside from its great issue of regular stock, the South Sea Company had put out £1,213,575 of fictitious stock of a nominal value of £574,000.

[15] *Ibid.*, p. 40.

[16] *Ibid.*, p. 62.

[17] *Ibid.*, pp. 55–56, 62.

[18] The latter history of the South Sea Company was published in the report "State of the South Sea Company's Affairs, Great Britain Parliament, Sessional Papers," 1834, Vol. XLI, No. 235.

[19] *Ibid.*, p. 3. Nearly one-half of the 1,017 stock owners at this time were small holders, most of them receiving incomes of from £100 to £200 a year. Only thirteen stockholders received £2,000, and only five £4,000 a year.

[20] The details of the arrangement were published in Vol. XXXIX, "Sessional Papers," 1854, No. 48.

[21] Under the pretence of gathering a supply of wheat for popular benefit, he built storehouses, crowded them with wheat and cornered the market. "He gave such serious attention to this speculation that those admitted to his private rooms saw on his desk accurate records of the prices of wheat, day by day, on the different markets of his kingdom." Simultaneously, lesser monopolies in the king's service were conducting their operations.—"The Private Life of Louis X," by Mouffle D'Angerville, pp. 303–304. (Boni & Liveright.)

[22] Act of 7 George II, Cap. 8.

[23] "The Complete English Tradesman in Familiar Letters" (London, 1732), Vol. 2, p. 29.

[24] "Horace Walpole's England," p. 46.

CHAPTER VIII

SECRET FRAUD AND THE REVOLUTION

[1] Copious details from documentary sources have been given in my "History of the Great American Fortunes," "History of the Supreme Court of the United States" and "History of Tammany Hall."

[2] Hansard, "The Parliamentary History of England," Vol. XXVIII, p. 458. These volumes gave in detail the debates in Parliament.

[3] Samuel Johnson, for instance. He acknowledged that in an Exeter Street garret he concocted the famous speech "on the atrocious crime of being a young man," represented to have been made by Pitt in reply to sneering observations by Walpole upon Pitt's youth.

[4] Hansard, "The Parliamentary History of England," Vol. XIX, pp. 205, 210–211.

[5] *Ibid.,* pp. 649–650.

[6] *Ibid.,* pp. 1089–1095.

[7] "The Report of the Commissioners Appointed to Examine, Take and State the Public Accounts of the Kingdom, Presented to His Majesty and to Both Houses of Parliament by William Molleson, Secretary to the Commissioners, June 18, 1782" (published in 1783), Vol. 1, pp. 130–133.

[8] *Ibid.,* Appendix No. 5, pp. 432–433.

[9] *Ibid.,* p. 137. The Commissioners presented figures of the highest costs of horses and wagons and hire of attendants, and the amounts charged to the Government. The price of labor was then seven pence to two shillings a day.

[10] *Ibid.,* pp. 133–135.

[11] *Ibid.,* p. 444.

[12] *Ibid.,* p. 136. Cornwallis testified that the regimental Quarter-Masters gave the Commissary-General receipts for the full ration without distinguishing whether it consisted of provisions obtained from England, or procured in America where provisions were often seized or bought at a price much below the European price (p. 433).

[13] *Ibid.,* p. 143.

[14] *Ibid.,* p. 144.

[15] What became of this money was a mystery. Of Lincoln's large defalcation Burke's "Peerage" (1839 edit. p. 765) contained not a word. It did relate, however, that in the time of Queen Anne, Lincoln so ingratiated himself in the graces of the Earl of Torrington, that the Earl bequeathed to him the greater part of his estates. Summoned in 1780 by the Commissioners, the Duke of Newcastle, Lincoln's son, informed them that he (Newcastle) had never had any of the public money possessed by his father, nor any of his accounts or vouchers. Further, that his father had died intestate, leaving him and several other children, then infants, and that such effects as he bequeathed were administered by the widow, the Countess of Lincoln.

[16] "The Report of the Commissioners," etc., p. 71.

[17] *Ibid.,* p. 50.

[18] *Ibid.,* p. 65.

[19] *Ibid.,* p. 27. In its biography of Lord Anthony Falkland, Burke's "Peerage" (1839 edit., p. 394) said nothing of his defalcation but it did say that, as a member of the House of Commons, that body, on January 17, 1693–1694, declared him guilty of a high misdemeanor and committed him to the Tower

for having begged and received £2,000 from the king, contrary to the ordinary method of obtaining benefactions.

[20] "The Report of the Commissioners," etc., pp. 36–38.

[21] *Ibid.*, p. 76. The Comissioners reported that "so large a sum of fees," paid in a single year to one officer "demanded our attention." The amount of "poundage" fees in 1780 was £39,198.

[22] *Ibid.*, p. 85.

[23] *Ibid.*, p. 80.

[24] *Ibid.*, p. 87.

[25] *Ibid.*, p. 110.

[26] *Ibid.*, p. 107.

[27] *Ibid.*, p. 111.

[28] In the House of Commons Henry Flood, during a debate, told its members that the Commons were not what the name purported but were merely "a second-rate aristocracy." Hansard, "The Parliamentary History of England," Vol. XXVIII, p. 458.

[29] "The Report of the Commissioners," etc., p. 72.

[30] "The Parliamentary History of England," Vol. XXVIII, p. 458.

CHAPTER IX

AN ONRUSH OF CRITICS

[1] "The American Museum or Universal Magazine," July, 1788.

[2] Doc. No. 91, Eighth Congress, First Session.

[3] "History of the Phelps and Gorham Purchase," pp. 140–144.

[4] "History of the Holland Company," N. Y. Assembly Doc. No. 224, "Assembly Documents," Vol. 3, 1837.

[5] See for example, the case, in 1843, of William Willinck, Jr. vs. the Morris Canal and Banking Company involving litigation growing out of a loan of $750,000. "New Jersey Chancery Reports," Vol. 3, p. 377.

[6] See "Peters' Reports," Supreme Court of the United States, Vol. 6, pp. 431–434. Delivering the court's decision in a case growing out of this transaction, Justice Thompson recounted the facts.

[7] "American State Papers: Public Lands," Vol. 1, pp. 29–30.

[8] *Ibid.*, Vol. 2, p. 253.

[9] See "American State Papers: Public Lands," Vol. 1, pp. 141–158. (Doc. No. 74). Also, "Cranch's Reports," Supreme Court of the United States, Vol. 6, p. 87.

[10] See Judge Huston's historical review, written some years later, of this contest in "Watt's Reports" (Supreme Court of Pennsylvania), Vol. 1, pp. 70–109. On the ground that Indian Wars prevented the Holland Company from making full and actual settling of its lands, Chief Justice Marshall of the Supreme Court of the U. S. later validated the Holland Company's title to the lands. See "Cranch's Reports," Supreme Court of the United States, Vol. 3, pp. 1–73.

[11] "American State Papers: Public Lands," Vol. 1, pp. 29–30.

[12] "American State Papers: Public Lands," Vol. 2, p. 441. The report does not state the number of individuals. But that a great part of this vast area was held for speculative purposes is distinctly set forth in the report.

[13] "Travels Through the States of North America, etc., During the years

1795, 1796 and 1797." I am quoting from the third edition, brought out in London in 1800, Vol. 1, pp. 126–127.

[14] *Ibid.*, Vol. 1, pp. 113–114.

[15] *Ibid.*, Vol. 1, p. 192.

[16] "The Parliamentary History of England," Vol. XXXVI, p. 833–834.

[17] "Great Britain Parliament, Sessional Papers," 1831–1832, Vol. V, "Report from the Select Committee on the Bill Relating to the Cruel and Improper Treatment of Animals," p. 73, etc.

[18] "Travels Through the United States of North America and Upper Canada in the years 1795, 1796 and 1797." (London, 1799), pp. xi and xii. Rochefoucauld was not allowed by Lord Dorchester, having supreme jurisdiction in Canada, to visit Lower Canada, as the Province of Quebec was then called.

[19] *Ibid.*, Vol. 3, pp. 31–32.

[20] *Ibid.*, Vol. 4, p. 577.

[21] *Ibid.*, Vol. 4, pp. 562, 579, etc.

[22] "The British Critic," October, 1800, p. 405, in a review of his volumes.

[23] "A Tour in America, in 1798, 1799 and 1800 Exhibiting Society and Manners, and a Particular Account of the American System of Agriculture."

[24] *Ibid.*, Vol. I, pp. 26, 30 and 31.

[25] *Ibid.*, p. 26, and Vol. 2, p. 652.

[26] *Ibid.*, Vol. 2, p. 652.

[27] "The Stranger in America," by Charles William Janson (London, 1807), p. ix.

[28] "Travels in America, Performed in 1806," by Thomas Ashe (London, 1808), Vol. 1, pp. 3, 4, 63, 143, etc.

[29] "Travels in the Interior of America in the Years 1809, 1810 and 1811" by John Bradbury, F.L.S., pp. 304–306. His book was privately printed in Liverpool in 1817.

[30] "Travels in the United States of America and Lower Canada Performed in the Year 1817." (London, 1818), pp. 3 and 4.

[31] "The Quarterly Review," November, 1809, pp. 321–327. The occasion chosen for the attack was a pretended review of Abiel Holmes' "American Annals," under cover of which page after page was given to sheer vilification of Americans.

[32] "Great Britain Parliament, Sessional Papers," 1803, No. 122, and *Ibid.*, 1813–1814, Nos. 206 and 207, Vol. XII.

[33] "Parliamentary Debates," 1807, Vol. 9, pp. 1001–1003. H. Thornton, a member of Parliament, and one of the company's directors, spoke in defence of the company.

[34] "The Portfolio," November 21, 1801, p. 271.

[35] *Ibid.*, December, 1811, pp. 585–587.

[36] "A Discourse Delivered on the Day Preceding the Annual Commencement of Union College, July 26, 1836," published in bound volume, pp. 15 and 55.

CHAPTER X

IN THEIR OWN LANDS

[1] See Dispatch of Lieutenant-Governor Stirling of Australia to George Murray, Colonial Department, London, January 20, 1830. "Great Britain Parliament, Sessional Papers," No. 675, Vol. XXI, 1830.

[2] "Great Britain Parliament, Sessional Papers," 1822, No. 448. Vol. XX.

[3] "Imperial Blue Books on Affairs Relating to Canada," Vol. X, pp. 53, 63, 78–86, etc.

[4] Usually the captain informed immigrants that they need not take along provisions for more than three weeks or a month—immigrants then had to supply their own food—he well knowing that the average passage was six weeks, frequently eight or nine weeks. Laying in a large stock of provisions, the captain, after the immigrants' supply had run out, compelled them to pay as much as 400 per cent on the cost price of the food (which often was bad) that he sold to them. See testimony of Quebec immigrant officers, "Imperial Blue Books on Affairs Relating to Canada," Vol. X, Appendix B., p. 83.

[5] "Report on Canadian Archives, Report of the Archivist," 1899, p. xiv.

[6] "Imperial Blue Books on Affairs Relating to Canada," Lord Durham's Report, Vol. X, Appendix B., pp. 86–87.

[7] "Report on Canadian Archives," 1899, p. xiii.

[8] Borthwick's "History of Montreal," p. 94. Even in the mid-nineteenth century boys as young as eight years were sentenced to Canadian Penitentiaries in which tortures and other cruelties were inflicted by keepers upon inmates. See "Ontario Legislative Council Sessional Papers," 1846, No. 2, Vol. 5, Appendix G and *Ibid.*, Vols. 8 and 9, Appendices.

[9] "Imperial Blue Books" etc., Lord Durham's Report, Vol. X, p. 92.

[10] "Report on Canadian Archives," 1892, p. 145.

[11] *Ibid.*, Note E., pp. 135–136.

[12] *Ibid.*, pp. 139–140.

[13] "Report from the Select Committee of the Hudson Bay Company," House of Commons, 1857, Appendix No. XVIII, p. 449, and Appendix XVI, pp. 444, etc.

[14] Borthwick's "History of Montreal," p. 398.

[15] "Report from the Select Committee on the Hudson Bay Company" etc., 1857, p. 326.

[16] "The Parliamentary History of England," Vol. XXXVI, p. 358.

[17] Niles' "Principles and Acts of the Revolution in America," etc., giving in detail the proceedings of this meeting, p. 205.

[18] Perry Walton's "The Story of Textiles," p. 174. (George Sully & Co.)

[19] "The American Museum or Universal Magazine," March, 1789, and May, 1792.

[20] Seventy members of the House of Commons were elected by 35 boroughs where there were hardly any voters; 90 were elected by 46 boroughs in none of which the voters exceeded 50; 37 were elected by 19 boroughs not having more than 200 voters; 20 more elected by Scotland counties each having less than 100 electors, etc.—"The Parliamentary History of England," Vol. XXX, pp. 787–799.

[21] "The Parliamentary History of England," Vol. XXX, p. 439.

[22] *Ibid.*, p. 907.

[23] "Parliamentary Debates," 1807, Vol. 9, pp. 738–746.

[24] "The Parliamentary History of England," Vol. XXX, p. 439.

[25] "Report of Accountant-General, Estimates from the East India Company, Great Britain Parliament, Sessional Papers," 1802–1803, 1–50.

[26] The figures here given were reported in "Great Britain Parliament, Sessional Papers," 1806, No. 264, "Report of the Inspector General of Exports and Imports of Great Britain."

[27] "Great Britain Census, 1800," Part 2, p. 497. The British census was confined to population, giving number of houses, occupants and occupations.

The United States census was restricted to number of population and its division into whites and slaves.

²⁸ These riots caused great uneasiness to authority. See "Great Britain Parliament, Sessional Papers," 1812, Vol. 1, p. 209, and *Ibid.*, 1816, Vol. II, p. 755.

²⁹ "Reports of the Proceedings and Debates of the Convention of 1821" (to amend and revise the Constitution), pp. 218, 221–222.

³⁰ Here is an instance: "America has, comparatively speaking, no manufactures; and how intimately the prosperity of the arts and sciences is connected with these, it is unnecessary even for the author to demonstrate." Janson's "The Stranger in America" (London, 1807), p. xiii.

³¹ "Great Britain Parliament, Sessional Papers," 1803, Vol. VII, "Minutes of Evidence Taken before the Select Committee on the Bill Respecting the Laws Relating to the Woolen Trade," pp. 34–35, 104, 119, 159, etc. Also "Report from the Select Committee on the Woolen Trade," 1821, pp. 62, 63, 68.

³² *Ibid.*, Vol. II, 1812, containing two reports on the subject, pp. 9–13.

³³ *Ibid.*, Vol. V, 1819, p. 23.

³⁴ *Ibid.*, Vol. VI, 1817, p. 285.

³⁵ *Ibid.*, 1824, Vol. 1, No. 385, and 1825, Vol. 1, No. 144.

³⁶ *Ibid.*, 1815, Vol. V, pp. 24, 32, 33, 79, 97, etc., and 1821, Vol. V, pp. 4, 14.

³⁷ These figures I take from the 1830 edition of "The American Almanac," citing "The Englishman's Almanac."

³⁸ "Studies in Millionaires," by James Bromley, "Chambers' Journal," 1901, pp. 212–217.

CHAPTER XI

AND STILL NO CHANGE

¹ "Metcalf's Reports" (Supreme Court of Massachusetts), Vol. 1, p. 111.

² While "The Edinburgh Review" constantly reviled America it did occasionally print truths as to British corruption. Following the introduction of a bill for "the better securing the independence and purity of Parliament by preventing the procuring or obtaining of seats by corrupt practices," it commented (February, 1811): "At present seats are exchanged for various equivalents; some for money, others for preferment, others for titles." But, it pointed out, unless the bill was cautiously drawn, newer ways of evading laws could be found; controlling borough voters, noblemen could have their creatures elected, dictate their votes in Parliament, and get what they asked from the Ministry.

³ The dread of these tumults, feared as a result of "universal" suffrage, "excites so much apprehension in this country." In thus stating (December, 1818) "The Edinburgh Review" admitted that no tumults had occurred in America.

⁴ "Great Britain Parliament, Sessional Papers," 1818, Vol. VI, No. 276, pp. 7, 19, 51.

⁵ "The Resources of the United States of America; or a View of the Agricultural, Commercial, Financial, Political, Literary, Moral and Religious Character of the American People," pp. 459, 460, etc.

⁶ "Sketches of America. A Narrative of a Journey of Five Thousand Miles through the Eastern and Western States of America," pp. 39, 48, 80, 166, 168, 262, 273, 368, etc.

[7] Robert Walsh, Jr., "An Appeal from the Judgments of Great Britain Respecting the United States of America, an Historical Outline of their Merits and Wrongs as Colonies, and Strictures upon the Calumnies of British Writers," pp. v–viii.

[8] "The Records of the Colony of Massachusetts Bay in New England," Vol. 2, p. 167; Vol. 4, p. 486; Vol. 5, p. 414, etc. The purpose of these early schools was both educational and religious. Teachers had to qualify by orthodoxy of faith.

[9] "The Public Records of the Colony of Connecticut," Vol. 2, p. 176, 307–308; Vol. 3, pp. 9, 29, 158; Vol. 4, pp. 31, 97, 331; Vol. 5, p. 462.

[10] "Pennsylvania Archives, Fourth Series," Vol. 1, p. 31.

[11] This, in 1812, received aid from the State school fund, and was further granted the support of a city tax.

[12] "History of the Public School Society of the City of New York," by William Oland Bourne (1870), p. 15–16.

[13] "Parliamentary Debates," 1807, Vol. 9, p. 799.

[14] *Ibid.*, pp. 1177–1178.

[15] Expenses of elementary schools were now borne by the commons: fees were authorized in all schools, but free tuition was given to all indigent children; after the regular school hours, schoolrooms were at the disposal of the several religious denominations.

[16] Heinrich von Treitschke's "History of Germany in the Nineteenth Century," Vol. 2, p. 516. (New York: McBride, Nast & Co.)

[17] See account in "Great Britain Parliament, Sessional Papers," 1834, Vol. IX, "Report from the Select Committee on the State of Education," pp. 41–44, etc.

[18] "Great Britain Parliament, Sessional Papers," 1818, Vol. IV, "Reports of Committees: Education of the Lower Orders," p. 9.

[19] *Ibid.*

[20] *Ibid.*, pp. 58–59.

[21] "Parliamentary Debates," 1833, Vol. 20, p. 203.

[22] *Ibid.*, p. 130.

[23] *Ibid.*, p. 242.

[24] "Travels through Part of the United States and Canada in 1818 and 1819" (Glasgow, 1823), Vol. I, pp. vii and 110; Vol. 2, pp. 325–327, 328, 335.

[25] One example of many instances: "There is no subject which ought to awaken deeper interest than that of free and common education. Let it be remembered that we have established free and universal suffrage. Can it be doubted that the means of common education ought to be co-extensive with this right . . . ?"—"New York Evening Post," December 17, 1828.

[26] "Annals of the Boston Primary School Committee," Compiled by Joseph M. Wightman (1860), p. 53.

[27] "Journal of the Rhode Island Institute of Instruction" (1846–1847).

[28] "Ohio Senate Journal," 1836, pp. 606–607.

[29] "Travels in North America in the Years 1827–1828," Vol. 1, pp. 216, 299, 305, 307, etc.

[30] "Great Britain Parliament, Sessional Papers," 1825, Vols. VIII and IX, "Report from the Select Committee of the House of Lords, Appointed to Inquire into the State of Ireland," pp. 50, 61–66, 108–112, 570–571, etc.

[31] "Parliamentary Debates," 1833, Vol. 15, p. 1154.

[32] "Sessional Papers," 1821, Nos. 379, 562, etc.

[33] "Great Britain Parliament, Sessional Papers," 1826–1827, Vol. III, Report No. 234, pp. 14, 17, 32. This was one of the very rare occasions on which the

chairman of a Parliamentary select committee allowed newspaper reporters to report testimony.

[34] "Parliamentary Debates," 1830, Vol. 22, pp. 727–734.

[35] *Ibid.*, 1837, Vol. 37, pp. 458–464 and 800.

[36] "Great Britain Parliament, Sessional Papers," 1818, Vol. VI, No. 227. "Report of the Select Committee on the Usury Laws," pp. 3–19. The same evasion of usury laws was common in Holland and other European countries.

[37] "The American Almanac" for 1833, p. 129, citing "The New York Shipping and Commercial Register."

[38] Davenport's "Gazetteer of North America," 1836, pp. 46, 50–70, 82, 85–95, etc.

[39] "Great Britain Parliament, Sessional Papers," 1836, Vol. XLV, containing the data. The British census of 1831 showed 24,410,429, and that of ten years later, 27,019,558 population.

CHAPTER XII

INSULAR SELF-SATISFACTION

[1] "Parliamentary History of England," Vol. XIX, pp. 187–192.

[2] "Great Britain Parliament, Sessional Papers," 1805, No. 172; 1813–1814, No. 225; 1816, No. 161, etc.

[3] "Parliamentary Debates," 1824, N.S. Vol. 10, p. 636.

[4] *Ibid.*, Vol. 11, p. 102.

[5] *Ibid.*, p. 103.

[6] See "The Almanac of the Fine Arts," Edited by R. W. Buss (London, 1850), p. 768.

[7] "Great Britain Parliament, Sessional Papers," 1842–1843, Vol. XXIX, "Report of the Council of the School of Design," pp. 11–12.

[8] "The New Monthly Magazine," London, November, 1829.

[9] "Impressions of America During the Years 1833, 1834 and 1835" (London, 1836), pp. 345–346.

[10] "A Letter to His Countrymen," by J. Fenimore Cooper (New York, 1834), pp. 3, 4, 59, 95–96.

[11] "The Edinburgh Review," January, 1833. Also Mill's anonymous article in "The Westminster," July, 1830, telling: "The unfortunate voter is in the power of some opulent man; the opulent man informs him how he must vote."

[12] "Parliamentary Debates," 1829, N.S. No. 21, p. 1106.

[13] See Samuel Smiles' "Lives of the Engineers" (1874), Vol. 5, p. 241.

[14] See "A Plan of Church Reform. With a letter to the King." By Lord Henley (London, 1832). British Government returns in 1827 showed that of 10,533 benefices in England and Wales, only 4,413 were served by clergymen actually resident.

[15] "Great Britain Parliament, Sessional Papers," 1833, Vol. XX, "Factories Inquiry Commission, First Report," pp. 7, 15, 18–20, 25–31.

[16] "Parliamentary Debates," 1847, Vol. 90, p. 134. Sir A. L. Hay pointed out that in America cotton mill spinners received higher wages and were given long vacations.

[17] *Ibid.*, 1840, Vol. 51, p. 1226, etc. "Discontent Among the Working Classes."

[18] "Great Britain Parliament, Sessional Papers," 1834, Vol. VIII, "Report from the Select Committee on Inquiry into Drunkenness," pp. x, 362, 404–407, etc.

¹⁹ "Great Britain Parliament, Sessional Papers," 1838, Vol. VIII, "First Report from the Select Committee on Combinations of Workmen," pp. 167–168.

²⁰ "Parliamentary Debates," 1837, Vol. 37, pp. 170–178, 189, 198.

CHAPTER XIII

A CONFLICT OF OPINIONS

[1] "Views of Society and Manners in America," pp. 28, 312–314.

[2] "Democracy in America," pp. vii, 33, 35, 206, etc.

[3] "Aristocracy in America, by a German Nobleman," 1839, Vol. 2, p. 53.

[4] "America and the American People." Citation is from the translated edition brought out in New York in 1845, pp. 445, etc.

[5] Treitschke, "History of Germany in the Nineteenth Century," Vol. 4, pp. 210–211, 220–222, 240.

[6] "The Founding of the German Empire by William I," by Heinrich von Sybel, Vol. I, p. 148.

[7] "Germany and Its Evolution in Modern Times," by Professor Henri Lichtenberg, pp. 11–12.

[8] "The Americans in Their Moral, Social and Political Relations," by Francis J. Grund (2 vols., London, 1837).

[9] "Society, Manners and Politics in the United States," by Michael Chevalier. The citation here is from the 1839 Boston edition, p. 106.

[10] *Ibid.*, p. 298.

[11] "A Diary in America with Remarks on Its Institutions," by Captain Frederick Marryatt, C.B. The citation here is from the edition published in Paris in English, in 1839, p. 7.

[12] For example," "Memoirs of an American Lady," by Mrs. Anne Grant (London, 1808). She described America as a land "that has become a receptacle of the outcasts of society from every nation in Europe." And much more to the same purport. Pp. 206–209, etc.

[13] Marryatt, pp. 9, 207, 339.

[14] See "Great Britain Parliament, Sessional Papers," 1839, Vol. XXXVIII, "Accounts and Papers, Crime; Committals; Convicts," pp. 4, 366–369. The number of death sentences did not imply an equal number of executions. Of every hundred sentenced to death under the old laws, only about seven to ten had been actually executed—a considerable number for robbery, larceny, arson, sheep stealing, cattle and horse stealing, house breaking and other offences.

[15] "A Picture of Parliament," "The People's Journal," March, 1847.

[16] *Ibid.*

[17] "American Notes" (1842 edition), p. 293.

[18] "Change for the American Notes," "By an American Lady" (London, 1843).

[19] "The Economist" (London), September 23, 1843. This periodical additionally described itself as "a political, literary and general newspaper."

[20] "Parliamentary Debates," 1840, Vol. 53, pp. 748 and 844.

[21] "Great Britain Parliament, Sessional Papers," 1843, Vol. XXVI, p. 349, and Vol. XXXI, p. 377.

[22] Report in "The Times," London, December 23, 1844. Also "The Economist," December 28, 1844.

²³ "The Railway Monitor of the Economist, Weekly Times and Bankers' Gazette" (London), October 4, 1845.

²⁴ *Ibid.* Also "Great Britain Parliament, Sessional Papers," 1844, No. 159, and 1845, No. 637.

²⁵ See the numerous stock-selling advertisements of these companies in "The Railway Monitor of the Economist," etc., throughout 1844 and 1845. Also "The Times" (London), in the same years. Advertisements of banks, insurance and other companies showed many members of Parliament on their boards of directors.

²⁶ "The Economist," July 20, 1844.

²⁷ "A Short Account of England's Foreign Trade in the Nineteenth Century," by Professor Arthur L. Bowley (London, 1892), p. 57. (S. Sonnenschein & Co. New York: Charles Scribner's Sons.)

²⁸ *Ibid.*, p. 75.

²⁹ "Great Britain Parliament, Sessional Papers," 1843, Vol. XII, "Sanitary Report," pp. 38, 169, 197–199, etc.

³⁰ "The Times" (London), October 17, 1844. An investigation showed that the same conditions prevailed in Leeds, Liverpool, Birmingham and other cities.

³¹ "The Economist," March 13, 1852, credited these figures to an article "by a writer long resident in France," and published in "The Westminster Review," January, 1851. I have been unable to find any such article at the time stated or in other issues.

³² "The Economist," March 13, 1852.

³³ Upon the complaint of a clergyman, who then himself sat as a magistrate, a laborer who had shot a hare was, in 1844, at Ashendown Petty Sessions, sentenced to pay £5 and costs, or serve three months' imprisonment at hard labor. To a poor man payment of such a mulcting was not possible; consequently to jail he was sent.

CHAPTER XIV

POUNDS STERLING TRIUMPHANT

¹ "Travels in North America," by Sir Charles Lyell (London, 1845), Vol. 1, pp. 71, 264, 268.

² See "The Continental Monthly" (New York), August, 1862, giving a detailed account of McDonough's life and will.

³ "Parliamentary Debates," 1847, 3d Series, Vol. 91, pp. 1008–1026.

⁴ Of the American total, exports of manufactured products amounted to only $15,601,899 or about £3,185,821, while the bulk of Britain's exports were manufactured articles—more than £19,000,000 of cotton goods, nearly £8,000,000 of woolen fabrics, £3,579,000 of linen cloths, and millions of pounds more in manufactured yarn, silk, metal and brass work and glassware.

⁵ "Report from the Select Committee on the Hudson Bay Company," etc. Great Britain Parliament, 1857, p. 326, etc., as to profits, and Appendix 17 as to the full list of stockholders.

⁶ "The History of the Great American Fortunes," Vols. 2 and 3.

⁷ "Lord Sydenham, a Biography," by Adam Shortt, p. 251.

⁸ "Statutes of Canada," 1845, p. 146.

⁹ The full list of incorporators is given in "Imperial Blue Books on Affairs Relating to Canada," Vol. 27, "Railways," pp. 7–8, and 18–19 of "Enclosure, Correspondence," etc.

[10] "Statutes of Canada," 1848–1849, p. 9.

[11] "Statutes of Canada," 1853, p. 362. Often after having acquired charters, legislators sold or leased them to themselves, as heads of other railways, profiting exceedingly thereby.

[12] *Ibid.*, 1852, pp. 103–104.

[13] *Ibid.*, 1857, pp. 622, 638.

[14] "Canada Directory," 1857–1858, p. 628.

[15] The complete list of incorporators is set forth in "Imperial Blue Books on Affairs Relating to Canada," Vol. 27, "Railways," etc., p. 12 of "Enclosure, Further Correspondence."

[16] "Statutes of Canada," 1849, pp. 899, 916, 981, 1079; 1855, pp. 821, 836, 851, etc. There were many other instances of legislators vesting corporate charters in themselves and associates.

[17] See Keefer, "Eighty Years' Progress of British North America, 1781–1861," pp. 199–200.

[18] "Legislative Council Sessional Papers," First Session, Fifth Parliament, 1854–1855, Appendix, A.A.A.A., incorporating testimony and report.

[19] "Eighty Years Progress in British North America, 1781–1861," p. 209.

[20] *Ibid.*, p. 208.

[21] "Legislative Council Sessional Papers," etc. Vol. 13, 1854–1855, Appendix A.A.A.A. See also Hincks' "Reminiscences," p. 347.

[22] Keefer, "Eighty Years Progress in British North America, 1781 to 1861," p. 209.

[23] *Ibid.*, p. 210.

[24] "Dominion Parliament, Sessional Papers," 1869, Vol. 2, No. 7.

[25] "Legislative Council Sessional Papers, First Session, Fifth Parliament," 1854–1855, Vol. 13, Appendix A.A.A.A. giving the facts.

[26] The full testimony of the ramifications of fraud, bribery and plunder are published in "Journal of the Legislative Assembly, Province of Canada," 1857, Appendices to the 15th Vol., Appendix No. 6.

[27] *Ibid.*, 1858, Vol. 16, Appendix No. 4, and Vol. 17, Appendix No. 12.

[28] "Railway Reform," by David Mills, M.P. in "The Canadian Monthly and National Review," November, 1872. pp. 438–439.

[29] "America and Europe" (1857), pp. 67–71.

CHAPTER XV

A CHANGE OF TACTICS

[1] "North America," Vol. 1, pp. 284–285.

[2] "Documents of the [New York] Board of Aldermen," 1861, Vol. XXVIII, No. 5.

[3] "North America," Vol. 1, pp. 290–291.

[4] *Ibid.*, p. 147.

[5] See Professor Emerson David Fite's detailed and excellent book "Social and Industrial Conditions in the North During the Civil War" (1910), pp. 17–19, etc. (The Macmillan Company.)

[6] "North America," Vol. 1, pp. 147–148, 410–411, 425.

[7] "America Before Europe" (1862), pp. 370–371.

[8] "London," Vol. 4, p. 17.

[9] "The Economist," March 19, 1864.

[10] "Parliamentary Debates," 1867, Series 3, Vol. 186, p. 1027.

[11] "A Short Account of England's Foreign Trade in the Nineteenth Century," p. 75.

[12] France's merchant marine at this time was 700,000 tons; Germany's about the same; Britain's 5,500,000, soon to expand to 7,000,000. Of French and German vessels, the great preponderance consisted of sail, and only one-tenth to one-twelfth of steamships. Britain had seven and twelve times, respectively, as many steam vessels as they.

[13] "Parliamentary Debates," 1861, 3d Series, Vol. 161, p. 1070.

[14] *Ibid.*, pp. 1063–1065.

[15] See "The Economist" (London), July 6, 1861.

[16] *Ibid.*, Dec. 19, 1857.

[17] *Ibid.*, Dec. 21, 1861.

[18] "The Economist" (London), March 19, 1864.

[19] *Ibid.*, January 13, 1866, and February 3, 1866.

[20] *Ibid.*, April 16, 1864.

[21] "The Spectator," of London, on November 2, 1862, gave specific details.

[22] "The Quarterly Review," July, 1863.

[23] "Chambers' Journal" (London), March 15, 1862.

[24] "The Times" (London), September 17, 1863.

[25] "The Post" (London), June 9, 1867.

[26] "Report of the Commissioners on the Existence of Corrupt Practices at the Last Election for Members to Serve in Parliament for Lancaster, with Evidence," Sessional Papers, 1867, Vol. XXVII, No. 1. Also "Parliamentary Debates," 1867, Series 3, Vol. 186, pp. 983–988.

[27] "Parliamentary Debates," 1867, 3d Series, Vol. 188, p. 638.

[28] *Ibid.*, Vol 187, pp. 63–66. An official compilation covering the years 1830–1870 showed that during the tenure of successive Prime Ministers of both parties 171 new peers had been created. "Great Britain Parliament, Sessional Papers," 1871, Vol. LVI, No. 81.

[29] "The Economist," May 19, 1866.

[30] "The Spectator," May 16, 1868.

[31] "Parliamentary Debates," 1870, 3d Series, Vol. 199, p. 441.

[32] *Ibid.*, Vol. 200, pp. 240–241.

[33] *Ibid.*, Vol. 202, p. 906.

CHAPTER XVI

"WANT OF SOUL AND DELICACY"

[1] Matthew Arnold, "Civilization in the United States—First and Last Impressions," Boston, 1888, pp. 112–113. (Cupples & Hurd.)

[2] George William Erskine Russell, "Matthew Arnold," New York, 1904, pp. 119–129. (Charles Scribner's Sons.)

[3] "Matthew Arnold, Prose and Poetry," New York, 1927, pp. 330–349. The essay on "Equality" was originally delivered as an address at the Royal Institution (London), and was printed in "The Fortnightly Review," March, 1878. (Charles Scribner's Sons.)

[4] But cf. "Listeners English and American," by Vera Brittain, in "The Atlantic Monthly," June, 1935.

[5] Matthew Arnold, "Discourses in America," London, 1885, New York, 1906 (The Macmillan Company), pp. 65–66; and "Civilization in the United States," Boston, 1888, pp. 183–187.

[6] "Report from the Select Committee on Loans to Foreign States, Great Britain Parliament," Sessional Papers, 1875, Vol. XI, p. v.

[7] "Parliamentary Debates," 1875, Vol. 223, pp. 787–811.

[8] *Ibid.*, pp. 1150–1152.

[9] *Ibid.*, p. 1451.

[10] See account in *Ibid.*, p. 1694.

[11] "Report from the Select Committee on Loans to Foreign States, Great Britain Parliament, Sessional Papers," 1875, Vol. XI, pp. xlv–xlix, etc.

[12] "Parliamentary Debates," 1875, 3d Series, Vol. 225, pp. 1824–1825.

[13] *Ibid.*, Vol. 226, pp. 232–235. The use of decayed or otherwise dangerous ships was by no means confined to Britain. America afforded many instances of this gruesome business, and several multimillionaire fortunes there came partly or largely from great profits derived from their operation or from their sale to the Union Government for transport service during the Civil War. See "The History of the Great American Fortunes," Vol. 2, pp. 125–137.

[14] "Great Britain Parliament, Reports on Adulteration of Food, Drinks and Drugs, Sessional Papers," 1854–1855, Vol. VIII, Nos. 221 and 373; 1856, Vol. VIII, No. 1; 1874, Vol. VI, No. 343.

[15] "Parliamentary Debates," 1875, 3d Series, Vol. 222, p. 609.

[16] "Report from the Select Committee on London Corporation (Charges of Malversation), Great Britain Parliament, Sessional Papers," 1887, Vol. X, No. 161, pp. iv–xiv.

[17] "Special Report from the Select Committee on the Merchandise Act, etc. Great Britain Parliament, Sessional Papers," 1887, Vol. X, No. 203, pp. 41, 90, 98, 141, etc.

(G. W. Steevens' "The Land of the Dollar," referred to in this chapter, was published by Dodd, Mead & Co.)

(Rudyard Kipling's "Letters of Travel," referred to in this chapter, was published by Doubleday, Page & Co.)

CHAPTER XVII

SPEAKING OF COMPARISONS

[1] "The American Commonwealth," Vol. 2, pp. 24–25 and 207. (Macmillan & Co., London.)

[2] "Great Britain Parliament, Report of the Select Committee on the Caledonian and other Railway Companies, Sessional Papers," 1890, Vol. XI, No. 27.

[3] For an account of the Broadway franchise bribery and its results, see "The History of Public Franchises in New York City," pp. 137–144.

[4] "Jonathan and His Continent" (New York edition, 1889), pp. 20–27. (Cassell & Co.)

[5] United States Senate Report, No. 1394, 1893.

[6] Testimony "United States Committee on Education and Labor," 1883, Vol. 3, p. 405.

[7] "The Diamond Mines of South Africa," by Gardner F. Williams, M.A., General Manager of the DeBeers Consolidated Mines, Limited, pp. 281–288.

[8] "Diamonds and Gold in South Africa," by Theodore Reunert, M. Inst., M.E., etc., published at Cape Town and Johannesburg, 1893, p. 39. This book was a serious account dealing with conditions technical, financial, social, and other.

[9] *Ibid.*, pp. 42–43.

[10] "The Economist," London, March 10, 1888.

[11] *Ibid.*, June 20, 1891.

[12] Reunert, "Diamonds and Gold in South Africa," p. 120.

[13] Report of David Magdola of the Transkeian General Council, "Great Britain Parliament, Sessional Papers," 1904, Vol. LXII, "Correspondence Relating to the Conditions of Native Labor Employed in the Transvaal Mines," p. 28.

[14] *Ibid.*, p. 46.

[15] "Native laborers are being sjamborked and beaten, and ill-treated in many other ways by their European overseers and indumas; so much so that the boys [native workers] wish to call back the days of the Republic, when the Boer dominated, stating that they were better treated then and received better wages for their work. This brutal treatment, combined as it is with very low wages, is enough to keep natives away from Johannesburg." Report of Chief Sipendu, delegate, on his visit to Johannesburg. *Ibid.*, p. 27.

[16] "Great Britain Parliament, Sessional Papers," 1904, Vol. LXII, Africa, No. 3, "Correspondence Respecting Introduction of Chinese Labor into the Transvaal."

[17] "Parliamentary Debates" (1913), N.S. Vol. 54, pp. 515–520 and 796. The death rate among native negro mine workers, one member of Parliament— Fell—stated, was seven times greater than among the Chinese formerly employed at the mines. Harcourt did not agree to that precise figure, but he admitted that the mortality was many times greater than in former years.

[18] P. Collier, "America and the Americans—From a French Point of View," 1897, p. 140. (Charles Scribner's Sons.)

[19] Paul Bourget, "Outre-Mer; Impressions of America," 1895, pp. 149, 423, et seq. (Charles Scribner's Sons.)

[20] "The American Commonwealth," Vol. 2, p. 604.

CHAPTER XVIII

"THE BITCH-GODDESS SUCCESS"

[1] "The Philosophy of William James," with Introduction by Horace M. Kallen. (The Modern Library.)

[2] H. G. Wells, "The Future in America. A Search After Realities," 1906, pp. 90–100. "He complained sourly that American magazine editors sought him out only after he became famous, but had neglected him in the days of his early struggles"—Extract from an article "Magazine Scouting Abroad" by William C. Lengle, Associate Editor, "Liberty" Magazine, and former Associate Editor, "Cosmopolitan Magazine" in "The American Spectator," October, 1934. (Harper & Bros., published Wells' book.)

[3] Arnold Bennett, "Your United States. Impressions of a First Visit." (Harper & Bros.)

[4] John Moody, "The Truth about the Trusts," 1904, pp. xi, xx.

[5] "Great Britain Parliament, Sessional Papers," 1909, Vol. LXVII, "Report of the Royal Commission on Shipping Rings," pp. 85, 91, 114.

[6] "The Economist," London, April 14, 1900, which advised: "It behooves investors to look closely into the question of capitalization, and particularly the loading of good-will."

[7] *Ibid.*, December 26, 1896, "Stock Watering in Excelsis."

8 "The Economist," London, March 8 and April 25, 1896.

9 "The Spectator," London, August 20, 1898.

10 Hooley's testimony and that of other witnesses was stenographically reported in "The Times," of London, on July 28, August 2, 11, 13, 16, 23, November 3, 8, 15, etc., 1898.

11 U. S. Senate Report No. 485, Fifty-third Congress, Second Session, June 21, 1894.

12 "The Spectator," London, November 19 and 5, 1898.

13 "The Economist," February 3, 1912.

14 "Parliamentary Debates," 1914, Vol. 62, pp. 1794–1795.

15 "London Gazette," December 20, 1889.

16 "Great Britain Parliament, Sessional Papers," 1900, Vol. XLV, "British South Africa Company," pp. 37–42.

17 Seventeenth annual stockholders' meeting, "The Economist," London, February 14, 1912.

18 "Parliamentary Debates," 1900, Vol. 88, pp. 397–421.

19 *Ibid.*, 1913, N.S. Vol. 50, p. 1637, and Vol. 51, pp. 551–552.

20 *Ibid.*, 1912, N.S. Vol. 42, pp. 667–726.

21 *Ibid.*, 1913, N.S. Vol. 54, pp. 556–557, 670.

CHAPTER XIX

RUBBER MADNESS AND WORLD TRADE

1 "Great Britain Parliament, Sessional Papers," 1904, Vol. LXII (Africa, No. 14), pp. 2–3.

2 *Ibid.*, pp. 9–16.

3 *Ibid.*, 1904 (Africa, No. 1), "Correspondence and Report from the British Consul at Boma," pp. 31–65.

4 *Ibid.*, 1912–1913, Vol. LIX, "Correspondence Respecting the Affairs of the Congo," pp. 1–4, 6–8.

5 *Ibid.*, pp. 23–24.

6 "Great Britain Parliament, Sessional Papers," 1912–1913, Vol. LIX, "Report on the Alienation of Native Lands in the Gold Coast Colony and Ashanti," p. 9.

7 *Ibid.*, 1909, Vol. XL, "Report of the Committee of Inquiry into the Liquor Trade in Southern Nigeria," pp. 4–23.

8 "The Economist," London, January 2, 1909.

9 One of numerous instances: Maple and Company, big British manufacturers of house furnishings, maintained stores in London, Paris and Buenos Aires. From 1908 to 1911 the company paid annual dividends of 12 to 15 per cent on the common stock, and it additionally placed amounts in its reserve funds. Assurances at a stockholders' meeting in London that the company had proved its capacity for substantially increasing dividends was greeted by a stockholders' outburst of "Hear, hear." "The Economist," London, March 2, 1912.

10 "Great Britain Parliament, Sessional Papers," 1913, Vol. XIV, "Special Report on Putumayo Atrocities, with Proceedings of the Committee," pp. iv-xx. Also, "Parliamentary Debates," 1913, Vol. 56, p. 2327.

11 "The Economist," London, May 4, 1912.

12 *Ibid.*, April 26, 1913.

13 *Ibid.*, March 22, 1913.

14 These mines were very ancient. Probably the Phoenicians worked them;

the Carthaginians, Romans and Moors certainly did. In a spasmodic way they were worked for centuries by the Spanish Government until 1873, when the Rothschilds' Rio Tinto Company acquired them.

[15] "Japan in the Beginning of the 20th Century," Published by Japan's Department of Agriculture and Commerce, Tokio, 1904, pp. 412–413.

[16] "Fifty Years of New Japan," 1919, Vol. 2, p. 567.

[17] *Ibid.*

[18] *Ibid.*, Chapter on "Joint Stock Enterprises in Japan," by Baron Yeiichi Shibusawa, president of the First National Bank, Vol. 1, pp. 474–475.

[19] "The Political Development of Japan, 1867–1909," by George Etsujiro Uyehara (1910), pp. 266–268. (London: Constable & Co.)

[20] The annals of official corruption would compel an extended account. A recent instance will be noted: A bribery scandal in July, 1934, involved a Vice-Minister of Finance, two Cabinet Ministers and others, and caused the resignation of Premier Saito and his Cabinet. The scandal concerned the alleged acceptance of bribes to facilitate a large-scale manipulation of Imperial Rayon shares.

[21] William Harbutt Dawson, "The Evolution of Modern Germany," London, 1908, pp. vi, 10–14, etc. (T. Fisher Unwin.)

[22] "The Economist," London, April 6, 1912.

[23] *Ibid.*, March 23, 1912.

[24] "Report of the Committee Appointed Pursuant to House Resolutions 429 and 504 to Investigate the Concentration of Money and Credit," February 28, 1913, pp. 159–160.

[25] "Report of Investigation of the Financial Affairs of the New York, New Haven & Hartford Railroad Company," Interstate Commerce Commission, No. 6569, 1914, pp. 1–39.

CHAPTER XX

ARMAMENTS AND PROFITEERING

[1] House Report No. 1468, Fifty-third Congress, Second Session.

[2] "The Economist," London, June 5, 1915.

[3] *Ibid.*, June 3, 1916.

[4] *Ibid.*, June 9, 1917.

[5] See the account in "Krupp's and the International Armaments Ring, the Scandal of Modern Civilization," by H. Robertson Murray, London (1915?), pp. 152–155. (London: Holden & Haringham.)

[6] "The Naval Annual," 1906, p. 107.

[7] "Parliamentary Debates," 1911, N.S. Vol. 24, pp. 453 and 845.

[8] "Alleged Activities at the Geneva Conference. Hearings Before a Sub-Committee on Naval Affairs, U. S. Senate," 1929 and 1930, pp. 508–509.

[9] See "U. S. Senate Document, No. 415, 64th Congress, First Session, Final Report and Testimony, Commission on Industrial Relations," 1916, Vol. 8, pp. 7897–7916, Vol. 9, pp. 8715–8730, etc.

[10] "Parliamentary Debates," 1913, N.S. Vol. 46, pp. 186 and 984.

[11] See the shining but partial list in H. Robertson Murray's book, pp. 162, 173–174.

[12] "The Economist," London, April 29, 1922.

[13] *Ibid.*, June 9, 1923.

[14] *Ibid.*, January 1, 1921.

[15] *Ibid.*, June 2, 1917.

[16] *Ibid.*, June 1, 1918.

[17] "Parliamentary Debates," 1919, Vol. N.S. 114, p. 2481, and Vol. 115, p. 217.

[18] See pp. 48–56. Lehmann-Russbüldt pointed out that in fictional disguises, the best known of which was "The Man in the Shadow," the story of Zarahoff's life had been written. "But," he added, "there is no need to resort to fiction; the available facts are picturesque and astonishing in themselves." (Alfred H. King.)

[19] "The Saturday Review," London, January 20, 1917.

[20] "The Economist," London, January 20, 1917.

[21] "The Saturday Review," London, August 18, 1917.

[22] "Great Britain Parliament, Sessional Papers," 1919, Vol. V, "Special Report from the Select Committee on High Prices and Profits, together with the Minutes of Evidence," pp. 3, 13.

[23] "Parliamentary Debates," 1919, N.S. Vol. 119, pp. 926, 995, 1010, etc.

[24] *Ibid.*, 1919, N.S. Vol. 115, pp. 469–471.

CHAPTER XXI

A SERIES OF EXHIBITS

[1] "The New York Times," May 12, 1920.

[2] "My Impressions of America" (New York), 1922, p. 200. (George H. Doran & Co.)

[3] "America Revisited" (Boston), 1924, pp. 4 and 49. (Little, Brown & Co.)

[4] See G. B. Shaw's signed article in "The New York Times," December 19, 1930.

[5] "The Congressional Record," Seventieth Congress, Second Session, Vol. 70, Part I, p. 682.

[6] Cable despatch published in "The World," New York, October 12, 1925.

[7] See "Representative International Cartels, Combines and Trusts," U. S. Department of Commerce, Bureau of Foreign and Domestic Commerce, Trade Promotion Series, No. 81, 1929, pp. 45, 73, etc.

[8] "The Economist," London, May 29, 1926.

[9] "Parliamentary Debates," 1904, Fourth Series, Vol. 129, p. 163.

[10] *Ibid.*, Vol. 130, p. 900.

[11] "Great Britain Parliament, Sessional Papers," 1918, Vol. XIII, No. 789.

[12] "The Economist," February 9, 1924.

[13] See their "The National Income, 1924," giving the data.

[14] "Installment Selling of Motor Vehicles in Europe," U. S. Department of Commerce, Bureau of Foreign and Domestic Commerce, Trade Information Bulletin, No. 550, 1928.

[15] "The Economist," London, December 18 and 25, 1926, and January 1, 1927, with the additional observation: "Something like 90 or 95 per cent of our capital is British owned, while the greater part has crossed no sea wider than the Irish channel."

[16] *Ibid.*, July 19, 1930.

[17] *Ibid.*, December 8, 1928.

[18] *Ibid.*, June 18, 1927.

[19] *Ibid.*, December 8, 1928.

[20] *Ibid.*, December 24, 1927. The company's capital had been doubled in 1920; hence care was taken to point out that this great profit was on original investment. Figuring on old and new stock the total was 552½ per cent.

[21] *Ibid.*, December 21, 1929. Address of Chairman of Scindia Steam Navigation Company, Bombay.

[22] See "Kings of Commerce," by Thomas C. Bridges and H. Hessell Titlman (London), 1928. Before this time wealthy commercial men had usually been eulogized as "great traders." Such was the distinction accorded, for instance, to Sir Robert Jardine and to his son of the same name, the one succeeding the other as head of a firm which had long held an almost complete monopoly of the importation of Indian opium into China. The paternal Jardine had made so extensive a fortune as to bequeath to his son a sum estimated at $20,000,000 and an estate of 200,000 acres in Scotland. Sir Robert Jardine, the son, died in 1927.

(Mencken's "Notes on Democracy," referred to in this chapter, was published by Alfred A. Knopf.)

(Dean Inge's "Outspoken Essays," referred to in this chapter, was published by Longmans, Green & Co., London and his "England" by Ernest Benn, London.)

CHAPTER XXII

UNCLE SHYLOCK

[1] See "American Direct Investments in Foreign Countries," United States Department of Commerce, Bureau of Foreign and Domestic Commerce, Trade Information Bulletin, No. 731, 1930, pp. 8, 37, etc.

[2] "Rights of Foreign Shareholders of European Corporations," U. S. Department of Commerce, Bureau of Foreign and Domestic Commerce Trade Information Bulletin No. 659, 1929, pp. 3, 5, 12.

[3] "The Promotion of Tourist Travel by Foreign Countries," U. S. Department of Commerce, Bureau of Foreign and Domestic Commerce, Trade Promotion Series No. 113, 1931, pp. 1–3.

[4] See "The Balance of International Payments in the United States in 1928," U. S. Department of Commerce, Bureau of Foreign and Domestic Commerce, Trade Information Bulletin No. 625, 1929, pp. 19–20.

[5] Illiteracy among native whites in America, as a whole, was, according to the 1930 census, only 1.5 per cent; it was more than eight times higher among foreign-born whites, and fifteen times higher among negroes. In France, in 1930, about 8.04 per cent of French men conscripted in its army were illiterates. France's public school system was an affair of class distinctions. To poor children primary instruction only was given, up to the age of 13. The system precluded any higher education except to children whose parents were able to pay for the privilege. Recreational facilities were not provided for school children in France.

As far back as 1878 a French Educational Commission on Public Instruction in the United States had enthusiastically reported on the free nature and high value of public high schools in America. Think, it commented in part on American high schools, of poor boys and girls "cultivating their minds by studies that everywhere else are reserved for the well-to-do, and tell us if these institutions do not bear the very seal and impress of American civilization."

[6] See Faÿ's signed article in "The New York Times Magazine," February 28, 1932.

7 See "The Monthly Labor Review," United States Department of Labor, Bureau of Labor Statistics, June, 1929, pp. 1–10, and March, 1930, p. 137, for data on the extent of this movement.

8 "International Labor Office" (League of Nations), Geneva, 1929, Vol. XXXII, No. 4, p. 154.

9 "Bulletin de l'Office du Travail," 1901, p. 856.

10 "International Labor Office," Geneva, 1929, Vol. XXXII, No. 4, pp. 166–167.

11 See "The American Illusion," pp. 12, 16, 21, 25, 55, 58, 60, etc. (The Century Co.)

12 Computations of the amount were loosely stated. The U. S. Senate Committee on Banking and Currency estimated $25,000,000 in ten years; Senator Fletcher, the committee's chairman, in a speech in the Senate, said $50,000,000. See "The Congressional Record," Seventy-third Congress, First Session, Vol. 77, Part 4, p. 3801.

(Duhamel's "America the Menace," referred to in this chapter, was published by Houghton, Mifflin Co.)

CHAPTER XXIII

REVAMPING THE OLD THEME

1 "The Political Science Quarterly," March, 1929.

2 See "The New York Times Magazine," December 11, 1927. This article was advertised in a foreword as that of "the widely read author of philosophic works."

3 For more of Keyserling's opinions see "America Set Free." Also "Harpers Magazine," August, 1929, and "The Atlantic Monthly," September, 1929.

4 "The New York Times," July 12, 1929.

5 "Hearings before the Special (United States Senate) Committee Investigating the Munitions Industry," 1934, p. 1169.

6 *Ibid.,* pp. 739–749, 1674–1683, 1965, 2515–2518, 2550–2557.

7 *Ibid.,* p. 193.

8 "Great Britain Parliament, Sessional Papers," Vol. XIII, 1931, "Report of the Committee on Finance and Industry," p. 256.

9 W. T. Stead, "Why the Lords Must Go," London, 1909, pp. 13–14. (Stead Publishing House, London.)

10 The point of this endorsement of an "ideal member" of the House of Commons is more fully seen when we turn to the attempts of some American intellectuals to disparage the American Congress as of all legislative bodies the most unfit and misfit. "Dull as a Congressman" was one of Mencken's favorite sayings. Of the House of Lords membership, seldom did more than 200 vote on bills at any specific time. Scores of Lords were in attendance but once or twice a session.

11 See "Parliamentary Debates," 1917, N.S. Vol. 26, pp. 835–885, for the full record of these highly interesting disclosures.

12 Mallet's "Lloyd George, A Study" (London), 1930, pp. 248, 251, 252, 254, 286, etc. (Ernest Benn, London, and E. P. Dutton & Co., New York.)

13 "Presidential Campaign Expenditures," United States Senate Report No. 823, Sixty-sixth Congress, Third Session (February 24, 1921), pp. 3, 12.

14 United States Senate Report, No. 1480, Seventieth Congress, Second Session, 1929, pp. 2, 14, 27, 31, etc. Also Report No. 2024, 1929, pp. 5–6.

15 See "Senatorial Campaign Expenditures," United States Senate Report

No. 1197, Part 2, 1926, followed by the confirmatory Report No. 1858, 1929, p. 92. A method was found of evading the Pennsylvania Corrupt Practices Act. Under that law the payment of poll watchers was a recognized and legitimate item of expense. The organizations of the two chief competitors paid tens of thousands of persons designated as watchers $5 to $10 each—which was equivalent to ensuring their votes as well as their services. Report No. 1197, p. 30.

[16] United States Senate Report No. 1197, 1926, p. 6.

[17] "Parliamentary Debates," N.S. Vol. 51–52, 1922, pp. 135–136. Carson had been created a peer in 1900. From that date to 1906 he was Solicitor-General; he was Attorney-General in 1915; and First Lord of the Admiralty in 1917.

[18] *Ibid.*, N.S. Vol. 49–50, 1922, pp. 1127–1130.

[19] *Ibid.*, N.S. Vol. 49–50, pp. 1138–1139.

[20] *Ibid.*, N.S. Vol. 51–52, pp. 128–129.

[21] "Great Britain Parliament, Sessional Papers," 1923, Vol. XI, "Report of the Royal Commission on Honors," pp. 7–11.

[22] "Parliamentary Debates," N.S. Vol. 210, 1927, pp. 356, 786.

[23] "Lloyd George, A Study," pp. 286–288.

(Owens' "The American Illusion," to which reference was made in this chapter, was published by Ernest Benn, London. Joad's "The Babbitt Warren" was brought out by Harper & Bros.)

CHAPTER XXIV

THE TRUE CONTRAST

[1] "Stock Exchange Practices," Hearing Before the Committee on Banking and Currency, Seventy-third Congress, First Session, Part 1, p. 23.

[2] "Stock Exchange Practices," Report of the United States Senate Committee on Banking and Currency (submitted by Senator Fletcher, June 6, 1934), p. 186.

[3] See Committee's Report, "Review of Evidence," 1913, p. 136.

[4] "Stock Exchange Practices," etc., Report, p. 101.

[5] *Ibid.*, p. 148.

[6] *Ibid.*, p. 85, 148–150.

[7] *Ibid.*, p. 189.

[8] *Ibid.*, p. 172.

[9] "Great Britain Parliament, Sessional Papers," Vol. XIII, 1931, "Report of the Committee on Finance and Industry."

INDEX

Abercorn, Duke of, 252, 308.
Aborigines' Protection Society, 107, 259.
Addington, Henry, 109.
Addison, Dr. Christopher, 290-291.
Adulteration of foods and liquors, 11-14, 216.
Africa, 27, 39, 258-263, 317.
African Society of London, 130.
Aislabie, John, 63.
Albermarle, Duke of, 34.
Albermarle, Lord, 247.
Alison, Archibald, 150.
Allegheny Mountains, 42.
Allen, Colonel Samuel, 33.
America, 3, 30-31, 93, 94, 96, 115, 119, 122, 126, 132, 156, 165, 175, 177-178, 216, 218, 220, 223, 237, 241, 268, 291, 302-303, 316, 337, 358.
American Brown Boveri Electric Corporation, 286.
American colonies, 40-41.
American Fur Company, 106.
American Marconi Company, 255-256.
American Museum or Universal Magazine, 83.
American Revolution, 68-70, 77, 84, 100, 119, 124, 146, 156.
American Smelting & Refining Company, 267.
Americans, strictures by foreign critics on, 82-83, 87-88, 89, 92, 93-94, 109, 118, 122, 123, 131, 133, 147, 154, 156-159, 189-191, 207-209, 220-221, 229, 237-238, 240-242, 258, 271, 297-300, 316, 323-328, 330-331, 335-336, 339-341, 343, 346, 349-350.
American Sugar & Refining Company, 267.
Amsterdam, 45, 84, 306, 361.
Anstruther, Sir William, 281.
Antrobus, Sir Edmund, 175.
Argentina, 341-342.
Arlington, Lord, 34.

Armor plate, 280, 282-284.
Armstrong, George William, 283.
Armstrong, Whitworth & Company, 283-284, 289.
Army, British, frauds and corruption in, 71-74.
Arnold, Matthew, 207-210.
Art, counterfeiting of in France, 334-335.
Art, state of in England, 138-143.
Ashanti, 262.
Ashburton, Lord, 246.
Ashe, Thomas, 94-96.
Ashley, Lord, 147.
Asquith, H. H., 254-256.
Asquith, Margot, 298.
Astor, John Jacob, 106, 172, 201.
Australia, 102-104, 245.
Ayen, Duc d', 314.

Baker, George F., 274.
Baldwin, Stanley, 287.
Bank Géneralé, 51-52, 60.
Bank of England, 7, 50, 59, 64, 158, 167, 368.
Bank of Montreal, 179.
Banks, American, 274, 363-365.
Banks, British, 193-194, 213, 244, 274, 360, 366-368.
Banks, French, 336.
Barker, Sir John, 273.
Barrington, Lord, 75.
Bass, Ratcliffe & Gretton, Limited, 321.
Basutoland, 234.
Bathurst, Earl, 104.
Bayard, Nicholas, 33.
Bechuanaland, 234.
Beecham, Sir Joseph, 320.
Beekman, Henry, 33.
Beit, Alfred, 252.
Belgium, 178, 258-263, 282, 311-312, 314, 337.

397

INDEX